10577819

SIX PLAYS BY

Lillian Hellman

SIX PLAYS BY

Lillian Hellman

THE CHILDREN'S HOUR

DAYS TO COME

THE LITTLE FOXES

WATCH ON THE RHINE

ANOTHER PART OF THE FOREST

THE AUTUMN GARDEN

With an introduction by the author

THE MODERN LIBRARY · NEW YORK

Random House IS THE PUBLISHER OF *The Modern Library*

BENNETT CERF · DONALD S. KLOPFER

Manufactured in the United States of America

Contents

INTRODUCTION

by LILLIAN HELLMAN

LAST night I finished reading the proofs of these four plays. I had never read them before, nor, beyond the rehearsal period, have I ever seen them played through. I had, of course, read parts of the plays—always the parts I liked, and I have seen parts of the plays once they had opened—always the parts I liked. There is a blessed door that leads from the orchestra out to the lobby. With practice you close it without a creak and what you don't like is behind you. Reading the proofs last night, carefully, slowly, thinking I was reading for the errors of the printer, I soon forgot the printer and was reading for myself.

Long ago I made a rule not to return to finished work: communion with what was ended seemed to me unhealthy. If you returned too often to what you had already done, I thought, you would come to like it and yourself too well, or dislike it and yourself too much. The work of the years before, or last year, or last month, was as far away as childhood, and your chance was ahead and not behind. Stirring the pole of memory in depths long buried, Henry James said it could be. My extreme dislike of that pole ended in a kind of pseudo-forgetfulness. I cannot remember: I cannot forget: I have always to be reminded that I had problems in writing the plays. I have to be told the first three drafts of *The Children's Hour* had a third set and three or four more people; *Days to Come* once had a scene in the town's main street; in *The Little Foxes* Addie had a daughter and Horace another disease; *Watch on the Rhine* started out in

Ohio. I have always to be told writing was hard work, and will be again.

Last night, finishing the proofs, I began to examine this state of forgetfulness with less amusement. There must be many reasons for it, but one came clear and simple: I have never before *really* wished to see, to examine, to evaluate myself. It is true that I, more than many writers, pay polite lip-service to criticism, to my own and to that of the few people for whose judgment I would give a penny. I have thought I was a cold audience for myself only because I was somewhat less warm than some other writers were about themselves. But comparative coldness is not necessarily cold at all. Last night, however, I think I saw most of what was wrong in the plays and—although I do not like these words, I will not apologize for them—most of what was right.

I started reading the proofs, as I started writing these plays, with *The Children's Hour*. It took a year and a half of stumbling stubbornness to do the play. I remembered, in the hodge-podge that came back last night, how many times I tore it up, how many characters I took out and put back and took out again; how I reached back into my own childhood and found the day I finished *Mlle. de Maupin;* the day I faked a heart attack; the day I saw an arm get twisted. And I thought again of the world of the half-remembered, the half-observed, the half-understood which you need so much as you begin to write. It is always there for you. God help you to use it right. Right? Right for what? Right to have something to say and to say it well.

There are, of course, many things wrong with *The Children's Hour*. (Even with my new clarity I have not seen them all, which is just as well, and better for my health.) The play probably should have ended with Martha's suicide: the last scene is tense and over-burdened. I knew this at the time, but I could not help myself. I am a moral writer, often too moral a writer, and I cannot avoid, it seems, that last summing-up. I think that is only a mistake when it fails to achieve its purpose, and I would rather make the attempt, and fail, than fail to make the attempt.

The theme of *The Children's Hour* was good and evil. The theme of *Days to Come* is good and evil: evil, this time, in the hands of people who don't understand it. *Days to Come* was a failure. It got bad reviews in the press, played six performances, and closed. Reading it now, I have no apologies for it. I spoiled a good play. I returned to the amateur's mistake: everything you think and feel must be written *this* time, because you may never have another chance to write it. I knew a woman like Cora and I hated her, and *that* hate had to go in the play; I knew a woman like Julie, I pitied her, and *that* pity had to go in the play; I had been raised with the Ellicotts of the world, and what I felt about them had to go in the play, too; I knew Leo Whalen and I wanted to say how much I respected men who work for other men. I wanted to say too much. And I began thinking of new ways to say it. People in life, I told myself, don't always make the direct answer, or follow the immediately preceding thought. (That is why, in the play, people answer, or understand, much later than the question or answer is offered them.) If you had lived in another place, or been richer or been poorer, or worked harder or worked less, or read a different book, perhaps you might have been. . . . And so I gave the leading characters their counterparts: Leo Whalen is the good Wilkie; Firth the simple Andrew Rodman; Cora the sick Hannah. I played this theme all alone: a solitary composer with a not very interesting quarter note. The subtleties of failures are seldom discovered, and that is just as well.

But with all that is wrong, all the confusion, the jumble, the attempt to do too much, I stand on the side of *Days to Come*. I am only sorry that the confusion in the script confused the best director in the theatre, who, in turn, managed to confuse one of its most inadequate casts.

(There were exceptions, of course.) On the opening night actors moved as figures in the dream of a frightened child. The death-dance of collapse was slow and unreal. It was my fault, I suppose, that it happened. I do not believe actors break plays, or make them, either. And nothing would have affected the play if I had done what the writer must do: kick and fight his way through until the whole is good, and the audience will not stop to worry about the parts. If he cannot do that, he has failed. In that sense, *Days to Come* failed, and only in that sense does its failure matter to me now.

It was with *Days to Come*, or perhaps it was with *The Little Foxes*—this forgetting has its cheery side—that I began to examine the two descriptions that some critics have found so handy for me: the plays are too well-made, the plays are melodramas. By the well-made play, I think is meant the play whose effects are contrived, whose threads are knit tighter than the threads in life and so do not convince.

Obviously, I can have no argument with those whom my plays do not convince. Something does not convince you. Very well, and that is all. But if they convince you, or partly convince you, then the dislike of their being well-made makes little sense. The theatre has limitations: it is a tight, unbending, unfluid, meager form in which to write. And for these reasons, compared to the novel, it is a second-rate form. (I speak of the form, not the content.) Let us admit that. Having admitted it—a step forward, since most of us are anxious to claim the medium by which we earn a living is a fine and fancy thing—we can stop the pretentious lie that the stage is unhampered. What the author has to say is unhampered: his means of saying it are not. He may do without scenery, he may use actors not as people but as animals or clouds, and he still must *pretend* the empty stage is a garden or an arena, and he still must *pretend* that living people are animals. He has three walls of a theatre and he has begun his pretense with the always rather comic notion that the audience is the fourth wall. He must pretend and he must represent. And if there is something vaguely awry, for me, about the pretense of representation—since by the nature of the stage it can never be done away with—it is not that I wish to deny to other writers their variations of the form, but that, for me, the realistic form has interested me most.

Within this form there must be tricks—the theatre is a trick—and they are, I think, only bad when they are used trickily and stop you short. But if they are there, simple, and come to hand, they are justified. In the last act of *Watch on the Rhine*, Kurt Müller is about to leave. He wants to say good-bye to his children who are upstairs. He asks his wife to bring them down. Now it is most probable that in real life a man would go upstairs, find the children in their room, say good-bye there. But it seemed to me, when this problem came up, that kind of un-well-madeness was not worth the candle. It seemed messy to ring in another set, to bring down the curtain, to interfere with a mood and a temper. The playwright, unlike the novelist, must—and here is where I think the charge of well-madeness should be made—trick up the scene. This is how he has to work. It is too bad, but it is not his fault. If he is good, and drives ahead, it will not matter much. If he is not good, the situation will worry him, and he will begin to pretend it doesn't exist and, by so pretending, fret and lengthen it.

I think the word melodrama, in our time, has come to be used in an almost illiterate manner. By definition it is a violent dramatic piece, with a happy ending. But I think we can add that it uses its violence for no purpose, to point no moral, to say nothing, in say-nothing's worse sense. (This, of course, does not mean, even by inference, that violence plus the *desire* to say something will raise the level of the work. A great many bad writers want to say something: their intention may make them fine men, but it does not make them fine writers. Winning the girl, getting the job, vanquishing the slight foe, are not enough.) But when violence is actually the needed stuff of the work and comes toward a large enough end, it has been and always will be in the good writer's field. George Moore said there was so much in *War and Peace* that Tolstoi must surely have awakened in the night frightened that he had left out a yacht race or a High Mass. There is a needed return to the correct use of the word melodrama. It is only then the critic will be able to find out whether a writer justifies his use of violence, and to scale him against those who have used it.

I do not want to talk here of *Watch on the Rhine.* Only eleven months have gone by since it was finished, and that is not time enough for me to see it clearly. Even now, of course, I know many ideas should have come clearer, many speeches cleaner, many things should have been said with more depth and understanding. I have not wanted to write here any final word on the plays. Some day, perhaps. Some day when I have greater faith that I will be the writer I now, on January 14, 1942, want to be. In any case, while there is much in all the plays that is wrong—and it did not hurt me to see it last night, as it once would have hurt me to half-see it— this much has been right: I tried. I did the best I could do at the time each play was written. Within the limitations of my own mind and nature, my own understanding, my own knowledge, it was the best I could do with what I had. If I did not hope to grow, I would not hope to live.

There have been two people—there have been others, good friends—who have been closely connected with these plays. I shall not, because I should not, thank them. One thanks for candy or a kindness, but not for what I owe them both. Herman Shumlin has directed and produced all four of the plays. On all four he has worked with the high seriousness which is the first requirement of a good artist.

He has done more than interpret these plays: he has wrung from them more than was in them, and hidden things in them which should not be seen. Mr. Shumlin's patient work on the plays has only been exceeded by his patient work with their author, and that is patience and sympathy of a high degree. It is one of the mysteries of the theatre—a mystery which irritates those who really *work* in the theatre —that very little is known, by the critics and the public, of the director's function. When a director is as good as Mr. Shumlin, his work is very important indeed. Important to the play and important to the actors who must interpret the play. Mr. Shumlin has made many an actor into a star, and many a star into a decent actor. The theatre, for him, is not a place to show off; not for himself, not for the actor. He is one of the few directors who believes in the *play:* he is one of the very few who has the sharp clarity, the sensitivity, the understanding, which should be the director's gift to the play.

By 1930 I had decided not to be a writer. I had tried, all my life, not too hard, I suppose, and certainly not too well. That year I thought I wouldn't ever be a good writer and if I couldn't be a good writer I didn't want to write at all. I had accepted that, but it made me sad. That I tried again is entirely due to Dashiell Hammett. Patiently and persistently, he hammered away. He began by attacking most of what I had written, teaching me along the way that writers must go to school at writing, and learn and read and think and study. He had made me believe that I should try once more. When I tried to write a play, he spared me nothing. Over and over again he would tell me how bad was the first draft, the second, the fifth, the sixth; over and over again I would bring the next drafts, giving them to him with what I thought was the truthful notice that if this wasn't any good I would never write again and might kill myself. It was meant to intimidate him, and it never did. If I never wrote again, he said, what difference did it make? If I wasn't going to be any good, I should stop writing anyway. Go back now and try again.

All that was more than friendship. It was the care and sacrifice of a scholarly and warm-hearted man who knows about writing, who wants it to be good, who is generous enough to give help. If he had never said much more to me—but that with pride—than that he thought I would be all right some day, it would still be the nicest compliment I have ever had.

January, 1942

RANDOM HOUSE, about to add two plays to this volume of four, has asked if I would like to write a new introduction. Every writer wants to make better, add to, do without, even make worse, what was written long ago or yesterday.

But if there is something in this introduction, written eighteen years ago, that now seems a little too young, a little too earnest, then that's what I was, and maybe still am, and no amount of more delicate phrasing or more shaded thought would hide it.

I said then that I wanted to live to be a better writer. I still want just that. No need to write about it again.

April, 1960

THE CHILDREN'S HOUR

FOR

D. HAMMETT

WITH THANKS

The Children's Hour was first produced at Maxine Elliot's Theatre, New York City, on November 20, 1934, with the following cast:

(In the order of their appearance)

PEGGY ROGERS	EUGENIA RAWLS
MRS. LILY MORTAR	ALINE MCDERMOTT
EVELYN MUNN	ELIZABETH SECKEL
HELEN BURTON	LYNNE FISHER
LOIS FISHER	JACQUELINE RUSLING
CATHERINE	BARBARA LEEDS
ROSALIE WELLS	BARBARA BEALS
MARY TILFORD	FLORENCE MCGEE
KAREN WRIGHT	KATHERINE EMERY
MARTHA DOBIE	ANNE REVERE
DOCTOR JOSEPH CARDIN	ROBERT KEITH
AGATHA	EDMONIA NOLLEY
MRS. AMELIA TILFORD	KATHERINE EMMET
A GROCERY BOY	JACK TYLER

Produced and directed by HERMAN SHUMLIN

Settings designed by ALINE BERNSTEIN

SCENE

ACT ONE

Living room of the Wright-Dobie School.
Late afternoon in April.

ACT TWO

Scene I. Living room at Mrs. Tilford's. A few hours later.
Scene II. The same. Later that evening.

ACT THREE

The same as Act One. November.

THE CHILDREN'S HOUR

ACT ONE

SCENE: *A room in the Wright-Dobie School for girls, a converted farm-house eighteen miles from the town of Lancet. It is a comfortable, unpretentious room used as an afternoon study-room and at all other times as the living room.*
A large door Left Center faces the audience. There is a single door Right. Against both back walls are bookcases. A large desk is at Right; a table, two sofas, and eight or ten chairs.
It is early in an afternoon in April.

AT RISE: MRS. LILLY MORTAR *is sitting in a large chair Right Center, with her head back and her eyes closed. She is a plump, florid woman of forty-five with obviously touched-up hair. Her clothes are too fancy for a class-room.*
Seven girls, from twelve to fourteen years old, are informally grouped on chairs and sofa. Six of them are sewing with no great amount of industry on pieces of white material. One of the others, EVELYN MUNN, *is using her scissors to trim the hair of* ROSALIE, *who sits, nervously, in front of her. She has* ROSALIE'S *head bent back at an awkward angle and is enjoying herself.*
The eighth girl, PEGGY ROGERS, *is sitting in a higher chair than the others. She is reading aloud from a book. She is bored and she reads in a singsong, tired voice.*

PEGGY (*reading*). "It is twice blest; it blesseth him that gives and him that takes: 'tis mightiest in the mightiest; it becomes the throned monarch better than his crown; his sceptre shows the force of temporal power, the attribute to awe and majesty, wherein . . ." (MRS. MORTAR *suddenly opens her eyes and stares at the haircutting. The children make efforts to warn* EVELYN. PEGGY *raises her voice until she is shouting*) "doth sit the dread and fear of kings; but mercy is above . . ."

MRS. MORTAR. Evelyn! What are you doing?

EVELYN (*inanely. She lisps*). Uh—nothing, Mrs. Mortar.

MRS. MORTAR. You are certainly doing something. You are ruining the scissors, for one thing.

PEGGY (*loudly*). "But mercy is above. It . . ."

MRS. MORTAR. Just a moment, Peggy. It is very unfortunate that you girls cannot sit quietly with your sewing and drink in the immortal words of the immortal bard. (*She sighs*) Evelyn, go back to your sewing.

EVELYN. I can't get the hem thtraight. Honeth, I've been trying for three weekth, but I jutht can't do it.

MRS. MORTAR. Helen, please help Evelyn with the hem.

HELEN (*rises, holding up the garment* EVELYN *has been working on. It is soiled and shapeless, and so much has been cut off that it is now hardly large enough for a child of five. Giggling*). She can't ever wear *that*, Mrs. Mortar.

MRS. MORTAR (*vaguely*). Well, try to do something with it. Make some handkerchiefs or something. Be clever about it. Women must learn these tricks. (*To* PEGGY) Continue. "Mightiest in the mightiest."

PEGGY. "'Tis mightiest in the mightiest; it becomes the throned monarch better than his crown; his sceptre—his sceptre shows the force of temporal power, the attribute to awe and majesty, wherein—"

LOIS (*from the back of the room chants softly and mo-*

notonously through the previous speech). Ferebam, ferebas, ferebat, ferebamus, ferebatis, fere, fere—

CATHERINE (*two seats away, the book propped in front of her*). Fere*bant*.

LOIS. Ferebamus, ferebatis, fere*bant*.

MRS. MORTAR. Who's doing that?

PEGGY (*the noise ceases. She hurries on*). "Wherein doth sit the dread and fear of kings; but mercy is above this sceptred sway, it is enthroned in the hearts of kings, it is an attribute to God himself—"

MRS. MORTAR (*sadly, reproachfully*). Peggy, can't you imagine yourself as Portia? Can't you read the lines with some feeling, some pity? (*Dreamily*) Pity. Ah! As Sir Henry said to me many's the time, pity makes the actress. Now, why can't *you* feel pity?

PEGGY. I guess I feel pity.

LOIS. Ferebamus, ferebatis, fere—fere—fere—

CATHERINE. Fere*bant*, stupid.

MRS. MORTAR. How many people in this room are talking? Peggy, read the line again. I'll give you the cue.

PEGGY. What's a cue?

MRS. MORTAR. A cue is a line or word given the actor or actress to remind them of their next speech.

HELEN (*softly*). To remind *him* or *her*.

ROSALIE (*a fattish girl with glasses*). Weren't you ever in the movies, Mrs. Mortar?

MRS. MORTAR. I had many offers, my dear. But the cinema is a shallow art. It has no—no— (*Vaguely*) no fourth dimension. Now, Peggy, if you would only try to submerge yourself in this problem. You are pleading for the life of a man. (*She rises and there are faint sighs from the girls, who stare at her with blank, bored faces. She recites hammily, with gestures*) "But mercy is above this sceptred sway; it is enthroned in the hearts of kings, it is an attribute to God himself; and earthly power doth then show likest God's when mercy seasons justice."

LOIS (*almost singing it*). Utor, fruor, fungor, potior, and vescor take the dative.

CATHERINE. Take the *ablative*.

LOIS. Oh, dear. Utor, fruor, fung—

MRS. MORTAR (*to* LOIS, *with sarcasm*). You have something to tell the class?

LOIS (*apologetically*). We've got a Latin exam this afternoon.

MRS. MORTAR. And you intend to occupy the sewing and elocution hour learning what should have been learnt yesterday?

CATHERINE (*wearily*). It takes her more than yesterday to learn it.

MRS. MORTAR. Well, I cannot allow you to interrupt us like this.

CATHERINE. But we're finished sewing.

LOIS (*admiringly*). I bet you were good at Latin, Mrs. Mortar.

MRS. MORTAR (*conciliated*). Long ago, my dear, long ago. Now, take your book over by the window and don't disturb our enjoyment of Shakespeare. (CATHERINE and LOIS *rise, go to window, stand mumbling and gesturing*) Let us go back again. "It is an attribute of—" (*At this point the door opens far enough to let* MARY TILFORD, *clutching a slightly faded bunch of wild flowers, squeeze cautiously in. She is fourteen, neither pretty nor ugly. She is an undistinguished-looking girl, except for the sullenly dissatisfied expression on her face*) "And earthly power doth then show likest God's when mercy seasons justice. We do pray for mercy, and that same prayer doth teach—"

PEGGY (*happily*). You've skipped three lines.

MRS. MORTAR. In my entire career I've never missed a line.

PEGGY. But you did skip three lines. (*Goes to* MRS. MORTAR *with book*) See?

MRS. MORTAR (*seeing* MARY *sidling along wall toward other end of the room, turns to her to avoid* PEGGY *and the book*). Mary!

HELEN (*in whisper to* MARY). You're going to catch it now.

MRS. MORTAR. Mary!

MARY. Yes, Mrs. Mortar?

MRS. MORTAR. This is a pretty time to be coming to your sewing class, I must say. Even if you have no interest in your work you might at least remember that you owe me a little courtesy. Courtesy is breeding. Breeding is an excellent thing. (*Turns to class*) Always re-member that.

ROSALIE. Please, Mrs. Mortar, can I write that down?

MRS. MORTAR. Certainly. Suppose you all write it down

PEGGY. But we wrote it down last week.

(MARY *giggles.*)

MRS. MORTAR. Mary, I am still awaiting your explanation. Where have you been?

MARY. I took a walk.

MRS. MORTAR. So you took a walk. And may I ask, young lady, are we in the habit of taking walks when we should be at our classes?

MARY. I am sorry, Mrs. Mortar, I went to get you these flowers. I thought you would like them and I didn't know it would take so long to pick them.

MRS. MORTAR (*flattered*). Well, well.

MARY (*almost in tears*). You were telling us last week how much you liked flowers, and I thought that I would bring you some and—

MRS. MORTAR. That was very sweet of you, Mary; I always like thoughtfulness. But you must not allow anything to interfere with your classes. Now run along, dear, and get a vase and some water to put my flowers in. (MARY *turns, sticks out her tongue at* HELEN, *says:* "A-a-a," *and exits Left*) You may put that book away, Peggy. I am sure your family need never worry about your going on the stage.

PEGGY. I don't want to go on the stage. I want to be a lighthouse-keeper's wife.

MRS. MORTAR. Well, I certainly hope you won't read to him.

(*The laughter of the class pleases her.* PEGGY *sits down among the other girls, who are making a great show of doing nothing.* MRS. MORTAR *returns to her chair, puts her head back, closes her eyes.*)

CATHERINE. How much longer, O Cataline, are you going to abuse our patience? (*To* LOIS) Now translate it, and for goodness' sakes try to get it right this time.

MRS. MORTAR (*for no reason*). "One master passion in the breast, like Aaron's serpent, swallows all the rest."

(*She and* LOIS *are murmuring during* KAREN WRIGHT'S *entrance.* KAREN *is an attractive woman of twenty-eight, casually pleasant in manner, without sacrifice of warmth or dignity. She smiles at the girls, goes to the desk. With her entrance there is an immediate change in the manner of the girls: they are fond of her and they respect her. She gives* MORTAR, *whose quotation has reached her, an annoyed look.*)

LOIS. "Quo usque tandem a*bute*re. . . ."

KAREN (*automatically*). "Abutere." (*Opens drawer in desk*) What's happened to your hair, Rosalie?

ROSALIE. It got cut, Miss Wright.

KAREN (*smiling*). I can see that. A new style? Looks as though it has holes in it.

EVELYN (*giggling*). I didn't mean to do it that bad, Mith Wright, but Rothalie'th got funny hair. I thaw a picture in the paper, and I wath trying to do it that way.

ROSALIE (*feels her hair, looks pathetically at* KAREN). Oh, what shall I do, Miss Wright? (*Gesturing*) It's long here, and it's short here and—

KAREN. Never mind. Come up to my room later and I'll see if I can fix it for you.

MRS. MORTAR. And hereafter we'll have no more hair-cutting.

KAREN. Helen, have you found your bracelet?

HELEN. No, I haven't, and I've looked everywhere.

KAREN. Have another look. It must be in your room somewhere.

(MARY *comes in Right, with her flowers in a vase. When she sees* KAREN, *she loses some of her assurance.* KAREN *looks at the flowers in surprise.*)

MARY. Good afternoon, Miss Wright. (*Sits down, looks at* KAREN, *who is staring hard at the flowers.*)

KAREN. Hello, Mary.

MRS. MORTAR (*fluttering around*). Peggy has been reading Portia for us.

(PEGGY *sighs.*)

KAREN (*smiling*). Peggy doesn't like Portia?

MRS. MORTAR. I don't think she quite appreciates it, but—

KAREN (*patting* PEGGY *on the head*). Well, I didn't either. I don't think I do yet. Where'd you get those flowers, Mary?

MRS. MORTAR. She picked them for me. (*Hurriedly*) It made her a little late to class, but she heard me say I loved flowers, and she went to get them for me. (*With a sigh*) The first wild flowers of the season.

KAREN. But not the very first, are they, Mary?

MARY. I don't know.

KAREN. Where did you get them?

MARY. Near Conway's cornfield, I think.

KAREN. It wasn't necessary to go so far. There was a bunch exactly like this in the garbage can this morning.

MRS. MORTAR (*after a second*). Oh, I can't believe it!

What a nasty thing to do! (*To* MARY) And I suppose
you have just as fine an excuse for being an hour late to
breakfast this morning, and last week— (*To* KAREN) I
haven't wanted to tell you these things before, but—

KAREN (*hurriedly, as a bell rings off stage*). There's the
bell.

LOIS (*walking toward door*). Ad, ab, ante, in, de, inter,
con, post, præ— (*Looks up at* KAREN) I *can't* seem to
remember the rest.

KAREN. Præ, pro, sub, super. Don't worry, Lois. You'll
come out all right. (LOIS *smiles, exits.* MARY *attempts
to make a quick exit*) Wait a minute, Mary. (*Reluctantly* MARY *turns back as the girls file out.* KAREN *moves
the small chairs, clearing the room as she talks*) Mary,
I've had the feeling—and I don't think I'm wrong—
that the girls here were happy; that they liked Miss
Dobie and me, that they liked the school. Do you think
that's true?

MARY. Miss Wright, I have to get my Latin book.

KAREN. I thought it was true until you came here a year
ago. I don't think you're very happy here, and I'd like
to find out why. (*Looks at* MARY, *waits for an answer,
gets none, shakes her head*) Why, for example, do you
find it necessary to lie to us so often?

MARY (*without looking up*). I'm not lying. I went out
walking and I saw the flowers and they looked pretty
and I didn't know it was so late.

KAREN (*impatiently*). Stop it, Mary! I'm not interested
in hearing that foolish story again. I *know* you got the
flowers out of the garbage can. What I do want to know
is why you feel you have to lie out of it.

MARY (*beginning to whimper*). I *did* pick the flowers
near Conway's. You never believe me. You believe
everybody but me. It's always like that. Everything I
say you fuss at me about. Everything I do is wrong.

KAREN You know that isn't true. (*Goes to* MARY, *puts her*

arm around her, waits until the sobbing has stopped)
Look, Mary, look at me. (*Raises* MARY'S *face with her
hand*) Let's try to understand each other. If you feel
that you *have* to take a walk, or that you just *can't* come
to class, or that you'd like to go into the village by
yourself, come and tell me—I'll try and understand.
(*Smiles*) I don't say that I'll always agree that you
should do exactly what you want to do, but I've had
feelings like that, too—everybody has—and I won't be
unreasonable about yours. But this way, this kind of
lying you do, makes everything wrong.

MARY (*looking steadily at* KAREN). I got the flowers near
Conway's cornfield.

KAREN (*looks at* MARY, *sighs, moves back toward desk
and stands there for a moment*). Well, there doesn't
seem to be any other way with you; you'll have to be
punished. Take your recreation periods alone for the
next two weeks. No horseback-riding and no hockey.
Don't leave the school grounds for any reason what-
soever. Is that clear?

MARY (*carefully*). Saturday, too?

KAREN. Yes.

MARY. But you said I could go to the boat-races.

KAREN. I'm sorry, but you can't go.

MARY. I'll tell my grandmother. I'll tell her how everybody treats me here and the way I get punished for
every little thing I do. I'll tell her, I'll—

MRS. MORTAR. Why, I'd slap her hands!

KAREN (*turning back from door, ignoring* MRS. MORTAR'S
speech. To MARY). Go upstairs, Mary.

MARY. I don't feel well.

KAREN (*wearily*). Go upstairs now.

MARY. I've got a pain. I've had it all morning. It hurts
right here (*pointing vaguely in the direction of her
heart*). Really it does.

KAREN. Ask Miss Dobie to give you some hot water and bicarbonate of soda.

MARY. It's a bad pain. I've never had it before.

KAREN. I don't think it can be very serious.

MARY. My heart! It's my heart! It's stopping or something. I can't breathe. (*She takes a long breath and falls awkwardly to the floor.*)

KAREN (*sighs, shakes her head, kneels beside* MARY. *To* MRS. MORTAR). Ask Martha to phone Joe.

MRS. MORTAR (*going out*). Do you think—? Heart trouble is very serious in a child.

(KAREN *picks* MARY *up from the floor and carries her off Right. After a moment* MARTHA DOBIE *enters Center. She is about the same age as* KAREN. *She is a nervous, high-strung woman.*)

KAREN (*enters Right*). Did you get Joe?

MARTHA (*nodding*). What happened to her? She was perfectly well a few hours ago.

KAREN. She probably still is. I told her she couldn't go to the boat-races and she had a heart attack.

MARTHA. Where is she?

KAREN. In there. Mortar's with her.

MARTHA. Anything really wrong with her?

KAREN. I doubt it. (*Sits down at desk and begins to mark papers*) She's a problem, that kid. Her latest trick was kidding your aunt out of a sewing lesson with those faded flowers we threw out. Then she threatened to go to her grandmother with some tale about being mistreated.

MARTHA. And, please God, Grandma would believe her and take her away.

KAREN. Which would give the school a swell black eye. But we ought to do something.

MARTHA. How about having a talk with Mrs. Tilford?

KAREN (*smiling*). You want to do it? (MARTHA *shakes her*

head) I hate to do it. She's been so nice to us. (*Shrugging her shoulders*) Anyway, it wouldn't do any good. She's too crazy about Mary to see her faults very clearly —and the kid knows it.

MARTHA. How about asking Joe to say something to her? She'd listen to him.

KAREN. That would be admitting that we can't do the job ourselves.

MARTHA. Well, we can't, and we might as well admit it. We've tried everything we can think of. She's had more attention than any other three kids put together. And we still haven't the faintest idea what goes on inside her head.

KAREN. She's a strange girl.

MARTHA. That's putting it mildly.

KAREN (*laughs*). It's funny. We always talk about the child as if she were a grown woman.

MARTHA. It's not so funny. There's something the matter with the kid. That's been true ever since the first day she came. She causes trouble here; she's bad for the other girls. I don't know what it is—it's a feeling I've got that it's wrong somewhere—

KAREN. All right, all right, we'll talk it over with Joe. Now what about our other pet nuisance?

MARTHA (*laughs*). My aunt the actress? What's she been up to now?

KAREN. Nothing unusual. Last night at dinner she was telling the girls about the time she lost her trunks in Butte, Montana, and how she gave her best performance of Rosalind during a hurricane. Today in the kitchen you could hear her on what Sir Henry said to her.

MARTHA. Wait until she does Hedda Gabler standing on a chair. Sir Henry taught her to do it that way. He said it was a test of great acting.

KAREN. You must have had a gay childhood.

MARTHA (*bitterly*). Oh, I did. I did, indeed. God, how I used to hate all that—

KAREN. Couldn't we get rid of her soon, Martha? I hate to make it hard on you, but she really ought not to be here.

MARTHA (*after a moment*). I know.

KAREN. We can scrape up enough money to send her away. Let's do it.

MARTHA (*goes to her, affectionately pats her head*). You've been very patient about it. I'm sorry and I'll talk to her today. It'll probably be a week or two before she can be ready to leave. Is that all right?

KAREN. Of course. (*Looks at her watch*) Did you get Joe himself on the phone?

MARTHA. He was already on his way. Isn't he always on his way over here?

KAREN (*laughs*). Well, I'm going to marry him some day, you know.

MARTHA (*looking at her*). You haven't talked of marriage for a long time.

KAREN. I've talked of it with Joe.

MARTHA. Then you *are* thinking about it—soon?

KAREN. Perhaps when the term is over. By that time we ought to be out of debt, and the school should be paying for itself.

MARTHA (*nervously playing with a book on the table*). Then we won't be taking our vacation together?

KAREN. Of course we will. The three of us.

MARTHA. I had been looking forward to some place by the lake—just you and me—the way we used to at college.

KAREN (*cheerfully*). Well, now there will be three of us. That'll be fun, too.

MARTHA (*after a pause*). Why haven't you told me this before?

KAREN. I'm not telling you anything we haven't talked about often.

MARTHA. But you're talking about it as *soon* now.

KAREN. I'm glad to be able to. I've been in love with Joe a long time. (MARTHA *crosses to window and stands looking out, her back to* KAREN. KAREN *finishes marking papers and rises*) It's a big day for the school. Rosalie's finally put an "l" in could.

MARTHA (*in a dull, bitter tone, not turning from window*). You really *are* going to leave, aren't you?

KAREN. I'm not going to leave, and you know it. Why do you say things like that? We agreed a long time ago that my marriage wasn't going to make any difference to the school.

MARTHA. But it will. You know it will. It can't help it.

KAREN. That's nonsense. Joe doesn't want me to give up here.

MARTHA (*turning from window*). I don't understand you. It's been so damned hard building this thing up, slaving and going without things to make ends meet—think of having a winter coat without holes in the lining again! —and now when we're getting on our feet, you're all ready to let it go to hell.

KAREN. This is a silly argument, Martha. Let's quit it. You haven't listened to a word I've said. I'm not getting married tomorrow, and when I do, it's not going to interfere with my work here. You're making something out of nothing.

MARTHA. It's going to be hard going on alone afterward.

KAREN. For God's sake, do you expect me to give up my marriage?

MARTHA. I don't mean that, but it's so—

(*Door Center opens and* DOCTOR JOSEPH CARDIN *comes in. He is a large, pleasant-looking, carelessly dressed man of about thirty-five.*)

CARDIN. Hello, darling. Hi, Martha. What's the best news?

MARTHA. Hello, Joe.

KAREN. We tried to get you on the phone. Come in and look at your little cousin.

CARDIN. Sure. What's the matter with her now? I stopped at Vernie's on the way over to look at that little black bull he bought. He's a baby! There's going to be plenty of good breeding done in these hills.

KAREN. You'd better come and see her. She says she has a pain in her heart. (*Goes out Right.*)

CARDIN (*stopping to light a cigarette*). Our little Mary pops up in every day's dispatches.

MARTHA (*impatiently*). Go and see her. Heart attacks are nothing to play with.

CARDIN (*looks at her*). Never played with one in my life. (*Exits Right.*)

(MARTHA *walks around room and finally goes to stare out window.*)

(MRS. MORTAR *enters Right.*)

MRS. MORTAR. *I* was asked to leave the room. (MARTHA *pays no attention*) It seems that I'm not wanted in the room during the examination.

MARTHA (*over her shoulder*). What difference does it make?

MRS. MORTAR. What difference does it make? Why, it was a deliberate snub.

MARTHA. There's very little pleasure in watching a man use a stethoscope.

MRS. MORTAR. Isn't it natural that the child should have me with her? Isn't it natural that an older woman should be present? (*No answer*) Very well, if you are so thick-skinned that you don't resent these things—

MARTHA. What are you talking about? Why, in the name of heaven, should *you* be with her?

MRS. MORTAR. It—it's customary for an older woman to be present during an examination.

MARTHA (*laughs*). Tell that to Joe. Maybe he'll give you a job as duenna for his office.

MRS. MORTAR (*reminiscently*). It was I who saved Delia Lampert's life the time she had that heart attack in Buffalo. We almost lost her that time. Poor Delia! We went over to London together. She married Robert Laffonne. Not seven months later he left her and ran away with Eve Cloun, who was playing the Infant Phenomenon in Birmingham—

MARTHA. Console yourself. If you've seen one heart attack, you've seen them all.

MRS. MORTAR. So you don't resent your aunt being snubbed and humiliated?

MARTHA. Oh, Aunt Lily!

MRS. MORTAR. Karen is consistently rude to me, and you know it.

MARTHA. I know that she is very polite to you, and—what's more important—very patient.

MRS. MORTAR. Patient with me? *I*, who have worked my fingers to the bone!

MARTHA. Don't tell yourself that too often, Aunt Lily; you'll come to believe it.

MRS. MORTAR. I *know* it's true. Where could you have gotten a woman of my reputation to give these children voice lessons, elocution lessons? Patient with me! Here I've donated my services—

MARTHA. I was under the impression you were being paid.

MRS. MORTAR. That small thing! I used to earn twice that for one performance.

MARTHA. The gilded days. It was very extravagant of them to pay you so much. (*Suddenly tired of the whole thing*) You're not very happy here, are you, Aunt Lily?

MRS. MORTAR. Satisfied enough, I guess, for a poor relation.

MARTHA (*makes a motion of distaste*). But you don't like the school or the farm or—

MRS. MORTAR. I told you at the beginning you shouldn't have bought a place like this. Burying yourself on a farm! You'll regret it.

MARTHA. We like it here. (*After a moment*) Aunt Lily, you've talked about London for a long time. Would you like to go over?

MRS. MORTAR (*with a sigh*). It's been twenty years, and I shall never live to see it again.

MARTHA. Well, you can go any time you like. We can spare the money now, and it will do you a lot of good. You pick out the boat you want and I'll get the passage. (*She has been talking rapidly, anxious to end the whole thing*) Now that's all fixed. You'll have a grand time seeing all your old friends, and if you live sensibly I ought to be able to let you have enough to get along on. (*She begins to gather books, notebooks, and pencils.*)

MRS. MORTAR (*slowly*). So you want me to leave?

MARTHA. That's not the way to put it. You've wanted to go ever since I can remember.

MRS. MORTAR. You're trying to get rid of me.

MARTHA. That's it. We don't want you around when we dig up the buried treasure.

MRS. MORTAR. So? You're turning me out? At my age! Nice, grateful girl you are.

MARTHA. Oh, my God, how can anybody deal with you? You're going where you want to go, and we'll be better off alone. That suits everybody. You complain about the farm, you complain about the school, you complain about Karen, and now you have what you want and you're still looking for something to complain about.

MRS. MORTAR (*with dignity*). Please do not raise your voice.

MARTHA. You ought to be glad I don't do worse.

MRS. MORTAR. I absolutely refuse to be shipped off three thousand miles away. I'm not going to England. I shall go back to the stage. I'll write to my agents tomorrow, and as soon as they have something good for me—

MARTHA. The truth is I'd like you to leave soon. The three

of us can't live together, and it doesn't make any difference whose fault it is.

MRS. MORTAR. You wish me to go tonight?

MARTHA. Don't act, Aunt Lily. Go as soon as you've found a place you like. I'll put the money in the bank for you tomorrow.

MRS. MORTAR. You think I'd take your money? I'd rather scrub floors first.

MARTHA. I imagine you'll change your mind.

MRS. MORTAR. I should have known by this time that the wise thing is to stay out of your way when *he's* in the house.

MARTHA. What are you talking about now?

MRS. MORTAR. Never mind. I should have known better. You always take your spite out on me.

MARTHA. Spite? (*Impatiently*) Oh, don't let's have any more of this today. I'm tired. I've been working since six o'clock this morning.

MRS. MORTAR. Any day that he's in the house is a bad day.

MARTHA. When *who* is in the house?

MRS. MORTAR. Don't think you're fooling me, young lady. I wasn't born yesterday.

MARTHA. Aunt Lily, the amount of disconnected unpleasantness that goes on in your head could keep a psychologist busy for years. Now go take your nap.

MRS. MORTAR. I know what I know. Every time that man comes into this house, you have a fit. It seems like you just can't stand the idea of them being together. God knows what you'll do when they get married. You're jealous of him, that's what it is.

MARTHA (*her voice is tense and the previous attitude of good-natured irritation is gone*). I'm very fond of Joe, and you know it.

MRS. MORTAR. You're fonder of Karen, and I know that. And it's unnatural, just as unnatural as it can be. You don't like their being together. You were always like that even as a child. If you had a little girl friend, you always got mad when she liked anybody else. Well, you'd better get a beau of your own now—a woman of your age.

MARTHA. The sooner you get out of here, the better. Your vulgarities are making me sick and I won't stand for them any longer. I want you to leave—

(*At this point there is a sound outside the large doors Center.* MARTHA *breaks off, angry and ashamed. After a moment she crosses to the door and opens it.* EVELYN *and* PEGGY *are to be seen on the staircase. For a second she stands still as they stop and look at her. Then, afraid that her anger with her aunt will color anything she might say to the children, she crosses the room again and stands with her back to them.*)

MARTHA. What were you doing outside the door?

EVELYN (*hurriedly*). We were going upththairth, Mith Dobie.

PEGGY. We came down to see how Mary was.

MARTHA. And you stopped long enough to see how we were. Did you deliberately listen?

PEGGY. We didn't mean to. We heard voices and we couldn't help—

MRS. MORTAR (*fake social tone*). Eavesdropping is something nice young ladies just don't do.

MARTHA (*turning to face the children*). Go upstairs now. We'll talk about this later. (*Slowly shuts door as they begin to climb the stairs.*)

MRS. MORTAR. You mean to say you're not going to do anything about that? (*No answer. She laughs nastily*) That's the trouble with these new-fangled notions of discipline and—

MARTHA (*thoughtfully*). You know, it's really bad having you around children.

MRS. MORTAR. What exactly does that mean?

MARTHA. It means that I don't like them hearing the things you say. Oh, I'll "do something about it," but the truth is that this is their home, and things shouldn't be said in it that they can't hear. When you're at your best, you're not for tender ears.

MRS. MORTAR. So now it's my fault, is it? Just as I said, whenever he's in the house you think you can take it out on me. You've got to have some way to let out steam and—

(*Door opens Right and* CARDIN *comes in.*)

MARTHA. How is Mary?

(MRS. MORTAR, *head in air, gives* MARTHA *a malicious half-smile and makes what she thinks is majestic exit Center.*)

MRS. MORTAR. Good day, Joseph.

CARDIN. What's the matter with the Duchess? (*Nods at door Center.*)

MARTHA. Just keeping her hand in, in case Sir Henry's watching her from above. What about Mary?

CARDIN. Nothing. Absolutely nothing.

MARTHA (*sighs*). I thought so.

CARDIN. I could have managed a better faint than that when I was six years old.

MARTHA. Nothing the matter with her at all, then?

CARDIN (*laughs*). No, ma'am, not a thing. Just a little something she thought up.

MARTHA. But it's such a silly thing to do. She knew we'd have you in. (*Sighs*) Maybe she's not so bright. Any idiots in your family, Joe? Any inbreeding?

CARDIN. Don't blame her on me. It's another side of the family. (*Laughs*) You can look at Aunt Amelia and tell: old New England stock; never married out of Boston; still thinks honor is honor and dinner's at eight thirty. Yes, ma'am, we're a proud old breed.

MARTHA. The Jukes were an old family, too. Look, Joe, have you any idea what is the matter with Mary? I mean, has she always been like this?

CARDIN. She's always been a honey. Aunt Amelia's spoiling hasn't helped any, either.

MARTHA. We're reaching the end of our rope with her. This kind of thing—

CARDIN (*looking at her*). Aren't you taking this too seriously?

MARTHA (*after a second*). I guess I am. But you stay around kids long enough and you won't know what to take seriously, either. But I do think somebody ought to talk to Mrs. Tilford about her.

CARDIN. You wouldn't be meaning me now, would you, Miss Dobie?

MARTHA. Well, Karen and I were talking about it this afternoon and—

CARDIN. Listen, friend, I'm marrying Karen, but I'm not writing Mary Tilford in the contract. (MARTHA *moves slightly.* CARDIN *takes her by the shoulders and turns her around to face him again. His face is grave, his voice gentle*) Forget Mary for a minute. You and I have got something to fight about. Every time anything's said about marrying—about Karen marrying me—you—(*She winces*) There it is. I'm fond of you. I always thought you liked me. What is it? I know how fond you are of Karen, but our marriage oughtn't to make a great deal of difference—

MARTHA (*pushing his hands from her shoulders*). God damn you. I wish— (*She puts her face in her hands.* CARDIN *watches her in silence, mechanically lighting a cigarette. When she takes her hands from her face, she holds them out to him. Contritely*) Joe, please, I'm sorry. I'm a fool, a nasty, bitter—

CARDIN (*takes her hands in one of his, patting them with his other hand*). Aw, shut up. (*He puts an arm around*

*her, and she leans her head against his lapel. They are
standing like that when* KAREN *comes in Right.*)

MARTHA (*to* KAREN, *as she wipes her eyes*). Your friend's
got a nice shoulder to weep on.

KAREN. He's an admirable man in every way. Well, the
angel child is now putting her clothes back on.

MARTHA. The angel child's influence is abroad even while
she's unconscious. Her room-mates were busy listening
at the door while Aunt Lily and I were yelling at each
other.

KAREN. We'll have to move those girls away from one
another.

(*A bell rings from the rear of the house.*)

MARTHA. That's my class. I'll send Peggy and Evelyn
down. You talk to them.

KAREN. All right. (*As* MARTHA *exits Center,* KAREN *goes
toward door Right. As she passes* CARDIN *she kisses
him*) Mary!

(MARY *opens door, comes in, stands buttoning the neck
of her dress.*)

CARDIN (*to* MARY). How's it feel to be back from the
grave?

MARY. My heart hurts.

CARDIN (*laughing. To* KAREN). Science has failed. Try a
hairbrush.

MARY. It's *my* heart, and it hurts.

KAREN. Sit down.

MARY. I want to see my grandmother. I want to—

(EVELYN *and* PEGGY *timidly enter Center.*)

KAREN. Sit down, girls, I want to talk to you.

PEGGY. We're awfully sorry, really. We just didn't think
and—

KAREN. I'm sorry too, Peggy. (*Thoughtfully*) You and
Evelyn never used to do things like this. We'll have to
separate you three.

EVELYN. Ah, Mith Wright, we've been together almotht a year.

KAREN. It was evidently too long. Now don't let's talk about it. Peggy, you will move into Lois's room, and Lois will move in with Evelyn. Mary will go in with Rosalie.

MARY. Rosalie hates me.

KAREN. That's a very stupid thing to say. I can't imagine Rosalie hating anyone.

MARY (*starting to cry*). And it's all because I had a pain. If anybody else was sick they'd be put to bed and petted. You're always mean to me. I get blamed and punished for everything. (*To* CARDIN) I do, Cousin Joe. All the time for everything.

(MARY *by now is crying violently and as* KAREN *half moves toward her,* CARDIN, *who has been frowning, picks* MARY *up and puts her down on the couch.*)

CARDIN. You've been unpleasant enough to Miss Wright. Lie here until you've stopped working yourself into a fit. (*Picks up his hat and bag, smiles at* KAREN) I've got to go now. She's not going to hurt herself crying. The next time she faints, I'd wait until she got tired lying on the floor. (*Passing* MARY, *he pats her head. She jerks away from him.*)

KAREN. Wait a minute. I'll walk to the car with you. (*To girls*) Go up now and move your things. Tell Lois to get her stuff ready.

(*She and* CARDIN *exit Center. A second after the door is closed,* MARY *springs up and throws a cushion at the door.*)

EVELYN. Don't do that. She'll hear you.

MARY. Who cares if she does? (*Kicks table*) And she can hear that, too.

(*Small ornament falls off table and breaks on floor.* EVELYN *and* PEGGY *gasp, and* MARY'S *bravado disappears for a moment.*)

EVELYN (*frightened*). Now what are you going to do?

PEGGY (*stooping down in a vain effort to pick up the pieces*). You'll get the devil now. Dr. Cardin gave it to Miss Wright. I guess it was kind of a lover's gift. People get awfully angry about a lover's gift.

MARY. Oh, leave it alone. She'll never know we did it.

PEGGY. *We* didn't do it. You did it yourself.

MARY. And what will you do if I say *we* did do it? (*Laughs*) Never mind, I'll think of something else. The wind could've knocked it over.

EVELYN. Yeh. She'th going to believe that one.

MARY. Oh, stop worrying about it. I'll get out of it.

EVELYN. Did you really have a pain?

MARY. I fainted, didn't I?

PEGGY. I wish I could faint sometimes. I've never even worn glasses, like Rosalie.

MARY. A lot it'll get you to faint.

EVELYN. What did Mith Wright do to you when the clath left?

MARY. Told me I couldn't go to the boat-races.

EVELYN. Whew!

PEGGY. But we'll remember everything that happens and we'll give you all the souvenirs and things.

MARY. I won't let you go if I can't go. But I'll find some way to go. What were *you* doing?

PEGGY. I guess we shouldn't have done it, really. We came down to see what was happening to you, but the doors were closed and we could hear Miss Dobie and Mortar having an awful row. Then Miss Dobie opens the door and there we were.

MARY. And a lot of crawling and crying you both did too, I bet.

EVELYN. We were thort of thorry about lithening. I gueth it wathn't—

MARY. Ah, you're always sorry about everything. What were they saying?

PEGGY. What was who saying?

MARY. Dobie and Mortar, silly.

PEGGY (*evasively*). Just talking, I guess.

EVELYN. Fighting, you mean.

MARY. About what?

EVELYN. Well, they were talking about Mortar going away to England and—

PEGGY. You know, it really wasn't very nice to've listened, and I think it's worse to tell.

MARY. You do, do you? You just don't tell me and see what happens.

(PEGGY *sighs*.)

EVELYN. Mortar got awful thore at that and thaid they juth wanted to get rid of her, and then they thtarted talking about Dr. Cardin.

MARY. What about him?

PEGGY. We'd better get started moving; Miss Wright will be back first thing we know.

MARY (*fiercely*). Shut up! Go on, Evelyn.

EVELYN. They're going to be married.

MARY. Everybody knows that.

PEGGY. But everybody doesn't know that Miss Dobie doesn't want them to get married. How do you like that?

(*The door opens and* ROSALIE WELLS *sticks her head in.*)

ROSALIE. I have a class soon. If you're going to move your things—

MARY. Close that door, you idiot. (ROSALIE *closes door, stands near it*) What do you want?

ROSALIE. I'm trying to tell you. If you're going to move your things—not that I want you in with me—you'd better start right now. Miss Wright's coming in a minute.

MARY. Who cares if she is?

ROSALIE (*starts for door*). I'm just telling you for your own good.

PEGGY (*getting up*). We're coming.

MARY. No. Let Rosalie move our things.

ROSALIE. You crazy?

PEGGY (*nervously*). It's all right. Evelyn and I'll get your things. Come on, Evelyn.

MARY. Trying to get out of telling me, huh? Well, you won't get out of it that way. Sit down and stop being such a sissy. Rosalie, you go on up and move my things and don't say a word about our being down here.

ROSALIE. And who was your French maid yesterday, Mary Tilford?

MARY (*laughing*). You'll do for today. Now go on, Rosalie, and fix our things.

ROSALIE. You crazy?

MARY. And the next time we go into town, I'll let you wear my gold locket and buckle. You'll like that, won't you, Rosalie?

ROSALIE (*draws back, moves her hands nervously*). I don't know what you're talking about.

MARY. Oh, I'm not talking about anything in particular. You just run along now and remind me the next time to get my buckle and locket for you.

ROSALIE (*stares at her a moment*). All right, I'll do it this time, but just 'cause I got a good disposition. But don't think you're going to boss me around, Mary Tilford.

MARY (*smiling*). No, indeed. (ROSALIE *starts for door*) And get the things done neatly, Rosalie. Don't muss my white linen bloomers—

(*The door slams as* MARY *laughs.*)

EVELYN. Now what do you think of that? What made her tho agreeable?

MARY. Oh, a little secret we got. Go on, now, what else did they say?

PEGGY. Well, Mortar said that Dobie was jealous of them, and that she was like that when she was a little girl, and that she'd better get herself a beau of her own because it was unnatural, and that she never wanted anybody to like Miss Wright, and that was unnatural. Boy! Did Miss Dobie get sore at that!

EVELYN. Then we didn't hear any more. Peggy dropped a book.

MARY. What'd she mean Dobie was jealous?

PEGGY. What's unnatural?

EVELYN. Un for not. Not natural.

PEGGY. It's funny, because everybody gets married.

MARY. A lot of people don't—they're too ugly.

PEGGY (*jumps up, claps her hand to her mouth*). Oh, my God! Rosalie'll find that copy of *Mademoiselle de Maupin*. She'll blab like the dickens.

MARY. Ah, she won't say a word.

EVELYN. Who getth the book when we move?

MARY. You can have it. That's what I was doing this morning—finishing it. There's one part in it—

PEGGY. What part?

(MARY *laughs*.)

EVELYN. Well, what wath it?

MARY. Wait until you read it.

EVELYN. Don't forget to give it to me.

PEGGY. It's a shame about being moved. I've got to go in with Helen, and she blows her nose all night. Lois told me.

MARY. It was a dirty trick making us move. She just wants to see how much fun she can take away from me. She hates me.

PEGGY. No, she doesn't, Mary. She treats you just like the rest of us—almost better.

MARY. That's right, stick up for your crush. Take her side against mine.

PEGGY. I didn't mean it that way.

EVELYN (*looks at her watch*). We'd better get upthtairth.

MARY. I'm not going.

PEGGY. Rosalie isn't so bad.

EVELYN. What you going to do about the vathe?

MARY. I don't care about Rosalie and I don't care about the vase. I'm not going to be here.

EVELYN *and* PEGGY (*together*). Not going to be here! What do you mean?

MARY (*calmly*). I'm going home.

PEGGY. Oh, Mary—

EVELYN. You can't do that.

MARY. Can't I? You just watch. (*Begins to walk around the room*) I'm not staying here. I'm going home and tell Grandma I'm not staying any more. (*Smiles to herself*) I'll tell her I'm not happy. They're scared of Grandma—she helped 'em when they first started, you know—and when she tells 'em something, believe me, they'll sit up and listen. They can't get away with treating me like this, and they don't have to think they can.

PEGGY (*appalled*). You just going to walk out like that?

EVELYN. What you going to tell your grandmother?

MARY. Oh, who cares? I'll think of something to tell her. I can always do it better on the spur of the moment.

PEGGY. She'll send you right back.

MARY. You let me worry about that. Grandma's very fond of me, on account my father was her favorite son. I can manage *her* all right.

PEGGY. I don't think you ought to go, really, Mary. It's just going to make an awful lot of trouble.

EVELYN. What'th going to happen about the vathe?

MARY. Say I did it—it doesn't make a bit of difference any more to me. Now listen, you two got to help. They won't miss me before dinner if you make Rosalie shut the door and keep it shut. Now, I'll go through the field to French's, and then I can get the bus to Homestead.

EVELYN. How you going to get to the thtreet-car?

MARY. Taxi, idiot.

PEGGY. How are you going to get out of here in the first place?

MARY. I'm going to walk out. You know where the front door is, or are you too dumb even for that? Well, I'm going right out that front door.

EVELYN. Gee, I wouldn't have the nerve.

MARY. Of course you wouldn't. You'd let 'em do anything to you they want. Well, they can't do it to me. Who's got any money?

EVELYN. Not me. Not a thent.

MARY. I've got to have at least a dollar for the taxi and a dime for the bus.

EVELYN. And where you going to find it?

PEGGY. See? Why don't you just wait until your allowance comes Monday, and then you can go any place you want. Maybe by that time—

MARY. I'm going today. *Now.*

EVELYN. You can't *walk* to Lanthet.

MARY (*goes to* PEGGY). You've got money. You've got two dollars and twenty-five cents.

PEGGY. I—I—

MARY. Go get it for me.

PEGGY. No! No! I won't get it for you.

EVELYN. You can't have *that* money, Mary—

MARY. Get it for me.

PEGGY (*cringes, her voice is scared*). I won't. I won't. Mamma doesn't send me much allowance—not half as much as the rest of you get—I saved this so long—you took it from me last time—

EVELYN. Ah, she wantth that bithycle tho bad.

PEGGY. I haven't gone to the movies, I haven't had any candy, I haven't had anything the rest of you get all the time. It took me so long to save that and I—

MARY. Go upstairs and get me the money.

PEGGY (*hysterically, backing away from her*). I won't. I won't. I won't.

(MARY *makes a sudden move for her, grabs her left arm, and jerks it back, hard and expertly.* PEGGY *screams softly.* EVELYN *tries to take* MARY's *arm away. Without releasing her hold on* PEGGY, MARY *slaps* EVELYN's *face.* EVELYN *begins to cry.*)

MARY. Just say when you've had enough.

PEGGY (*softly, stiflingly*). All—all right—I'll get it.

(MARY *smiles, nods her head as the Curtain falls.*)

ACT TWO

SCENE I

SCENE: *Living room at* MRS. TILFORD'S. *It is a formal room, without being cold or elegant. The furniture is old, but excellent. The exit to the hall is Left; glass doors Right lead to a dining room that cannot be seen.*

AT RISE: *Stage is empty. Voices are heard in the hall*

AGATHA (*off-stage*). What are *you* doing here? Well, come on in—don't stand there gaping at me. Have they given you a holiday or did you just decide you'd get a better dinner here? (AGATHA *enters Left, followed by* MARY. AGATHA *is a sharp-faced maid, not young, with a querulous voice*) Can't you even say hello?

MARY. Hello, Agatha. You didn't give me a chance. Where's Grandma?

AGATHA. Why aren't you in school? Look at your face and clothes. Where have you been?

MARY. I got a little dirty coming home. I walked part of the way through the woods.

AGATHA. Why didn't you put on your middy blouse and your old brown coat?

MARY. Oh, stop asking me questions. Where's Grandma?

AGATHA. Where ought any clean person be at this time of day? She's taking a bath.

MARY. Is anybody coming for dinner?

AGATHA. She didn't say anything about you coming.

MARY. How could she, stupid? She didn't know.

AGATHA. Then what are you doing here?

MARY. Leave me alone. I don't feel well.

AGATHA. Why don't you feel well? Who ever heard of a person going for a walk in the woods when they didn't feel well?

MARY. Oh, leave me alone. I came home because I was sick.

AGATHA. You look all right.

MARY. But I don't feel all right. (*Whining*) I can't even come home without everybody nagging at me.

AGATHA. Don't think you're fooling me, young lady. You might pull the wool over some people's eyes, but—I bet you've been up to something again. (*Stares suspiciously at* MARY, *who says nothing*) Well, you wait right here till I tell your grandmother. And if you feel so sick, you certainly won't want any dinner. A good dose of rhubarb and soda will fix you up. (*Exits Left.*)

(MARY *makes a face in the direction* AGATHA *has gone and stops sniffling. She looks nervously around the room, then goes to a low mirror and tries several experiments with her face in an attempt to make it look sick and haggard.*)

(MRS. TILFORD, *followed by* AGATHA, *enters Left.* MRS. TILFORD *is a large, dignified woman in her sixties, with a pleasant, strong face.*)

AGATHA (*to* MRS. TILFORD, *as she follows her into the room*). Why didn't you put some cold water on your chest? Do you want to catch your death of cold at your age? Did you have to hurry so?

MRS. TILFORD. Mary, what are you doing home?

(MARY *rushes to her and buries her head in* MRS. TILFORD'S *dress, crying.* MRS. TILFORD *lets her cry for a moment while she pats her head, then puts an arm around the child and leads her to a sofa.*)

MRS. TILFORD. Never mind, dear; now stop crying and tell me what is the matter.

MARY (*gradually stops crying, fondling* MRS. TILFORD'S

hand). It's so good to see you, Grandma. You didn't come to visit me all last week.

MRS. TILFORD. I couldn't, dear. But I was coming tomorrow.

MARY. I missed you so. (*Smiling up at* MRS. TILFORD) I was awful homesick.

MRS. TILFORD. I'm glad that's all it was. I was frightened when Agatha said you were not well.

AGATHA. Did I say that? I said she needed a good dose of rhubarb and soda. Most likely she only came home for Wednesday night fudge cake.

MRS. TILFORD. We all get homesick. But how did you get here? Did Miss Karen drive you over?

MARY. I—I walked most of the way, and then a lady gave me a ride and—(*Looks timidly at* MRS. TILFORD.)

AGATHA. Did she have to walk through the woods in her very best coat?

MRS. TILFORD. Mary! Do you mean you left without permission?

MARY (*nervously*). I ran away, Grandma. They didn't know—

MRS. TILFORD. That was a very bad thing to do, and they'll be worried. Agatha, phone Miss Wright and tell her Mary is here. John will drive her back before dinner.

MARY (*as* AGATHA *starts toward telephone*). No, Grandma, don't do that. Please don't do that. Please let me stay.

MRS. TILFORD. But, darling, you can't leave school any time you please.

MARY. Oh, please, Grandma, don't send me back right away. You don't know how they'll punish me.

MRS. TILFORD. I don't think they'll be that angry. Come, you're acting like a foolish little girl.

MARY (*hysterically, as she sees* AGATHA *about to pick up the telephone*). Grandma! Please! I can't go back! I can't! They'll kill me! They will, Grandma! They'll kill me!

(MRS. TILFORD *and* AGATHA *stare at* MARY *in amazement. She puts her head in* MRS. TILFORD'S *lap and sobs.*)

MRS. TILFORD (*motioning with a hand for* AGATHA *to leave the room*). Never mind phoning now, Agatha.

AGATHA. If you're going to let her—

(MRS. TILFORD *repeats the gesture.* AGATHA *exits Right, with offended dignity.*)

MRS. TILFORD. Stop crying, Mary.

MARY (*raising her head from* MRS. TILFORD'S *lap*). It's so nice here, Grandma.

MRS. TILFORD. I'm glad you like being home with me, but at your age you can hardly—(*More seriously*) What made you say such a terrible thing about Miss Wright and Miss Dobie? You know they wouldn't hurt you.

MARY. Oh, but they would. They—I—(*Breaks off, looks around as if hunting for a clue to her next word; then dramatically*) I fainted today!

MRS. TILFORD (*alarmed*). Fainted?

MARY. Yes, I did. My heart—I had a pain in my heart. I couldn't help having a pain in my heart, and when I fainted right in class, they called Cousin Joe and he said I didn't. He said it was maybe only that I ate my breakfast too fast and Miss Wright blamed me for it.

MRS. TILFORD (*relieved*). I'm sure if Joseph said it wasn't serious, it wasn't.

MARY. But I did have a pain in my heart—honest.

MRS. TILFORD. Have you still got it?

MARY. I guess I haven't got it much any more, but I feel a little weak, and I was so scared of Miss Wright being so mean to me just because I was sick.

MRS. TILFORD. Scared of Karen? Nonsense. It's perfectly possible that you had a pain, but if you had really been sick your Cousin Joseph would certainly have known it. It's not nice to frighten people by pretending to be sick when you aren't.

MARY. I didn't *want* to be sick, but I'm always getting punished for everything.

MRS. TILFORD (*gently*). You mustn't imagine things like that, child, or you'll grow up to be a very unhappy woman. I'm not going to scold you any more for coming home this time, though I suppose I should. Run along upstairs and wash your face and change your dress, and after dinner John will drive you back. Run along.

MARY (*happily*). I can stay for dinner?

MRS. TILFORD. Yes.

MARY. Maybe I could stay till the first of the week. Saturday's your birthday and I could be here with you.

MRS. TILFORD. We don't celebrate my birthday, dear. You'll have to go back to school after dinner.

MARY. But—(*She hesitates, then goes up to* MRS. TILFORD *and puts her arms around the older woman's neck. Softly*) How much do you love me?

MRS TILFORD (*smiling*). As much as all the words in all the books in all the world.

MARY. Remember when I was little and you used to tell me that right before I went to sleep? And it was a rule nobody could say another single word after you finished? You used to say: "Wor-rr-ld," and then I had to shut my eyes tight.

MRS. TILFORD. And sometimes you were naughty and didn't shut them.

MARY. I miss you an awful lot, Grandma.

MRS. TILFORD. And I miss you, but I'm afraid my Latin is too rusty—you'll learn it better in school.

MARY. But couldn't I stay out the rest of this term? After the summer maybe I won't mind it so much. I'll study hard, honest, and—

MRS. TILFORD. You're an earnest little coaxer, but it's out of the question. Back you go tonight. (*Gives* MARY *a playful slap*) Let's not have any more talk about it now, and let's have no more running away from school ever.

MARY (*slowly*). Then I really have to go back there to-night?

MRS. TILFORD. Of course.

MARY. You don't love me. You don't care whether they kill me or not.

MRS. TILFORD. Mary.

MARY. You don't! You don't! You don't care what happens to me.

MRS. TILFORD (*sternly*). But I *do* care that you're talking this way.

MARY (*meekly*). I'm sorry I said that, Grandma. I didn't mean to hurt your feelings. (*Puts her arms around* MRS. TILFORD's *neck*) Forgive me?

MRS. TILFORD. What made you talk like that?

MARY (*in a whisper*). I'm scared, Grandma, I'm scared. They'll do dreadful things to me.

MRS. TILFORD. Dreadful? Nonsense. They'll punish you for running away. You deserve to be punished.

MARY. It's not that. It's not anything I do. It never is. They —they just punish me anyhow, just like they got something against me. I'm afraid of them, Grandma.

MRS. TILFORD. That's ridiculous. What have they ever done to you that is so terrible?

MARY. A lot of things—all the time. Miss Wright says I can't go to the boat-races and—(*Realizing the inadequacy of this reply, she breaks off, hesitates, hunting for a more telling reply, and finally stammers*) It's—it's after what happened today.

MRS. TILFORD. You mean something else besides your naughtiness in pretending to faint and then running away?

MARY. I *did* faint. I didn't pretend. They just said that to make me feel bad. Anyway, it wasn't anything that I did.

MRS. TILFORD. What was it, then?

MARY. I can't tell you.

MRS. TILFORD. Why?

MARY (*sulkily*). Because you're just going to take their part.

MRS. TILFORD (*a little annoyed*). Very well. Now run upstairs and get ready for dinner.

MARY. It was—it was all about Miss Dobie and Mrs. Mortar. They were talking awful things and Peggy and Evelyn heard them and Miss Dobie found out, and then they made us move our rooms.

MRS. TILFORD. What has that to do with you? I don't understand a word you're saying.

MARY. They made us move our rooms. They said we couldn't be together any more. They're afraid to have us near them, that's what it is, and they're taking it out on me. They're scared of you.

MRS. TILFORD. For a little girl you're imagining a lot of big things. Why should they be scared of me? Am I such an unpleasant old lady?

MARY. They're afraid you'll find out.

MRS. TILFORD. Find out what?

MARY (*vaguely*). Things.

MRS. TILFORD. Run along, Mary. I hope you'll get more coherent as you get older.

MARY (*slowly starting for door*). All right. But there're a lot of things. They have secrets or something, and they're afraid I'll find out and tell you.

MRS. TILFORD. There's not necessarily anything wrong with people having secrets.

MARY (*coming back in the room again*). But they've got funny ones. Peggy and Evelyn heard Mrs. Mortar telling Miss Dobie that she was jealous of Miss Wright marrying Cousin Joe.

MRS. TILFORD. You shouldn't repeat things like that.

MARY. But that's what she said, Grandma. She said it was unnatural for a girl to feel that way.

MRS. TILFORD. What?

MARY. I'm just telling you what she said. She said there was something funny about it, and that Miss Dobie had always been like that, even when she was a little girl, and that it was unnatural—

MRS. TILFORD. Stop using that silly word, Mary.

MARY (*vaguely realizing that she is on the right track, hurries on*). But that was the word *she* kept using, Grandma, and then they got mad and told Mrs. Mortar she'd have to get out.

MRS. TILFORD. That was probably not the reason at all.

MARY (*nodding vigorously*). I bet it was, because honestly, Miss Dobie does get cranky and mean every time Cousin Joe comes, and today I heard her say to him: "God damn you," and then she said she was just a jealous fool and—

MRS. TILFORD. You have picked up some very fine words, haven't you, Mary?

MARY. That's just what she said, Grandma, and one time Miss Dobie was crying in Miss Wright's room, and Miss Wright was trying to stop her, and she said that all right, maybe she wouldn't get married right away if—

MRS. TILFORD. How do you know all this?

MARY. We couldn't help hearing because they—I mean Miss Dobie—was talking awful loud, and their room is right next to ours.

MRS. TILFORD. Whose room?

MARY. Miss Wright's room, I mean, and you can just ask Peggy and Evelyn whether we didn't hear. Almost always Miss Dobie comes in after we go to bed and stays a long time. I guess that's why they want to get rid of us—of me—because we hear things.

That's why they're making us move our room, and they punish me all the time for—

MRS. TILFORD. For eavesdropping, I should think. (*She has said this mechanically. With nothing definite in her mind, she is making an effort to conceal the fact that* MARY's *description of the life at school has shocked her*) Well, now I think we've had enough gossip, don't you? Dinner's almost ready, and I can't eat with a girl who has such a dirty face.

MARY (*softly*). I've heard other things, too.

MRS. TILFORD (*abstractedly*). What? What did you say?

MARY. I've heard other things. Plenty of other things, Grandma.

MRS. TILFORD. What things?

MARY. Bad things.

MRS. TILFORD. Well, what were they?

MARY. I can't tell you.

MRS. TILFORD. Mary, you're annoying me very much. If you have anything to say, then say it and stop acting silly.

MARY. I mean I can't say it out loud.

MRS. TILFORD. There couldn't possibly be anything so terrible that you couldn't say it out loud. Now either tell the truth or be still.

MARY. Well, a lot of things I don't understand. But it's awful, and sometimes they fight and then they make up, and Miss Dobie cries and Miss Wright gets mad, and then they make up again, and there are funny noises and we get scared.

MRS. TILFORD. Noises? I suppose you girls have a happy time imagining a murder.

MARY. And we've seen things, too. Funny things. (*Sees the impatience of her grandmother*) I'd tell you, but I got to whisper it.

MRS. TILFORD. Why must you whisper it?

MARY. I don't know. I just got to. (*Climbs on the sofa*

next to MRS. TILFORD *and begins whispering. At first the whisper is slow and hesitant, but it gradually works itself up to fast, excited talking. In the middle of it* MRS. TILFORD *stops her.*)

MRS. TILFORD (*trembling*). Do you know what you're saying? (*Without answering,* MARY *goes back to the whispering until the older woman takes her by the shoulders and turns her around to stare in her face*) Mary! *Are you telling me the truth?*

MARY. Honest, honest. You just ask Peggy and Evelyn and—(*After a moment* MRS. TILFORD *gets up and begins to pace about the room. She is no longer listening to* MARY, *who keeps up a running fire of conversation*) They know too. And maybe there're other kids who know, but we've always been frightened and so we didn't ask, and one night I was going to go and find out, but I got scared and we went to bed early so we wouldn't hear, but sometimes I couldn't help it, but we never talked about it much, because we thought they'd find out and— Oh, Grandma, don't make me go back to that awful place.

MRS. TILFORD (*abstractedly*). What? (*Starts to move about again.*)

MARY. Don't make me go back to that place. I just couldn't stand it any more. Really, Grandma, I'm so unhappy there, and if only I could stay out the rest of the term, why, then—

MRS. TILFORD (*makes irritated gesture*). Be still a minute. (*After a moment*) No, you won't have to go back.

MARY (*surprised*). Honest?

MRS. TILFORD. Honest.

MARY (*hugging* MRS. TILFORD). You're the nicest, loveliest grandma in all the world. You—you're not mad at me?

MRS. TILFORD. I'm not mad at you. Now go upstairs and get ready for dinner. (MARY *kisses her and runs hap-*

pily out Left. MRS. TILFORD *stands staring after her for a long moment; then, very slowly, she puts on her eye-glasses and crosses to the phone. She dials a number)* Is Miss Wright—is Miss Wright in? (*Waits a second, hurriedly puts down the receiver)* Never mind, never mind. (*Dials another number)* Dr. Cardin, please. Mrs. Tilford. (*She remains absolutely motionless while she waits. When she does speak, her voice is low and tense)* Joseph? Joseph? Can you come to see me right away? Yes, I'm perfectly well. No, but it's important, Joseph, very important. I must see you right away. I—I can't tell you over the phone. Can't you come sooner? It's not about Mary's fainting—I said it's not about Mary, Joseph; in one way it's about Mary— (*Suddenly quiet)* But will the hospital take so long? Very well, Joseph, make it as soon as you can. (*Hangs up the receiver, sits for a moment undecided. Then, taking a breath, she dials another number)* Mrs. Munn, please. This is Mrs. Tilford. Miriam? This is Amelia Tilford. I have some-thing to tell you—something very shocking, I'm afraid —something about the school and Evelyn and Mary—

Curtain

SCENE II

SCENE: *The same as Scene I. The curtain has been lowered to mark the passing of a few hours.*

AT RISE: MARY *is lying on the floor playing with a puzzle.* AGATHA *appears lugging blankets and pillows across the room. Almost at the door, she stops and gives* MARY *an annoyed look.*

AGATHA. And see to it that she doesn't get my good quilt all dirty, and let her wear your green pajamas.

MARY. Who?

AGATHA. Who? Don't you ever keep your ears open? Rosalie Wells is coming over to spend the night with you.

MARY. You mean she's going to sleep *here?*

AGATHA. You heard me.

MARY. What for?

AGATHA. Do I know all the crazy things that are happening around here? Your grandmother phones Mrs. Wells all the way to New York, three dollars and eighty-five cents and families starving, and Mrs. Wells wanted to know if Rosalie could stay here until tomorrow.

MARY (*relieved*). Oh. Couldn't Evelyn Munn come instead?

AGATHA. Sure. We'll have the whole town over to entertain you.

MARY. I won't let Rosalie Wells wear my new pajamas.

AGATHA (*exits as the front door-bell rings*). Don't tell me what you won't do. You'll act like a lady for once in your life. (*Off-stage*) Come on in, Rosalie. Just go on in there and make yourself at home. Have you had your dinner?

ROSALIE (*off-stage*). Good evening. Yes'm.

AGATHA (*off-stage*). Hang up your pretty coat. Have you had your bath?

ROSALIE (*off-stage*). Yes, ma'am. This morning.

AGATHA (*off-stage*). Well, you better have another one. (*She is climbing the stairs as* ROSALIE *comes into the room.* MARY, *lying in front of the couch, is hidden from her. Gingerly* ROSALIE *sits down on a chair.*)

MARY (*softly*). Whoooooo. (ROSALIE *jumps*) Whoooooo. (ROSALIE, *frightened, starts hurriedly for the door.* MARY *sits up, laughs*) You're a goose.

ROSALIE (*belligerently*). Oh, so it's you. Well, who likes to hear funny noises at night? You could have been a werewolf.

MARY. A werewolf wouldn't want you.

ROSALIE. You know everything, don't you? (MARY *laughs.* ROSALIE *comes over, stands staring at puzzle*) Isn't it funny about school?

MARY. What's funny about it?

ROSALIE. Don't act like you can come home every night.

MARY. Maybe I can from now on. (*Rolls over on her back luxuriously*) Maybe I'm never going back.

ROSALIE. Am I going back? I don't want to stay home.

MARY. What'll you give to know?

ROSALIE. Nothing. I'll ask Mamma.

MARY. Will you give me a free T. L. if I tell you?

ROSALIE (*thinks for a moment*). All right. Lois Fisher told Helen that you were very smart.

MARY. That's an old one. I won't take it.

ROSALIE. You got to take it.

MARY. Nope.

ROSALIE (*laughs*). You don't know, anyway.

MARY. I know what I heard, and I know Grandma phoned your mother in New York to come and get you right away. You're just going to spend the night here. I wish Evelyn could come instead of you.

ROSALIE. But what's happened? Peggy and Helen and Evelyn and Lois went home tonight, too. Do you think somebody's got scarlet fever or something?

MARY. No.

ROSALIE. Do *you* know what it is? How'd you find out? (*No answer*) You're always pretending you know everything. You're just faking. (*Flounces away*) Never mind, don't bother telling me. I think curiosity is very unladylike, anyhow. I have no concern with your silly secrets.

MARY. Suppose I told you that I just may have said that you were in on it?

ROSALIE. In on what?

MARY. The secret. Suppose I told you that I *may have* said that you told me about it?

ROSALIE. Why, Mary Tilford! You can't do a thing like that. I didn't tell you about anything. (MARY *laughs*) Did you tell your grandmother such a thing?

MARY. Maybe.

ROSALIE. Did you?

MARY. Maybe.

ROSALIE. Well, I'm going right up to your grandmother and tell her I didn't tell you anything—whatever it is. You're just trying to get me into trouble and I'm not going to let you. (*Starts for door.*)

MARY. Wait a minute, I'll come with you.

ROSALIE. What for?

MARY. I want to tell her about Helen Burton's bracelet.

ROSALIE (*sits down suddenly*). What about it?

MARY. Just that you stole it.

ROSALIE. Shut up. I didn't do any such thing.

MARY. Yes, you did.

ROSALIE (*tearfully*). You made it up. You're always making things up.

MARY. You can't call me a fibber, Rosalie Wells. That's a kind of a dare and I won't take a dare. I guess I'll go tell Grandma, anyway. Then she can call the police and they'll come for you and you'll spend the rest of your life in one of those solitary prisons and you'll get older and older, and when you're very old and can't see anymore, they'll let you out maybe with a big sign on your back saying you're a thief, and your mother and father will be dead and you won't have any place to go and you'll beg on the streets—

ROSALIE. I didn't steal anything. I borrowed the bracelet and I was going to put it back as soon as I'd worn it to the movies. I never meant to keep it.

MARY. Nobody'll believe that, least of all the police. You're just a common, ordinary thief. Stop that bawling. You'll have the whole house down here in a minute.

ROSALIE. You won't tell? Say you won't tell.

MARY. Am I a fibber?

ROSALIE. No.

MARY. Then say: "I apologize on my hands and knees."

ROSALIE. I apologize on my hands and knees. Let's play with the puzzle.

MARY. Wait a minute. Say: "From now on, I, Rosalie Wells, am the vassal of Mary Tilford and will do and say whatever she tells me under the solemn oath of a knight."

ROSALIE. I won't say that. That's the worse oath there is. (MARY *starts for the door*) Mary! Please don't—

MARY. Will you swear it?

ROSALIE (*sniffling*). But then you could tell me to do anything.

MARY. And you'd have to do it. Say it quick or I'll—

ROSALIE (*hurriedly*). From now on, I, Rosalie Wells, am the vassal of Mary Tilford and will do and say whatever she tells me under the solemn oath of a knight. (*She gasps, and sits up straight as* MRS. TILFORD *enters.*)

MARY. Don't forget that.

MRS. TILFORD. Good evening, Rosalie, you're looking very well.

ROSALIE. Good evening, Mrs. Tilford.

MARY. She's getting fatter every day.

MRS. TILFORD (*abstractedly*). Then it's very becoming. (*Door-bell rings*) That must be Joseph. Mary, take Rosalie into the library. There's some fruit and milk on the table. Be sure you're both fast asleep by half past ten. (*Leans down, kisses them both.* ROSALIE *starts to exit Right, sees* MARY, *stops and hesitates.*)

MARY. Go on, Rosalie. (*Waits until* ROSALIE *reluctantly exits*) Grandma.

MRS. TILFORD. Yes?

MARY. Grandma, Cousin Joe'll say I've got to go back. He'll say I really wasn't—

(CARDIN *enters and she runs from the room.*)

CARDIN. Hello, Amelia. (*Looks curiously at the fleeing* MARY) Mary home, eh?

MRS. TILFORD (*watching* MARY *as she leaves*). Hello, Joseph. Sit down. (*He sits down, looks at her curiously, waits for her to speak*) Whisky?

CARDIN. Please. How are you feeling? Headaches again?

MRS. TILFORD (*puts drink on table*). No.

CARDIN. Those are good powders. Bicarbonate of soda and water. Never hurt anybody yet.

MRS. TILFORD. Yes. How have you been, Joseph?

CARDIN. My good health is monotonous.

MRS. TILFORD (*vaguely, sparring for time*). I haven't seen you the last few weeks. Agatha misses you for Sunday dinners.

CARDIN. I've been busy. We're getting the results from the mating-season right about now.

MRS. TILFORD. Did I take you away from a patient?

CARDIN. No. I was at the hospital.

MRS. TILFORD. How's it getting on?

CARDIN. Just the same. No money, badly equipped, a lousy laboratory, everybody growling at everybody else— Amelia, you didn't bring me here to talk about the hospital. We're talking like people waiting for the muffins to be passed around. What's the matter with you?

MRS. TILFORD. I—I have something to tell you.

CARDIN. Well, out with it.

MRS. TILFORD. It's a very hard thing to say, Joseph.

CARDIN. Hard for you to say to *me*? (*No answer*) Don't be worried about Mary. I guessed that she ran home to tell you about her faint. It was caused by nothing but bad temper and was very clumsily managed, at that. Amelia, she's a terribly spoilt—

MRS. TILFORD. I heard about the faint. That's not what is worrying me.

CARDIN (*gently*). Are you in some trouble?

MRS. TILFORD. We all are in trouble. Bad trouble.

CARDIN. We? Me, you mean? Nothing's the matter with me.

MRS. TILFORD. When did you last see Karen?

CARDIN. Today. This afternoon.

MRS. TILFORD. Oh. Not since seven o'clock?

CARDIN. What's happened since seven o'clock?

MRS. TILFORD. Joseph, you've been engaged to Karen for a long time. Are your plans any more definite than they were a year ago?

CARDIN. You can get ready to buy the wedding present. We'll have the wedding here, if you don't mind. The smell of clean little girls and boiled linen would worry me.

MRS. TILFORD. Why has Karen decided so suddenly to make it definite?

CARDIN. She has not suddenly decided anything. The school is pretty well on its feet, and now that Mrs. Mortar is leaving—

MRS. TILFORD. I've heard about their putting Mrs. Mortar out.

CARDIN. Putting her out? Well, maybe. But a nice sum for a trip and a promise that a good niece will support you the rest of your life is an enviable way of being put out.

MRS. TILFORD (*slowly*). Don't you find it odd, Joseph, that they want so much to get rid of that silly, harmless woman?

CARDIN. I don't know what you're talking about, but it isn't odd at all. Lily Mortar is not a harmless woman, although God knows she's silly enough. She's a nasty, tiresome, spoilt old bitch. If you're forming a Mortar Welfare Society, you're wasting your time. (*Gets up, puts down his glass*) It's not like you to waste your time. Now, what's it that's really on your mind?

MRS. TILFORD. You must not marry Karen.

CARDIN (*shocked, he grins*). You're a very impertinent

lady. Why must I—(*imitates her*) not marry Karen?

MRS. TILFORD. Because there's something wrong with Karen—something horrible.

(*The door-bell is heard to ring loud and long.*)

CARDIN. I don't think I can allow you to say things like that, Amelia.

MRS. TILFORD. I have good reason for saying it. (*Breaks off as she hears voices off-stage*) Who is that?

KAREN (*off-stage*). Mrs. Tilford, Agatha. Is she in?

AGATHA (*off-stage*). Yes'm. Come on in.

MRS. TILFORD. I won't have her here.

CARDIN (*angrily*). What are you talking about?

MRS. TILFORD. I won't have her here.

CARDIN (*picks up his hat*). Then you don't want me here either. (*Turns to face* KAREN, *who, with* MARTHA, *has rushed in*) Darling, what?—

KAREN (*stops when she sees him, puts her hand over her eyes*). Is it a joke, Joe?

MARTHA (*with great force to* MRS. TILFORD). We've come to find out what you are doing.

CARDIN (*kissing* KAREN). What is it?

KAREN. It's crazy! It's crazy! What did she do it for?

CARDIN. What are you talking about? What do you mean?

MRS. TILFORD. You shouldn't have come here.

CARDIN. What is all this? What's happened?

KAREN. I tried to reach you. Hasn't she told you?

CARDIN. Nobody's told me anything. I haven't heard anything but wild talk. What is it, Karen? (*She starts to speak, then dumbly shakes her head*) What's happened, Martha?

MARTHA (*violently*). An insane asylum has been let loose. How do we know what's happened?

CARDIN. What was it?

KAREN. We didn't know what it was. Nobody would talk to us, nobody would tell us anything.

MARTHA. I'll tell you, I'll tell you. You see if you can

make any sense out of it. At dinner-time Mrs. Munn's chauffeur said that Evelyn must be sent home right away. At half past seven Mrs. Burton arrived to tell us that she wanted Helen's things packed and that she'd wait outside because she didn't want to enter a place like ours. Five minutes later the Wells's butler came for Rosalie.

CARDIN. What was it?

MARTHA. It was madhouse. People rushing in and out, the children being pushed into cars—

KAREN (*quiet now, takes his hand*). Mrs. Rogers finally told us.

CARDIN. What? What?

KAREN. That—that Martha and I are—in love with each other. In love with each other. Mrs. Tilford told them.

CARDIN (*for a moment stands staring at her incredulously. Then he walks across the room, stares out of the window, and finally turns to* MRS. TILFORD). Did you tell them that?

MRS. TILFORD. Yes.

CARDIN. Are you sick?

MRS. TILFORD. You know I'm not sick.

CARDIN (*snapping the words out*). Then what did you do it for?

MRS. TILFORD (*slowly*). Because it's true.

KAREN (*incredulously*). You think it's true, then?

MARTHA. You fool! You damned, vicious—

KAREN. Do you realize what you're saying?

MRS. TILFORD. I realize it very well. And—

MARTHA. You realize nothing, nothing, nothing.

MRS. TILFORD. And that's why I don't think you should have come here. (*Quietly, with a look at* MARTHA) I shall not call you names, and I will not allow you to call me names. It comes to this: I can't trust myself to talk about it with you now or ever.

KAREN. What's she talking about, Joe? What's she mean?

What is she trying to do to us? What is everybody doing to us?

MARTHA (*softly, as though to herself*). Pushed around. We're being pushed around by crazy people. (*Shakes herself slightly*) That's an awful thing. And we're standing here— (CARDIN *puts his arm around* KAREN, *walks with her to the window. They stand there together*) We're standing here taking it. (*Suddenly with violence*) Didn't you know we'd come here? Were we supposed to lie down and grin while you kicked us around with these lies?

MRS. TILFORD. This can't do any of us any good, Miss Dobie.

MARTHA (*scornfully imitating her*). "This can't do any of us any good." Listen, listen. Try to understand this: you're not playing with paper dolls. We're human beings, see? It's our lives you're fooling with. *Our* lives. That's serious business for us. Can you understand that?

MRS. TILFORD (*for the first time she speaks angrily*). I can understand that, and I understand a lot more. *You've* been playing with a lot of children's lives, and that's why I stopped you. (*More calmly*) I know how serious this is for you, how serious it is for all of us.

CARDIN (*bitterly*). I don't think you do know.

MRS. TILFORD. I wanted to avoid this meeting because it can't do any good. You came here to find out if I had made the charge. You've found out. Let's end it there. *I don't want you in this house.* I'm sorry this had to be done to you, Joseph.

CARDIN. I don't like your sympathy.

MRS. TILFORD. Very well. There's nothing I mean to do, nothing I want to do. There's nothing anybody can do.

CARDIN (*carefully*). You have already done a terrible thing.

MRS. TILFORD. I have done what I had to do. What they are may possibly be their own business. It becomes a great deal more than that when children are involved.

KAREN (*wildly*). It's not true. Not a word of it is true; can't you understand that?

MRS. TILFORD. There won't be any punishment for either of you. But there mustn't be any punishment for me, either—and that's what this meeting is. This—this thing is your own. Go away with it. I don't understand it and I don't want any part of it.

MARTHA (*slowly*). So you thought we would go away?

MRS. TILFORD. I think that's best for you.

MARTHA. There must be something we can do to you, and, whatever it is, we'll find it.

MRS. TILFORD. That will be very unwise.

KAREN. You are right to be afraid.

MRS. TILFORD. I am not afraid, Karen.

CARDIN. But you *are* old—and you *are* irresponsible.

MRS. TILFORD (*hurt*). You know that's not true.

KAREN (*goes to her*). I don't want to have anything to do with your mess, do you hear me? It makes me feel dirty and sick to be forced to say this, but here it is: there isn't a single word of truth in anything you've said. We're standing here defending ourselves—and against what? Against a lie. A great, awful lie.

MRS. TILFORD. I'm sorry that I can't believe that.

KAREN. Damn you!

CARDIN. But you can believe this: they've worked eight long years to save enough money to buy that farm, to start that school. They did without everything that young people ought to have. You wouldn't know about that. That school meant things to them: self-respect, and bread and butter, and honest work. Do you know what it is to try so hard for anything? Well, now it's gone. (*Suddenly hits the side of the table with his hand*) What the hell did you do it for?

MRS. TILFORD (*softly*). It had to be done.

CARDIN. Righteousness is a great thing.

MRS. TILFORD (*gently*). I know how you must feel.

CARDIN. You don't know anything about how I feel. And you don't know how they feel, either.

MRS. TILFORD. I've loved you as much as I loved my own boys. I wouldn't have spared them; I couldn't spare you.

CARDIN (*fiercely*). I believe you.

MARTHA. What is there to do to you? What can we do to you? There must be something—something that makes you feel the way we do tonight. You don't want any part of this, you said. But you'll get a part. More than you bargained for. (*Suddenly*) Listen: are you willing to stand by everything you've said tonight?

MRS. TILFORD. Yes.

MARTHA. All right. That's fine. But don't get the idea we'll let you whisper this lie: you made it and you'll come out with it. Shriek it to your town of Lancet. We'll *make* you shriek it—and we'll make you do it in a court room. (*Quietly*) Tomorrow, Mrs. Tilford, you will have a libel suit on your hands.

MRS. TILFORD. That will be very unwise.

KAREN. Very unwise—for you.

MRS. TILFORD. It is you I am thinking of. I am frightened for you. It was wrong of you to brazen it out here tonight; it would be criminally foolish of you to brazen it out in public. That can bring you nothing but pain. I am an old woman, Miss Dobie, and I have seen too many people, out of pride, act on that pride. In the end they punish themselves.

MARTHA. And you feel that you are too old to be punished? That we should spare you?

MRS. TILFORD. You know that is not what I meant.

CARDIN (*turns from the window*). So you took a child's word for it?

MARTHA (*looks at him, shakes her head*). I knew it, too.

KAREN. That is really where you got it? I can't believe— it couldn't be. Why, she's a child.

MARTHA. She's not a child any longer.

KAREN. Oh, my God, it all fits so well now. That girl has hated us for a long time. We never knew why, we never could find out. There didn't seem to be any reason—

MARTHA. There wasn't any reason. She hates everybody and everything.

KAREN. Your Mary's a strange girl, a bad girl. There's something very awful the matter with her.

MRS. TILFORD. I was waiting for you to say that, Miss Wright.

KAREN. I'm telling you the truth. We should have told it to you long ago. (*Stops, sighs*) It's no use.

MARTHA. Where is she? Bring her out here and let us hear what she has to say.

MRS. TILFORD. You cannot see her.

CARDIN. Where is she?

MRS. TILFORD. I won't have that, Joseph.

CARDIN. I'm going to talk to her.

MRS. TILFORD. *I won't have her go through with that again.* (*To* KAREN *and* MARTHA) You came here demanding explanations. It was I who should have asked them from you. You attack me, you attack Mary. I've told you I didn't mean you any harm. I still don't. You claim that it isn't true; it may be natural that you should say that, but I *know* that it is true. No matter what you say, you know very well I wouldn't have acted until I was absolutely sure. All I wanted was to get those children away. That has been done. There won't be any talk about it or about you—I'll see to that. You have been in my house long enough. Get out.

KAREN (*gets up*). The wicked very young, and the wicked very old. Let's go home.

CARDIN. Sit down. (*To* MRS. TILFORD) When two people come here with their lives spread on the table for you to cut to pieces, then the only honest thing to do is to give them a chance to come out whole. Are you honest?

MRS. TILFORD. I've always thought so.

CARDIN. Then where is Mary? (*After a moment she moves her head to door Right. Quickly* CARDIN *goes to the door and opens it*) Mary! Come here.

(*After a moment* MARY *appears, stands nervously near door. Her manner is shy and afraid.*)

MRS. TILFORD (*gently*). Sit down, dear, and don't be afraid.

MARTHA (*her lips barely moving*). Make her tell the truth.

CARDIN (*walking about in front of* MARY). Look: everybody lies all the time. Sometimes they have to, sometimes they don't. I've lied myself for a lot of different reasons, but there was never a time when, if I'd been given a second chance, I wouldn't have taken back the lie and told the truth. You're lucky if you ever get that chance. I'm telling you this because I'm about to ask you a question. Before you answer the question, I want to tell you that if you've l—, if you made a mistake, you must take this chance and say so. You won't be punished for it. Do you get all that?

MARY (*timidly*). Yes, Cousin Joe.

CARDIN (*grimly*). All right, let's get started. Were you telling your grandmother the truth this afternoon? The exact truth about Miss Wright and Miss Dobie?

MARY (*without hesitation*). Oh, yes.

(KAREN *sighs deeply,* MARTHA, *her fists closed tight, turns her back to the child.* CARDIN *smiles as he looks at* MARY.)

CARDIN. All right, Mary, that was your chance; you passed it up. (*Pulls up a chair, sits down in front of her*) Now let's find out things.

MRS. TILFORD. She's told you. Aren't you through?

CARDIN. Not by a long shot. You've started something, and I'm going to finish it for you. Will you answer some more questions, Mary?

MARY. Yes, Cousin Joe.

MARTHA. Stop that sick, sweet tone.

(MRS. TILFORD *half rises;* CARDIN *motions her back.*)

CARDIN. Why don't you like Miss Dobie and Miss Wright?

MARY. Oh, I do like them. They just don't like me. They never have liked me.

CARDIN. How do you know?

MARY. They're always picking on me. They're always punishing me for everything that happens. No matter what happens, it's always me.

CARDIN. Why do you think they do that?

MARY. Because—because they're—because they— (*Stops, turns*) Grandma, I—

CARDIN. All right, we'll skip that one. Did you get punished today?

MARY. Yes, and it was just because Peggy and Evelyn heard them and so they took it out on me.

KAREN. That's a lie.

CARDIN. Sssh. Heard what, Mary?

MARY. Mrs. Mortar told Miss Dobie that there was something funny about her. She said that she had a funny feeling about Miss Wright, and Mrs. Mortar said that was unnatural. That was why we got punished, just because—

KAREN. That was not the reason they got punished.

MRS. TILFORD (*to* MARTHA). Miss Dobie?

MARTHA. My aunt is a stupid woman. What she said was unpleasant; it was said to annoy me. It meant nothing more than that.

MARY. And, Cousin Joe, she said every time you came to the school Miss Dobie got jealous, and that she didn't want you to get married.

MARTHA (*to* CARDIN). She said that, too. For God's sake,

can't you see what's happening? This—this child is taking little things, little family things, and making them have meanings that— (*Stops, suddenly regards* MARY *with a combination of disgust and interest*) Where did you learn so much in so little time?

CARDIN. What do you think Mrs. Mortar meant by all that, Mary?

MRS. TILFORD. Stop it, Joseph!

MARY. I don't know, but it was always kind of funny and she always said things like that and all the girls would talk about it when Miss Dobie went and visited Miss Wright late at night—

KAREN (*angrily*). And we go to the movies at night and sometimes we read at night and sometimes we drink tea at night. Those are guilty things, too, Mrs. Tilford.

MARY. And there are always funny sounds and we'd stay awake and listen because we couldn't help hearing and I'd get frightened because the sounds were like—

MARTHA. Be still!

KAREN (*with violence*). No, no. You don't want her still now. What else did you hear?

MARY. Grandma, I—

MRS. TILFORD (*bitterly to* CARDIN). You are trying to make her name it, aren't you?

CARDIN (*ignoring her, speaks to* MARY). Go on.

MARY. I don't know; there were just sounds.

CARDIN. But what did you think they were? Why did they frighten you?

MARY (*weakly*). I don't know.

CARDIN (*smiles at* MRS. TILFORD). She doesn't know.

MARY (*hastily*). I saw things, too. One night there was so much noise I thought somebody was sick or something and I looked through the keyhole and they were kissing and saying things and then I got scared because it was different sort of and I—

MARTHA (*her face distorted, turns to* MRS. TILFORD). That child—that child is sick.

KAREN. Ask her again how she could see us.

CARDIN. How could you see Miss Dobie and Miss Wright?

MARY. I—I—

MRS. TILFORD. Tell him what you whispered to me.

MARY. It was at night and I was leaning down by the keyhole.

KAREN. *There's no keyhole on my door.*

MRS. TILFORD. What?

KAREN. There—is—no—keyhole—on—my—door.

MARY (*quickly*). It wasn't her room, Grandma, it was the other room, I guess. It was *Miss Dobie's* room. I saw them through the keyhole in Miss Dobie's room.

CARDIN. How did you know anybody was in Miss Dobie's room?

MARY. I told you, I told you. Because we heard them. Everybody heard them—

MARTHA. I share a room with my aunt. It is on the first floor at the other end of the house. It is impossible to hear anything from there. (*To* CARDIN) Tell her to come and see for herself.

MRS. TILFORD (*her voice shaken*). What is this, Mary? Why did you say you saw through a keyhole? *Can* you hear from your room?—

MARY (*starts to cry*). Everybody is yelling at me. I don't know what I'm saying with everybody mixing me all up. I did see it! I did see it!

MRS. TILFORD. *What* did you see? *Where* did you see it? I want the truth, now. The truth, whatever it is.

CARDIN (*gets up, moves his chair back*). We can go home. We are finished here. (*Looks around*) It's not a pleasant place to be.

MRS. TILFORD (*angrily*). Stop that crying, Mary. Stand up.

(MARY *gets up, head down, still crying hysterically.* MRS. TILFORD *goes and stands directly in front of her.*)

MRS. TILFORD. *I want the truth.*

MARY. All—all right.

MRS. TILFORD. What is the truth?

MARY. It was Rosalie who saw them. I just said it was me so I wouldn't have to tattle on Rosalie.

CARDIN (*wearily*). Oh, my God!

MARY. It *was* Rosalie, Grandma, she told us all about it. She said she had read about it in a book and she knew. (*Desperately*). You ask Rosalie. You just ask Rosalie. She'll tell you. We used to talk about it all the time. That's the truth, that's the honest truth. She said it was when the door was open once and she told us all about it. I was just trying to save Rosalie, and everybody jumps on me.

MRS. TILFORD (*to* CARDIN). Please wait a minute. (*Goes to library door*) Rosalie!

CARDIN. You're giving yourself an awful beating, Amelia, and you deserve whatever you get.

MRS. TILFORD (*stands waiting for* ROSALIE, *passes her hand over her face*). I don't know. I don't know, any more. Maybe it's what I do deserve. (*As* ROSALIE, *frightened, appears at the door, making bows to everybody, she takes the child gently by the hand, brings her down Center, talking nervously*) I'm sorry to keep you up so late, Rosalie. You must be tired. (*Speaks rapidly*) Mary says there's been a lot of talk in the school lately about Miss Wright and Miss Dobie. Is that true?

ROSALIE. I—I don't know what you mean.

MRS. TILFORD. That things have been said among you girls.

ROSALIE (*wide-eyed, frightened*). What things? I never—— I—I—

KAREN (*gently*). Don't be frightened.

MRS. TILFORD. What was the talk about, Rosalie?

ROSALIE (*utterly bewildered*). I don't know what she means, Miss Wright.

KAREN. Rosalie, Mary has told her grandmother that certain things at school have been—er—puzzling you girls. You, particularly.

ROSALIE. History puzzles me. I guess I'm not very good at history, and Helen helps me sometimes, if that—

KAREN. No, that's not what she meant. She says that you told her that you saw certain—certain acts between Miss Dobie and myself. She says that once, when the door was open, you saw us kissing each other in a way that—(*Unable to bear the child's look, she turns her back*) women don't kiss one another.

ROSALIE. Oh, Miss Wright, I didn't, didn't, I didn't. I *never* said such a thing.

MRS. TILFORD (*grimly*). That's true, my dear?

ROSALIE. I never saw any such thing. Mary always makes things up about me and everybody else. (*Starts to weep in excitement*) I never said any such thing ever. Why, I never even could have thought of—

MARY (*staring at her, speaks very slowly*). Yes, you did, Rosalie. You're just trying to get out of it. I remember just when you said it. I remember it, because it was the day Helen Burton's bracelet was—

ROSALIE (*stands fascinated and fearful, looking at* MARY). I never did. I—I—you're just—

MARY. It was the day Helen's bracelet was stolen, and nobody knew who did it, and Helen said that if her mother found out, she'd have the thief put in jail.

KAREN (*puzzled, as are the others, by the sudden change in* ROSALIE'S *manner*). There's nothing to cry about. You must help us by telling the truth. Why, what's the matter, Rosalie?

MARY. Grandma, there's something I've got to tell you that—

ROSALIE (*with a shrill cry*). Yes. Yes. I did see it. I told Mary. What Mary said was right. I said it, I said it— (*Throws herself on the couch, weeping hysterically;* MARTHA *stands leaning against the door;* KAREN, CARDIN, *and* MRS. TILFORD *are staring at* ROSALIE; MARY *slowly sits down as the Curtain falls.*)

ACT THREE

SCENE: *The same as Act One. Living room of the school.*

AT RISE: *The room has changed. It is not dirty, but it is dull and dark and uncared for. The windows are tightly shut, the curtains tightly drawn. KAREN is sitting in a large chair, Right Center, feet flat on floor. MARTHA is lying on the couch, her face buried against the pillows, her back to KAREN. It is a minute or two after the rise of the curtain before either speaks.*

MARTHA. It's cold in here.

KAREN. Yes.

MARTHA. What time is it?

KAREN. I don't know. What's the difference?

MARTHA. None. I was hoping it was time for my bath.

KAREN. Take it early today.

MARTHA (*laughs*). Oh, I couldn't do that. I look forward all day to that bath. It's my last touch with the full life. It makes me feel important to know that there's one thing ahead of me, one thing I've *got* to do. You ought to get yourself something like that. I tell you, at five o'clock every day you comb your hair. How's that? It's better for you, take my word. You wake up in the morning and you say to yourself, the day's not entirely empty, life is rich and full: at five o'clock I'll comb my hair.

(*They fall back into silence. A moment later the phone rings. Neither of them pays the slightest attention to it. But the ringing becomes too insistent. KAREN rises, takes the receiver off, goes back to her chair and sits down.*)

KAREN. It's raining.

MARTHA. Hungry?

KAREN. No. You?

MARTHA. No, but I'd like to be hungry again. Remember how much we used to eat at college?

KAREN. That was ten years ago.

MARTHA. Well, maybe we'll be hungry in another ten years. It's cheaper this way.

KAREN. What's the old thing about time being more nourishing than bread?

MARTHA. Yeah? Maybe.

KAREN. Joe's late today. What time is it?

MARTHA (*turns again to lie on her side*). We've been sitting here for eight days asking each other the time. Haven't you heard? There isn't any time any more.

KAREN. It's been days since we've been out of this house.

MARTHA. Well, we'll have to get off these chairs sooner or later. In a couple of months they'll need dusting.

KAREN. What'll we do when we get off?

MARTHA. God knows.

KAREN (*almost in a whisper*). It's awful.

MARTHA. Let's not talk about it. (*After a moment*) What about eggs for dinner?

KAREN. All right.

MARTHA. I'll make some potatoes with onions, the way you used to like them.

KAREN. It's a week ago Thursday. It never seemed real until the last day. It seems real enough now, all right.

MARTHA. Now and forever after.

KAREN (*suddenly*). Let's go out.

MARTHA (*turns over, stares at her*). Where to?

KAREN. We'll take a walk.

MARTHA. Where'll we walk?

KAREN. Why shouldn't we take a walk? We won't see anybody, and suppose we do, what of it? We'll jus—

MARTHA (*slowly gets up*). Come on. We'll go through the park.

KAREN. They might see us. (*They stand looking at each other*) Let's not go. (MARTHA *goes back, lies down again*) We'll go tomorrow.

MARTHA (*laughs*). Stop kidding yourself.

KAREN. But Joe says we've got to go out. He says that all the people who don't think it's true will begin to wonder if we keep hiding this way.

MARTHA. If it makes you feel better to think there *are* such people, go ahead.

KAREN. He says we ought to go into town and go shopping and act as though—

MARTHA. Shopping? That's a sound idea. There aren't three stores in Lancet that would sell us anything. Hasn't he heard about the ladies' clubs and their meetings and their circulars and their visits and their—

KAREN (*softly*). Don't tell him.

MARTHA (*gently*). I won't. (*There are footsteps in the hall, and the sound of something being dragged*) There's our friend.

(*A* GROCERY BOY *appears lugging a box. He brings it into the room, stands staring at them, giggles a little. Walks toward* KAREN, *stops, examines her. She sits tense, looking away from him. Without taking his eyes from* KAREN, *he speaks.*)

GROCERY BOY. I knocked on the kitchen door but nobody answered.

MARTHA. You said that yesterday. All right. Thanks. Good-bye.

KAREN (*unable any longer to stand the stare*). Make him stop it.

GROCERY BOY. Here are the things. (*Giggles, moves toward* MARTHA, *stands looking at her. Suddenly* MARTHA *thrusts her hand in the air.*)

MARTHA. I've got eight fingers, see? I'm a freak.

GROCERY BOY (*giggling*). There's a car comin' here. (*Gets no answer, starts backing out of door, still looking. Familiarly*) Good-bye. (*Exits.*)

MARTHA (*bitterly*). You still think we should go into town?

KAREN. I don't know. I don't know about anything any more. (*After a moment*) Martha, Martha, Martha—

MARTHA (*gently*). What is it, Karen?

KAREN. What are we going to do? It's all so cold and unreal and—. It's like that dark hour of the night when, half awake, you struggle through the black mess you've been dreaming. Then, suddenly, you wake up and you see your own bed or your own nightgown and you know you're back again in a solid world. But now it's all the nightmare; there is no solid world. Oh, Martha, *why* did it happen? *What* happened? What are we doing here like this?

MARTHA. Waiting.

KAREN. For what?

MARTHA. I don't know.

KAREN. We've got to get out of this place. I can't stand it any more.

MARTHA. You'll be getting married soon. Everything will be all right then.

KAREN (*vaguely*). Yes.

MARTHA (*looks up at the tone*). What is it?

KAREN. Nothing.

MARTHA. There mustn't be anything wrong between you and Joe. Never.

KAREN (*without conviction*). Nothing's wrong. (*As footsteps are heard in the hall, her face lights up*) There's Joe now.

(MRS. MORTAR, *small suitcase in hand, stands in the doorway, her face pushed coyly forward.*)

MRS. MORTAR. And here I am. Hello, hello.

MARTHA (*she has turned over on her back and is staring*

at her aunt. She speaks to KAREN). The Duchess, isn't
it? Returned at long last. (*Too jovially*) Come on in.
We're delighted to see you. Are you tired from your
journey? Is there something I can get you?

MRS. MORTAR (*surprised*). I'm very glad to see you both,
and (*looks around*) I'm very glad to see the old place
again. How is everything?

MARTHA. Everything's fine. We're splendid, thank you.
You're just in time for tea.

MRS. MORTAR. You know, I should like some tea, if it isn't
too much trouble.

MARTHA. No trouble at all. Some small sandwiches and a
little brandy?

MRS. MORTAR (*puzzled finally*). Why, Martha.

MARTHA. Where the hell have you been?

MRS. MORTAR. Around, around. I had a most interesting
time. Things—

MARTHA. Why didn't you answer my telegrams?

MRS. MORTAR. Things have changed in the theater—drasti-
cally changed, I might say.

MARTHA. *Why didn't you answer my telegrams?*

MRS. MORTAR. Oh, Martha, there's your temper again.

MARTHA. Answer me and don't bother about my temper.

MRS. MORTAR (*nervously*). I was moving around a great
deal. (*Conversationally*) You know, I think it will
throw a very revealing light on the state of the new
theater when I tell you that the Lyceum in Rochester
now has a toilet back stage.

MARTHA. To hell with the toilet in Rochester. Where were
you?

MRS. MORTAR. Moving around, I tell you.

KAREN. What difference does it all make now?

MRS. MORTAR. Karen is quite right. Let bygones be bygones. As I was saying, there's an effete something in
the theater now, and that accounts for—

MARTHA (*to* KAREN). Isn't she wonderful? (*To* MRS.

MORTAR) Why did you refuse to come back here and testify for us?

MRS. MORTAR. Why, Martha, I didn't refuse to come back at all. That's the wrong way to look at it. I was on a tour; that's a moral obligation, you know. Now don't let's talk about unpleasant things any more. I'll go up and unpack a few things; tomorrow's plenty of time to get my trunk.

KAREN (*laughs*). Things have changed here, you know.

MARTHA. She doesn't know. She expected to walk right up to a comfortable fire and sit down and she very carefully waited until the whole thing was over. (*Leans forward, speaking to* MRS. MORTAR) Listen: Karen Wright and Martha Dobie brought a libel suit against a woman called Tilford because her grandchild had accused them of having what the judge called "sinful sexual knowledge of one another." (MRS. MORTAR *holds up her hand in protest, and* MARTHA *laughs*) Don't like that, do you? Well, a great part of the defense's case was based on remarks made by Lily Mortar, actress in the toilets of Rochester, against her niece, Martha. And a greater part of the defense's case rested on the telling fact that Mrs. Mortar would not appear in court to deny or explain those remarks. Mrs. Mortar had a moral obligation to the theater. As you probably read in the papers, we lost the case.

MRS. MORTAR. I didn't think of it that way, Martha. It couldn't have done any good for all of us to get mixed up in that unpleasant notoriety— (*Sees* MARTHA's *face. Hastily*) But now that you've explained it, why, I do see it your way, and I'm sorry I didn't come back. But now that I am here, I'm going to stand shoulder to shoulder with you. I know what you've gone through, but the body and heart *do* recover, you know. I'll be here working right along with you and we'll—

MARTHA. There's an eight o'clock train. Get on it.

MRS. MORTAR. Martha.

MARTHA. You've come back to pick the bones dry. Well, there aren't even bones anymore. There's nothing here for you.

MRS. MORTAR (*sniffling a little*). How can you talk to me like that?

MARTHA. Because I hate you. I've always hated you.

MRS. MORTAR (*gently*). God will punish you for that.

MARTHA. He's been doing all right.

MRS. MORTAR. When you wish to apologize, I will be temporarily in my room. (*Starts to exit, almost bumps into* CARDIN, *steps back with dignity*) How do you do?

CARDIN (*laughs*). Look who's here. A little late, aren't you?

MRS. MORTAR. So it's you. Now, I call *that* loyal. A lot of men wouldn't still be here. They would have felt—

MARTHA. Get out of here.

KAREN (*opening door*). I'll call you when it's time for your train.

(MRS. MORTAR *looks at her, exits.*)

CARDIN. Now, what do you think brought her back?

KAREN. God knows.

MARTHA. I know. She was broke.

CARDIN (*pats* MARTHA *on the shoulder*). Don't let her worry you this time, Martha. We'll give her some money and get rid of her. (*Pulls* KAREN *to him*) Been out today, darling?

KAREN. We started to go out.

CARDIN (*shakes his head*). Feel all right?

(KAREN *leans over to kiss him. Almost imperceptibly he pulls back.*)

KAREN. Why did you do that?

MARTHA. Karen.

CARDIN. Do what?

KAREN. Draw back that way.

CARDIN (*laughs, kisses her*). If we sit around here much

longer, we'll all be bats. I sold my place today to Foster.

KAREN. You did what?

CARDIN. We're getting married this week. Then we're going away—all three of us.

KAREN. You can't leave here. I won't have you do this for me. What about the hospital and—

CARDIN. Shut up, darling, it's all fixed. We're going to Vienna and we're going quick. Fischer wrote that I can have my old place back.

KAREN. No! No! I'm not going to let you.

CARDIN. It's already done. Fischer can't pay me much, but it'll be enough for the three of us. Plenty if we live cheap.

MARTHA. I couldn't go with you, Joe.

CARDIN. Nonsense, Martha, we're all going. We're going to have fun again.

KAREN (*slowly*). You don't want to go back to Vienna.

CARDIN. No.

KAREN. Then why?

CARDIN. Look: I don't want to go to Vienna; I'd rather have stayed here. But then you don't want to go to Vienna; you'd rather have stayed here. Well, to hell with that. We *can't* stay here, and Vienna offers enough to eat and sleep and drink beer on. Now don't object any more, please, darling. All right?

KAREN. All right.

MARTHA. I can't go. It's better for all of us if I don't.

CARDIN (*puts his arm around her*). Not now. You stay with us now. Later on, if you want it that way. All right?

MARTHA (*smiles*). All right.

CARDIN. Swell. I'll buy you good coffee cakes and take you both to Ischl for a honeymoon.

MARTHA (*picking up grocery box, she starts for door*). A big coffee cake with a lot of raisins. It would be nice to like something again. (*Exits.*)

CARDIN (*with a slightly forced heartiness*). I'll be going back with a pretty girl who belongs to me. I'll show you off all over the place—to Dr. Engelhardt, and the nurse at the desk, and to the fat gal in the cake shop, and to Fischer. (*Laughs*) The last time I saw him was at the railroad station. He took me back of the baggage car. (*With an imitation of an accent*) "Joseph," he said, "you'll be a good doctor; I would trust you to cut up my Minna. But you're not a great doctor, and you never will be. Go back where you were born and take care of your sick. Leave the fancy work to the others." I came home.

KAREN. You'll be coming home again some day.

CARDIN. No. Let's not talk about it. (*After a moment*) You'll need some clothes?

KAREN. A few. Oh, your Dr. Fischer was so right. This is where you belong.

CARDIN. I need an overcoat and a suit. You'll need a lot of things—heavy things. It's cold there now, much colder than you'd expect—

KAREN. I've done this to you. I've taken you away from everything you want.

CARDIN. But it's lovely in the mountains, and that's where we'll go for a month.

KAREN. They—*they've* done it. They've taken away every chance we had. Everything we wanted, everything we were going to be.

CARDIN. And we've got to stop talking like that. (*Takes her by the shoulder*) We've got a chance. But it's just one chance, and if we miss it we're done for. It means that we've got to start putting the whole business behind us now. *Now*, Karen. What you've done, you've done—and that's that.

KAREN. What *I've* done?

CARDIN (*impatiently*). What's been done to you.

KAREN. What did you mean? (*When there is no answer*)

What did you mean when you said: "What you've done"?

CARDIN (*shouting*). Nothing. Nothing. (*Then very quietly*) Karen, there are a lot of people in this world who've had bad trouble in their lives. We're three of those people. We could sit around the rest of our lives and exist on that trouble, until in the end we had nothing else and we'd want nothing else. That's something I'm not coming to and I'm not going to let you come to.

KAREN. I know. I'm sorry. (*After a moment*) Joe, can we have a baby right away?

CARDIN (*vaguely*). Yes, I guess so. Although we won't have much money now.

KAREN. You used to want one right away. You always said that was the way you wanted it. There's some reason for your changing.

CARDIN. My God, we *can't* go on like this. Everything I say to you is made to mean something else. We don't talk like people any more. Oh, let's get out of here as fast as we can.

KAREN (*as though she is finishing the sentence for him*). And every word will have a new meaning. You think we'll be able to run away from that? Woman, child, love, lawyer—no words that we can use in safety any more. (*Laughs bitterly*) Sick, high-tragic people. That's what we'll be.

CARDIN (*gently*). No, we won't, darling. Love is casual— that's the way it should be. We must find that out all over again. We must learn again to live and love like other people.

KAREN. It won't work.

CARDIN. What?

KAREN. The two of us together.

CARDIN (*sharply*). Stop talking like that.

KAREN. It's true. (*Suddenly*) I want you to say it now.

CARDIN. I don't know what you're talking about.

KAREN. Yes, you do. We've both known for a long time. I knew surely the day we lost the case. I was watching your face in court. It was ashamed—and sad at being ashamed. Say it now, Joe. Ask it now.

CARDIN. I have nothing to ask. Nothing— (*Quickly*) All right. Is it—was it ever—

KAREN (*puts her hand over his mouth*). No. Martha and I have never touched each other. (*Pulls his head down on her shoulder*) That's all right, darling. I'm glad you asked. I'm not mad a bit, really.

CARDIN. I'm sorry, Karen, I'm sorry. I didn't mean to hurt you, I—

KAREN. I know. You wanted to wait until it was all over, you really never wanted to ask at all. You didn't know for sure; you thought there might be just a little truth in it all. (*With great feeling*) You've been good to me and loyal. You're a fine man. (*Afraid of tears, she pats him, walks away*) Now go and sit down, Joe. I have things to say. They're all mixed up and I must get them clear.

CARDIN. Don't let's talk any more. Let's forget and go ahead.

KAREN (*puzzled*). Go ahead?

CARDIN. Yes, Karen.

KAREN. You believe me, then?

CARDIN. Of course I believe you. I only had to hear you say it.

KAREN. No, no, no. That isn't the way things work. Maybe you believe me. I'd never know whether you did or not. You'd never know whether you did, either. We couldn't do it that way. Can't you see what would happen? We'd be hounded by it all our lives. I'd be frightened, always, and in the end my own fright would make me—would make me hate you. (*Sees slight movement he makes*) Yes, it would; I know it would. I'd hate you for what I thought I'd done to you. And

I'd hate myself, too. It would grow and grow until we'd be ruined by it. (*Sees him about to speak*) Ah, Joe, you've seen all that yourself. You knew it first.

CARDIN (*softly*). I didn't mean it that way; I don't now.

KAREN (*smiles*). You're still trying to spare me, still trying to tell yourself that we might be all right again. But we won't be all right. Not ever, ever, ever. I don't know all the reasons why. Look, I'm standing here. I haven't changed. (*Holds out her hands*) My hands look just the same, my face is the same, even my dress is old. We're in a room we've been in so many times before; you're sitting where you always sit; it's nearly time for dinner. I'm like everybody else. I can have all the things that everybody has. I can have you and a baby, and I can go to market, and we can go to the movies, and people will talk to me and— (*Suddenly notices the pain in his face*) Oh, I'm sorry. I mustn't talk like that. That couldn't be true any more.

CARDIN. It could be, Karen. We'll make it be like that.

KAREN. No. That's only what we'd like to have had. It's what we can't have now. Go home, darling.

CARDIN (*with force*). Don't talk like that. No matter what it is, we can't leave each other. I can't leave you—

KAREN. Joe, Joe. Let's do it now and quick; it will be too hard later on.

CARDIN. No, no, no. We love each other. (*His voice breaks*) I'd give anything not to have asked questions, Karen.

KAREN. It had to be asked sooner or later—and answered. You're a good man—the best I'll ever know—and you've been better to me than— But it's no good now, for either of us; you can see that.

CARDIN. It can be. You say I helped you. Help me now; help me to be strong and good enough to— (*Goes toward her with his arms out*) Karen!

KAREN (*drawing back*). No, Joe! (*Then, as he stops*) Will you do something for me?

CARDIN. No. I won't—

KAREN. Will you—will you go away for two days—a day —and think this all over by yourself—away from me and love and pity? Will you? And then decide.

CARDIN (*after a long pause*). Yes, if you want, but it won't make any difference. We will—

KAREN. Don't say anything. Please go now. (*She sits down, smiles, closes her eyes. For a moment he stands looking at her, then slowly puts on his hat*) And all my heart goes with you.

CARDIN (*at door, leaving*). I'll be coming back. (*Exits, slowly, reluctantly, closing door.*)

KAREN (*a moment after he has gone*). No, you won't. Never, darling. (*Stays as she is until* MARTHA *enters Right.*)

MARTHA (*goes to lamp, lights it*). It gets dark so early now. (*Sits down, stretches, laughs*) Cooking always makes me feel better. Well, I guess we'll have to give the Duchess some dinner. When the hawks descend, you've got to feed 'em. Where's Joe? (*No answer*) Where's Joe?

KAREN. Gone.

MARTHA. A patient? Will he be back in time for dinner?

KAREN. No.

MARTHA (*watching her*). We'll save dinner for him, then. Karen! What's the matter?

KAREN (*in a dull tone*). He won't be back any more.

MARTHA (*speaking slowly and carefully*). You mean he won't be back any more tonight.

KAREN. He won't be back at all.

MARTHA (*quickly, walks to* KAREN). What happened? (KAREN *shakes her head*) What happened, Karen?

KAREN. He thought that we had been lovers.

MARTHA (*tensely*). I don't believe you.

(*Wearily* KAREN *turns her head away.*)

KAREN. All right.

MARTHA (*automatically*). I don't believe it. He's never said a word all these months, all during the trial— (*Suddenly grabs* KAREN *by the shoulder, shakes her*) Didn't you tell him? For God's sake, didn't you tell him it wasn't true?

KAREN. Yes.

MARTHA. He didn't believe you?

KAREN. I guess he believed me.

MARTHA (*angrily*). Then what have you done?

KAREN. What had to be done.

MARTHA. It's all wrong. It's silly. He'll be back in a little while and you'll clear it all up— (*Realizes why that can't be, covers her mouth with her hand*) Oh, God, I wanted that for you so much.

KAREN. Don't. I feel sick to my stomach.

MARTHA (*goes to couch opposite* KAREN, *puts her head in her arms*). What's happened to us? What's really happened to us?

KAREN. I don't know. I want to be sleepy. I want to go to sleep.

MARTHA. Go back to Joe. He's strong; he'll understand. It's too much for you this way.

KAREN (*irritably*). Stop talking about it. Let's pack and get out of here. Let's take the train in the morning.

MARTHA. The train to where?

KAREN. I don't know. Some place; any place.

MARTHA. A job? Money?

KAREN. In a big place we could get something to do.

MARTHA. They'd know about us. We've been famous.

KAREN. A small town, then.

MARTHA. They'd know more about us.

KAREN (*as a child would say it*). Isn't there anywhere to go?

MARTHA. No. There'll never be any place for us to go.

We're bad people. We'll sit. We'll be sitting the rest of our lives wondering what's happened to us. You think this scene is strange? Well, get used to it; we'll be here for a long time. (*Suddenly pinches* KAREN *on the arm*) Let's pinch each other sometimes. We can tell whether we're still living.

KAREN (*shivers, listlessly gets up, starts making a fire in the fireplace*). But this isn't a new sin they tell us we've done. Other people aren't destroyed by it.

MARTHA. They are the people who believe in it, who want it, who've chosen it. We aren't like that. We don't love each other. (*Suddenly stops, crosses to fireplace, stands looking abstractedly at* KAREN. *Speaks casually*) I don't love you. We've been very close to each other, of course. I've loved you like a friend, the way thousands of women feel about other women.

KAREN (*only half listening*). Yes.

MARTHA. Certainly that doesn't mean anything. There's nothing wrong about that. It's perfectly natural that I should be fond of you, that I should—

KAREN (*listlessly*). Why are you saying all this to me?

MARTHA. Because I love you.

KAREN (*vaguely*). Yes, of course.

MARTHA. I love you that way—maybe the way they said I loved you. I don't know. (*Waits, gets no answer, kneels down next to* KAREN) Listen to me!

KAREN. What?

MARTHA. *I have loved you the way they said.*

KAREN. You're crazy.

MARTHA. There's always been something wrong. Always —as long as I can remember. But I never knew it until all this happened.

KAREN (*for the first time looks up, horrified*). Stop it!

MARTHA. You're afraid of hearing it; I'm more afraid than you.

KAREN (*puts her hands over her ears*). I won't listen to you.

MARTHA. Take your hands down. (*Leans over, pulls* KAREN'S *hands away*) You've got to know it. I can't keep it any longer. I've got to tell you how guilty I am.

KAREN (*deliberately*). You are guilty of nothing.

MARTHA. I've been telling myself that since the night we heard the child say it; I've been praying I could convince myself of it. I can't, I can't any longer. It's there. I don't know how, I don't know why. But I did love you. I do love you. I resented your marriage; maybe because I wanted you; maybe I wanted you all along; maybe I couldn't call it by a name; maybe it's been there ever since I first knew you—

KAREN (*tensely*). It's a lie. You're telling yourself a lie. We never thought of each other that way.

MARTHA (*bitterly*). No, of course *you* didn't. But who says I didn't? I never felt that way about anybody but you. I've never loved a man— (*Stops. Softly*) I never knew why before. Maybe it's that.

KAREN (*carefully*). You are tired and sick.

MARTHA (*as though she were talking to herself*). It's funny; it's all mixed up. There's something in you, and you don't know it and you don't do anything about it. Suddenly a child gets bored and lies—and there you are, seeing it for the first time. (*Closes her eyes*) I don't know. It all seems to come back to *me*. In some way I've ruined your life. I've ruined my own. I didn't even *know*. (*Smiles*) There's a big difference between us now, Karen. I feel all dirty and—(*Puts out her hand, touches* KAREN'S *head*) I can't stay with you any more, darling.

KAREN (*in a shaken, uncertain tone*). All this isn't true. You've never said it; we'll forget it by tomorrow—

MARTHA. Tomorrow? That's a funny word. Karen, we

would have had to invent a new language, as children do, without words like tomorrow.

KAREN (*crying*). Go and lie down, Martha. You'll feel better.

MARTHA (*looks around the room, slowly, carefully. She is very quiet. Exits Right, stands at door for a second looking at* KAREN, *then slowly shuts the door behind her*).

(KAREN *sits alone without moving. There is no sound in the house until, a few minutes after* MARTHA'S *exit, a shot is heard. The sound of the shot should not be too loud or too strong. For a few seconds after the noise has died out,* KAREN *does not move. Then, suddenly, she springs from the chair, crosses the room, pulls open door Right. Almost at the same moment footsteps are heard on the staircase.*)

MRS. MORTAR. What was that? Where is it? (*Enters door Center, frightened, aimlessly moving about*) Karen! Martha! Where are you? I heard a shot. What was— (*Stops as she sees* KAREN *reappear Right. Walks toward her, still talking. Stops when she sees* KAREN'S *face*) What—what is it? (KAREN *moves her hands, shakes her head slightly, passes* MRS. MORTAR, *and goes toward window.* MRS. MORTAR *stares at her for a moment, rushes past her through door Right. Left alone,* KAREN *leans against the window.* MRS. MORTAR *re-enters crying. After a minute*) What shall we do? What shall we do?

KAREN (*in a toneless voice*). Nothing.

MRS. MORTAR. We've got to get a doctor—right away. (*Goes to phone, nervously, fumblingly starts to dial.*)

KAREN (*without turning*). There isn't any use.

MRS. MORTAR. We've got to do something. Oh, it's awful. Poor Martha. I don't know what we can do— (*Puts phone down, collapses in chair, sobs quietly*) You think she's dea—

KAREN. Yes.

MRS. MORTAR. Poor, poor Martha. I can't realize it's true. Oh, how could she—she was so—I don't know what— (*Looks up, still crying, surprised*) I'm—I'm frightened.

KAREN. Don't cry.

MRS. MORTAR. I can't help it. How can I help it? (*Gradually the sobs cease, and she sits rocking herself*) I'll never forgive myself for the last words I said to her. But I was good to her, Karen, and you know God will excuse me for that once. I always tried to do everything I could. (*Suddenly*) Suicide's a sin. (*No answer. Timidly*) Shouldn't we call somebody to—

KAREN. In a little while.

MRS. MORTAR. She shouldn't have done it, she shouldn't have done it. It was because of all this awful business. She would have got a job and started all over again—, she was just worried and sick and—

KAREN. That isn't the reason she did it.

MRS. MORTAR. What—why—?

KAREN (*wearily*). What difference does it make now?

MRS. MORTAR (*reproachfully*). You're not crying.

KAREN. No.

MRS. MORTAR. What will happen to me? I haven't anything. Poor Martha—

KAREN. She was very good to you; she was good to us all.

MRS. MORTAR. Oh, I know she was, Karen, and I was good to her too. I did everything I could. I—I haven't any place to go. (*After a few seconds of silence*) I'm afraid. It seems so queer—in the next room. (*Shivers.*)

KAREN. Don't be afraid.

MRS. MORTAR. It's different for you. You're young.

KAREN. Not any more.

(*The sound of the door-bell ringing.* MRS. MORTAR *jumps.* KAREN *doesn't move. It rings again.*)

MRS. MORTAR (*nervously*). Who is it? (*The bell rings again*) Shall I answer it? (KAREN *shrugs*) I think we'd better. (*Exits down the hall through Center doors. Returns in a minute followed by* MRS. TILFORD'S *maid,* AGATHA, *who stands in the door*) It's a woman. (*No answer*) It's a woman to see you, Karen. (*Getting no answer, she turns to* AGATHA) You can't come in now; we've had a—we've had trouble here.

AGATHA. Miss Karen, I've *got* to speak to you.

KAREN (*turns slowly, mechanically*). Agatha.

AGATHA (*goes to* KAREN). Please, Miss Karen. We've tried so hard to get you. I been phoning here all the time. Trying to get you. Phoning and phoning. Please, please let her come in. Just for a minute, Miss Karen. Please—

MRS. MORTAR. Who wants to come in here?

AGATHA. Mrs. Tilford. (*Looks at* KAREN) Don't you feel well? (KAREN *shakes her head*) You ain't mad at *me*?

MRS. MORTAR. That woman can't come in here. She caused all—

KAREN. I'm not mad at you, Agatha.

AGATHA. Can I—can I get you something?

KAREN. No.

AGATHA. You poor child. You look like you got a pain somewhere. (*Hesitates, takes* KAREN'S *hands*) I only came cause she's so bad off. She's got to see you, Miss Karen, she's just got to. She's been sittin' outside in the car, hoping you'd come out. She can't get Dr. Joe. He—he won't talk to her any more. I wouldn't a come—I always been on your side—but she's sick. If only you could see her, you'd let her come for just a minute.

KAREN. I couldn't do that, Agatha.

AGATHA. I don't blame you. But I had to tell you. She's old. It's going to kill her.

KAREN (*bitterly*). Kill her? Where is Mrs. Tilford?

AGATHA. Outside.

KAREN. All right.

AGATHA (*presses* KAREN'S *arm*). You always been a good girl. (*Hurriedly exits.*)

MRS. MORTAR. You going to allow that woman to come in here? With Martha lying there? How can you be so feelingless? (*She starts to cry*) I won't stay and see it. I won't have anything to do with it. I'll never let that woman— (*Rushes sobbing from the room.*)

(*A second after,* MRS. TILFORD *appears in the doorway Center. Her face, her walk, her voice have changed. She is feeble.*)

MRS. TILFORD. Karen, let me come in.

(*Without turning,* KAREN *bows her head.* MRS. TILFORD *enters, stands staring at the floor.*)

KAREN. Why have you come here?

MRS. TILFORD. I had to come. (*Stretches out her hand to* KAREN, *who does not turn. She drops her hand*) I know now; I know it wasn't true.

KAREN. What?

MRS. TILFORD (*carefully*). I know it wasn't true, Karen.

KAREN (*stares at her, shudders*). You know it wasn't true? I don't care what you know. It doesn't matter any more. If that's what you had to say, you've said it. Go away.

MRS. TILFORD (*puts her hand to her throat*). I've got to tell you.

KAREN. I don't want to hear you.

MRS. TILFORD. Last Tuesday Mrs. Wells found a bracelet in Rosalie's room. The bracelet had been hidden for several months. We found out that Rosalie had taken the bracelet from another girl, and that Mary—(*Closes her eyes*) that Mary knew that and used it to force Rosalie into saying that she had seen you and Miss Dobie together. I—I've talked to Mary. I've found out. (KAREN *suddenly begins to laugh, high and sharp*) Don't do that, Karen. I have only a little more to say. I've talked to Judge Potter. He will make all arrangements. There will be a public apology and an explanation. The damage suit will be paid to you in full and— and any more that you will be kind enough to take from me. I—I must see that you won't suffer any more.

KAREN. We're not going to suffer any more. Martha is dead. (MRS. TILFORD *gasps, shakes her head as though to shake off the truth, feebly falls into a chair, and covers her face.* KAREN *watches her for a minute*) So you've come here to relieve your conscience? Well, I won't be your confessor. It's choking you, is it? (*Violently*) And you want to stop the choking, don't you? You've done a wrong and you have to right that wrong or you can't rest your head again. You want to be "just," don't you, and you wanted us to help you be just? You've come to the wrong place for help. You want to be a "good" woman again, don't you? (*Bitterly*) Oh, I know. You told us that night you had to do what you did. Now you "have" to do this. A public apology and money paid, and you can sleep again and eat again. That done and there'll be peace for you. You're old, and the old are callous. Ten, fifteen years left for you. But what of me? It's a whole life for me. A whole God-damned life. (*Suddenly quiet, points to door Right*) And what of her?

MRS. TILFORD (*she is crying*). You are still living.

KAREN. Yes. I guess so.

MRS. TILFORD (*with a tremendous effort to control herself*). I didn't come here to relieve myself. I swear to God I didn't. I came to try—to try anything. I knew there wasn't any relief for me, Karen, and that there never would be again. (*Tensely*) But what I am or why I came doesn't matter. The only thing that matters is you and—You, now.

KAREN. There's nothing for me.

MRS. TILFORD. Oh, let's try to make something for you. You're young and I—I can help you.

KAREN (*smiles*). You can help me?

MRS. TILFORD (*with great feeling*). Take whatever I can give you. Take it for yourself and use it for yourself.

It won't bring me peace, if that's what's worrying you. (*Smiles*) Those ten or fifteen years you talk about! They will be bad years.

KAREN. I'm tired, Mrs. Tilford. (*Almost tenderly*) You will have a hard time ahead, won't you?

MRS. TILFORD. Yes.

KAREN. Mary?

MRS. TILFORD. I don't know.

KAREN. You can send her away.

MRS. TILFORD. No. I could never do that. Whatever she does, it must be to me and no one else. She's—she's——

KAREN. Yes. Your very own, to live with the rest of your life. (*For a moment she watches* MRS. TILFORD's *face*) It's over for me now, but it will never end for you. She's harmed us both, but she's harmed you more, I guess. (*Sits down beside* MRS. TILFORD) I'm sorry.

MRS. TILFORD (*clings to her*). Then you'll try for yourself.

KAREN. All right.

MRS. TILFORD. You and Joe.

KAREN. No. We're not together anymore.

MRS. TILFORD (*looks up at her*). Did I do that, too?

KAREN. I don't think anyone did anything, any more.

MRS. TILFORD (*makes a half-movement to rise*). I'll go to him right away.

KAREN. No, it's better now the way it is.

MRS. TILFORD. But he must know what I know, Karen. You must go back to him.

KAREN (*smiles*). No, not any more.

MRS. TILFORD. You must, you must— (*Sees her face, hesitates*) Perhaps later, Karen?

KAREN. Perhaps.

MRS. TILFORD (*after a moment in which they both sit silent*). Come away from here now, Karen. (KAREN *shakes her head*) You can't stay with— (*Moves her hand toward door Right.*)

KAREN. When she is buried, then I will go.

MRS. TILFORD. You'll be all right?

KAREN. I'll be all right, I suppose. Good-bye, now.

(*They both rise.* MRS. TILFORD *speaks, pleadingly.*)

MRS. TILFORD. You'll let me help you? You'll let me try?

KAREN. Yes, if it will make you feel better.

MRS. TILFORD (*with great feeling*). Oh, yes, oh, yes, Karen.

(*Unconsciously* KAREN *begins to walk toward the window.*)

KAREN (*suddenly*). Is it nice out?

MRS. TILFORD. It's been cold. (KAREN *opens the window slightly, sits on the ledge.* MRS. TILFORD *with surprise*) It seems a little warmer, now.

KAREN. It feels very good.

(*They smile at each other.*)

MRS. TILFORD. You'll write me some time?

KAREN. If I ever have anything to say. Good-bye, now.

MRS. TILFORD. You will have. I know it. Good-bye, my dear.

(KAREN *smiles, shakes her head as* MRS. TILFORD *exits. She does not turn, but a minute later she raises her hand.*)

KAREN. Good-bye.

Curtain

DAYS TO COME

FOR

JULIA AND MAX HELLMAN

Days to Come was first produced at the Vanderbilt Theatre, New York City, on December 15, 1936, with the following cast:

(In the order of their appearance)

HANNAH	CLARE WOODBURY
LUCY	MURIEL GALLICK
CORA RODMAN	FRIEDA ALTMAN
HENRY ELLICOTT	NED WEVER
ANDREW RODMAN	WILLIAM HARRIGAN
JULIE RODMAN	FLORENCE ELDRIDGE
THOMAS FIRTH	JOSEPH SWEENEY
LEO WHALEN	BEN SMITH
SAM WILKIE	CHARLES DINGLE
MOSSIE DOWEL	JACK CARR
JOE EASTER	THOMAS FISHER

Produced and directed by HERMAN SHUMLIN

Settings designed by ALINE BERNSTEIN

ACT ONE

Living room of the Rodman house.
Late morning in October.

SCENE: *The living room of the Rodman house in Callom, Ohio, two hundred miles from Cleveland. The room is deep and the Left stage window-wall is curved into the room. All furniture gives the impression of being arranged for the entrance doors which are on the Right Center stage wall. On the backstage wall, on the extreme Right, is a door leading into the library. On the curved Left stage wall are two high windows. These windows open on a circular porch and are used as an entrance by people who know the house well. Between the windows, and well out on the stage, is a large drum table. There are chairs on each side of the table. Back from the table is an antique flat topped table desk. Left downstage is a high circular cabinet, unglassed, in which there are many small figures of animals. Near the cabinet is a couch. The room is beautiful, simple. But the objects in the cabinet are too neatly placed and the effect is rigid and bad.*
Left and Right stage directions are always the audience's Left and Right.

AT RISE: *A large vigorous woman is sitting on the floor in front of the window, comfortably arranging flowers in several bowls. (The bowls and the flowers are on the porch.) She has on a house dress, but is not in servant's uniform.* LUCY, *in uniform, is dusting. On a chair next to* HANNAH *is a bowl of half shelled peas.*

LUCY (*finishes dusting the animals*). That's enough for them today.

HANNAH (*hands her a bowl of flowers and laughs*). Did you get your wages this morning? (*No answer*) Huh?

LUCY (*reluctantly*). Yes.

HANNAH (*cheerfully*). Then hand it over.

LUCY. I was going to. But Hannah, I got to keep five dollars out of it because I owe somebody the five dollars.

HANNAH. Is the five dollar somebody in this town?

LUCY. No.

HANNAH. Then don't pay 'em. The boys need it— (*Soberly*) and I got a hunch will need it more. (*As* LUCY *gives her the money from her apron pocket*) Thanks, Lucy. You're a nice kid. I'll tell them how it comes from you.

LUCY. But when's it going to be over? Seems funny, don't it?

HANNAH. I'm not laughing. (*She hands* LUCY *another bowl of flowers.* LUCY *takes it to a table near the couch and puts it very carefully in a certain spot*) I don't know when it's going to be over. But I guessed it was going to be. I haven't lived in this house twenty years for nothing. (HANNAH *has been watching* LUCY *place the bowl. She laughs and makes a this-way gesture with her hands*) Uh-uh. Bring it over.

LUCY (*as if this joke had been played before*). What's the use? Miss Cora will only— (*Makes imitative gestures on the table*) move it right back here.

HANNAH. I know. I like to see her do it.

LUCY. But Aunt Lundee says that all they do is sit around talking and that a man should be at work and that Uncle Jim and the rest should go on back and stop this crazy strike and—

HANNAH. Since when does anybody listen to your Aunt Lundee?

LUCY. I don't know.

HANNAH (*cheerfully*). Lucy, there were people made to think and people made to listen. I ain't sure either you or Lundee were made to do either.

LUCY (*pointing to the vase*). Miss Cora's been downtown already this morning. So was Mrs. Rodman, and when I came out of the butcher store there was Miss Cora standing on one side of the street, looking at Mrs. Rodman in the funniest way, and she didn't call to her, she just stood watching and not saying anything—

HANNAH. And *you* just stood watching and not saying anything, too, huh?

LUCY (*hurt*). What's wrong with that now?

HANNAH. Nothing. (*Then looks at her, half-seriously, half-teasingly*) As long as you just watch and don't say anything.

(CORA RODMAN *enters from the Center doors. She is a thin, nervous-looking woman of about forty-two. She has a small clay Chinese horse in her hand.* HANNAH *doesn't look up, but* LUCY *watches* CORA *as she crosses to the cabinet with the horse.*)

CORA. I brought this down. I'll take the elephant up for my desk. It will make a nice change.

LUCY. Yes'm.

CORA (*to* HANNAH). Did you make something sweet?

HANNAH (*to* CORA). Chocolate cake. All over.

CORA (*to* LUCY, *who has picked up carpet sweeper, rags, etc. and is exiting*). Well, don't cut me such a small piece. You didn't bring me enough butter on my tray this morning, and I had a roll left over.

LUCY. Yes'm. (*She exits.*)

CORA (*she crosses to flower bowl and, with the motions* LUCY *has imitated, moves it back to its particular spot*). Always seems to be something the matter with the breakfast tray. I read in the morning paper about a thirteen year old girl who had a baby in the county hospital. Why don't they watch those things?

HANNAH (*who has smiled maliciously as* CORA *moved the bowl*). Who's going to watch 'em?

CORA. It was a very dangerous Caesarian operation. Maybe that always happens when the mother is under age. What's the name of that man who boards with your sister?

HANNAH. Now you can go over and ask Doc Morris about the girl—and he can tell you, the way he did that time about cats, which you never gotten straight.

CORA. I asked you what is the name of that man.

HANNAH. I don't know which you mean. She's got five boarders regular.

CORA. He was walking up and down in front of the factory, the way they've been doing and wasting their time, and I said good morning and he didn't answer. I said it again and he walked to the other side. So I went right up and told him I didn't like rudeness—

HANNAH. That's Odave. He's only been here a year. Maybe that's not time enough to fall in love with the Rodman family. (*Thoughtfully*) You know, Miss Cora, they tell me that in places where there's a strike, the men forget sometimes to bow to the boss' sister.

CORA. There is never any need for rudeness.

HANNAH. She's getting a new boarder. Guess he's moved in by now. Leo Whalen.

CORA (*after a pause*). That's very wrong of your sister. And disloyal of you to let her. He's a bad character—

HANNAH. How do you know? You never spoke to him.

CORA. I know why he's here. That's enough. He's trying to make trouble and you know it. That's what he came here for—

HANNAH. Not my business. She's in the boarding house business and it's open to anybody who don't steal. (*Picks up bowl of peas and starts to exit*) Anyway, she likes him. Lots of people here like him. (*So casually that it has meaning*) Women, too, I guess.

(*She passes* HENRY ELLICOTT *who is entering. He has on a hat and overcoat. He is about forty, good-looking in a worldly kind of way.*)

ELLICOTT. Good morning. Did anyone call me, Cora?

CORA (*as he takes off his coat*). A woman called you about a month ago. I told you about that, although I don't see why she called you here.

ELLICOTT. You told me about that. Several times.

CORA. She hasn't called you since. I think I gave her to understand that you should conduct your affairs at your own house.

ELLICOTT. I'm not talking about women, Cora. I'm talking about my office.

CORA. *They* did *not* call.

HANNAH (*as* ELLICOTT *crosses to desk*). You be here for lunch? We got a good lunch.

CORA. Hannah, will you please allow *me* to invite Mr. Ellicott for lunch?

ELLICOTT. You, and you alone, may invite me to lunch.

CORA (*to* HANNAH). *I* have invited Mr. Ellicott to lunch.

(HANNAH *nods, pleased at the effect she has had on* CORA, *then exits.*)

ELLICOTT. You put your foot down very firmly on that important matter. Where is Julie? (*He is moving around the room.*)

CORA (*holds out a small box*). Don't move around so. Want one? They're pepsin drops with chocolate. Doctor Morris says they're good for me. I'm going to get a dog this week. I've ordered it. A male this time. Females are too difficult to take care of during, er, during. I was reading only this morning about a thirteen year old girl who had a baby. You travel around. Have you ever seen that before?

ELLICOTT. I haven't actually seen it. But they tell me that in warm countries—

CORA. In *warm* countries. But not in Cleveland. (*He goes*

to the window, and after a second she says softly) Julie is out, Henry.

ELLICOTT. Where is she?

CORA (*as if she had been waiting for it*). I don't know. I don't spy on Julie.

ELLICOTT (*turns and looks at her*). You've such a pleasant way of saying things. (*Then he looks at his watch and goes to the telephone, dials a number*) This is Mr. Ellicott. Joe still there? (*To* CORA) Andrew around?

CORA. I suppose so. I shall have to move my room if he doesn't stop walking up and down in the library all night. I sleep badly enough anyway and if a pin drops it wakes me. I've always been like that—

ELLICOTT (*into phone*). Joe? I've been waiting for you to call. Everything all right? Good. (ANDREW RODMAN *comes in through the library doors. He has a pleasant, serious face. His motions are those of a man who is puzzled and tired. He crosses to the desk and looks at some papers, idly, as he listens to* ELLICOTT *on the phone*) Take them off a few at a time. Then drive Wilkie up to Mr. Rodman's. (*Gets up, to* ANDREW) That's good. They'll be off the train about lunch time. The train will come in on the siding. They won't be noticed much.

ANDREW. Are these high-jinks necessary? As long as they're coming, let them in at the station.

ELLICOTT. There's no sense walking into trouble.

ANDREW (*nods his head*). So you're admitting now that there might be trouble? That they might not see it the way—the way we do?

CORA. But why should there be any trouble? We can run the factory when we want to. It's ours. I don't understand why there should be any trouble—

ELLICOTT (*sharply*). I didn't say there'd be any trouble.

CORA (*placatingly to* ANDREW). Now you see. Henry says there won't be a bit of trouble.

ELLICOTT (*smiles, obviously irritated*). Andrew, do we have to start this all over again now?

ANDREW. No. Don't pay any attention to me. We've made up our minds and that's that.

ELLICOTT. And a damn good thing! The loan's o. k. now. But Nelson says you couldn't've gotten a nickel in Cleveland if you hadn't made this decision. He had to swear to them that you wouldn't change your mind again.

CORA. See? As long as you have to spend the money anyway, you should have hired these new workers weeks ago. The way Henry and I told you to.

ANDREW. I didn't want to do it that way. I don't now.

CORA. No, of course you didn't. You thought kind talk and reason would do it. Well, it didn't work, did it? Papa would have known what to do. And without wasting time and money. Papa would have known—

(*Her speech is interrupted by* JULIE RODMAN *who comes in from the porch windows. She is a very attractive, slim, slightly tired-looking woman of about thirty-two. She is wearing a sweater and skirt, low shoes, a loose tweed coat, no hat. Her clothes are expensive and careless.*)

JULIE (*slowly, as if she didn't expect the room to be full: as if thinking of something else*). Good morning.

CORA. The man was here about the tree planting. I told him that you always did that. Forgetting about things.

JULIE. I did forget. You could have told him about the planting.

CORA (*smugly*). You know my rules. Not to interfere.

JULIE. There are so many rules. It's hard to remember them all. It's funny to go walking now. The Carlsen kids were coming from school. (*Smiles*) They had a bad minute wondering whether to say hello to me. (ANDREW *has moved on her speech as if he knew what*

*she meant, and didn't like hearing it. She has gone to
the decanters on the table*) Sherry? It's cold.

ELLICOTT. Your walks take you in all directions, don't they?

JULIE (*without answering, turns to* ANDREW, *motions to
sherry glass*). Andy? Do you good.

ANDREW. No, darling. (*As he gathers up papers*) I have
work to do before lunch.

ELLICOTT. Wilkie should be here soon.

ANDREW (*slowly, at door*). I haven't forgotten.

JULIE (*gently*). You look so tired.

CORA. Certainly he looks tired. He's worn himself out for
no reason. Papa would have settled this strike weeks
ago—

ANDREW (*at door, smiles, speaks slowly*). Yes. I suppose
so. Maybe Papa was a better man than I am.

CORA (*gets up, gently to* JULIE). I will see about the trees.
Before my headache gets worse. (JULIE *begins to protest, but is interrupted by* CORA's *wheeling sharply on*
ELLICOTT *as if she had just thought of something*) Inci-
dentally, I hope you didn't touch my securities for this
loan? You are my lawyer. You must protect me—

ELLICOTT (*smiles*). Certainly. Increased protection, increased fees.

CORA. I'm unmarried. It's different with me. I have no one
to support me. It's different when you're not married—

ELLICOTT. Unfortunately, in the business world there is
no reward for virginity. (*Sharply, quickly, as he sees
the question coming again*) No. Andrew wouldn't let
me take your securities. I don't know why—

CORA (*pleasantly now*). Because I'm his sister.

ELLICOTT. Really? Is that the reason? (*Annoyed at her
sudden turn to good nature*) However, when it's
cleaned up, you will pay your part of the expenses.

CORA. I don't understand that.

ELLICOTT. Then it's not because I haven't tried to explain

it to you. You own as much of the factory as Andy does. As you share the profits, you must share the losses.

CORA. Why should I pay for Andrew's mistakes? If we'd been able to make him do this three weeks ago—

ELLICOTT. You will still be well this side of starvation. You can have two pieces of cake instead of your usual three.

CORA. I shall have to talk the losses business over with Andrew. I don't understand why— (*As if she had just heard him*) And I shall eat just as much as I please. Just as much as I please. (*She closes the door as* ELLICOTT *looks after her.*)

JULIE (*smiling, watching him*). Cora worries you too much.

ELLICOTT. And you, happily, very little. She seems to be watching you these days— (*As her face changes*) Or am I imagining it? Where have you been, Julie?

JULIE. Walking.

ELLICOTT. In town?

JULIE. I must be getting old. I don't like autumn anymore. The river is full of leaves and it was too cold to walk very far.

ELLICOTT. Weren't you in town?

JULIE (*very deliberate*). The storm broke the big elm. The heavy branch is lying in the river. There's a big lizard on the branch that looks as if it grew there—

ELLICOTT. You were near the strike office. I saw you. I think Cora saw you, too.

JULIE (*annoyed*). Really? Were you both hiding?

ELLICOTT. That's the second time you've lied about being in town. Why?

JULIE. Maybe because I like to lie. (*Quietly, looking at him*) Maybe it's because I'm tired of your questions.

ELLICOTT (*quietly*). I don't like your being tired. (*After a second*) I'm going down to White Sulphur when things are cleared up here. Are you coming?

JULIE. No.

ELLICOTT (*suddenly, sharply*). I want to know where we stand, Julie. It's time for me to know.

JULIE (*lightly, kindly*). We stand nowhere. We've always stood nowhere. I knew about you—and you knew about me. (*Quickly*) Staying for lunch?

ELLICOTT. Yes, I knew about you. And what I didn't know our friends told me. (*Carefully*) But I find, more to my surprise than to yours, that you mean something to me. I think you have for a long time.

JULIE. I don't think so. (*Kindly*) Look. It doesn't mean anything to me—and that's where I've got to quit.

ELLICOTT. "And that's where I've got to quit." There isn't a man living who doesn't know about the woman who allows herself anything, but who invents the one rule that will keep her this side of what she thinks is respectable. She'll lie, but not on Thursdays. She'll sleep with you, but not immediately after lunch. Usually it's funny. In your case, for me, it's not so funny. (*Angrily*) What the hell did you expect me to mean to you?

JULIE (*puts her hand on his arm*). What did I expect you to mean to me? I don't know. I haven't any excuse, really. I've hoped for a very long time that everybody or anybody would mean something. (*Smiles*) Things start as hopes and end up as habits. (*Earnestly*) Look. Don't let's talk about it. You like civilized conversations about love too much, and I like them too little. One of the things that brings people like you and me together is the understanding that there won't be any talk about it at the end.

ELLICOTT. That's true. And it's too callous for me.

JULIE (*violently*). And for me, too. That's why I don't like it. I'm ashamed of its callousness—and I don't want any more of it. I don't mean to hurt you. (*She gets up, smiles, takes off her coat*) I asked you if you were staying for lunch.

ELLICOTT (*after a second, watching her*). Yes, I'm staying. If you ever saw what you wanted, Julie, would you know it?

JULIE (*quickly, unconsciously, very seriously, as if to herself*). Yes. I knew it. I knew about it quick.

ELLICOTT (*suddenly wheels about and takes her arm, tightly*). That's foolish what you're saying. Too foolish to believe. (*Tensely*) And what's more important, it's dangerous. Don't start anything, Julie—

JULIE (*softly*). I don't know what you are talking about.

(*They stand for a second as they are. He does not release her arm until the window-doors open and* THOMAS FIRTH *followed by* LEO WHALEN *appear on the porch. Then he quickly releases her arm and moves away.* FIRTH *taps on the window-wood. He is a big, lean, middle-aged American working-man. He is obviously nervous and excited.* WHALEN *is attractive in a simple, clean, undistinguished way. All his movements from this moment until the end of the play show calmness, and are the movements of a man who knows he can take care of himself.*)

FIRTH. Mrs. Rodman.

JULIE. Oh. (*Then cordially*) Hello, Tom. (*To* WHALEN, *her tone changed and nervous*) Hello, Mr. Whalen. Come in.

ELLICOTT (*to both*). Good morning.

FIRTH. I want to see Andrew. I came to see him.

JULIE (*surprised at the tenseness of his tone*). Yes. But come in, won't you? (*Abruptly* FIRTH *steps into the room, standing straight and rigid.* WHALEN *moves in casually*) I thought you were leaving us, Mr. Whalen. I haven't seen you in town the last few days.

WHALEN. Leaving? (*Looks at* FIRTH, *smiles*) Not for a while yet.

ELLICOTT (*to* FIRTH). Andrew's busy. Will I do?

FIRTH. No.

JULIE (*moves to the wall bell, presses it, speaks nervously to* WHALEN). I thought—I thought perhaps you would come and have dinner with us one night—

WHALEN (*laughs heartily*). The boss asks me for dinner. Well, that's very pleasant. It's never happened to me before. (*Looks at* FIRTH) But strange things happen in this town.

FIRTH. Mrs. Rodman, can I see Andrew now?

(LUCY *appears at the door.*)

JULIE. Tell Mr. Rodman that Tom Firth is here and wants to see him. (LUCY *disappears. To* WHALEN) Why should that be so strange? We don't get many visitors here and because you and my husband happen to be, well, happen to think differently, is no reason we can't eat together.

WHALEN (*pleasantly*). In my business it's a good reason.

ELLICOTT. Julie. Whalen is in the business of hating. It pays well, I imagine.

WHALEN. Very well. All labor organizers are racketeers, Mr. Ellicott, as you and I both know from the papers. (*He has started to roll a cigarette. Quickly* JULIE *offers him a box from the table*) But there's no hate *here*. The boss loves the workers, and the workers— (*To* FIRTH) the worker—loves the boss. In other towns I've heard that called something else.

FIRTH. Shut up.

(*There is a second's embarrassed silence.* WHALEN, *however, is pleased.*)

JULIE (*to* WHALEN). Old Mrs. Hicks tells me you like our river. That you walk there very often.

WHALEN. Yes. You've got a nice river. You've kept it clean.

JULIE (*to* WHALEN). When I first moved here I used to fish in it. Do you like to fish?

WHALEN. Yes. Very much. (*To* FIRTH) Maybe Mr. Rodman doesn't want to see you.

FIRTH. You don't have to wait.

ELLICOTT (*to* WHALEN). No. I'm sure you're busy—

WHALEN. I'll wait. (*To* JULIE) If it's all right.

JULIE (*smiles, warmly, quickly*). It's very all right. (*Still smiling, turns to* ELLICOTT) Mr. Ellicott is too concerned with your time.

FIRTH. You're staying to watch. I don't need you to watch me. You and nobody is going to make me act blind. You and nobody is going to make me hate a man who's been my friend.

ELLICOTT (*to* JULIE). He *is* in the business of hate. I was right.

WHALEN (*to* FIRTH). I don't give a damn who you hate and who you love. I'm trying to see that that Christian heart of yours doesn't do too much harm. (*To* ELLICOTT) You were right.

(*On* WHALEN's *words,* FIRTH *moves toward him angrily, and then turns and stands rigidly as* ANDREW *comes into the room.*)

ANDREW (*slowly*). Hello, Tom. (*Less friendly*) Hello, Mr. Whalen.

FIRTH. Andrew, I went out on strike with the rest. That was my duty. But I stood by you in a lot of ways.

WHALEN (*unpleasantly*). He did. I can vouch for it.

FIRTH. We've all been trying to see it from both our sides and we've been friends about it—

WHALEN. Ask your question.

FIRTH. He says that a trainload of strikebreakers came through Callom Junction this morning. And I said I didn't believe it. I said you didn't know no more about things like that than we did, and that I knew you—

ANDREW. Tom, I wanted to talk to you this afternoon.

ELLICOTT (*looking at his watch*). Which would still be wisest. This afternoon.

FIRTH. I'm here. I don't want to wait. Talk to me now. (*After a second's silence, speaks to* WHALEN *over his shoulder*) Read him that fool thing.

WHALEN (*takes a telegram from his pocket, reads it in a pleasant, unconcerned way*). "Wilkie on way probably fifty sixty of the boys including Gans Easter Malloy which gives you rough idea stop Easter just out of jail with toothache so watch your heart and anything else." That's from a friend of mine in Cleveland. He's a wit.

FIRTH. I don't know about these people he's talking about. And neither do you. That's why I know it's got to be wrong. (*Watches* ANDREW, *gets no answer, then slowly, firmly*) Andrew. It's got to be wrong.

ANDREW. Tom, I've tried to explain. I tried from the first day you came to me. (*Touches a paper on the desk, looks at it*) The figures are here. They're as much yours to see as they are mine.

FIRTH. I don't have to see 'em again.

ANDREW. You don't. But I have to see them again and again and again. We've got to sell the brushes we make.

WHALEN. Some places make what they can sell.

ANDREW (*sharply*). Yes. They make them cheaper than we do— (*Slowly*) and they make them cheaper because they cost less. You know that Partee cut salaries two years ago—

FIRTH. I know that. I told you to cut us a little. That we'd take a little for you. And I told you to make three, four model brushes, not eighteen—

ANDREW. I can't, against the others.

WHALEN. Then make them the way they make them.

ANDREW. You mean cheaper brushes? Ask Tom what he thinks of that.

FIRTH. We make the best brush in America.

WHALEN (*laughs*). There. You've hit on something. That'll pay your rent. You can eat fine on that.

ANDREW (*to* FIRTH). You tell me a way out, I'll take it. Seven years ago we were making a lot of money. (*Touches the paper*) I can't stay in business losing it this way. We'd be out in another year.

WHALEN. You haven't been answering his question, Mr. Rodman.

ANDREW. I'm doing my best to answer him. (*After a second*) I knew the cuts had to come. I tried hard to keep them off as long as I could. I thought you'd see that the only way you could stay working and I could stay working was if we took the bad times together. I couldn't do anything else.

FIRTH. And I know we can't live on forty-cent piece work. I told you it was too big a cut. And I told you they wouldn't take it.

ANDREW. Do you think I want to cut you that way? It's just for a little while—

FIRTH. And who's going to pay our bills for the little while?

ANDREW (*shakes his head*). I know. I don't blame you. But you mustn't blame us, either.

FIRTH (*quickly*). Who's us?

ANDREW. Me, I mean. That's the story. I wish I'd known what else to do.

(*Slowly* WHALEN *rises, smiling.* FIRTH *turns and looks at him, looks around the room, and then crosses quickly to* ANDREW *as if he didn't believe the answer had been made.*)

FIRTH. All right. We knew all that. That's what I been saying to myself, and I ain't got the answer for either of us. (*Hits the table*) But that's something between us to settle. We ain't foreigners. Our people came here with your people, and worked along with them and helped them, too. In twelve when they came and tried to make a union, we threw 'em out. There ain't never been any trouble here, Andrew—

ELLICOTT (*to* ANDREW). It's late.

ANDREW. Let him say what he wants to say.

FIRTH. I ain't believing that you're bringing foreigners—

ANDREW (*slowly*). You've been out three weeks. The place had to start running again.

FIRTH (*slowly*). You mean you're giving away our jobs. You mean other people are taking our work— (*Breaks off sharply and stands staring at* ANDREW, *shaking his head.*)

WHALEN (*rises, smiles to* JULIE). Sad to grow up, isn't it? (*To* FIRTH) Well, come on. Cry at home. You've wasted enough time now. The world is a bad place and you're a big boy.

ELLICOTT (*to* FIRTH). You could have talked this over with me. It may be all right for you to walk out, but it is also all right for Andrew to keep his own machines going his own way.

FIRTH (*shouting*). And this was his way of keeping 'em going, eh? I could've known you had a hand in it.

ELLICOTT (*sharply*). He's got to start making brushes again. If you've made up your mind not to make them, then somebody else has to.

WHALEN. No? You're kidding. (*To* ANDREW) Who sold you the idea Wilkie's boys can run machines? (*Makes the motion of pointing a pistol*) That's the kind they meant. That's the kind you'll get run—and they do that fine. (*To* FIRTH) And be sure you're there to make speeches about the boat your grandfather came over on, and God is love, and your heart's breaking. Turn the other cheek, and crawl back. It hurts less that way, I guess.

FIRTH (*slowly*). I told the boys we'd be settling it like friends. I was wrong. (*To* WHALEN) I won't be turning the other cheek. I won't be crawling back. Nobody else will either. (*Without turning to look at* ANDREW, *he moves quickly to the window and out.*)

ANDREW (*quietly, to* JULIE). He's been a good friend. For a long time.

ELLICOTT (*slowly, to* WHALEN). We don't want trouble

here. We're sorry that you do want it. But I suppose that's your job.

WHALEN (*getting up*). Sometimes it is. Sometimes it isn't. But what you and I want won't make much difference. When the guns start popping and the skulls start cracking, they won't be thinking about us.

ANDREW (*angrily*). There won't be any guns here—on either side.

ELLICOTT. Unless you have them.

WHALEN. I? No, sir. I'm scared to death of them. (*To* ANDREW, *moving toward the window*) I hope you're right, Mr. Rodman.

(*As* WHALEN *moves toward the window the front door bell starts to ring, steadily, loudly. They have all turned, startled by it.* HANNAH, *calm, quiet, appears in the door.*)

JULIE. What is it, Hannah?

HANNAH. Lucy's watching my oven so the things don't burn.

ANDREW (*looking at her*). Then you answer it, Hannah.

HANNAH. No, Mr. Andrew. If what I heard is right, that's one bell I ain't going to answer. I can't help what other people do, but I don't have to help 'em out.

JULIE. Hannah—

HANNAH. And Lucy can't answer because she's watching my oven so the things don't burn, if she's got the sense. (ELLICOTT, *quickly, angrily, moves past* HANNAH *and out into the hall. To* WHALEN) Like boarding at my sister's?

WHALEN. Sure. It's a good place. (*Smiles at her warmly*) I'm no boarder, I'm charity.

HANNAH. She can afford it. But watch her. She don't always like to get the dust from under things. (*She exits.*)

(WHALEN, *in the first quick motion he has made, moves to* ANDREW'*s desk, leans over it, speaks tensely, hurriedly.*)

WHALEN. Rodman. It's hard to believe, but I'm believing it. You don't know. (*He points toward Center doors*) about things like this. I do. This is a nice town. I hate to see it hurt. (*Then quietly*) Give them their sixty-cent hour. Give them their union. They'll be back to work in ten minutes.

ANDREW. They can have any union they want. But I can't pay the salaries. I want to—and I can't. I don't know what you've seen in the past. But there won't be any trouble here. I won't let there be. I hope you won't either.

(ELLICOTT, *followed by* SAMUEL WILKIE, *comes in from the hall.* WILKIE *is of medium height, heavy. He looks like any husky business man. Directly behind him are* MOSSIE DOWEL *and* JOE EASTER. MOSSIE *is fat and pleasant-looking.* EASTER *is thin, nervous, tough.* MOSSIE *and* EASTER *stand stiffly at the door.*)

WILKIE. Mr. Rodman. I'm Samuel Wilkie. (*He bows to* JULIE) How do you do?

ELLICOTT (*as* WILKIE *looks at* WHALEN). This is Mr. Whalen. You'll meet, I think.

WHALEN (*pleasantly*). I've heard of Mr. Wilkie.

WILKIE. Seems I've heard of you, too. (*To the others*) We're in the same line, you might say.

WHALEN. You knew my friend Cliff Taylor?

WILKIE. I knew who he was.

WHALEN (*conversationally to the others*). Taylor was an organizer. He had his throat cut last year in Gainesville.

WILKIE. They tell me he was a nice guy.

WHALEN. Yeah. And they tell me a side-burn guy did it. He worked for you, I think, and he played with knives a lot.

WILKIE (*thoughtfully*). No. I don't think he worked for me. But you can't tell. Lot of people come in and out of the office. Were you in Gainesville?

WHALEN (*laughs*). No. (*Touches his throat*) Fortunately, I was in Akron.

WILKIE. Now we're talking. That's the job I wanted. That's money for you. But they pieced it out in New York. You been here long?

WHALEN. About two weeks. I haven't done much. How many men you got?

WILKIE. Fifty-two, three. (WHALEN *says "um"*) Yes. That's what I say. I been trying to tell these gentlemen that it isn't enough. Better to spend it now than later. (*Hastily, as he sees* ELLICOTT'*s face*) But they're paying, and they should know.

ANDREW. The men with you are good brush makers?

MOSSIE (*unconsciously*). Huh?

WILKIE (*puzzled, turns to look at* WHALEN, *who is smiling*). Good? Well, we'll hope so.

WHALEN (*laughs*). They are also skilled motormen, miners, car loaders, longshoremen—and anything you like. They're the best.

WILKIE (*laughs*). Now that's the kind of recommendation we want. (*To* WHALEN) How many men you signed? What kind?

ANDREW. What I need, and what I ordered, were brush workers.

WILKIE (*looks at him*). We'll see how it works out.

WHALEN. Hundred and ninety-two men and not bad for a new union. Decent and—(*Looks at* WILKIE) peaceful, the right way.

WILKIE (*heartily*). And that's the way we like it.

WHALEN (*laughs*). Yes. That's the way we like it.

ELLICOTT. If you gentlemen are finished with your conference, perhaps, Wilkie—

WHALEN. Certainly. I talk too much. (*Moves toward windows, and as he passes* JULIE) And if I promise not to talk at all, may I still walk by your river?

JULIE (*smiles*). Yes. But I hope you will talk. I like to listen.

(*As he exits, he collides with* CORA, *who is coming in from the porch.*)

WHALEN. Oh. Sorry.

JULIE. This is Mr. Whalen, Cora. (CORA *looks up at him, then lowers her eyes, says "Hum," and marches past him into the room.* WHALEN *looks at her, amazed, then grins and runs off the porch.* JULIE, *violently, to* CORA) Don't ever do that in my house again.

CORA. What? What did you say to me?

JULIE. I said you were never to do that in my house again.

LUCY (*at door*). Lunch is ready, Mrs. Rodman.

ELLICOTT (*looks at* JULIE, *smiles*). You're very upset, aren't you?

CORA. How dare you talk to me that way—

JULIE (*to* ANDREW, *touching his arm*). I'm sorry, Andy.

ANDREW. There's nothing to be sorry for, darling. Cora acted like a fool.

CORA (*to* JULIE). So it's *your* house now? My father built it, but it's your house now.

JULIE. Please. I'm sorry.

CORA. You've thought that all these years. It's very strange that you waited to tell me until something happened about *that* man—

ANDREW (*sharply*). Stop that silly shouting.

JULIE. I don't want lunch, Andy. Go in without me.

(*She pats his arm and exits quickly through library door.* CORA *sits down and begins to sniffle.* ANDREW *and* ELLICOTT *stare after* JULIE.)

WILKIE (*after a moment*). Um.

ELLICOTT (*turns*). It's late. You'd better have lunch here, Wilkie. It'll save time.

ANDREW (*has turned and is looking at* MOSSIE *and* JOE). Who are these gentlemen, Mr. Wilkie?

WILKIE. Mr. Easter, Mr. Dowel. I'll be staying at the hotel. They'll be here with you. (*To* ELLICOTT) Thank you. Can I wash up?

ANDREW. Staying here? Why should they be staying here? (*To* CORA, *who is sniffling and arranging the figures in the cabinet*) Please stop that, Cora.

WILKIE. They're here to take good care of you and your family, Mr. Rodman. You won't have anything to worry about.

ANDREW (*carefully*). I don't think I understand what you are talking about. Neither I nor my family need any taking care of.

WILKIE. I hope not. I believe not. But I don't like taking chances with people who pay my bills.

ANDREW (*to* ELLICOTT). What kind of nonsense is this? (*To* WILKIE) They'll stay at the hotel.

CORA. It's not nonsense. It's not nonsense. I'm paying my share of this and it's my house, too, and if Julie is going to have people like that around—(*Motions toward window*) in and out of the house, we will all need protection. She treats that man like—

ELLICOTT (*sharply*). Cora.

CORA. I insist on my rights. If you don't care what happens to me, then *I* must care—

WILKIE (*pleasantly to* ANDREW). If you'd prefer the boys stay at the hotel—?

ANDREW (*wearily*). My sister needs protection. It makes no difference. (*Starts slowly for the door.*)

LUCY (*back at door*). Lunch is getting cold.

ANDREW (*at door, over his shoulder to* ELLICOTT). I don't want lunch. Go ahead.

ELLICOTT (*stares after him for a moment. Then to* CORA). We're a small party. But that will leave more food for you. Let's go in now. You can take up the hysterics again after lunch. (CORA *rises, sweeps past him, exits.*

ELLICOTT, *as he starts out, to* WILKIE) Miss Rodman is a nervous lady.

WILKIE. Yes. They're all nervous, aren't they?

(*Without answering,* ELLICOTT *exits.*)

MOSSIE. It's like a society picture, what they were doing. (*Touches his throat*) They talk so high. (*Watches* WILKIE *who is standing in the middle of the room*) You look like you're puzzling something, boss. What's a brush worker? (*He cracks his knuckles.*)

WILKIE (*laughs*). I don't know. Somebody who makes a brush, I guess.

EASTER (*suddenly, as* MOSSIE *cracks knuckles again*). For Christ's sake quit that. You're getting me crazy.

WILKIE (*turns*). Sit down. Both of you. Try to act like you've been in a house with a bathroom before. (*Looks at* EASTER) I don't want to have to worry about your nerves this time. (*He exits.*)

MOSSIE (*sits down near cabinet*). I couldn't follow what they were saying. They talk fast, don't they? (EASTER *has wandered over to desk. Idly he looks at papers on it, examines a few things on it*) They were mad. I got that. But it don't sound bad when you talk high. (*He cracks his knuckles.*)

EASTER. I liked it for myself in Cleveland. Fifty of us. What kind of piker job is this? That Wilkie goes crazy when he smells a dollar. Always has.

MOSSIE. I don't get what he's doing. The boys sit in the factory and we sit here, huh? What's that for?

EASTER. Something he made up. We're going to get a lot extra sitting here.

MOSSIE (*cheerfully*). Well, we're eating on him. (MOSSIE *cracks his knuckles.*)

EASTER. Just keep that up for a few days, hear me? I can feed myself. I told him that.

MOSSIE (*laughs*). Yeah. But it tastes better when somebody else buys it.

EASTER. There might be street car trouble on the coast next month. I found out. I told him about it. So would he stay and wait and play for big stuff? No. He's got to take this, 'cause they let him smell a dollar bill first.

MOSSIE (*thoughtfully*). Well, he ain't working for us. He don't care about us. Car stuff, huh? Who's going to get it?

EASTER. How do I know? (MOSSIE *cracks his knuckles*) Stop it.

MOSSIE. Jesus Christ. Passing up street car work. He made enough money in New Orleans to keep him for a year.

EASTER. So did you.

MOSSIE. And so did you. More'n me, with the dice. I got some of mine yet. I took a little insurance for my mother. That's what you should've done. Instead of that sucker diamond Phil walked you in to—

EASTER (*irritated*). You said that before. (*Looks at his watch*) What do we do? Cook our food in here?

MOSSIE. They couldn't invite us to eat inside. We're out here protecting her. (*Cracks his knuckles. During his next speech* EASTER *has idly started to play with a cigarette lighter on the desk. After the second light, it stops working. He picks up a paper-knife and begins fixing it.* MOSSIE *looks down at his hand, smiles*) Everybody's got a habit. That's a good one. Protecting her. Bet there ain't even an inch anymore to protect. But the other one looks good. You can't tell about people like this. They say, in the papers, talking fine, what they wouldn't do, and then they sneak off and take a shot in bed at the first thing that comes along— (*He has cracked his knuckles again. Quickly,* EASTER *throws the paper-knife at him.* MOSSIE *ducks, the knife misses him and knocks over a vase on a small table. Slowly,* MOSSIE *adjusts his chair, shakes his head, stares at the vase*) Starting it again, huh? When you get time, Joe, you ought to take a rest cure. Ain't natural to be so nervous with knives. (*Shakes his head, looking at the vase*) You certainly ain't neat with other people's things.

Curtain

ACT TWO

SCENE I

Four weeks later.

AT RISE: MOSSIE DOWEL *is seated and* JOE EASTER *is stand-*
ing at the table between the windows. They are playing
two-handed poker. MOSSIE *has his chair turned.* WILKIE,
in hat and overcoat, is sitting on the arm of a chair,
looking idly out of the window. The radio is playing
softly. For a few seconds after the rise of the curtain
there are no sounds but the shuffling of cards, the sound
of money on the table, the radio.

EASTER (*after a second, sharply*). All right. All right. Show
'em. Stop flirting with 'em.

(MOSSIE *puts his hand down, smiles, rakes in the center*
money. EASTER *puts down his cards, crosses to radio,*
angrily snaps it off.)

MOSSIE. Funny. Losers never like music. It's good luck
for me, on the contrary. (*To* WILKIE) It's after nine.
Must be something big keeping you out of bed.

EASTER. I guess. It's got to be money to keep him out of
those woolen nightgowns.

WILKIE. It's pay day, or it should be. That always gives
me insomnia. (*They have started to play again*) Ellicott been here?

EASTER. Nope.

MOSSIE. He's coming. Always is. Looking for Mrs. Rodman
with the legs.

EASTER (*to* WILKIE, *pointing upstairs*). You think Rodman
knows about 'em?

WILKIE (*unpleasantly*). What do you know?

MOSSIE. What does he know? He's guessing. He sees it everywhere. It comes from watching the flies go to it on cell doors.

WILKIE (*sharply, to* EASTER). I'd get the shakedown out of my head, if I were you.

EASTER. You think I'm crazy? (MOSSIE *cracks his knuckles*) Deal 'em. And stop that cracking. (*He wins a small hand and begins to shuffle the cards. Maliciously, casually to* WILKIE) So things ain't going so good, huh?

MOSSIE (*cheerfully*). It's nice and easy here. I like a rest job once in a while.

WILKIE. Another few weeks like this and you'll get a long rest.

MOSSIE. It ain't our fault, Sam.

EASTER. When you got nothing to do, we can't do it for you.

MOSSIE. Finger tried a fight. Eddie tried a fight. I even had Sig chase the old guy Firth's girl around. (*Puzzled*) Any guy'd protect his thirteen year old kid.

EASTER. Three sevens.

MOSSIE. But nobody'll fight. No matter what you do, they don't fight. Must be some kind of new religion, maybe. (*Turns up his hand, cracks his knuckles*) Three nines easy.

EASTER (*through his teeth*). They *are* running pretty easy the last two days, huh? (*To* WILKIE) I'm crazy for this place. Losing to him and following that dame around.

WILKIE. Just keep on doing it. I'll tell you when you're fit for anything else.

(ELLICOTT *appears at the Center doors. He looks around the room, then after a second, coldly.*)

ELLICOTT. Good evening. I hear you were looking for me today. You're active on pay day, aren't you?

WILKIE. Yes, sir. (*Pointing to desk*) The account's over there.

ELLICOTT (*as he passes* MOSSIE *and* JOE). I'm glad to see that nothing has disturbed your game, gentlemen. (*Picks up the sheet*) Yes. It's a very full account. Well, you're right to get it while you can. I'm not so sure how many more pay days there are going to be. You do nothing and your bills get bigger.

WILKIE. That's the way it seems to have worked out.

ELLICOTT. The Cincinnati Herald is crying its eyes out tonight over model town being over-run with toughs. None of that helps any. (*Looking at* MOSSIE *and* JOE) Do you think they could have meant these gentlemen and the other friends you brought with you?

WILKIE. I read the papers. (*Looks speculatively at* MOSSIE *and* JOE) They don't look like anything Oscar Wilde would have wanted, do they? But no job's ever paid me enough to have their faces pushed pretty. (*Gets up*) Well, I know I haven't done too much, and I like it less than you. We're in hunting country. You didn't tell me that.

ELLICOTT. What?

WILKIE. The people around here hunt. In the season, I mean. That right?

ELLICOTT. What's that got to do with it?

WILKIE. It's got a lot to do with it. Every man for five miles owns a gun. Flintlocks, maybe, but clean. But they won't use 'em on me. They won't use 'em at all. You know why? Because somebody in Cleveland made a mistake and sent down a smart organizer. He won't let 'em use 'em. There hasn't even been a nose bleed for me to stop. I can't work with nothing.

ELLICOTT. We didn't bargain to cut the plan out for you. That's your business, and you've done a bad job of it.

WILKIE (*coldly, still pleasantly*). Now, now. It's not all my fault. Even if there had been something to do, I couldn't have done it. Because I'm working for a man who doesn't want me to do anything. I'm working for

a man who doesn't want me to work for him. That's a
bad set-up, Mr. Ellicott.

ELLICOTT (*starting to exit, slowly*). You'd better come up
and see Mr. Rodman. (*Looks up at him*) As a lawyer,
I have found that for my client's own good, it is often
wise not to ask his permission on little details.

(WILKIE *has turned to stare at him as he reaches the door
and passes* CORA, *who is entering.*)

CORA (*to* ELLICOTT). Don't you ever stay in your own
house anymore? There are people who can never stay
quietly at home and read a book. (*He exits without
answering her*) Good evening. Rain. Rain. Rain. Are
there several types of detectives, Mr. Wilkie?

WILKIE. Only one kind, Miss Rodman. Lousy.

CORA. I mean, very funny things are happening here.
Things are missing from the pantry— (*Coquettishly*)
Or is that too unimportant work for you?

WILKIE. Not at all. I don't seem to be doing much else.

CORA (*goes to cabinet*). On Thursday, I was taking my
weekly supply list. Just as a matter of routine. Mrs.
Rodman was out—

WILKIE. Mrs. Rodman is out a good deal, isn't she?

CORA. Yes, Mrs. Rodman always manages to go off by
herself. Well, when I looked in the closet I was amazed
to find that at least eight or ten dollars' worth of canned
goods—

WILKIE (*rises, politely*). Mr. Dowel is a specialist at just
such detection. He's at your service, Miss Rodman. I'll
be down later and we can lay our trap. (*He exits.*)

MOSSIE (*giggles*). Sure. Who, me? Sure.

CORA. I like to see a nice little card game. Do you know
that night club singer who got killed in the paper this
morning?

MOSSIE. No ma'am. I don't know ladies who get into
trouble.

EASTER (*motioning to the cards*). Beat the straight.

MOSSIE. Easy. (*He rakes in the money as* EASTER *stares at him.*)

CORA (*to* EASTER). My. You were beaten. Are you playing for money?

(HANNAH *enters with a tray of drinks which she puts on the other side of the room.* CORA *watches her as she empties ash trays into a saucer.*)

HANNAH (*slamming ash tray on table, pointing to the floor*). Ain't it *more* trouble to lean over the ash trays to get the ashes on the rug? Pigs.

MOSSIE. My Ma used to say ashes were good for rugs.

HANNAH. Your Ma never saw a rug.

CORA. Hannah. We were just talking about the things that were stolen from the pantry.

HANNAH. Were you now? Anybody in jail?

CORA. It's ridiculous that you shouldn't know where they've disappeared to—

HANNAH (*has picked up* JOE'S *cigarette which is lying on the table, and carefully placed the lighted end nearer the wood*). Put it like this. It'll burn the table faster.

EASTER (*angrily, under his breath, as she starts to exit*). Mind your business.

CORA. Hannah! You haven't been listening to a word I've said— (ANDREW *enters from the rear library door. Goes to desk*) Henry and Mr. Wilkie are upstairs. Henry's been here three times today. In, out. In, out.

ANDREW (*as* EASTER *has noisily slammed down his cards*). Would you play in the other room, please?

MOSSIE (*softly, not paying any attention and not moving*). Yes sir.

CORA (*as* HANNAH *goes to the door*). Andrew. It's time for you to know that groceries have been missing from the kitchen. Regularly. Hannah refuses to tell me who's been doing it and I can't allow it to go on. I have asked Mr. Wilkie to take a hand.

HANNAH (*turning*). Have you? (*Laughs. The noise of the*

*game, the words, the raking in of the money has be-
come sharp once more.*)

ANDREW. *Get out of this room.* (*They turn, surprised. Then
slowly, without hurry, they gather up their things and
move out.*)

CORA (*after a second*). Andrew. I was telling you that—

HANNAH (*crossing to him quickly*). Miss Cora was telling
you that food's been missing. It has. I've been taking
it. I wish I could've taken more. (*Motions with her hand
toward windows*) I don't know what you feel, but I
don't like to see the boys go hungry. Do what you want
about it, Mr. Andrew.

ANDREW (*slowly, staring at her*). I don't want to do anything about it, Hannah.

(HANNAH *without answering exits. She passes* JULIE, *in
hat and coat, entering. For a fraction,* JULIE *draws back
when she sees the room is not empty.*)

CORA. Sometimes I think you're crazy. And sometimes I
think you are doing things just to humiliate me.

ANDREW. It's raining, darling.

JULIE. I know. But I'd like a walk anyway.

CORA. I say one thing. You say another. Telling her it's all
right to steal. What *right* have you to humiliate me in
front of servants?

JULIE (*gently*). Cora, do stop nagging at Andy—

CORA. Nagging at him. Nagging at him. He's gone crazy—

ANDREW. I like my wife. Could I ever, anymore, be alone
with her? For just a few minutes? And then you can
start with me all over again.

CORA (*at door*). Certainly you can be alone. I daresay
you have a great many things to ask.

JULIE. She has one of her bad headaches. She's upset.
(ANDREW *smiles, shakes his head. She looks around the
room*) How messy this room looks.

ANDREW (*comes up to her as he speaks*). Our friends have
been using it as a club. I don't blame you for wanting

to go out. (*Leans down, kisses her hair*) But not tonight, Julie. It's cold and it's raining, and—

JULIE (*slowly*). I want to go.

ANDREW (*moves away from her to chair*). And I'm lonely.

JULIE (*on the "want to go" she has moved again to the window. On his speech she turns, looks at him, puzzled*). You? Lonely?

ANDREW (*smiles*). Yes. I. Lonely. I always thought loneliness meant alone, without people. It means something else.

JULIE (*softly*). That's a late discovery. You're lucky.

ANDREW (*laughs*). Why do people always think it's lucky to find out the simple things long after one should have known them?

JULIE. Because each year you can put off knowing about them gives you one more year of peace.

ANDREW. I don't think so. Unless you can put it off forever. (*Smiles*) I think that's what I was trying to do. But I'm at a bad age to start looking at the world, to start looking at myself. (*Very simply*) It confuses me, Julie. I am mixed up.

JULIE. I know. I've guessed. But I'm no one to help. I'm more mixed up than you.

ANDREW. I've walked up and down this room so much for so many nights, that I'm (*Angrily*) sick of it and sick of myself. I try to tell myself that I can think things straight, and every night I start the same way, —by taking stock of this house. Bums walking in and out, followed by Henry, as undisturbed and as anxious to get down to White Sulphur as always; Hannah, trying to make me into the villain she wants me to be. And Cora. Taking up one unpleasant sentence where she left off the last. (*Softly*) And you. I've missed you.

JULIE. Missed me?

ANDREW (*looks at her, laughs*). You're embarrassed. Strange. We've lived together so long it seems almost indecent to talk about ourselves. We used to talk about ourselves. Remember?

JULIE (*smiles*). Yes. When we were young. We belonged to the time when talk was part of the marriage ceremony. Such cynical, smooth talk, about marriage and life and freedom. Not you. Me, I mean.

ANDREW. I suppose. I remember I used to be a little puzzled by it. But that's what we were then. (*Affectionately*) You always hate yesterday, don't you, Julie?

JULIE. Yes. (*She moves again to window and then turns back suddenly*) Andy. We haven't talked about it much. I knew you didn't want to. But the strike, these people here—it's wrong for you. I know it's so wrong for you. Settle it now. It doesn't make any difference who wins—

ANDREW (*sharply*). I don't care who wins. If it were that simple, it would be fine. But it isn't that simple. (*Leans forward, slowly*) I can't fit the pieces together. That's what is happening to me. I suddenly don't know where my place in the whole thing is. Don't tell me that's one of the things I was lucky to worry about late. That doesn't do any good. I've only loved two things in my whole life: you and this town. Papa never loved it. He just wanted to be boss and get to Carlsbad for the season. But my grandfather loved it. I think the way I do. Remember how I never wanted to go to Europe or to any place else,—even when you went? This was my home, these were my people, I didn't want much else. (*With feeling*) But that's been changed. I don't know how. And I don't know where I stand anymore.

JULIE (*softly*). Try to set it right again.

ANDREW. I wish I knew how. I worked well because I worked one way, without thinking about any other. They worked one way, without thinking about any other. How do I set that right again? Don't you see? It would be like us. If anything ever happened to us we could come together again and pretend it had never happened. But what good would that be if it had really happened, and we couldn't be the same anymore? (*Laughs suddenly*) Well, I'm not the strong man Papa was, and Cora will be down in a minute to remind me of it.

JULIE (*after a second, she kneels on the floor in front of him*). Andy. Look at me. You've talked because you wanted help. You wanted me to help you, about yourself. I can't do that. I need help myself. It's a mean thing I'm saying: that I can't stay and listen, because I want to talk myself. I want help, too.

ANDREW (*after a second he nods, smiles, pats her head*). Where are you going, Julie? Down by the river in the rain?

JULIE. I don't know. Probably the river. I always do. (*Then suddenly, softly*) And perhaps not.

ANDREW (*rises*). Good night, darling.

JULIE (*quietly*). Good night, Andy.

(*He watches her move toward the window and exit. He stands for a moment looking after her as* MOSSIE *opens the library door.*)

MOSSIE. Mr. Ellicott says he's waiting for you. (ANDREW, *his eyes on the window, pays no attention to* MOSSIE, *who, after a minute*) Mr. Ellicott's waiting.

(*For a second longer,* ANDREW *stands looking out of the window. Then slowly, without looking at* MOSSIE, *he exits from Center doors.* MOSSIE *comes into the room, idly, pushes the door shut with his foot as he turns on the radio. The radio is playing something banal and loud. Then he sits down—the corner near the cabinet has no light on it—comfortably leans back to listen to the music. After a second,* EASTER *comes slowly in from the library door. He has a pack of cards in his hand and is playing with them. He crosses to the large table and lays out six or seven of them, face-down on the table.*)

MOSSIE. Funny how a lot of rich people don't like noise.

I like that. I once took piano lessons for two months. (*No answer*) What you doing, Joe?

EASTER (*through his teeth*). Playing solitaire. (*As he leans very close to look at the backs of the cards*) A new way. (*As* MOSSIE *cracks his knuckles*) You doing it worse today. *Stop it.*

MOSSIE (*looks at cabinet*). Screwy. The way she plays with these things. And the other one. Walking up and down, up and down. Tim says she's had him crazy trying to follow her. Bet she's doing it tonight, in the rain. She just went out.

EASTER (*looks up*). Your finger nails need cutting, Mossie.

MOSSIE (*looks at him, laughs*). Yeah. You buying me a manicure?

EASTER. That'd be better than having you wear them down making marks on the back of these cards—and it wouldn't cost me as much.

MOSSIE. You're nuts.

EASTER (*straightens up*). Put the sixty-five bucks you won over here on the table, Mossie.

MOSSIE. *You* got the cards out of *that* drawer. My God, Joe, you don't mean to tell me you think rich people like this would fool around with wrong cards—Jesus, Joe, I been telling you you'd better take a rest cure. Books and milk and just laying in a bed. You're getting too nervous about nothing. You're seeing things. Rodman fixing the cards— (*Laughs, then quietly*) Was it Rodman's dice you made that killing with at Phil's? Joe, you're getting good and batty.

EASTER. The cards are scratched. Put that money on the table.

MOSSIE (*slowly, as he cracks his knuckles, turns toward the radio*). You don't want to get so excited, Joe. You don't want to come over here and get the dough, Joe, and I don't blame you. So stay over there and quiet yourself. Sit down and whittle yourself some straight dice.

EASTER (*slowly*). For the last time. Put the money on the table.

MOSSIE (*quietly*). No.

(*As he turns back to the radio,* EASTER, *pressing the spring of his knife, lets it fly through the air.* MOSSIE *screams softly, pushes with his feet from the ground as he topples from the chair. He falls noisily to the floor. For a second* EASTER *stands watching him, listening to the two soft groans. The groans cease and* EASTER *suddenly begins to move. His movements are quick but aimless, as if he didn't know what to do first. He turns out the lamp nearest him, shuts the library door, and moves to Center doors. As he starts to turn the key, the door is violently pushed open by* WILKIE. EASTER *steps back, frightened.*)

WILKIE. What's it? (EASTER *looks out in the hall for a second, then quickly closes the door, nods his head toward* MOSSIE *and the chair.* WILKIE *crosses quickly, leans down, looks at* MOSSIE. *Then quickly, he moves toward* EASTER, *grabs the lapel of his coat with one hand as he hits him in the face with the other*) You tough guy. You God damned tough guy.

EASTER (*hoarsely*). I couldn't help it, Sam—he had his gun out.

WILKIE. Yeah, out in his pocket. O. K. the hell with you. (*Lets go his lapels and shoves him.*)

EASTER. Sam. Give me some money. Please. Sam. Please.

WILKIE. I'll give you money—to get your hair waved for the chair.

EASTER. I'm telling you, I'm telling you. What could I do? He tried the gun. I'm telling you—- (*Hysterically, as he watches* WILKIE *move toward telephone*) Sam. Sam. What are you doing—

WILKIE. I'm trying to think which cop would like to have you most. (*Turning on him violently*) This whole damn job wasn't lousy enough. You got to make it better. That boy scout upstairs you got to spell words in front of is going to like this in his house. I can sit in the office now and knit for a year—until they forget you worked for me. (*Picks up telephone*) Well, I'll take you in myself and make a pretty speech about how I didn't know your record, and the only dope who'll believe that is some guy milking a cow, and I'd never have worked for him anyway. You tough guy.

EASTER. No. No. Sam. No—

WILKIE (*as he starts to dial*). You son of a bitch. I can't get a nose bleed where I want it, but you've got to start carving— (*His last words have become slower, as if he were thinking. Then he looks up at* EASTER, *and slowly puts the receiver back on the hook. Stands at the table, staring at it, as* EASTER *watches him. After a long silence*) This way you'd hang during the warm weather. My way might keep you alive for the winter—maybe. (*Comes over and stands in front of* EASTER) Take that knife out of him. Take him out and dump him. (*Carefully*) Dump him in the right place—with no fancy work. Do you hear me? (EASTER *nods quickly, and as he starts to move*, WILKIE *jerks him back*) Remember, I don't promise you anything. If it goes wrong, you slob, it goes wrong for you. I'll turn you in myself if I have to—and with plenty of story to keep me in the clear. Do you understand me? (*Waits, gets no answer*) Do you understand me?

EASTER (*very quietly*). Yes.

Curtain

SCENE II

*The same evening. The time is immediately following
Scene I.*

SETTING: *A bare, clean office-room, the empty side of a
store. The office is in an alley. The entrance is Left
stage. There is a desk, a few chairs, a filing cabinet, a
typewriter, a mimeographing machine, an electric stove.*

AT RISE: WHALEN *is sitting at the desk chair, leaning over
to hammer on a box.* FIRTH *is sitting by the window,
staring idly out into the alley. Neither of them speaks
for a minute after the curtain rises. Then* FIRTH *gets
slowly to his feet and goes to the chair on which his hat
and raincoat are lying.*

FIRTH. Well. Want to come to my house for a bowl of
something hot?

WHALEN (*shakes his head, points to a cardboard container
on his desk*). Odave treated me to a pint of whisky. It
tastes like he made it on the picket line.

FIRTH. Bad for your stomach.

WHALEN. Don't worry about my stomach. It'll last another
few years. (*Waves toward the window*) Worry about
the stomachs out there.

FIRTH. I been worrying enough.

WHALEN. How much we got?

FIRTH. Enough, maybe. Hannah brought down canned
stuff and Richmondville sent over a pig.

WHALEN. That's enough for a month, if you take a little
caviar with it.

FIRTH. Well, it ain't enough. I don't say anybody's starving, but it's tough to watch kids not get enough. It ain't
only my kid, it's kids.

WHALEN. Yep!

FIRTH. I had a hundred sixty-two dollars left in my savings bank. Clyde needed it. Nobody's got much left. Clyde coughs too much.

WHALEN. Didn't anybody ever tell you that Christians aren't supposed to act like Christians?

FIRTH. Funny. All the boys had a little something. But we were talking last night how you work all your life to save it, then it runs out fast. Funny.

WHALEN. Very funny.

FIRTH (*suddenly, as if he had been thinking of it all along*). I couldn't tell her what they meant. I was so ashamed for the kid. (*Violently*) I'll kill 'em if they ever go near my girl again. I'll kill 'em—

WHALEN (*looks at him, slowly, calmly*). That's just what they want you to do. You boys were hot stuff Thursday. You couldn't take a little pushing around. You got to push back. So what? So it winds up Wilkie gets half his boys sworn in as deputy sheriffs. They're law and order now and you're un-American.

FIRTH. There's some things you can't take. Nobody can. Nobody.

WHALEN. Speak for yourself. There's not much I can't take, if I have to. (*Slowly*) You gave me your word that you wouldn't fight again, and that you'd keep the boys from fighting.

FIRTH. And I've kept my word. But it gets too much—

WHALEN (*wearily*). We've been over all this before. Try to believe that I'm telling you the truth. The longer you're quiet the sooner you'll win. Wilkie's been in this business for a long time. They've all got one gag—to make you fight. And no matter what *they* do to start it, you'll be surprised to read in the paper, and to hear from the police, that *you* started it. (*Slowly, with force*) And once they start a real fight here, you're lost.

FIRTH. You don't believe we can take care of ourselves, do you? You don't—

WHALEN. No. I don't believe it. There are men in your spot who know what it's about and who can take what's coming. I believe in *their* fighting, but not *you*. Your idea of fighting is not to hit below the waist— (*Laughs*) And that's no good. Now be good. And don't let your kid or anybody else go out alone.

FIRTH (*shakes his head, passes his hand over his face wearily, and begins to put on his coat*). Hannah says Andrew don't like things much. Might be a good sign. He's an easy going man. I don't believe he'd have ever got us into this if it hadn't been for the others.

WHALEN (*smiles*). That's the stuff. That kind of talk will do you a lot of good.

FIRTH (*sighs*). I don't know how much longer we can hold out here, when kids aren't getting enough. (*As he turns he looks at* WHALEN, *who is paying no attention to him*) I wouldn't be the one to know. What do you think?

WHALEN. I told you what I thought. Wilkie wants a fight, and as long as we're not giving him one we're sitting not bad. Now go on home. And if they cut your grandmother in half, don't lift a hand. Wait'll they cut her in slices and then maybe, but I don't promise, I'll let you take a sock at one of 'em.

FIRTH. That ain't what I meant. That ain't telling me how much longer we can feed. You ain't never told me.

WHALEN (*finally irritated*). And I'm never going to. That may be part of my job, too, but it's not for me. You pick your own minute. You'll get no speeches from me about the beauty of starving for what you think. I don't mind doing it for myself, but I don't do it for other people. (*Gets up*) Because it's a waste of time, and I'm busy. I guess you'll hold out as long as you've got the guts to. That I can't put in you.

FIRTH (*angrily*). We don't need you to tell us about guts—

WHALEN (*smiles*). That's all right. I'm no hero-worshiper.

FIRTH. We've got more guts around here than you'll ever see. Our folks have always had. We—

WHALEN (*wearily, goes back to his desk and starts working again on the box*). Go on home and boast to your wife.

(FIRTH *stands watching him. After a second he sighs, moves toward the door.*)

FIRTH (*softly*). I could bring you back something hot.

WHALEN (*affectionately*). Good night, Tom.

FIRTH (*affectionately*). Don't worry about the boys here. We'll be all right when you're crying for a rotten apple.

(*He exits.* WHALEN *watches him, smiling. Then with a few loud hammerings, he finishes with the box and gets up, carrying it to the other side of the room. He goes to a basin, washes his hands, dabs at his face, lights a cigarette, pours himself a drink. He stands smoking as the door opens and* JULIE RODMAN *comes slowly in. She stands away from the door, waiting for him to speak.*)

WHALEN (*turns, looks at her, then after a moment's silence, says loudly, as if he is talking for somebody outside*). Please close the door, Mrs. Rodman—unless there is somebody with you.

JULIE (*closing the door, without turning*). There is nobody with me. (*She stands waiting for him to speak*) I—I— Can't I come in?

WHALEN (*slowly, pleasantly*). I'm guessing. But I want to save you time. You can go back and tell them that I don't want any bribes—and that the gag is too stale.

JULIE (*crosses to him. Intensely*). No. No. Really, no. I haven't come for any reason—I mean, any reason except my own. Really, really, Mr. Whalen—

WHALEN (*picks up two cheap glasses from the window sill*). Well, whatever your reason, you look cold. Like a drink? (*She nods, shy, embarrassed, watching him*) It's filthy, but it's a drink. (*He hands her a glass, sits down at desk, smiles, pours himself a drink*) Don't listen to the doctors. Cheap whisky is good for you. Why did you come, Mrs. Rodman?

JULIE. I—er—I— (*Looks up at him*) It won't sound like the truth. I wanted to talk to you. Just talk to you. Not about anything. I just wanted to talk to you—

WHALEN (*looks at her, then after a pause*). Well. That sounds too pleasant. Don't you know that you're not supposed to feel friendly enough for a visit and— (*Slowly, seriously*) and that I'm not supposed to let you make the visit?

JULIE (*rises, softly*). Yes, I suppose I knew it. I'm sorry. I just wanted to talk to you.

WHALEN (*kindly*). What did you want to say?

JULIE. I don't know. Although I've thought about it a lot. (*Turns to him and smiles*) You don't remember, but I do. The first evening you came here, you talked to me.

WHALEN. I do remember. I didn't know who you were.

JULIE. I've walked past your alley often. Tonight I didn't think. I just came in. (*Quickly*) Haven't you ever wanted to talk to somebody you thought knew more about things than you did, and you just hoped the talk would start, and—(*Smiles*) there wouldn't be any questions about why you came?

WHALEN (*pours himself another drink*). Yes. Once. When I was in college. I thought that Lafayette— (*Bows*) Lafayette, of all people—was a fake and I wanted to know about it. But the professor was eating his dinner, and he thought Lafayette was fine. It never seems to work out very well.

JULIE (*without snobbishness*). College?

WHALEN (*laughs*). Yes, ma'am. No, it's not as good as it sounds. I only went to college for seven months. That

cost four hundred dollars. (*Bows*) Almost half of what
my father could earn in a year. The old story. (*Leans
forward, nastily*) My mother sacrificed herself.

JULIE. I went to college, too. But it cost more than that.
(*Smiles*) And it wasn't any sacrifice for my mother.

WHALEN. No? You shouldn't have denied her that. My
mother found great happiness in it, crowing over our
half-starved neighbors. My mother hated what she was
and what she came from. None of that love of beauty
stuff in my mother. I was to become a priest.

JULIE (*smiling*). I'd have guessed that.

WHALEN (*smiles*). You would have been wrong. When
that failed, she just wanted me to get rich enough to
hate what I was and what I came from. (*Leans over
to light a cigarette*) I fooled her. I hated her instead.
I always had. I kind of liked my father, and that four
hundred bucks would have been plenty of carfare for
him. He had rheumatism bad and the places where
they could pay a gardener were in the suburbs and he
had to walk most of the way. He'd come home at night
and it would hurt him to take his pants off and he'd
sit in a chair and hold them out from his legs so the
goods couldn't touch the skin. He wasn't much. But
he was nice. Anyway, what for? Four years of dopes
and faking that I had as much as they had. I quit.
(*Stops, leans over to look at her, then slowly*) What is
your reason for coming here?

JULIE (*puts up her hand, as if to detail him, softly*). In
a minute. In a minute. (*Then politely, loudly*) What
did you do then?

WHALEN (*sits back, looks at her, then after a second*).
Nothing. I hoboed. Once in a while I'd work. But not
when I could help it. Then one day, or one month, or
one year, I began to get worried. I couldn't understand
about things, and it scared hell out of me. (*Laughs,
pours himself out a drink, pours her one*) When you

don't feel yourself anything, I mean any part of anything, that's when you get scared. I was that way for a long time.

JULIE (*softly*). My husband said he felt that.

WHALEN. I imagine he would. Well it took me a long time. I had listened too much to what was wrong with the world from every louse from New Orleans to Seattle. I was sick of it all. I hated the rich. I hated the poor I couldn't figure either of them. (*Smiles at her*) I'm not bright, but I'm stubborn. And I came out with something. (*Slowly, seriously*) I've been working ever since.

JULIE. Then you didn't hate. Not the poor anyway. You loved them.

WHALEN (*laughs*). Love them? No. Do you think you can love the smell that comes from dirty skin, or the scum on dishes, or the holes in the floor with the bugs coming through— (*Sharply*) Or the meanness and the cowardice that comes with poverty? (*Leans forward*) I hate the poor, Mrs. Rodman. But I love what they could be. (*Then lightly*) Do you hate the poor, Mrs. Rodman?

JULIE. No. And I don't know what they could be.

WHALEN. Not even hate? You've never thought that much about them?

JULIE (*simply*). No. I've never seen many poor people.

WHALEN. Some bright Sunday you must lift your hem from the mud and have a try.

JULIE. I'd like to.

WHALEN. I imagine one of the ladies' charities would be delighted to let you peep over the fence. (*Nastily*) It would not be unpleasant, since the poor *they* will show you will lick your boots—in gratitude for nothing. Or rather for the gift of seeing a handsome, clean lady who can eat three meals every day. The people *they* will show you haven't the— (*Uses the word carefully*) dignity to want those things for themselves. The church has taught them to be grateful that *you* have them. When you have left, with your empty bag of groceries, they will tell themselves that it is easier for a camel to go through the eye of a needle, than for a rich lady to enter the Kingdom of God. That has consoled them for a long time.

JULIE (*angrily*). That's not what I am. That's not what I want to see. You have no reason for thinking it is.

WHALEN. Perhaps not. But people like me always make symbols of people like you.

JULIE. I never wanted to see a selected world: I never knew how to see any other. I think that is one of the reasons I wanted to talk to you.

WHALEN (*laughs mockingly*). Are you in a hurry? Or can I show you my world in fifteen minutes? I'm not a teacher, Mrs. Rodman. (*Looks at her*) And I believe that if one wants to see the world, one knows where to find it. It's all about you. They tell me you've been married here a long time and that they don't know you very well.

JULIE. No, they don't. They're a hard people with strangers —as you've probably found out.

WHALEN (*smiles*). Yes.

JULIE. But it's really my fault. I've been busy. Busy, like you, finding out. (*Bitterly*) I was finding out about myself. That took all my time.

WHALEN. A psychoanalyst?

JULIE (*begins to be angry, then laughs*). No.

WHALEN. Oh. I thought that was the rich man's gin. What were you finding out?

JULIE. I don't know. When I was young, I guess I was looking for something I could do. Then for something I could be. (*Smiles*) Finally, just for something to want, or to think, or to believe in. I always wanted somebody to show me the way.

WHALEN (*smiles*). Certainly. That's what we all want. It's easy. Were you lucky?

JULIE. Lucky in finding them? No.

WHALEN (*looks at his watch, begins to put papers away in desk*). Then you should try for yourself. That works sometimes.

JULIE. No. I decided a long time ago that there were people who had to learn from other people. I'm one of them. (*Gets up, slowly*) That's why I wanted to talk to you.

WHALEN (*looks up at her, laughs, shakes his head*). To me? Is that why you came?

JULIE (*slowly*). Yes. And I'd like to stay.

WHALEN (*slowly, puzzled*). To stay?

JULIE. Sounds crazy, doesn't it? It isn't crazy for me. I know the things you're going to say about a silly, rich woman. But I've thought about it too much, and I know it isn't that. I have no right to come here and talk to you like this—

WHALEN (*gets up, looks at her*). What are you talking about, Mrs. Rodman?

JULIE (*angrily*). I've told you. I've told you. (*Then softly, quietly*) I want to stay, I want to stay here. I mean, I—

WHALEN (*there is a second's silence. Then he moves to her quickly, takes her roughly by the arm*). All right. Now go back and tell Wilkie this isn't a new one either. (*She draws her face away from him, sharply*) Don't look so hurt. What am I supposed to think?

JULIE. I've told you the truth. I don't care what you think. (*He looks at her, drops her arm, moves back to desk, turns to look at her again.*)

WHALEN. Who have you told this nonsense to?

JULIE (*carefully*). I haven't told this—this nonsense to anybody.

WHALEN (*angrily*). What the hell do you think I am?

JULIE. I don't blame you for anything you think. I know
what a fool I've sounded. But it's been the truth.
(*Softly*) I've never in my life talked that way before.
(*To herself*) I should have known that when I did, I
wouldn't be believed.

WHALEN. And if I do believe you, then you are a silly
rich woman who doesn't know what to do with her life
and who sees the solution for it in the first man she
meets who doesn't stutter: sick of your own world,
aren't you, and you think I know another? What do
you think mine is? A new game to be learned in an
evening and played for a week? (*Takes her arm*) I don't
like that kind of playing, Mrs. Rodman.

JULIE (*after a second, slowly, carefully*). Maybe what
you've said is true. Maybe it isn't. But I'm not playing
—and you don't think I am.

WHALEN (*stares at her, as if he were thinking of something else*). You could blow me out of here with this.
(*Carefully*) Please. Don't mention your—don't mention your coming here.

JULIE (*softly*). I won't. (*Her face hurt and tight, she begins to move toward the door. As she passes the desk,
he stops her.*)

WHALEN. I'd like to say something kind. But I'm worrying about my job. (*Smiles*) I'm tired and I've got a lot
of work to do.

JULIE (*without turning*). Do you think I'm pretty?

WHALEN (*as he starts to speak, there is the noise of a car
outside, and he stops to listen. When he hears nothing
more, he smiles*). No. Better than pretty. (*Looks at
her, nods*) Yes, that I feel. Sure. I feel a lot of that.
You'd be fun. If you ever feel like it, and I'm not working, you bring your maids, and your trunks, and your
cars, and—

JULIE (*simply*). No.

WHALEN (*laughs*). All right. (*Pleasantly*) And now, good night.

(*As she walks toward the door, the noise of a car, the grinding of gears, becomes very sharp and close. She stops, and he looks quickly toward the door and window. Then, as if he is wondering whether the noise means anything to her, he looks at her. Quickly, he moves toward the door, jerks it open, runs out, as she draws back into the room. A minute later he returns, stands staring as if unconscious that she was there.*)

JULIE. What is it?

WHALEN (*slowly, looking at her*). It's a big night for me. Your friends have been playing tricks.

JULIE. What do you mean?

WHALEN. I mean that the dead body of that fat thug who was living in your house has just been planted in the alley.

JULIE. Dead? He's dead? I don't understand—

WHALEN. It's very simple. You heard the car. He was put there to get somebody in trouble. (*Stops, thinks*) Yep. (*Moves quickly to the telephone. Into phone*) Corley? Run next door and get me Tom Firth. Quick. (*Puts phone down. Crosses back to her*) Go out the other end of the alley, Mrs. Rodman. Please don't let anybody see you.

JULIE. But you—

WHALEN (*quickly, firmly*). Good night. (*She turns, stares at him, hesitates, and begins to run out of the door. He watches her, shuts the door, moves quickly back to the telephone*) Tom. One of Wilkie's boys is outside in the alley, dead. They planted him there. I don't know. For me or you or anybody else. Listen to me. I'm going to be in jail in a few minutes, sleeping tight. (*Sharply*) Stay where you are and don't worry about me. I don't know what he's going to start, but I know he's going to start something. Stop worrying about me, and listen. (*Very carefully*) No matter what he starts, let him alone. *Don't fight with him.* (*Loudly*) Do you hear me? Let him do what he wants and don't fight with him. (*Pleasantly*) Just get ready to do nothing. That'll take all the guts you've got. No. I'll be all right. Good night. (*He hangs up, sits quietly for a second, then gets up and takes his hat and coat from the floor behind the desk, puts them on, sits down again, turns his chair to face the door, lights a cigarette. A second later there is a loud knocking on the door. He smiles, starts to rise, as the curtain falls.*)

Curtain

SCENE III

Same as Act One.

AT RISE: *The living room of the Rodman house. Some of the lamps have been turned off, as if to keep attention off the room.* WILKIE *has moved a large chair to face the Center doors. A second after the curtain rises, there is the noise of someone descending the hall stairs.* WILKIE *lights a cigarette, slowly, and leans forward.*

WILKIE. Mr. Ellicott.

ELLICOTT (*coming into the room, putting on his overcoat*). I thought you'd gone home long ago. (*Slowly*) What are you doing here, Wilkie?

WILKIE (*shakes his head, gets up, waits, then slowly, nodding his head toward card table*). My man Dowel was found knifed, dead, down near strike headquarters.

ELLICOTT. Oh. (*After a second, puzzled*) But he was here—

WILKIE (*watching him*). He went out.

ELLICOTT (*carefully*). You think they killed him?

WILKIE (*looks at him, amused, laughs*). I think so.

ELLICOTT. Why?

WILKIE. Whalen was there. Any of the others could have been there, too.

ELLICOTT (*carefully*). They got into a fight and killed him—

WILKIE (*smiles*). Maybe. Or maybe they thought he was snooping around and jumped him.

ELLICOTT. Well?

WILKIE. Well. That gives us a little job of law enforcement to do. The boys we had sworn in as deputy sheriffs last week will have to pass up their crap game, and— (*Smiles broadly*) go to work for justice.

ELLICOTT (*sharply, irritated*). What do you intend to do?

WILKIE. Find the guy who put the knife in Mossie, and find the guys he did it for.

ELLICOTT. And where does that lead?

WILKIE. Well, we'll hope it leads somewhere. (*Casually*) Is this Judge Alcott a good enough friend of yours that I can count on his not getting up out of bed to issue any silly court orders that could get in my way?

ELLICOTT (*slowly*). Yes.

WILKIE. And could you ask your marshal to go home and go to bed?

ELLICOTT (*carefully*). Rodman isn't going to stand for your making any trouble here, Wilkie.

WILKIE. I'm not going to make any and I'm going to leave it to you to tell him what's happened and to make him see it right.

ELLICOTT. I'll talk to him. (*Starts for door, stops, turns back to look at* WILKIE) You needn't wait. I should think you'd be needed downtown.

WILKIE. My boys know what to do. I'm waiting for Mrs. Rodman.

ELLICOTT (*after a second*). Why are you waiting for Mrs. Rodman?

WILKIE. Your guess should be pretty good. (*Looks at his watch*) She's taking a long time.

ELLICOTT (*after a second*). Where's Whalen?

WILKIE. In jail, I hope.

ELLICOTT. You think he—

WILKIE. I don't know. I'm only thinking for a little while. It don't hurt to have him in jail while I'm thinking. That—

(*The window doors open and* JULIE *comes quickly in. She looks as if she has been running. She starts for the door, ignores* WILKIE, *speaks to* ELLICOTT.)

JULIE. Where's Andy?

WILKIE. Mrs. Rodman. (*Sharply, as she does not turn*) Mrs. Rodman. (*Crosses in front of her*) I think Mr. Rodman's gone to bed. But I've been waiting for you. I thought you'd like to talk to me first.

JULIE. Yes. I'd like to talk to you. (*To* ELLICOTT) Do you know what's happened? (*He nods, slowly*) Do you know that he had that man's body put in the alley—

ELLICOTT (*sharply*). Julie. Those are dangerous guesses.

JULIE. They're not guesses. I was there.

ELLICOTT. I knew where you were. So your adventures finally carried you to an unpleasant place at an unpleasant hour? I—

WILKIE. I'd like to talk to Mrs. Rodman. (*Looks toward the hall*) Will you—?

ELLICOTT (*exiting*). Yes.

JULIE (*suddenly, furiously*). How dare you think you can do a thing like this in Mr. Rodman's name?

WILKIE. Mr. Ellicott was right. You are making very dangerous guesses.

JULIE. I am making no guesses. I was there to see and hear.

WILKIE. So you're going to tell your husband where you were?

JULIE (*staring at him*). Of course. (*She starts again for door.*)

WILKIE. I thought you would. That's why I waited. You're a noble lady, and I'm frightened of noble ladies. They usually land the men they know in cemeteries. (*As she opens the door*) And that's where you're getting ready to land Leo Whalen. (*She takes her hand off the door, stands without turning*) You're throwing a monkey-wrench, Mrs. Rodman, and it's going to hit both Whalen and Mr. Rodman.

JULIE (*softly, without turning*). What did you mean about —about Whalen?

WILKIE (*casually, sits down on arm of chair*). I meant several things. Now you tell me that you're going up-stairs to tell your husband that Whalen couldn't have had anything to do with Mossie, because you were with him?

JULIE. Yes.

WILKIE. And that's too bad. Right this minute Whalen's probably playing checkers— (*Smiles*) somewhere. But your way, he won't be for long.

JULIE. I don't know what you're talking about.

WILKIE. Then it's because you haven't thought about it. (*Pleasantly*) You see, Mrs. Rodman, *your husband* might believe you, *I* might believe you, but the police might take your noble gesture not as an alibi— (*Softly, as she turns*) but as a motive. It sounds foolish, since you and I know better, but they might think that— (*Makes a mocking gallant stop*) that Mossie caught you together and Whalen killed him for it. (*She has been staring at him. Then she moves past him, as if she were thinking*) That's my guess, and I've been in the business a long time. And even if my guess is wrong—and there's always a good chance that police will be boobs —he'll be through anyway. When the strikers found out he'd been carrying on with the boss's wife—

JULIE (*furiously*). He was not carrying on—

WILKIE (*smiles*). It's going to look like a sell out, and if he gets out all in one piece he's lucky.

JULIE (*defiance gone from her voice*). Why do you care what happens to him?

WILKIE. I don't. But I'm working for your husband. It's my job to keep him— (*Slowly*) and his wife out of trouble. (*Looks at his watch*) For a little while.

JULIE (*sits down slowly, then after a second*). Have you been telling me the truth? Will he be—

WILKIE. Oh, some of it's the truth, and some of it isn't. (*As he speaks,* CORA *opens the library door and comes in. She has on a warm woolen robe.*)

CORA (*crossing to bell, ringing it*). My milk and fruit aren't upstairs. We can't help it if he got killed. Whatever we do now isn't going to do him any good.

WILKIE (*to* JULIE). Yes. He'll be all right.

CORA. Henry just told me. He puts everything so badly, that it came as a shock. (HANNAH *appears carrying milk and a small plate of fruit*) Yes. You forgot it, didn't you?

HANNAH (*looking at* WILKIE, *curiously*). I didn't think you'd starve. (*Watches* CORA *drink the milk*) Funny how you drink it just like you need it— (*Motions to the window*) And those kids down town don't say anything.

CORA (*hysterical, childish voice*). Take it. Take it. Everything is begrudged me.

HANNAH (*to* JULIE, *gruffly, kindly*). Do you want something Mrs. Rodman?

JULIE (*softly, without looking up*). No, thank you, Hannah.

(ANDREW *and* ELLICOTT *enter from the Center doors.* ANDREW *comes directly into the room,* ELLICOTT *stands at the door.* JULIE *gets up as if she were going to turn to* ANDREW, *then slowly turns away again.*)

ANDREW (*to* WILKIE). I'm sorry about Dowel, Wilkie.

(*Then slowly*) But I won't pretend that I am not more sorry that murder happened in this town. We're not a tough people here, and we're not used to it.

WILKIE. Somebody was tough enough.

ANDREW. Yes. That's true, and that shocks me most. But that means that I pushed them into it, and that I'm responsible for it. I know these people here.

CORA. Do you know that they won't come around to murder us, too?

ANDREW (*to* WILKIE). This murder is for the police. Not for you and me. Your bill will be paid for the week, of course. Wilkie, I want you and your people out of here tonight.

JULIE (*turns quickly*). Yes. Yes. That's right for you, Andy—

CORA. Are you crazy?

ELLICOTT. I told you upstairs that the decision wasn't entirely up to you.

ANDREW (*to* ELLICOTT). But my part *is* up to me. (*To* WILKIE) I know I've been a hard man to work for. I didn't want you here, and I was right. We can't undo what's been done. But we can stop any further trouble.

WILKIE (*quietly*). I want the people who did it, Mr. Rodman.

ANDREW. I understand. The police will do that for you.

WILKIE (*pleasantly*). I don't think you do understand. I'm not talking about Mossie. I'm not crying about that. That was his job. He got paid for it. But somebody's been killed and that somebody worked for me. If I'm going to stay in business I can't let people get the idea they can slice up my folks. (*Less pleasantly*) And I won't. I can't make you let me keep this job. But I can't leave tonight. I'm the police here, Mr. Rodman, and if I wasn't worrying about finishing a job I was hired for, I'd have to think of that.

ANDREW (*with force*). *I won't have any more trouble.*

WILKIE. That's just what I'm trying to avoid for you. I want the guns and the knives and the bricks cleaned out, and no more murders. That's what you want too, isn't it? When the guns get put away in a nice, safe spot you and your boys can talk things over. But before I leave here, they're going to be put away. (*Gets up, looks at his watch*) That's the way it'll have to be, Mr. Rodman. No reason why things shouldn't be swell and peaceful. All I want is the guns, and if they don't intend to use 'em, they should be glad to give 'em up.

CORA. That's right. That's the nice way to do it—

ANDREW (*furiously*). No. That's not what I want done. No—

HANNAH. You can't let him do that. They can't walk in a house and take anything. Maybe the government can take things, but you— (*Motioning to the others in the room*) you can't take them. Why you let him go near one of their houses and they'll think you're crazy. You ain't got any rights they haven't got. They could come in here and take from you—

ELLICOTT. Andrew. We want this thing finished. It's gone on for weeks now. We've got to get it over soon—

JULIE (*to* ELLICOTT). Andy's right. There's been trouble enough.

CORA (*to* ANDREW). I don't know why you're so worried about *them*. You should protect us—

JULIE (*to* CORA). What are you talking about? How can you talk that way about people you went to school with, people you've known all your life—

HANNAH (*bitterly*). She never liked them. I know. I remember the school days.

ANDREW (*sharply*). Stop it. (*To* ELLICOTT) I won't have any more trouble.

ELLICOTT. He's told you there won't be any trouble—

(*As he speaks, there is the sudden, distant sound of firing. They all turn slowly to stare at the window.* WILKIE *puts*

*his watch back into his pocket, moves toward his over-
coat, as the firing starts again, this time four or five shots
in rapid succession.*)

WILKIE (*shakes his head*). That's too bad. Too bad. (*Starts
for door*) Rest easy, Miss Cora, the law will protect you.
(*He exits as they stand stiff and silent. Then suddenly,
HANNAH bursts into tears and begins to run from the
room. The others do not move until CORA rises, brushes
off her robe, starts for the door.*)

CORA. It is too bad. Well, all this excitement has made me
very tired and nervous. We all get far too worked up
about everything. (*As she gets to door*) Mr. Wilkie
knows more about these things than we do.

Curtain

ACT THREE

The same as Act One. Seven-thirty the next morning.

AT RISE: JULIE *is sitting in a chair, wrapped in a coat, her head thrown back. Several of the lamps are still lit, although the dull early light of a rainy morning is beginning to come through. The room is as it was at the end of the second act, but it has the mussed, unaired look of a morning-after living room. A few seconds after the rise of the curtain,* ANDREW, *in an overcoat, opens the Center doors. He comes in slowly, tired. Automatically, he puts the bunch of front door keys back into his pocket.*

JULIE (*without looking up*). It stopped a little while ago. Thank God. (*She shudders, looks up at him*) Are you all right, Andy?

ANDREW (*slowly*). Remember the last time we went riding early in the morning? Well, when we came to the high point on Tucker's Road, I thought that I didn't like to ride much anymore. When you don't know anything about poetry, you know how you feel sometimes when you see things? That's the way I always felt about the high point, because I could look down on the town and that made me happy. It always looks so scrubbed and clean and I thought the way I used to, when I was a kid: that I could stop in any house and have a good breakfast and they'd be glad to see me. (*Violently*) It doesn't look so pretty this morning. And they wouldn't be glad to have me for breakfast. (*Turns away, then quickly*) Yes, I'm all right. The partnership of Ellicott

144

and Wilkie practically locked me in the office. They were busy and I'd only have been a nuisance.

JULIE (*again*). It stopped a while ago. Why did it stop? Did you stop it?

ANDREW (*bitterly*). No. Not me. I didn't stop it. (*Slowly*) People got hurt. I guess that's why it stopped.

JULIE (*gets up, starts to turn out lamps*). I've been using guns all my life— (*Turns*) Who got hurt?

ANDREW. But the guns sound different when they're not for fun, don't they? I don't know who got hurt. There was some fuss around Corley's house and— (*Softly*) around Firth's.

JULIE (*carefully*). Was Whalen—was Leo Whalen—was he hurt?

ANDREW. He's in jail.

JULIE (*sharply*). In jail? What for? Wilkie told me—

ANDREW (*wearily*). I don't know. Something about that fat man. They think he got into a fight with him and— (*Sits down suddenly*) My God, I'm tired.

JULIE. He can't—I can't— (*She stands watching him, then turns away as if she had changed her mind.*)

ANDREW. I tried to get down to Firth's, but they wouldn't let me.

JULIE (*as if she were thinking of something else*). Maybe it was just a fight. Maybe no one was hurt.

ANDREW. Maybe. Maybe.

JULIE (*suddenly, violently*). Why didn't you stop it? Why did you let it go on like this? They talked you into it. Why did you let them?

ANDREW (*smiles*). You make me sound like a child. And you're right.

JULIE. You didn't want any of this. Why did you ever have to start it? Then why didn't you stop it?

ANDREW. You asked me that before. (*Slowly, with force*) There are a lot of reasons. The reason I tell myself is that I couldn't stop anything. I owe money. A lot of money. (*Bitterly*) I've been borrowing it for a long time. I've borrowed on the factory and on this house and on how many brushes I thought I could make in five years—

JULIE. Oh. (*Carefully*) From Henry?

ANDREW. Oh, from everybody. From banks, from dealers— Mostly from Henry.

JULIE. But why did you borrow it? We didn't need it—

ANDREW. Oh, I got pushed and pushed until—until I couldn't help myself. (*Looks up at her, smiles*) Don't worry about it. If I were another kind of man, I guess I wouldn't have let that make any difference.

JULIE. I didn't know any of that. (*After a second*) There are a lot of things we don't know about each other.

ANDREW. I suppose so, darling. That's the way with most marriages, I guess.

JULIE. Andy. He can't stay in jail. He had nothing to do with that man. I was with him last night when it happened. With Whalen.

ANDREW (*there is a pause. Then he slowly raises his head to look at her, speaks quietly, carefully*). Then you shouldn't let him stay in jail, Julie. That's not right. (*Sharply*) Why are you acting so strange? Why didn't you say so and get him out? There's nothing to be ashamed of— (*She looks at him, nods, starts for windows*) Julie! (*She turns*) Never mind. I'll do it. (*He rises as she watches him go to telephone. Into phone*) Operator, call Judge Alcott's house. (*To* JULIE) Didn't you know he'd been arrested?

JULIE. No. I'd been told—

ANDREW (*through her last words, into phone*). Jim? This is Andrew Rodman. I want you to let Leo Whalen out of jail immediately. We—er—I know where he was last night. I'll be down later and explain. (*Sharply*) Jim. I don't give a damn what anybody said. Let him out. (*Wearily*) Yes. Yes. Thanks. No. Everything's all right.

JULIE. Thank you, Andy.

ANDREW. What are you thanking me for? (*As if for himself*) It's not important. You don't have to thank me.

JULIE (*quietly*). We've been dealing with people shrewder than we are.

ANDREW. Yes, I suppose so. I suppose that's it.

(*He passes his hand over his eyes. She makes a half motion toward him, changes her mind, turns away. A second later,* FIRTH *appears in the Center doors. He is dirty, bruised and tired-looking. In his hand is a gun. It is hanging at his side, as if he had forgotten it. Through all his speeches, through his exit, he holds the gun, unconscious that he has it. He stands in the doorway as they both look up.*)

FIRTH (*aimlessly*). The front door's open. The rain's coming in. (*Then shakes his head, bewildered*) I don't know what to do with you, Andrew.

JULIE (*in a whisper*). What is it, Tom? What is it?

(ANDREW *is standing by the desk, staring at* FIRTH.)

FIRTH. When you can't have a kid, that's bad. It makes a man feel funny, like he can't do anything, and not the way it should be. Specially a big man. You feel like you can't do what you're here for. (*Directly to* ANDREW) Remember once when you were at that college and you came home for Christmas and you came to a meal and after Miriam went up, I told you about it. I cried. Remember? (ANDREW *stares, nods slowly*) They hit her here. (*Puts his hand on the back of his head*) They said she threw a brick. A little kid threw a brick. They broke something.

ANDREW (*horror in his voice*). Where's Morris? Where is he?

FIRTH (*shakes his head as if he were drunk*). It's worse, I guess, when it's an adopted kid. You like it better that way. It makes up for the other thing and you like it better— (*Quietly*) Doc Morris? He's down there. Talking. Telling me what broke. Telling me why it happened. Talking and talking. Talking won't make her live again.

JULIE (*in a whisper*). Oh my God.

ANDREW (*looks up, softly*). They killed her. (*He nods slowly, puts his hand to his mouth, comes to* FIRTH, *takes him by the arm, then lets him go suddenly.*)

FIRTH. I don't know what to do. I beat everybody up for a while like crazy, telling myself what I was going to do to you. (*Violently, shaking his finger at* ANDREW) But I know you. I know you. It's better to tell you. It'll do worse for you. (*Suddenly, quietly*) I can't touch you, Andrew. I'm too tired. (*He sits down, as if he couldn't stand any longer. Then, as if it were an old familiar position between them,* ANDREW *sits opposite him. For a second, neither of them speaks. To* JULIE, *without looking up*) Once she saw you coming home from school and she told me you were pretty and I told her that you weren't half as pretty as her, and not an ounce as pretty as she'd grow to be. She laughed and got red and said she wasn't pretty and that I just liked her— (*Quietly, but with passion*) How can I go home? How can I live? How can I sit and eat with Miriam when only yesterday the kid sat between us—

JULIE (*choking, desperately, to* ANDREW). Do something for him.

ANDREW (*looks up at her in surprise*). What is there to do?

FIRTH. There's nothing to do. And I wouldn't let you do it. Ain't it funny how everything's changed? (ANDREW *nods*) I've known you all your life. All my life I worked for your father, or for you. I liked you more—more than anybody except my own, I guess. (*Puzzled*) I guess you can't know anybody. You must have been bad all along.

ANDREW (*leans over to touch his arm, nods*). I must have been.

JULIE. Tom, Andrew didn't know. He didn't know anything bad would happen—

FIRTH (*shakes his head*). That does a lot of good. (*Slowly*) If my kid had—had died any other way, you'd been the first I'd come to. I guess I never knew you. I don't understand that.

ANDREW (*simply*). I don't understand it, either.

FIRTH. Well, I can't fight anymore. I wouldn't know how. We ain't used to things like last night. Lundee got his hand shot off— (ANDREW *gets up and turns away sharply*) they burnt Carlsen's house all to pieces. We always used to play penny-ante there. We had to drag Berthe out, she was half crazy. She got burnt a little. (On *the next speech,* WHALEN *appears in the open Center doors.* EASTER *has him by the arm. All three people see him, and all three stare at him.* FIRTH's *voice becomes defiant, and the next speech is meant for* WHALEN, *but is said directly to* ANDREW) I don't know, but I guess I can speak for most of 'em. We can't fight you when you fight like this. It's our town more'n it's yours. Our folks came and built it. We can't watch it go like this. (*Gets up, wearily, quietly*) You call off your dogs. Keep 'em away from us, so there won't be no more killing. Get 'em out of here. I guess we'll have to go back to work.

EASTER. I picked him up trying to shove in the front door. There wouldn't been any door in a minute. He's in jail.

ANDREW (*to* EASTER). Get out of here.

EASTER. Oh. (*Looks at him and begins to exit.*)

WHALEN (*to* EASTER). What's Wilkie do? Keep you for the knife work? (*Motions toward hall*) Don't let you in the rough fights, huh? (EASTER *looks at him, exits.* WHALEN *comes into the room, smiles pleasantly*) Somebody got soft and let me out of jail. (*To* FIRTH) They told me where you were. I could have guessed.

FIRTH. They killed my kid.

WHALEN. I got all the news.

FIRTH. I feel bad. I can't fight anymore.

WHALEN. I heard you.

FIRTH (*angrily*). It wasn't your kid.

WHALEN (*angrily*). Didn't I tell you to give them what they wanted? Didn't I tell you not to fight?

FIRTH (*quietly*). You were right.

WHALEN (*looks at* FIRTH *and then at* RODMAN, *and laughs*). You both look the same kind of surprised. What are you surprised at? What the hell did you think he was after— (*To* ANDREW) Or do you still believe he came down to make brushes for you?

ANDREW (*slowly*). No.

WHALEN (*to* FIRTH). He wanted you to fight. He's been trying to make you fight for weeks. So as soon as he gets me out of the way for a couple of hours, you give him the fight he's been waiting for.

FIRTH. I couldn't do anything. When they come in talking and shoving, you don't think. Then they hit my kid— (*As if he hadn't said it before*) My girl's dead.

WHALEN (*shouting*). All right. She's dead. What are you trying to do, make Joan of Arc out of her? You wanted to fight—till the time came. Well, here's your time. If they killed my kid, I wouldn't come crawling back to any lousy job—

JULIE. There's been enough trouble. Don't let's make any more.

FIRTH. I don't want any more. We ain't used to this. We're tired. We don't care so much who wins, like you—

WHALEN (*quietly*). You *will* care. More than I do. For me, you're only one of a thousand fights. But you've only got one fight. This one. And someday you're going to have to settle it.

FIRTH. There's no use arguing. I'm trying to tell you why and what and you don't understand. (*Gets up, wearily.*)

WHALEN. Your why and what aren't any good to me.

FIRTH. I can't seem to say what I'm getting at. All I'm saying is that it came too quick. We didn't know about the things you know about. Everybody's got to see for themselves, I guess.

WHALEN. You haven't seen anything. They didn't scratch the surface here.

FIRTH (*nods his head*). Yeah? Well, maybe you were right, when you said that all the time. Wouldn't make any sense to hold out now. There wouldn't be any spirit to hold out with. I guess I'm worse than anybody, because of my kid. We'll go on back, make the best of it. (*Turns, quietly*) And if the time comes again, we'll be different. We'll know. I don't like him now. He killed my kid. They don't like him, either. We won't forget.

ANDREW (*with force, to* WHALEN). That's the truth. He's telling you the truth. They won't forget.

WHALEN (*to* FIRTH). He didn't kill your kid. Don't start that, or you'll get the wrong answer again. He hasn't much to do with it. He's got to go his way, and you've got to go yours. And they're not the same way.

FIRTH (*softly*). We used to be good friends.

WHALEN. I know. And you're as good as he is. It says so in the book. Until the time comes. Look. You're on one side. He's on the other. That's lesson number one. Don't let 'em tell you that because your grandfather voted for Jefferson, you're any different from some Polack in Pittsburgh whose grandfather couldn't write his name. You're on the same side the Polack is, and that's where you belong.

FIRTH. Well, maybe we'll try again some day.

WHALEN (*smiles, as if he were pleased*). I hope so. And the guy they send in my place, you give him a better chance.

FIRTH (*starts for door*). You coming? They'd like to see you.

WHALEN (*shakes his head*). No. I'm going to be busy for a while.

ANDREW (*softly*). Tom, would you let me do anything for you and Miriam and the others?

FIRTH (*without turning, puzzled*). What? (*Laughs, then quietly*) Stay away from downtown, Andrew. For a while. (JULIE, *watching the effect of this on* ANDREW, *moves to him, puts a hand on his sleeve.* FIRTH *speaks to* WHALEN) Well, if it comes again, I hope they'll be sending you.

WHALEN (*simply, sincerely*). I hope so, too. (FIRTH *exits. No one speaks for a second*) Well, it's time for me to see whether your pink-cheeked policeman is holding me for murder or because I've got two legs. He's having a tough time deciding. (*He has started for door.*)

JULIE (*quickly*). Wait. You don't have to go back there. They won't hold you— (*On her speech, he has turned.*)

ANDREW (*who is still looking at the door, as if he were thinking of* FIRTH). I've spoken to Judge Alcott. There's no need for you to go back. Everything will be straightened out.

WHALEN (*carefully*). Straightened out, Mr. Rodman?

JULIE (*after a second, softly*). I've told my husband that I was in your office last night when it happened.

WHALEN (*has turned to look at* ANDREW, *and then back to* JULIE). Is that what you are going to say?

JULIE. Yes. (*Not looking at him*) I wanted to before. But —but I was told that you weren't in any trouble, and that I'd be doing you harm.

WHALEN (*quietly*). You were told right. (*Looks quickly at them both*) Please. Don't do that. They've got nothing on me, and they know it. A few days of nuisance maybe, and that's all. That's my job. I don't want trouble for myself, ever, but when it comes it's part of my work

JULIE (*looking at him*). Why don't you want any help from us? From me?

WHALEN. It's not my job to take help from the boss, or—
(*Slowly*) the boss's wife. I can't take chances on anybody thinking I do.

(WILKIE *comes in through Center doors.*)

WILKIE. Good morning. (*To* ANDREW) Glad to see you
here. We were worried about you. (*To* WHALEN) Good
morning.

WHALEN. Had a good breakfast?

WILKIE. Pretty good. I'm like the English, I eat big in the
mornings.

WHALEN. I thought so. You look like you've been licking
the cream.

WILKIE. You need some breakfast?

WHALEN (*laughs*). No, thank you. I'm eating on the
county. With the marshal.

WILKIE (*looking toward* JULIE, *then back to* WHALEN).
That. Oh. That's yokel stuff. They got nothing to hold
you on.

WHALEN. They held me long enough to make it easy for
you.

WILKIE. My break this time. Maybe yours the next.

(ELLICOTT *appears in the hall. Comes in, throws his coat
and hat on a chair.*)

ELLICOTT (*looking at* JULIE *and* ANDREW, *quietly*). Good
morning.

WHALEN (*to* WILKIE). Your spick outside looks like a knife
thrower to me. What do you think?

WILKIE (*seriously*). I don't know. Maybe so. You can't
keep track of everybody. I don't like to see a man get
buried without finding who did it— If you know anything—

WHALEN (*laughs*). I don't know anything. Some other
time. (*Crosses to* JULIE *and says kindly, with meaning*)
Don't worry about last night. There's no honor involved
in any of it. And if there was it wouldn't be practical

to remember it. (*Holds out his hand to her*) Good-bye,
Mrs. Rodman.

JULIE (*touches his hand, speaks softly*). Good-bye.

WHALEN (*to* ANDREW). Good-bye.

ANDREW. Good-bye.

(WHALEN *exits.*)

ELLICOTT (*to* JULIE). You look tired. (*No answer. He looks
at his watch*) Almost eight o'clock. I haven't been up
this early in a long time.

WILKIE. Does you good sometimes.

JULIE (*to* ANDREW). What are they talking about? What
are they cheerful about?

ANDREW (*slowly*). I don't know.

JULIE (*to* ELLICOTT). Did you have a good time? Was it
more exciting than being at the club? Is it fun to see a
killing?

ELLICOTT (*sharply*). Stop it. (*After a second*) We've been
fighting your husband's battles for him.

ANDREW. Yes. That's quite true. The delicate prince in his
ivory tower— (*Carefully*) was carefully protected from
the dust and din of battle. You are noble warriors and
you've done a noble night's work. (*Sharply to* ELLI-
COTT) I'll see to it that when the history is written, it
won't be mentioned that you were fighting for yourself,
too.

ELLICOTT. I knew nothing about the child until Morris
told me.

WILKIE. I knew you were going to feel this way, Mr. Rodman. But nobody wanted any trouble. Sometimes these
things can't be helped. I understand it's going to be
settled now and I'm glad for you, and glad for me.
(*Smiles*) I don't like to take money for losing, and for
a while—

ANDREW. Send us your bill. We'll mail you a check.

WILKIE. Yes, sir. (*Goes to him, puts out his hand*) Thank
you, Mr. Rodman—

ANDREW (*ignores the hand*). That's all. Good-bye.

WILKIE (*looks down at his hand, laughs*). Well, that's your business. But I want to tell you, I've worked for a lot of men, some of them deacons of the church who were breaking strikes for the good of America, but I never worked for a man before who believed I could come in, run his factory, and break his strike without walking on anybody's toes. You actually believed that. I come in to break strikes. That's my business. It's *not* a tea room business. You ought to have known that. Well, I break your strike and now you're sitting on the right hand of Jesus, crying because it doesn't smell of violets.

ELLICOTT (*sharply*). Does this speech go on your bill?

WILKIE. No. I'm giving it free of charge. If you didn't like what I was doing, you should have stopped it. But you didn't stop it, and that doesn't leave you in any place to call names. The boys standing in your shoes need the boys standing in mine. But the next time I have to waste weeks acting like it was a tea party, the next time I have to nurse along a blind man— (*Laughs carefully*) a blind man who calls the turns when they're over—I'm going to charge extra. (*Picks up his hat as he passes* ELLICOTT) There'll be expense items on my bill.

ELLICOTT. You'll get your check.

WILKIE. Good morning.

(*There is a long silence.* ELLICOTT *lights a cigarette, looks at* JULIE, *moves uncomfortably about the room.*)

ELLICOTT. Well, Andy— (*No answer*) What's the matter with you?

ANDREW (*unpleasantly*). Very little. I'm over here thinking how I don't like being a murderer. You are fortunate. You don't seem to mind so much.

ELLICOTT (*angrily*). I knew nothing about the child. But I did know there had to be trouble. (*Carefully*) And I'm not willing to act the saint about it now.

ANDREW. That's wise for you. I hope the little trouble last night won't keep you from White Sulphur.

ELLICOTT. It won't. I'm going tonight.

ANDREW. I wish you a happy journey, and I hope that your dreams are free.

ELLICOTT (*angrily*). If it makes you feel better to enjoy your conscience, go ahead. There was a lot of truth in what that bum just said.

ANDREW. Yes. There was. But did he know that *you* were also his employer? You own so much of me now— (JULIE *has turned to look at them as* ANDREW *breaks off.* ANDREW *sees her, and speaks as if he had been thinking of her all along*) Why were you with Whalen last night?

(ELLICOTT *turns quickly to look at her.*)

JULIE. You don't want to hear about it, Andy.

(ANDREW *begins to speak as* LUCY *comes into the room, carrying a small table with breakfast on it. She is followed by* CORA, *in a bathrobe.*)

CORA. The noise that's been going on here this morning. (*Puts up a commanding hand*) Now. Please. Please. Don't tell me about last night. I've heard all about it. Lucy had it from Morris' nurse, and insisted upon telling it to me. It's awful. Simply awful. (*Leans over, smells the chocolate pot. Then to* LUCY) Did Hannah make this chocolate? Take it back.

LUCY. No, ma'am. I made it. Hannah's out.

CORA. Out? At this time of the morning? (*To everybody as* LUCY *exits*) What do you think of that? Out at this time of the morning.

ELLICOTT. Do you have to have your breakfast here? In this room?

CORA (*as she starts to eat*). Mind your business. I've had it here for thirty years. I shall continue—

ANDREW (*who has been staring at* JULIE, *paying no attention to* CORA). Julie! Why were you in Whalen's office?

JULIE (*desperately*). Andy, I don't want to— Don't let's talk about it now.

ANDREW. Julie. Answer me.

JULIE. I wanted to go away with him. I wanted to tell him that.

(ANDREW *rises from his chair, and then, slowly, sits down again.* CORA *puts down her spoon suddenly.*)

ELLICOTT. My God, you're a foolish woman.

JULIE (*quietly*). That wasn't foolish. It was what I wanted. It would have been right for me.

CORA (*looking around the room, in a daze*). Is she crazy?

ELLICOTT. But he didn't want you to go away with him?

JULIE. No.

ANDREW. Leave her alone.

CORA (*springing from her chair*). Look at you. So you're just finding out about your wife, are you? Then you're the only one who is. She's been doing this for years.

ELLICOTT. Cora. Cora—

CORA (*ignoring the interruption, to* ANDREW). Now she's decided to tell you, finally. (*With great scorn*) "Leave her alone" you tell him. How can he leave her alone? All that's his business, too.

ELLICOTT (*furiously*). Cora, I tell you—

JULIE (*quietly*). Let her say it. She's wanted to for a long time.

CORA. Yes. I could have told you about them a long time ago. She's just as much Henry's business as she is yours. Just as much. I knew. I made it my business to know. He's crazy about her. (*Shrieking*) You fool. You fool. All these years—

ANDREW (*he has been staring at her, then as if he were speaking to an insane person*). Control yourself. Get away from my desk. Go back to your breakfast.

CORA (*to* JULIE). You were never fooling me. Never for a minute fooling me.

JULIE. I'm glad.

ELLICOTT (*after a long silence, while* CORA *paces around restlessly*). Well, it's a nasty story, Andy. Your best friend and—

CORA. And his wife.

ANDREW (*looks up at* ELLICOTT, *smiles*). In what strange ways you think of things. Did you read somewhere that it was wicked to sleep with your best friend's wife? Was it a vulgar book you read it in? Or does the fact that it was *my* wife make it more sinful, and therefore more pleasant?

CORA (*to* JULIE). I knew what you were doing to my brother. I knew every bit of it.

JULIE (*comes toward* ANDREW, *slowly*). I wasn't doing anything to you. Not the way she means. (*She sits down, opposite him*) Andy. I wasn't in love with you when I married you. That was what I did to you. The rest had only to do with me. I didn't want to get married. I didn't want to live here. I wanted to make something for myself, something that would be right for me. I told you all that when we were young. I thought marriage would be all that for me. But it wasn't. (*Gets up*) And when I found it wasn't, I took the wrong way. I knew I should have stopped. But I thought someday I might find somebody who—

ELLICOTT. You found him, didn't you?

JULIE (*to* ANDREW). Yes. I found him. It didn't do me any good. I was going to tell you that, Andy. That I thought you ought to know. But the rest—the rest was just me and just exactly as shabby as she's made it sound. (*Leans across the desk, suddenly*) Darling, I told you the truth. I wasn't in love with you when we were married. I'm not in love with you now. But I love you. Not the way I want to. But another way. More than anybody I've ever known.

ANDREW (*softly*). Julie. Julie. (*Motioning toward* CORA

and ELLICOTT) Don't listen to what they say. I know what you mean. You have done nothing to me.

CORA. No? That's a strange way of looking at it. Done nothing to you. She's broken you, that's what she's done. She's why you owe money— (JULIE *has turned and is staring at her*) to Henry and to everybody else. She's why—

ELLICOTT (*violently*). Is that your business, too?

CORA. No, thank you. It's not my money he's lost. But you needn't think I didn't know. I knew where it was going. The year her family lost their money and how her mother had to have the best doctors and how her brother had to go to Paris to study, and how she always had to have trips and clothes, and a year in Europe— (*With scorn*) to make her happy. Thousands and thousands he had to borrow for it—

JULIE (*suddenly, her voice hysterical*). I didn't know that. I swear I didn't. We always had so much. Why didn't you tell me?

ANDREW. It wasn't your business. It isn't now. I wanted it that way. I suppose, underneath, I always knew. I wanted to keep you. That was my way of trying. You had nothing to do with it. Nothing at all.

CORA. And didn't it ever occur to you that was *why* Henry lent you the money. That *she* was the reason he lent you the money? Why shouldn't he—

ELLICOTT (*quietly*). That's not true.

ANDREW. No. It's not true. He made a good investment in my business. And he protected his investment, last night.

JULIE (*in a whisper*). That's why you couldn't stop— that's why—

ANDREW. That's the reason I tell myself. It's not a good one. (*Suddenly starts to laugh. They all watch him. Then, after a second, he leans on his desk, smiles, talks to* JULIE) Isn't it strange? The three of us— (*Pointing*

to CORA *and* ELLICOTT) have known each other since
we were born. My sister— (*Bows*) my best friend—
my best friend. We grew up in this town knowing all
about each other. Henry and I, for example, know that
Cora, all her life—

CORA. Be still.

ANDREW. All her life has been, well, slightly ill. Then
Cora and I know all about Henry, the rich and worldly
Henry, and all the very legal manipulating he does with
his money and with his life. They, on the other hand,
Cora and Henry know all about me. They've always
thought me a soft, weak man and they've always had
contempt for me. Hannah shares the secrets of all of us.
That's why Cora can't get rid of her, isn't it, Cora? Ten
years ago you married me and came here, and so you
were one of us, too. Our married life always had an
audience—my sister and my best friend and my cook.
All the things we knew about each other, all the things
that accumulate through a lifetime, or through ten
years, sat quietly, waiting for us, while we lived politely
and tried, like most people, to push them out of sight.
Polite and blind, we lived.

JULIE (*softly*). And then early one morning, it all blew up.

ANDREW. You don't understand. It blew up last night. All
the things we know, were there to know a long time
ago. But we were polite. We were doing our best to live
happily. Well, there's no need for being polite anymore.
You were my wife. (*To* ELLICOTT) You and I and Cora
made me a murderer. (*To* CORA) You hate me and I
hated you from the day I was old enough to think about
you. You hate my wife and you have always hated her.
(*To* ELLICOTT) Since we were old enough to play together, you've never had anything but toleration for
me—and I've never had anything but contempt for
you. That's a lot of hate, isn't it? It was all there before.
(*Pleasantly*) It can be said now.

ELLICOTT (*after a moment's silence*). I'm sorry all this had to come now, Andy. That's straight. (*Motioning toward* CORA) And I'm sorry it had to come from Cora.

CORA (*calmly*). I think both of you are drunk.

ELLICOTT (*to* JULIE). Do you want me to stay?

JULIE. What? Oh no. (*He looks at her for a second and then exits quickly. After his exit, nobody speaks. Then after a second,* JULIE *says softly*) What do you want me to do, Andy?

ANDREW (*after a second, puzzled*). What do you mean?

JULIE. Do you want me to go away? Do you want a divorce?

ANDREW (*quietly, sadly, reproachfully*). Oh, Julie. Even you haven't understood. I'm not sitting here in tears for you or me. A year ago, a month ago, what you told me about you, about us, would have broken my heart. It will again, but not now. Because last night I lost the place and the land where I was born. (*Laughs bitterly*) I can't go downtown, he said. It isn't safe. It isn't safe for *me* to go into that town. You see what I mean. I lost what I thought I was. (*Softly*) I lost Firth his child. (*Suddenly, violently*) Murder is worse than lost love. Murder is worse than a broken heart.

JULIE (*softly*). It is. Yes.

ANDREW. They said it would come again. I think they're right. I'll be hardened to it by then, I guess, and I won't mind what happens. In a little while I'll think about us. About how I lost you, and how I never had you, and how much I loved you. But now it seems so small beside what else has happened here. (*Smiles*) And it seems almost right that it should be this way and that you should have told me this morning. It was right that it should have come. I don't know what you should do, Julie. Go to White Sulphur, if you like.

JULIE. That would be what I deserved.

ANDREW. That's foolish. You don't deserve anything. Go

anywhere you like. Or nowhere. Whatever is left here is as much yours as it is mine. *That's* your punishment— if you're looking for it. For the rest of your life, my wife, for all the days to come— (*Laughs*) You can have half of all this. Half of me. I'm sorry for you. (*He has motioned with his arm around the room, toward* CORA. *Suddenly his face is dead and heavy, and he sits down in the desk chair.*)

JULIE (*turns and stares curiously at* CORA's *cabinet. She rises*). Your animals weren't touched, Cora. They're still all right. (*She exits.*)

CORA (*after a long silence, she pours herself some chocolate, and speaks timidly*). Things went entirely too far. It comes from everybody getting too excited. Now, you go get some sleep and nothing will seem as bad when you wake up. (*No answer. She takes a bite of toast*) People said a lot of things they didn't mean, Andy. (*Consolingly*) A lot of things they didn't mean. I'm sure of that.

ANDREW (*doesn't answer for a minute. Then he raises his head and with great force*). Take your breakfast out of here. (*She rises hurriedly, frightened*) Get out. (*As she moves toward the door*) Get out.

Curtain

THE LITTLE FOXES

*"Take us the foxes, the little foxes,
that spoil the vines; for our vines
have tender grapes."*

FOR

ARTHUR KOBER AND LOUIS KRONENBERGER

WHO HAVE BEEN MY GOOD FRIENDS

THE LITTLE FOXES

The Little Foxes was first produced at the National Theatre, New York City, on February 15, 1939, with the following cast:

(*In order of their appearance*)

ADDIE	ABBIE MITCHELL
CAL	JOHN MARRIOTT
BIRDIE HUBBARD	PATRICIA COLLINGE
OSCAR HUBBARD	CARL BENTON REID
LEO HUBBARD	DAN DURYEA
REGINA GIDDENS	TALLULAH BANKHEAD
WILLIAM MARSHALL	LEE BAKER
BENJAMIN HUBBARD	CHARLES DINGLE
ALEXANDRA GIDDENS	FLORENCE WILLIAMS
HORACE GIDDENS	FRANK CONROY

Produced and staged by HERMAN SHUMLIN

Settings designed by HOWARD BAY

Costumes designed by ALINE BERNSTEIN

SCENE

The scene of the play is the living room of the Giddens house, in a small town in the South.

ACT ONE

The Spring of 1900, evening.

ACT TWO

A week later, early morning.

ACT THREE

Two weeks later, late afternoon.

There has been no attempt to write Southern dialect. It is to be understood that the accents are Southern.

ACT ONE

SCENE: *The living room of the Giddens home, in a small town in the deep South, the spring of 1900. Upstage is a staircase leading to the second story. Upstage, right, are double doors to the dining room. When these doors are open we see a section of the dining room and the furniture. Upstage, left, is an entrance hall with a coat-rack and umbrella stand. There are large lace-curtained windows on the left wall. The room is lit by a center gas chandelier and painted china oil lamps on the tables. Against the wall is a large piano. Downstage, right, are a high couch, a large table, several chairs. Against the left back wall are a table and several chairs. Near the window there are a smaller couch and tables. The room is good-looking, the furniture expensive; but it reflects no particular taste. Everything is of the best and that is all.*

AT RISE: ADDIE, *a tall, nice-looking Negro woman of about fifty-five, is closing the windows. From behind the closed dining-room doors there is the sound of voices. After a second,* CAL, *a middle-aged Negro, comes in from the entrance hall carrying a tray with glasses and a bottle of port.* ADDIE *crosses, takes the tray from him, puts it on table, begins to arrange it.*

ADDIE (*pointing to the bottle*). You gone stark out of your head?

CAL. No, smart lady, I ain't. Miss Regina told me to get out that bottle. (*Points to bottle*) That very bottle for the mighty honored guest. When Miss Regina changes

167

orders like that you can bet your dime she got her reason.

ADDIE (*points to dining room*). Go on. You'll be needed.

CAL. Miss Zan she had two helpings frozen fruit cream and she tell that honored guest, she tell him that you make the best frozen fruit cream in all the South.

ADDIE (*smiles, pleased*). Did she? Well, see that Belle saves a little for her. She like it right before she go to bed. Save a few little cakes, too, she like—

(*The dining room doors are opened and quickly closed again by* BIRDIE HUBBARD. BIRDIE *is a woman of about forty, with a pretty, well-bred, faded face. Her movements are usually nervous and timid, but now, as she comes running into the room, she is gay and excited.* CAL *turns to* BIRDIE.)

BIRDIE. Oh, Cal. (*Closes door*) I want you to get one of the kitchen boys to run home for me. He's to look in my desk drawer and— (*To* ADDIE) My, Addie. What a good supper! Just as good as good can be.

ADDIE. You look pretty this evening, Miss Birdie, and young.

BIRDIE (*laughing*). Me, young? (*Turns back to* CAL) Maybe you better find Simon and tell him to do it himself. He's to look in my desk, the left drawer, and bring my music album right away. Mr. Marshall is very anxious to see it because of his father and the opera in Chicago. (*To* ADDIE) Mr. Marshall is such a polite man with his manners and very educated and cultured and I've told him all about how my mama and papa used to go to Europe for the music— (*Laughs. To* ADDIE) Imagine going all the way to Europe just to listen to music. Wouldn't that be nice, Addie? Just to sit there and listen and— (*Turns and steps to* CAL) Left drawer, Cal. Tell him that twice because he forgets. And tell him not to let any of the things drop out of the album and to bring it right in here when he comes back.

(*The dining-room doors are opened and quickly closed by* OSCAR HUBBARD. *He is a man in his late forties.*)

CAL. Yes'm. But Simon he won't get it right. But I'll tell him.

BIRDIE. Left drawer, Cal, and tell him to bring the blue book and—

OSCAR (*sharply*). Birdie.

BIRDIE (*turning nervously*). Oh, Oscar. I was just sending Simon for my music album.

OSCAR (*to* CAL). Never mind about the album. Miss Birdie has changed her mind.

BIRDIE. But, really, Oscar. Really I promised Mr. Marshall. I—

(CAL *looks at them, exits.*)

OSCAR. Why do you leave the dinner table and go running about like a child?

BIRDIE (*trying to be gay*). But, Oscar, Mr. Marshall said most specially he *wanted* to see my album. I told him about the time Mama met Wagner, and Mrs. Wagner gave her the signed program and the big picture. Mr. Marshall wants to see that. Very, very much. We had such a nice talk and—

OSCAR (*taking a step to her*). You have been chattering to him like a magpie. You haven't let him be for a second. I can't think he came South to be bored with you.

BIRDIE (*quickly, hurt*). He wasn't bored. I don't believe he was bored. He's a very educated, cultured gentleman. (*Her voice rises*) I just don't believe it. You always talk like that when I'm having a nice time.

OSCAR (*turning to her, sharply*). You have had too much wine. Get yourself in hand now.

BIRDIE (*drawing back, about to cry, shrilly*). What am I doing? I am not doing anything. What am I doing?

OSCAR (*taking a step to her, tensely*). I said get yourself in hand. Stop acting like a fool.

BIRDIE (*turns to him, quietly*). I don't believe he was

bored. I just don't believe it. Some people like music and like to talk about it. That's all I was doing.

(LEO HUBBARD *comes hurrying through the dining-room door. He is a young man of twenty, with a weak kind of good looks.*)

LEO. Mama! Papa! They are coming in now.

OSCAR (*softly*). Sit down, Birdie. Sit down now. (BIRDIE *sits down, bows her head as if to hide her face.*)

(*The dining-room doors are opened by* CAL. *We see people beginning to rise from the table.* REGINA GIDDENS *comes in with* WILLIAM MARSHALL. REGINA *is a handsome woman of forty.* MARSHALL *is forty-five, pleasant-looking, self-possessed. Behind them comes* ALEXANDRA GIDDENS, *a very pretty, rather delicate-looking girl of seventeen. She is followed by* BENJAMIN HUBBARD, *fifty-five, with a large jovial face and the light graceful movements that one often finds in large men.*)

REGINA. Mr. Marshall, I think you're trying to console me. Chicago may be the noisiest, dirtiest city in the world but I should still prefer it to the sound of our horses and the smell of our azaleas. I should like crowds of people, and theaters, and lovely women— *Very* lovely women, Mr. Marshall?

MARSHALL (*crossing to sofa*). In Chicago? Oh, I suppose so. But I can tell you this: I've never dined there with *three* such lovely ladies.

(ADDIE *begins to pass the port.*)

BEN. Our Southern women are well favored.

LEO (*laughs*). But one must go to Mobile for the ladies, sir. Very elegant worldly ladies, too.

BEN (*looks at him very deliberately*). Worldly, eh? *Worldly,* did you say?

OSCAR (*hastily, to* LEO). Your uncle Ben means that worldliness is not a mark of beauty in any woman.

LEO (*quickly*). Of course, Uncle Ben. I didn't mean—

MARSHALL. Your port is excellent, Mrs. Giddens.

REGINA. Thank you, Mr. Marshall. We had been saving that bottle, hoping we could open it just for you.

ALEXANDRA (*as* ADDIE *comes to her with the tray*). Oh. May I *really*, Addie?

ADDIE. Better ask Mama.

ALEXANDRA. May I, Mama?

REGINA (*nods, smiles*). In Mr. Marshall's honor.

ALEXANDRA (*smiles*). Mr. Marshall, this will be the first taste of port I've ever had.

(ADDIE *serves* LEO.)

MARSHALL. No one ever had their first taste of a better port. (*He lifts his glass in a toast; she lifts hers; they both drink*) Well, I suppose it is all true, Mrs. Giddens.

REGINA. What is true?

MARSHALL. That you Southerners occupy a unique position in America. You live better than the rest of us, you eat better, you drink better. I wonder you find time, or want to find time, to do business.

BEN. A great many Southerners don't.

MARSHALL. Do all of you live here together?

REGINA. Here with me? (*Laughs*) Oh, no. My brother Ben lives next door. My brother Oscar and his family live in the next square.

BEN. But we are a very close family. We've always wanted it that way.

MARSHALL. That is very pleasant. Keeping your family together to share each other's lives. My family moves around too much. My children seem never to come home. Away at school in the winter; in the summer, Europe with their mother—

REGINA (*eagerly*). Oh, yes. Even down here we read about Mrs. Marshall in the society pages.

MARSHALL. I dare say. She moves about a great deal. And all of you are part of the same business? Hubbard Sons?

BEN (*motions to* OSCAR). Oscar and me. (*Motions to* REGINA) My sister's good husband is a banker.

MARSHALL (*looks at* REGINA, *surprised*). Oh.

REGINA. I am so sorry that my husband isn't here to meet you. He's been very ill. He is at Johns Hopkins. But he will be home soon. We think he is getting better now.

LEO. I work for Uncle Horace. (REGINA *looks at him*) I mean I work for Uncle Horace at his bank. I keep an eye on things while he's away.

REGINA (*smiles*). Really, Leo?

BEN (*looks at* LEO, *then to* MARSHALL). Modesty in the young is as excellent as it is rare. (*Looks at* LEO *again.*)

OSCAR (*to* LEO). Your uncle means that a young man should speak more modestly.

LEO (*hastily, taking a step to* BEN). Oh, I didn't mean, sir—

MARSHALL. Oh, Mrs. Hubbard. Where's that Wagner autograph you promised to let me see? My train will be leaving soon and—

BIRDIE. The autograph? Oh. Well. Really, Mr. Marshall, I didn't mean to chatter so about it. Really I— (*Nervously, looking at* OSCAR) You must excuse me. I didn't get it because, well, because I had—I—I had a little headache and—

OSCAR. My wife is a miserable victim of headaches.

REGINA (*quickly*). Mr. Marshall said at supper that he would like you to play for him, Alexandra.

ALEXANDRA (*who has been looking at* BIRDIE). It's not I who play well, sir. It's my aunt. She plays just wonderfully. She's my teacher. (*Rises. Eagerly*) May we play a duet? May we, Mama?

BIRDIE (*taking* ALEXANDRA's *hand*). Thank you, dear. But I have my headache now. I—

OSCAR (*sharply*). Don't be stubborn, Birdie. Mr. Marshall wants you to play.

MARSHALL. Indeed I do. If your headache isn't—

BIRDIE (*hesitates, then gets up, pleased*). But I'd like to, sir. Very much. (*She and* ALEXANDRA *go to the piano.*)

MARSHALL. It's very remarkable how you Southern aristocrats have kept together. Kept together and kept what belonged to you.

BEN. You misunderstand, sir. Southern aristocrats have *not* kept together and have *not* kept what belonged to them.

MARSHALL (*laughs, indicates room*). You don't call this keeping what belongs to you?

BEN. But we are not aristocrats. (*Points to* BIRDIE *at the piano*) Our brother's wife is the only one of us who belongs to the Southern aristocracy.

(BIRDIE *looks toward* BEN.)

MARSHALL (*smiles*). My information is that you people have been here, and solidly here, for a long time.

OSCAR. And so we have. Since our great-grandfather.

BEN (*smiles*). Who was *not* an aristocrat, like Birdie's.

MARSHALL (*a little sharply*). You make great distinctions.

BEN. Oh, they have been made for us. And maybe they are important distinctions. (*Leans forward, intimately*) Now you take Birdie's family. When my great-grandfather came here they were the highest-tone plantation owners in this state.

LEO (*steps to* MARSHALL. *Proudly*). My mother's grandfather was *governor* of the state before the war.

OSCAR. They owned the plantation, Lionnet. You may have heard of it, sir?

MARSHALL (*laughs*). No, I've never heard of anything but brick houses on a lake, and cotton mills.

BEN. Lionnet in its day was the best cotton land in the South. It still brings us in a fair crop. (*Sits back*) Ah, they were great days for those people—even when I can remember. They had the best of everything. (BIRDIE *turns to them*) Cloth from Paris, trips to Europe, horses you can't raise any more, niggers to lift their fingers—

BIRDIE (*suddenly*). We were good to our people. Everybody knew that. We were better to them than—

(MARSHALL *looks up at* BIRDIE.)

REGINA. Why, Birdie. You aren't playing.

BEN. But when the war comes these fine gentlemen ride off and leave the cotton, *and* the women, to rot.

BIRDIE. My father was killed in the war. He was a fine soldier, Mr. Marshall. A fine man.

REGINA. Oh, certainly, Birdie. A famous soldier.

BEN (*to* BIRDIE). But that isn't the tale I am telling Mr. Marshall. (*To* MARSHALL) Well, sir, the war ends. (BIRDIE *goes back to piano*) Lionnet is almost ruined, and the sons finish ruining it. And there were thousands like them. Why? (*Leans forward*) Because the Southern aristrocrat can adapt himself to nothing. Too high-tone to try.

MARSHALL. Sometimes it is difficult to learn new ways. (BIRDIE *and* ALEXANDRA *begin to play.* MARSHALL *leans forward, listening.*)

BEN. Perhaps, perhaps. (*He sees that* MARSHALL *is listening to the music. Irritated, he turns to* BIRDIE *and* ALEXANDRA *at the piano, then back to* MARSHALL) You're right, Mr. Marshall. It is difficult to learn new ways. But maybe that's why it's profitable. *Our* grandfather and *our* father learned the new ways and learned how to make them pay. (*Smiles nastily*) *They* were in trade. Hubbard Sons, Merchandise. Others, Birdie's family, for example, looked down on them. (*Settles back in chair*) To make a long story short, Lionnet now belongs to *us*. (BIRDIE *stops playing*) Twenty years ago we took over their land, their cotton, and their daughter. (BIRDIE *rises and stands stiffly by the piano.* MARSHALL, *who has been watching her, rises.*)

MARSHALL. May I bring you a glass of port, Mrs. Hubbard?

BIRDIE (*Softly*). No, thank you, sir. You are most polite.

REGINA (*Sharply, to* BEN). You are boring Mr. Marshall with these ancient family tales.

BEN. I hope not. I hope not. I am trying to make an important point— (*Bows to* MARSHALL) for our future business partner.

OSCAR (*to* MARSHALL). My brother always says that it's folks like us who have struggled and fought to bring to our land some of the prosperity of your land.

BEN. Some people call that patriotism.

REGINA (*laughs gaily*). I hope you don't find my brothers too obvious, Mr. Marshall. I'm afraid they mean that this is the time for the ladies to leave the gentlemen to talk business.

MARSHALL (*hastily*). Not at all. We settled everything this afternoon. (MARSHALL *looks at his watch*) I have only a few minutes before I must leave for the train. (*Smiles at her*) And I insist they be spent with you.

REGINA. *And* with another glass of port.

MARSHALL. Thank you.

BEN (*to* REGINA). My sister is right. (*To* MARSHALL) I am a plain man and I am trying to say a plain thing. A man ain't only in business for what he can get out of it. It's got to give him something here. (*Puts hand to his breast*) That's every bit as true for the nigger picking cotton for a silver quarter, as it is for you and me. (REGINA *gives* MARSHALL *a glass of port*) If it don't give him some-thing here, then he don't pick the cotton right. Money isn't all. Not by three shots.

MARSHALL. Really? Well, I always thought it was a great deal.

REGINA. And so did I, Mr. Marshall.

MARSHALL (*leans forward. Pleasantly, but with meaning*). Now you don't have to convince me that you are the right people for the deal. I wouldn't be here if you hadn't convinced me six months ago. You want the mill here, and I want it here. It isn't my business to find out why you want it.

BEN. To bring the machine to the cotton, and not the cot-ton to the machine.

MARSHALL (*amused*). You have a turn for neat phrases, Hubbard. Well, however grand your reasons are, mine are simple: I want to make money and I believe I'll make it on you. (*As* BEN *starts to speak, he smiles*) Mind you, I have no objections to more high-minded reasons. They are mighty valuable in business. It's fine to have partners who so closely follow the teachings of Christ. (*Gets up*) And now I must leave for my train.

REGINA. I'm sorry you won't stay over with us, Mr. Marshall, but you'll come again. Any time you like.

BEN (*motions to* LEO, *indicating the bottle*). Fill them up, boy, fill them up. (LEO *moves around filling the glasses as* BEN *speaks*) Down here, sir, we have a strange custom. We drink the *last* drink for a toast. That's to prove that the Southerner is always still on his feet for the last drink. (*Picks up his glass*) It was Henry Frick, your Mr. Henry Frick, who said, "Railroads are the Rembrandts of investments." Well, *I* say, "Southern cotton mills *will be* the Rembrandts of investment." So I give you the firm of Hubbard Sons and Marshall, Cotton Mills, and to it a long and prosperous life. (*They all pick up their glasses.* MARSHALL *looks at them, amused. Then he, too, lifts his glass, smiles.*)

OSCAR. The children will drive you to the depot. Leo! Alexandra! You will drive Mr. Marshall down.

LEO (*eagerly, looks at* BEN *who nods*). Yes, sir. (*To* MARSHALL) Not often Uncle Ben lets *me* drive the horses. And a beautiful pair they are. (*Starts for hall*) Come on, Zan.

ALEXANDRA. May I drive tonight, Uncle Ben, please? I'd like to and—

BEN (*shakes his head, laughs*). In your evening clothes? Oh, no, my dear.

ALEXANDRA. But Leo always—(*Stops, exits quickly.*)

REGINA. I don't like to say good-bye to you, Mr. Marshall.

MARSHALL. Then we won't say good-bye. You have promised that you would come and let me show you Chicago. Do I have to make you promise again?

REGINA (*looks at him as he presses her hand*). I promise again.

MARSHALL (*touches her hand again, then moves to* BIRDIE). Good-bye, Mrs. Hubbard.

BIRDIE (*shyly, with sweetness and dignity*). Good-bye, sir.

MARSHALL (*as he passes* REGINA). Remember.

REGINA. I will.

OSCAR. We'll see you to the carriage. (MARSHALL *exits, followed by* BEN *and* OSCAR. *For a second* REGINA *and* BIRDIE *stand looking after them. Then* REGINA *throws up her arms, laughs happily.*)

REGINA. And there, Birdie, goes the man who has opened the door to our future.

BIRDIE (*surprised at the unaccustomed friendliness*). What?

REGINA (*turning to her*). *Our future.* Yours and mine, Ben's and Oscar's, the children— (*Looks at* BIRDIE's *puzzled face, laughs*) Our future! (*Gaily*) You were charming at supper, Birdie. Mr. Marshall certainly thought so.

BIRDIE (*pleased*). Why, Regina! Do you think he did?

REGINA. Can't you tell when you're being admired?

BIRDIE. Oscar said I bored Mr. Marshall. (*Then quietly*) But he admired *you.* He told me so.

REGINA. What did he say?

BIRDIE. He said to me, "I hope your sister-in-law will come to Chicago. Chicago will be at her feet." He said the ladies would bow to your manners and the gentlemen to your looks.

REGINA. Did he? He seems a lonely man. Imagine being lonely with all that money. I don't think he likes his wife.

BIRDIE. Not like his wife? What a thing to say.

REGINA. She's away a great deal. He said that several times. And once he made fun of her being so social and high-tone. But that fits in all right. (*Sits back, arms on back of sofa, stretches*) Her being social, I mean. She can introduce me. It won't take long with an introduction from her.

BIRDIE (*bewildered*). Introduce you? In Chicago? You mean you really might go? Oh, Regina, you can't leave here. What about Horace?

REGINA. Don't look so scared about everything, Birdie. I'm going to live in Chicago. I've always wanted to. And now there'll be plenty of money to go with.

BIRDIE. But Horace won't be able to move around. You know what the doctor wrote.

REGINA. There'll be millions, Birdie, millions. You know what I've always said when people told me we were rich? I said I think you should either be a nigger or a millionaire. In between, like us, what for? (*Laughs. Looks at* BIRDIE) But I'm not going away tomorrow, Birdie. There's plenty of time to worry about Horace when he comes home. If he ever decides to come home.

BIRDIE. Will we be going to Chicago? I mean, Oscar and Leo and me?

REGINA. You? I shouldn't think so. (*Laughs*) Well, we must remember tonight. It's a very important night and we mustn't forget it. We shall plan all the things we'd like to have and then we'll really have them. Make a wish, Birdie, any wish. It's bound to come true now. (BEN *and* OSCAR *enter*.)

BIRDIE (*laughs*). Well. Well, I don't know. Maybe. (REGINA *turns to look at* BEN) Well, I guess I'd know right off what I wanted. (OSCAR *stands by the upper window, waves to the departing carriage*.)

REGINA (*looks up at* BEN, *smiles. He smiles back at her*). Well, you did it.

BEN. Looks like it might be we did.

REGINA (*springs up, laughs*). Looks like it! Don't pretend. You're like a cat who's been licking the cream. (*Crosses to wine bottle*) Now we must all have a drink to celebrate.

OSCAR. The children, Alexandra and Leo, make a very handsome couple, Regina. Marshall remarked himself what fine young folks they were. How well they looked together!

REGINA (*sharply*). Yes. You said that before, Oscar.

BEN. Yes, sir. It's beginning to look as if the deal's all set. I may not be a subtle man—but— (*Turns to them. After a second*) Now somebody ask me how I know the deal is set.

OSCAR. What do you mean, Ben?

BEN. You remember I told him that down here we drink the *last* drink for a toast?

OSCAR (*thoughtfully*). Yes. I never heard that before.

BEN. Nobody's ever heard it before. God forgives those who invent what they need. I already had his signature. But we've all done business with men whose word over a glass is better than a bond. Anyway it don't hurt to have both.

OSCAR (*turns to* REGINA). You understand what Ben means?

REGINA (*smiles*). Yes, Oscar. I understand. I understood immediately.

BEN (*looks at her admiringly*). Did you, Regina? Well, when he lifted his glass to drink, I closed my eyes and saw the bricks going into place.

REGINA. And *I* saw a lot more than that.

BEN. Slowly, slowly. As yet we have only our hopes.

REGINA. Birdie and I have just been planning what we want. I know what I want. What will you want, Ben?

BEN. Caution. Don't count the chickens. (*Leans back, laughs*) Well, God would allow us a little daydreaming. Good for the soul when you've worked hard enough to deserve it. (*Pauses*) I think I'll have a stable. For a long time I've had my good eyes on Carter's in Savannah. A rich man's pleasure, the sport of kings, why not the sport of Hubbards? Why not?

REGINA (*smiles*). Why not? What will you have, Oscar?

OSCAR. I don't know. (*Thoughtfully*) The pleasure of seeing the bricks grow will be enough for me.

BEN. Oh, of course. Our greatest pleasure will be to see the bricks grow. But we are all entitled to a little side indulgence.

OSCAR. Yes, I suppose so. Well, then, I think we might take a few trips here and there, eh, Birdie?

BIRDIE (*surprised at being consulted*). Yes, Oscar. I'd like that.

OSCAR. We might even make a regular trip to Jekyll Island. I've heard the Cornelly place is for sale. We might think about buying it. Make a nice change. Do you good, Birdie, a change of climate. Fine shooting on Jekyll, the best.

BIRDIE. I'd like—

OSCAR (*indulgently*). What would you like?

BIRDIE. Two things. Two things I'd like most.

REGINA. Two! I should like a thousand. You are modest, Birdie.

BIRDIE (*warmly, delighted with the unexpected interest*). I should like to have Lionnet back. I know you own it now, but I'd like to see it fixed up again, the way Mama and Papa had it. Every year it used to get a nice coat of paint—Papa was very particular about the paint —and the lawn was so smooth all the way down to the river, with the trims of zinnias and red-feather plush. And the figs and blue little plums and the scuppernongs — (*Smiles. Turns to* REGINA) The organ is still there and it wouldn't cost much to fix. We could have parties for Zan, the way Mama used to have for me.

BEN. That's a pretty picture, Birdie. Might be a most pleasant way to live. (*Dismissing* BIRDIE) What do you want, Regina?

BIRDIE (*very happily, not noticing that they are no longer listening to her*). I could have a cutting garden. Just where Mama's used to be. Oh, I do think we could be happier there. Papa used to say that *nobody* had ever lost their temper at Lionnet, and *nobody* ever would. Papa would never let anybody be nasty-spoken or mean. No, sir. He just didn't like it.

BEN. What do you want, Regina?

REGINA. I'm going to Chicago. And when I'm settled there and know the right people and the right things to buy—because I certainly don't now—I shall go to Paris and buy them. (*Laughs*) I'm going to leave you and Oscar to count the bricks.

BIRDIE. Oscar. Please let me have Lionnet back.

OSCAR (*to* REGINA). You are serious about moving to Chicago?

BEN. She is going to see the great world and leave us in the little one. Well, we'll come and visit you and meet all the great and be proud you are our sister.

REGINA (*gaily*). Certainly. And you won't even have to learn to be subtle, Ben. Stay as you are. You will be rich and the rich don't have to be subtle.

OSCAR. But what about Alexandra? She's seventeen. Old enough to be thinking about marrying.

BIRDIE. And, Oscar, I have one more wish. Just one more wish.

OSCAR (*turns*). What is it, Birdie? What are you saying?

BIRDIE. I want you to stop shooting. I mean, so much. I don't like to see animals and birds killed just for the killing. You only throw them away—

BEN (*to* REGINA). It'll take a great deal of money to live as you're planning, Regina.

REGINA. Certainly. But there'll be plenty of money. You have estimated the profits very high.

BEN. I have—

BIRDIE (OSCAR *is looking at her furiously*). And you never let anybody else shoot, and the niggers need it so much to keep from starving. It's wicked to shoot food just because you like to shoot, when poor people need it so—

BEN (*laughs*). I have estimated the profits very high—for myself.

REGINA. What did you say?

BIRDIE. I've always wanted to speak about it, Oscar.

OSCAR (*slowly, carefully*). What are you chattering about?

BIRDIE (*nervously*). I was talking about Lionnet and—and about your shooting—

OSCAR. You are exciting yourself.

REGINA (*to* BEN). I didn't hear you. There was so much talking.

OSCAR (*to* BIRDIE). You have been acting very childish, very excited, all evening.

BIRDIE. Regina asked me what I'd like.

REGINA. What did you say, Ben?

BIRDIE. Now that we'll be so rich everybody was saying what they would like, so *I* said what *I* would like, too.

BEN. I said— (*He is interrupted by* OSCAR.)

OSCAR (*to* BIRDIE). Very well. We've all heard you. That's enough now.

BEN. I am waiting. (*They stop*) I am waiting for you to finish. You and Birdie. Four conversations are three too many. (BIRDIE *slowly sits down.* BEN *smiles, to* REGINA) I said that I had, and I do, estimate the profits very high—for myself, and Oscar, of course.

REGINA (*slowly*). And what does that mean? (BEN *shrugs, looks toward* OSCAR.)

OSCAR (*looks at* BEN, *clears throat*). Well, Regina, it's like this. For forty-nine per cent Marshall will put up four hundred thousand dollars. For fifty-one per cent— (*Smiles archly*) a controlling interest, mind you, we will put up two hundred and twenty-five thousand dollars besides offering him certain benefits that our (*looks at* BEN) local position allows us to manage. Ben means that two hundred and twenty-five thousand dollars is a lot of money.

REGINA. I know the terms and I know it's a lot of money.

BEN (*nodding*). It is.

OSCAR. Ben means that we are ready with our two-thirds of the money. Your third, Horace's I mean, doesn't seem to be ready. (*Raises his hand as* REGINA *starts to speak*) Ben has written to Horace, I have written, and you have written. He answers. But he never mentions this business. Yet we have explained it to him in great detail, and told him the urgency. Still he never mentions it. Ben has been very patient, Regina. Naturally, you are our sister and we want you to benefit from anything we do.

REGINA. And in addition to your concern for me, you do not want control to go out of the family. (*To* BEN) That right, Ben?

BEN. That's cynical. (*Smiles*) Cynicism is an unpleasant way of saying the truth.

OSCAR. No need to be cynical. We'd have no trouble raising the third share, the share that you want to take.

REGINA. I am sure you could get the third share, the share you were saving for me. But that would give you a strange partner. And strange partners sometimes want a great deal. (*Smiles unpleasantly*) But perhaps it would be wise for you to find him.

OSCAR. Now, now. Nobody says we *want* to do that. We would like to have you in and you would like to come in.

REGINA. Yes. I certainly would.

BEN (*laughs, puts up his hand*). But we haven't heard from Horace.

REGINA. I've given my word that Horace will put up the money. That should be enough.

BEN. Oh, it was enough. I took your word. But I've got to have more than your word now. The contracts will be signed this week, and Marshall will want to see our money soon after. Regina, Horace has been in Baltimore for five months. I know that you've written him to come home, and that he hasn't come.

OSCAR. It's beginning to look as if he doesn't want to come home.

REGINA. Of course he wants to come home. You can't move around with heart trouble at any moment you choose. You know what doctors are like once they get their hands on a case like this—

OSCAR. They can't very well keep him from answering letters, can they? (REGINA *turns to* BEN) They couldn't keep him from arranging for the money if he wanted to—

REGINA. Has it occurred to you that Horace is also a good businessman?

BEN. Certainly. He is a shrewd trader. Always has been. The bank is proof of that.

REGINA. Then, possibly, he may be keeping silent because he doesn't think he is getting enough for his money. (*Looks at* OSCAR) Seventy-five thousand he has to put up. That's a lot of money, too.

OSCAR. Nonsense. He knows a good thing when he hears it. He knows that we can make *twice* the profit on cotton goods manufactured here than can be made in the North.

BEN. That isn't what Regina means. (*Smiles*) May I interpret you, Regina? (*To* OSCAR) Regina is saying that Horace wants *more* than a third of our share.

OSCAR. But he's only putting up a third of the money. You put up a third and you get a third. What else could he expect?

REGINA. Well, *I* don't know. I don't know about these things. It would seem that if you put up a third you should only get a third. But then again, there's no law about it, is there? I should think that if you knew your money was very badly needed, well, you just might say, I want more, I want a bigger share. You boys have done that. I've heard you say so.

BEN (*after a pause, laughs*). So you believe he has deliberately held out? For a larger share? (*Leaning forward*) Well, I don't believe it. But I do believe that's what *you* want. Am I right, Regina?

REGINA. Oh, I shouldn't like to be too definite. But I could say that I wouldn't like to persuade Horace unless he did get a larger share. I must look after his interests. It seems only natural—

OSCAR. And where would the larger share come from?

REGINA. I don't know. That's not my business. (*Giggles*) But perhaps it could come off your share, Oscar. (REGINA *and* BEN *laugh.*)

OSCAR (*rises and wheels furiously on both of them as they laugh*). What kind of talk is this?

BEN. I haven't said a thing.

OSCAR (*to* REGINA). *You* are talking very big tonight.

REGINA (*stops laughing*). Am I? Well, you should know me well enough to know that I wouldn't be asking for things I didn't think I could get.

OSCAR. Listen. I don't believe you can even get Horace to come home, much less get money from him or talk quite so big about what you want.

REGINA. Oh, I can get him home.

OSCAR. Then why haven't you?

REGINA. I thought I should fight his battles for him, before he came home. Horace is a very sick man. And even if *you* don't care how sick he is, I do.

BEN. Stop this foolish squabbling. How can you get him home?

REGINA. I will send Alexandra to Baltimore. She will ask him to come home. She will say that she wants him to come home, and that *I* want him to come home.

BIRDIE (*suddenly*). Well, of course she wants him here, but he's sick and maybe he's happy where he is.

REGINA (*ignores* BIRDIE, *to* BEN). You agree that he will come home if she asks him to, if she says that I miss him and want him—

BEN (*looks at her, smiles*). I admire you, Regina. And I agree. That's settled now and— (*Starts to rise.*)

REGINA (*quickly*). But before she brings him home, I want to know what he's going to get.

BEN. What do you want?

REGINA. Twice what you offered.

BEN. Well, you won't get it.

OSCAR (*to* REGINA). I think you've gone crazy.

REGINA. I don't want to fight, Ben—

BEN. I don't either. You won't get it. There isn't any chance of that. (*Roguishly*) You're holding us up, and that's not pretty, Regina, not pretty. (*Holds up his hand as he sees she is about to speak*) But we need you, and I don't want to fight. Here's what I'll do: I'll give Horace forty per cent, instead of the thirty-three and a third he really should get. I'll do that, provided he is home and his money is up within two weeks. How's that?

REGINA. All right.

OSCAR. I've asked before: where is this extra share coming from?

BEN (*pleasantly*). From you. From your share.

OSCAR (*furiously*). From me, is it? That's just fine and dandy. That's my reward. For thirty-five years I've worked my hands to the bone for you. For thirty-five years I've done all the things you didn't want to do. And this is what I—

BEN (*turns slowly to look at* OSCAR. OSCAR *breaks off*). My, my. I am being attacked tonight on all sides. First by my sister, then by my brother. And I ain't a man who likes being attacked. I can't believe that God wants the strong to parade their strength, but I don't mind doing it if it's got to be done. (*Leans back in his chair*) You ought to take these things better, Oscar. I've made you money in the past. I'm going to make you more money now. You'll be a very rich man. What's the difference to any of us if a little more goes here, a little less goes there—it's all in the family. And it will stay in the family. I'll never marry. (ADDIE *enters, begins to gather the glasses from the table.* OSCAR *turns to* BEN) So my money will go to Alexandra and Leo. They may even marry some day and— (ADDIE *looks at* BEN.)

BIRDIE (*rising*). Marry—Zan and Leo—

OSCAR (*carefully*). That would make a great difference in my feelings. If they married.

BEN. Yes, that's what I mean. Of course it would make a difference.

OSCAR (*carefully*). Is that what *you* mean, Regina?

REGINA. Oh, it's too far away. We'll talk about it in a few years.

OSCAR. I want to talk about it now.

BEN (*nods*). Naturally.

REGINA. There's a lot of things to consider. They are first cousins, and—

OSCAR. That isn't unusual. Our grandmother and grandfather were first cousins.

REGINA (*giggles*). And look at us. (BEN *giggles.*)

OSCAR (*angrily*). You're both being very gay with my money.

BEN (*sighs*). These quarrels. I dislike them so. (*Leans forward to* REGINA) A marriage might be a very wise arrangement, for several reasons. And then, Oscar has given up something for you. You should try to manage something for him.

REGINA. I haven't said I was opposed to it. But Leo is a wild boy. There were those times when he took a little money from the bank and—

OSCAR. That's all past history—

REGINA. Oh, I know. And I know all young men are wild. I'm only mentioning it to show you that there are considerations—

BEN (*irritated because she does not understand that he is trying to keep* OSCAR *quiet*). All right, so there are. But please assure Oscar that you will think about it very seriously.

REGINA (*smiles, nods*). Very well. I assure Oscar that I will think about it seriously.

OSCAR (*sharply*). That is not an answer.

REGINA (*rises*). My, you're in a bad humor and you shall put me in one. I have said all that I am willing to say now. After all, Horace has to give his consent, too.

OSCAR. Horace will do what you tell him to.

REGINA. Yes, I think he will.

OSCAR. And I have your word that you will try to—

REGINA (*patiently*). Yes, Oscar. You have my word that I will think about it. Now do leave me alone. (*There is the sound of the front door being closed.*)

BIRDIE. I—Alexandra is only seventeen. She—

REGINA (*calling*). Alexandra? Are you back?

ALEXANDRA. Yes, Mama.

LEO (*comes into the room*). Mr. Marshall got off safe and sound. Weren't those fine clothes he had? You can always spot clothes made in a good place. Looks like maybe they were done in England. Lots of men in the North send all the way to England for their stuff.

BEN (*to* LEO). Were you careful driving the horses?

LEO. Oh, yes, sir. I was. (ALEXANDRA *has come in on* BEN'S *question, hears the answer, looks angrily at* LEO.)

ALEXANDRA. It's a lovely night. You should have come, Aunt Birdie.

REGINA. Were you gracious to Mr. Marshall?

ALEXANDRA. I think so, Mama. I liked him.

REGINA. Good. And now I have great news for you. You are going to Baltimore in the morning to bring your father home.

ALEXANDRA (*gasps, then delighted*). Me? Papa said I should come? That must mean— (*Turns to* ADDIE) Addie, he must be well. Think of it, he'll be back home again. We'll bring him home.

REGINA. You are going alone, Alexandra.

ADDIE (ALEXANDRA *has turned in surprise*). Going alone? Going by herself? A child that age! Mr. Horace ain't going to like Zan traipsing up there by herself.

REGINA (*sharply*). Go upstairs and lay out Alexandra's things.

ADDIE. He'd expect me to be along—

REGINA. I'll be up in a few minutes to tell you what to pack. (ADDIE *slowly begins to climb the steps. To* ALEXANDRA) I should think you'd like going alone. At your age it certainly would have delighted me. You're a strange girl, Alexandra. Addie has babied you so much.

ALEXANDRA. I only thought it would be more fun if Addie and I went together.

BIRDIE (*timidly*). Maybe I could go with her, Regina. I'd really like to.

REGINA. She is going alone. She is getting old enough to take some responsibilities.

OSCAR. She'd better learn now. She's almost old enough to get married. (*Jovially, to* LEO, *slapping him on shoulder*) Eh, son?

LEO. Huh?

OSCAR (*annoyed with* LEO *for not understanding*). Old enough to get married, you're thinking, eh?

LEO. Oh, yes, sir. (*Feebly*) Lots of girls get married at Zan's age. Look at Mary Prester and Johanna and—

REGINA. Well, she's not getting married tomorrow. But she is going to Baltimore tomorrow, so let's talk about that. (*To* ALEXANDRA) You'll be glad to have Papa home again.

ALEXANDRA. I wanted to go before, Mama. You remember that. But you said *you* couldn't go, and that *I* couldn't go alone.

REGINA. I've changed my mind. (*Too casually*) You're to tell Papa how much you missed him. and that he must come home now—for your sake. Tell him that you *need* him home.

ALEXANDRA. Need him home? I don't understand.

REGINA. There is nothing for you to understand. You are simply to say what I have told you.

BIRDIE (*rises*). He may be too sick. She couldn't do that—

ALEXANDRA. Yes. He may be too sick to travel. I couldn't make him think he had to come home for me, if he is too sick to—

REGINA (*looks at her, sharply, challengingly*). You *couldn't* do what I tell you to do, Alexandra?

ALEXANDRA (*quietly*). No. I couldn't. If I thought it would hurt him.

REGINA (*after a second's silence, smiles pleasantly*). But you are doing this for Papa's own good. (*Takes* ALEXANDRA's *hand*) You must let me be the judge of his condition. It's the best possible cure for him to come home and be taken care of here. He mustn't stay there any longer and listen to those alarmist doctors. You are doing this entirely for his sake. Tell your papa that I want him to come home, that I miss him very much.

ALEXANDRA (*slowly*). Yes, Mama.

REGINA (*to the others. Rises*). I must go and start getting Alexandra ready now. Why don't you all go home?

BEN (*rises*). I'll attend to the railroad ticket. One of the boys will bring it over. Good night, everybody. Have a nice trip, Alexandra. The food on the train is very good. The celery is so crisp. Have a good time and act like a little lady. (*Exits.*)

REGINA. Good night, Ben. Good night, Oscar— (*Playfully*) Don't be so glum, Oscar. It makes you look as if you had chronic indigestion.

BIRDIE. Good night, Regina.

REGINA. Good night, Birdie. (*Exits upstairs.*)

OSCAR (*starts for hall*). Come along.

LEO (*to* ALEXANDRA). Imagine your not wanting to go!

What a little fool you are. Wish it were me. What I could do in a place like Baltimore!

ALEXANDRA (*angrily, looking away from him*). Mind your business. I can guess the kind of things *you* could do.

LEO (*laughs*). Oh, no, you couldn't. (*He exits.*)

REGINA (*calling from the top of the stairs*). Come on, Alexandra.

BIRDIE (*quickly, softly*). Zan.

ALEXANDRA. I don't understand about my going, Aunt Birdie. (*Shrugs*) But anyway, Papa will be home again. (*Pats* BIRDIE'S *arm*) Don't worry about me. I can take care of myself. Really I can.

BIRDIE (*shakes her head, softly*). That's not what I'm worried about. Zan—

ALEXANDRA (*comes close to her*). What's the matter?

BIRDIE. It's about Leo—

ALEXANDRA (*whispering*). He beat the horses. That's why we were late getting back. We had to wait until they cooled off. He always beats the horses as if—

BIRDIE (*whispering frantically, holding* ALEXANDRA'S *hands*). He's my son. My own son. But you are more to me—more to me than my own child. I love you more than anybody else—

ALEXANDRA. Don't worry about the horses. I'm sorry I told you.

BIRDIE (*her voice rising*). *I am not worrying about the horses*. I am worrying about *you*. You are *not* going to marry Leo. I am not going to let them do that to you—

ALEXANDRA. Marry? To Leo? (*Laughs*) I wouldn't marry, Aunt Birdie. I've never even thought about it—

BIRDIE. But they have thought about it. (*Wildly*) Zan, I couldn't stand to think about such a thing. You and— (OSCAR *has come into the doorway on* ALEXANDRA'S *speech. He is standing quietly, listening.*)

ALEXANDRA (*laughs*). But I'm not going to marry. And I'm certainly not going to marry Leo.

BIRDIE. Don't you understand? They'll make you. They'll make you—

ALEXANDRA (*takes* BIRDIE's *hands, quietly, firmly*). That's foolish, Aunt Birdie. I'm grown now. Nobody can make me do anything.

BIRDIE. I just couldn't stand—

OSCAR (*sharply*). Birdie. (BIRDIE *looks up, draws quickly away from* ALEXANDRA. *She stands rigid, frightened. Quietly*) Birdie, get your hat and coat.

ADDIE (*calls from upstairs*). Come on, baby. Your mama's waiting for you, and she ain't nobody to keep waiting.

ALEXANDRA. All right. (*Then softly, embracing* BIRDIE) Good night, Aunt Birdie. (*As she passes* OSCAR) Good night, Uncle Oscar. (BIRDIE *begins to move slowly toward the door as* ALEXANDRA *climbs the stairs.* ALEXANDRA *is almost out of view when* BIRDIE *reaches* OSCAR *in the doorway. As* BIRDIE *quickly attempts to pass him, he slaps her hard, across the face.* BIRDIE *cries out, puts her hand to her face. On the cry,* ALEXANDRA *turns, begins to run down the stairs*) Aunt Birdie! What happened? What happened? I—

BIRDIE (*softly, without turning*). Nothing, darling. Nothing happened. (*Quickly, as if anxious to keep* ALEXANDRA *from coming close*) Now go to bed. (OSCAR *exits*) Nothing happened. I only—I only twisted my ankle. (*She goes out.* ALEXANDRA *stands on the stairs looking after her as if she were puzzled and frightened.*)

Curtain

ACT TWO

SCENE: *Same as Act One. A week later, morning.*

AT RISE: *The light comes from the open shutter of the right window; the other shutters are tightly closed.* ADDIE *is standing at the window, looking out. Near the dining room doors are brooms, mops, rags, etc. After a second,* OSCAR *comes into the entrance hall, looks in the room, shivers, decides not to take his hat and coat off, comes into the room. At the sound of the door,* ADDIE *turns.*

ADDIE (*without interest*). Oh, it's you, Mr. Oscar.

OSCAR. What is this? It's not night. What's the matter here? (*Shivers*) Fine thing at this time of the morning. Blinds all closed. (ADDIE *begins to open shutters*) Where's Miss Regina? It's cold in here.

ADDIE. Miss Regina ain't down yet.

OSCAR. She had any word?

ADDIE (*wearily*). No, sir.

OSCAR. Wouldn't you think a girl that age could get on a train at one place and have sense enough to get off at another?

ADDIE. Something must have happened. If Zan say she was coming last night, she's coming last night. Unless something happened. Sure fine disgrace to let a baby like that go all that way alone to bring home a sick man with-out—

OSCAR. You do a lot of judging around here, Addie, eh? Judging of your white folks, I mean.

ADDIE (*looks at him, sighs*). I'm tired. I been up all night watching for them.

REGINA (*speaking from the upstairs hall*). Who's down-stairs, Addie? (*She appears in a dressing gown, peers down from the landing.* ADDIE *picks up broom, dustpan and brush and exits*) Oh, it's you, Oscar. What are you doing here so early? I haven't been down yet. I'm not finished dressing.

OSCAR (*speaking up to her*). You had any word from them?

REGINA. No.

OSCAR. Then something certainly has happened. People don't just say they are arriving on Thursday night, and they haven't come by Friday morning.

REGINA. Oh, nothing has happened. Alexandra just hasn't got sense enough to send a message.

OSCAR. If nothing's happened, then why aren't they here?

REGINA. You asked me that ten times last night. My, you do fret so, Oscar. Anything might have happened. They may have missed connections in Atlanta, the train may have been delayed—oh, a hundred things could have kept them.

OSCAR. Where's Ben?

REGINA (*as she disappears upstairs*). Where should he be? At home, probably. Really, Oscar, I don't tuck him in his bed and I don't take him out of it. Have some coffee and don't worry so much.

OSCAR. Have some coffee? There isn't any coffee. (*Looks at his watch, shakes his head. After a second* CAL *enters with a large silver tray, coffee urn, small cups, news-paper*) Oh, there you are. Is everything in this fancy house always late?

CAL (*looks at him surprised*). You ain't out shooting this morning, Mr. Oscar?

OSCAR. First day I missed since I had my head cold. First day I missed in eight years.

CAL. Yes, sir. I bet you. Simon he say you had a mighty good day yesterday morning. That's what Simon say. (*Brings* OSCAR *coffee and newspaper.*)

OSCAR. Pretty good, pretty good.

CAL (*laughs, slyly*). Bet you got enough bobwhite and squirrel to give every nigger in town a Jesus-party. Most of 'em ain't had no meat since the cotton picking was over. Bet they'd give anything for a little piece of that meat—

OSCAR (*turns his head to look at* CAL). Cal, if I catch a nigger in this town going shooting, you know what's going to happen. (LEO *enters.*)

CAL (*hastily*). Yes, sir, Mr. Oscar. I didn't say nothing about nothing. It was Simon who told me and— Morning, Mr. Leo. You gentlemen having your breakfast with us here?

LEO. The boys in the bank don't know a thing. They haven't had any message. (CAL *waits for an answer, gets none, shrugs, moves to door, exits.*)

OSCAR (*peers at* LEO). What you doing here, son?

LEO. You told me to find out if the boys at the bank had any message from Uncle Horace or Zan—

OSCAR. I told you if they had a message to bring it here. I told you that if they didn't have a message to stay at the bank and do your work.

LEO. Oh, I guess I misunderstood.

OSCAR. You didn't misunderstand. You just were looking for any excuse to take an hour off. (LEO *pours a cup of coffee*) You got to stop that kind of thing. You got to start settling down. You going to be a married man one of these days.

LEO. Yes, sir.

OSCAR. You also got to stop with that woman in Mobile. (*As* LEO *is about to speak*) You're young and I haven't got no objections to outside women. That is, I haven't got no objections so long as they don't interfere with serious things. Outside women are all right in their place, but *now* isn't their place. You got to realize that.

LEO (*nods*). Yes, sir. I'll tell her. She'll act all right about it.

OSCAR. Also, you got to start working harder at the bank. You got to convince your Uncle Horace you going to make a fit husband for Alexandra.

LEO. What do you think has happened to them? Supposed to be here last night— (*Laughs*) Bet you Uncle Ben's mighty worried. Seventy-five thousand dollars worried.

OSCAR (*smiles happily*). Ought to be worried. Damn well ought to be. First he don't answer the letters, then he don't come home— (*Giggles.*)

LEO. What will happen if Uncle Horace don't come home or don't—

OSCAR. Or don't put up the money? Oh, we'll get it from outside. Easy enough.

LEO (*surprised*). But *you* don't want outsiders.

OSCAR. What do I care who gets my share? I been shaved already. Serve Ben right if he had to give away some of his.

LEO. Damn shame what they did to you.

OSCAR (*looking up the stairs*). Don't talk so loud. Don't you worry. When I die, you'll have as much as the rest. You might have yours *and* Alexandra's. I'm not so easily licked.

LEO. I wasn't thinking of myself, Papa—

OSCAR. Well, you should be, you should be. It's every man's duty to think of himself.

LEO. You think Uncle Horace don't want to go in on this?

OSCAR (*giggles*). That's my hunch. He hasn't showed any signs of loving it yet.

LEO (*laughs*). But he hasn't listened to Aunt Regina yet, either. Oh, he'll go along. It's too good a thing. Why wouldn't he want to? He's got plenty and plenty to invest with. He doesn't even have to sell anything. Eighty-eight thousand worth of Union Pacific bonds sitting right in his safe deposit box. All he's got to do is open the box.

OSCAR (*after a pause. Looks at his watch*). Mighty late breakfast in this fancy house. Yes, he's had those bonds for fifteen years. Bought them when they were low and just locked them up.

LEO. Yeah. Just has to open the box and take them out. That's all. Easy as easy can be. (*Laughs*) The things in that box! There's all those bonds, looking mighty fine. (OSCAR *slowly puts down his newspaper and turns to* LEO) Then right next to them is a baby shoe of Zan's and a cheap old cameo on a string, and, *and*—nobody'd believe this—a piece of an old violin. Not even a whole violin. Just a piece of an old thing, a piece of a violin.

OSCAR (*very softly, as if he were trying to control his voice*). A piece of a violin! What do you think of that!

LEO. Yes, sirree. A lot of other crazy things, too. A poem, I guess it is, signed with his mother's name, and two old schoolbooks with notes and— (LEO *catches* OSCAR's *look. His voice trails off. He turns his head away.*)

OSCAR (*very softly*). How do you know what's in the box, son?

LEO (*stops, draws back, frightened, realizing what he has said*). Oh, well. Well, er. Well, one of the boys, sir. It was one of the boys at the bank. He took old Manders' keys. It was Joe Horns. He just up and took Manders' keys and, and—well, took the box out. (*Quickly*) Then they all asked me if I wanted to see, too. So I looked a little, I guess, but then I made them close up the box quick and I told them never—

OSCAR (*looks at him*). Joe Horns, you say? He opened it?

LEO. Yes, sir, yes, he did. My word of honor. (*Very nervously looking away*) I suppose that don't excuse *me* for looking— (*Looking at* OSCAR) but I did make him close it up and put the keys back in Manders' drawer—

OSCAR (*leans forward, very softly*). Tell me the truth, Leo. I am not going to be angry with you. Did you open the box yourself?

LEO. *No, sir, I didn't.* I told you I didn't. No, I—

OSCAR (*irritated, patient*). I am *not* going to be angry with you. (*Watching* LEO *carefully*) Sometimes a young fellow deserves credit for looking round him to see what's going on. Sometimes that's a good sign in a fellow your age. (OSCAR *rises*) Many great men have made their fortune with their eyes. Did you open the box?

LEO (*very puzzled*). No. I—

OSCAR (*moves to* LEO). Did you open the box? It may have been—well, it may have been a good thing if you had.

LEO (*after a long pause*). I opened it.

OSCAR (*quickly*). Is that the truth? (LEO *nods*) Does anybody else know that you opened it? Come, Leo, don't be afraid of speaking the truth to me.

LEO. No. Nobody knew. Nobody was in the bank when I did it. But—

OSCAR. Did your Uncle Horace ever know you opened it?

LEO (*shakes his head*). He only looks in it once every six months when he cuts the coupons, and sometimes Manders even does that for him. Uncle Horace don't even have the keys. Manders keeps them for him. Imagine not looking at all that. You can bet if I had the bonds, I'd watch 'em like—

OSCAR. If you had them. (LEO *watches him*) *If* you had them. Then you could have a share in the mill, you and me. A fine, big share, too. (*Pauses, shrugs*) Well, a man can't be shot for wanting to see his son get on in the world, can he, boy?

LEO (*looks up, begins to understand*). No, he can't. Natural enough. (*Laughs*) But I haven't got the bonds and Uncle Horace has. And now he can just sit back and wait to be a millionaire.

OSCAR (*innocently*). You think your Uncle Horace likes

you well enough to lend you the bonds if he decides
not to use them himself?

LEO. Papa, it must be that you haven't had your breakfast!
(*Laughs loudly*) Lend me the bonds! My God—

OSCAR (*disappointed*). No, I suppose not. Just a fancy of
mine. A loan for three months, maybe four, easy enough
for us to pay it back then. Anyway, this is only April—
(*Slowly counting the months on his fingers*) and if he
doesn't look at them until Fall, he wouldn't even miss
them out of the box.

LEO. That's it. He wouldn't even miss them. Ah, well—

OSCAR. No, sir. Wouldn't even miss them. How could he
miss them if he never looks at them? (*Sighs as* LEO *stares
at him*) Well, here we are sitting around waiting for
him to come home and invest his money in something
he hasn't lifted his hand to get. But I can't help thinking he's acting strange. You laugh when I say he could
lend you the bonds if he's not going to use them himself. But would it hurt him?

LEO (*slowly looking at* OSCAR). No. No, it wouldn't.

OSCAR. People ought to help other people. But that's not
always the way it happens. (BEN *enters, hangs his coat
and hat in hall. Very carefully*) And so sometimes you
got to think of yourself. (*As* LEO *stares at him,* BEN *appears in the doorway*) Morning, Ben.

BEN (*coming in, carrying his newspaper*). Fine sunny
morning. Any news from the runaways?

REGINA (*on the staircase*). There's no news or you would
have heard it. Quite a convention so early in the morning, aren't you all? (*Goes to coffee urn.*)

OSCAR. You rising mighty late these days. Is that the way
they do things in Chicago society?

BEN (*looking at his paper*). Old Carter died up in Senateville. Eighty-one is a good time for us all, eh? What do
you think has really happened to Horace, Regina?

REGINA. Nothing.

BEN (*too casually*). You don't think maybe he never started from Baltimore and never intends to start?

REGINA (*irritated*). Of course they've started. Didn't I have a letter from Alexandra? What is so strange about people arriving late? He has that cousin in Savannah he's so fond of. He may have stopped to see him. They'll be along today some time, very flattered that you and Oscar are so worried about them.

BEN. I'm a natural worrier. Especially when I am getting ready to close a business deal and one of my partners remains silent *and* invisible.

REGINA (*laughs*). Oh, is that it? I thought you were worried about Horace's health.

OSCAR. Oh, that too. Who could help but worry? I'm worried. This is the first day I haven't shot since my head cold.

REGINA (*starts toward dining room*). Then you haven't had your breakfast. Come along. (OSCAR *and* LEO *follow her.*)

BEN. Regina. (*She turns at dining-room door*) That cousin of Horace's has been dead for years and, in any case, the train does not go through Savannah.

REGINA (*laughs, continues into dining room, seats herself*). Did he die? You're always remembering about people dying. (BEN *rises*) Now I intend to eat my breakfast in peace, and read my newspaper.

BEN (*goes toward dining room as he talks*). This is second breakfast for me. My first was bad. Celia ain't the cook she used to be. Too old to have taste any more. If she hadn't belonged to Mama, I'd send her off to the country.

(OSCAR *and* LEO *start to eat.* BEN *seats himself.*)

LEO. Uncle Horace will have some tales to tell, I bet. Baltimore is a lively town.

REGINA (*to* CAL). The grits isn't hot enough. Take it back.

CAL. Oh, yes'm. (*Calling into the kitchen as he exits*) Grits didn't hold the heat. Grits didn't hold the heat.

LEO. When I was at school three of the boys and myself took a train once and went over to Baltimore. It was so big we thought we were in Europe. I was just a kid then—

REGINA. I find it very pleasant (ADDIE *enters*) to have breakfast alone. I hate chattering before I've had something hot. (CAL *closes the dining-room doors*) Do be still, Leo.

(ADDIE *comes into the room, begins gathering up the cups, carries them to the large tray. Outside there are the sounds of voices. Quickly* ADDIE *runs into the hall. A few seconds later she appears again in the doorway, her arm around the shoulders of* HORACE GIDDENS, *supporting him.* HORACE *is a tall man of about forty-five. He has been good looking, but now his face is tired and ill. He walks stiffly, as if it were an enormous effort, and carefully, as if he were unsure of his balance.* ADDIE *takes off his overcoat and hangs it on the hall tree. She then helps him to a chair.*)

HORACE. How are you, Addie? How have you been?

ADDIE. I'm all right, Mr. Horace. I've just been worried about you.

(ALEXANDRA *enters. She is flushed and excited, her hat awry, her face dirty. Her arms are full of packages, but she comes quickly to* ADDIE.)

ALEXANDRA. Don't tell me how worried you were. We couldn't help it and there was no way to send a message.

ADDIE (*begins to take packages from* ALEXANDRA). Yes, sir, I was mighty worried.

ALEXANDRA. We had to stop in Mobile over night. Papa— (*Looks at him*) Papa didn't feel well. The trip was too much for him, and I made him stop and rest— (*As* ADDIE *takes the last package*) No, don't take that. That's father's medicine. I'll hold it. It mustn't break. Now, about the stuff outside. Papa must have his wheel chair. I'll get that and the valises—

ADDIE (*very happy, holding* ALEXANDRA's *arms*). Since when you got to carry your own valises? Since when I ain't old enough to hold a bottle of medicine? (HORACE *coughs*) You feel all right, Mr. Horace?

HORACE (*nods*). Glad to be sitting down.

ALEXANDRA (*opening package of medicine*). He doesn't feel all right. (ADDIE *looks at her, then at* HORACE) He just says that. The trip was very hard on him, and now he must go right to bed.

ADDIE (*looking at him carefully*). Them fancy doctors, they give you help?

HORACE. They did their best.

ALEXANDRA (*has become conscious of the voices in the dining room*). I bet Mama was worried. I better tell her we're here now. (*She starts for door.*)

HORACE. Zan. (*She stops*) Not for a minute, dear.

ALEXANDRA. Oh, Papa, you feel bad again. I knew you did. Do you want your medicine?

HORACE. No, I don't feel that way. I'm just tired, darling. Let me rest a little.

ALEXANDRA. Yes, but Mama will be mad if I don't tell her we're here.

ADDIE. They're all in there eating breakfast.

ALEXANDRA. Oh, are they all here? Why do they *always* have to be here? I was hoping Papa wouldn't have to see anybody, that it would be nice for him and quiet.

ADDIE. Then let your papa rest for a minute.

HORACE. Addie, I bet your coffee's as good as ever. They don't have such good coffee up north. (*Looks at the urn*) Is it as good, Addie? (ADDIE *starts for coffee urn.*)

ALEXANDRA. No. Dr. Reeves said not much coffee. Just now and then. I'm the nurse now, Addie.

ADDIE. You'd be a better one if you didn't look so dirty.

Now go and take a bath. Change your linens, get out a fresh dress and give your hair a good brushing—go on—

ALEXANDRA. Will you be all right, Papa?

ADDIE. Go on.

ALEXANDRA (*on stairs, talks as she goes up*). The pills Papa must take once every four hours. And the bottle only when—only if he feels very bad. Now don't move until I come back and don't talk much and remember about his medicine, Addie—

ADDIE. Ring for Belle and have her help you and then I'll make you a fresh breakfast.

ALEXANDRA (*as she disappears*). How's Aunt Birdie? Is she here?

ADDIE. It ain't right for you to have coffee? It will hurt you?

HORACE (*slowly*). Nothing can make much difference now. Get me a cup, Addie. (*She looks at him, crosses to urn, pours a cup*) Funny. They can't make coffee up north. (ADDIE *brings him a cup*) They don't like red pepper, either. (*He takes the cup and gulps it greedily*) God, that's good. You remember how I used to drink it? Ten, twelve cups a day. So strong it had to stain the cup. (*Then slowly*) Addie, before I see anybody else, I want to know why Zan came to fetch me home. She's tried to tell me, but she doesn't seem to know herself.

ADDIE (*turns away*). I don't know. All I know is big things are going on. Everybody going to be high-tone rich. Big rich. You too. All because smoke's going to start out of a building that aint' even up yet.

HORACE. I've heard about it.

ADDIE And, er— (*Hesitates—steps to him*) And—well, Zan, she going to marry Mr. Leo in a little while.

HORACE (*looks at her, then very slowly*). What are you talking about?

ADDIE. That's right. That's the talk, God help us.

HORACE (*angrily*). *What's* the talk?

ADDIE. I'm telling you. There's going to be a wedding— (*Angrily turns away*) Over my dead body there is.

HORACE (*after a second, quietly*). Go and tell them I'm home.

ADDIE (*hesitates*). Now you ain't to get excited. You're to be in your bed—

HORACE. Go on, Addie. Go and say I'm back. (ADDIE *opens dining-room doors. He rises with difficulty, stands stiff, as if he were in pain, facing the dining room.*)

ADDIE. Miss Regina. They're home. They got here—

REGINA. Horace! (REGINA *quickly, rises, runs into the room. Warmly*) Horace! You've finally arrived. (*As she kisses him, the others come forward, all talking together.*)

BEN (*in doorway, carrying a napkin*). Well, sir, you had us all mighty worried. (*He steps forward. They shake hands.* ADDIE *exits.*)

OSCAR. You're a sight for sore eyes.

HORACE. Hello, Ben.

(LEO *enters, eating a biscuit.*)

OSCAR. And how you feel? Tip-top, I bet, because that's the way you're looking.

HORACE (*coldly, irritated with* OSCAR's *lie*). Hello, Oscar. Hello, Leo, how are you?

LEO (*shaking hands*). I'm fine, sir. But a lot better now that you're back.

REGINA. Now sit down. What did happen to you and where's Alexandra? I am so excited about seeing you that I almost forgot about her.

HORACE. I didn't feel good, a little weak, I guess, and we stopped over night to rest. Zan's upstairs washing off the train dirt.

REGINA. Oh, I am so sorry the trip was hard on you. I didn't think that—

HORACE. Well, it's just as if I had never been away. All of you here—

BEN. Waiting to welcome you home.

(BIRDIE *bursts in. She is wearing a flannel kimono and her face is flushed and excited.*)

BIRDIE (*runs to him, kisses him*). Horace!

HORACE (*warmly pressing her arm*). I was just wondering where you were, Birdie.

BIRDIE (*excited*). Oh, I would have been here. I didn't know you were back until Simon said he saw the buggy. (*She draws back to look at him. Her face sobers*) Oh, you don't look well, Horace. No, you don't.

REGINA (*laughs*). Birdie, what a thing to say—

HORACE (*looking at* OSCAR). Oscar thinks I look very well.

OSCAR (*annoyed. Turns on* LEO). Don't stand there holding that biscuit in your hand.

LEO. Oh, well. I'll just finish my breakfast, Uncle Horace, and then I'll give you all the news about the bank— (*He exits into the dining room.*)

OSCAR. And what is that costume you have on?

BIRDIE (*looking at* HORACE). Now that you're home, you'll feel better. Plenty of good rest and we'll take such fine care of you. (*Stops*) But where is Zan? I missed her so much.

OSCAR. I asked you what is that strange costume you're parading around in?

BIRDIE (*nervously, backing toward stairs*). Me? Oh! It's my wrapper. I was so excited about Horace I just rushed out of the house—

OSCAR. Did you come across the square dressed that way? My dear Birdie, I—

HORACE (*to* REGINA, *wearily*). Yes, it's just like old times.

REGINA (*quickly to* OSCAR). Now, no fights. This is a holiday.

BIRDIE (*runs quickly up the stairs*). Zan! Zannie!

OSCAR. Birdie! (*She stops.*)

BIRDIE. Oh. Tell Zan I'll be back in a little while. (*Whispers*) Sorry, Oscar. (*Exits.*)

REGINA (*to* OSCAR *and* BEN). Why don't you go finish your breakfast and let Horace rest for a minute?

BEN (*crossing to dining room with* OSCAR). Never leave a meal unfinished. There are too many poor people who need the food. Mighty glad to see you home, Horace. Fine to have you back. Fine to have you back.

OSCAR (*to* LEO *as* BEN *closes dining-room doors*). Your mother has gone crazy. Running around the streets like a woman—

(*The moment* REGINA *and* HORACE *are alone, they become awkward and self-conscious.*)

REGINA (*laughs awkwardly*). Well. Here we are. It's been a long time. (HORACE *smiles*) Five months. You know, Horace, I wanted to come and be with you in the hospital, but I didn't know where my duty was. Here, or with you. But you know how much I *wanted* to come.

HORACE. That's kind of you, Regina. There was no need to come.

REGINA. Oh, but there was. Five months lying there all by yourself, no kinfolks, no friends. Don't try to tell me you didn't have a bad time of it.

HORACE. I didn't have a bad time. (*As she shakes her head, he becomes insistent*) No, I didn't, Regina. Oh, at first when I—when I heard the news about myself— but after I got used to that, I liked it there.

REGINA. You *liked* it? (*Coldly*) Isn't that strange. You liked it so well you didn't want to come home?

HORACE. That's not the way to put it. (*Then, kindly, as he sees her turn her head away*) But there I was and I got kind of used to it, kind of to like lying there and thinking. (*Smiles*) I never had much time to think before. And time's become valuable to me.

REGINA. It sounds almost like a holiday.

HORACE (*laughs*). It was, sort of. The first holiday I've had since I was a little kid.

REGINA. And here I was thinking you were in pain and—

HORACE (*quietly*). I was in pain.

REGINA. And instead you were having a holiday! A holiday of thinking. Couldn't you have done that here?

HORACE. I wanted to do it before I came here. I was thinking about us.

REGINA. About us? About you and me? Thinking about you and me after all these years. (*Unpleasantly*) You shall tell me everything you thought—some day.

HORACE (*there is silence for a minute*). Regina. (*She turns to him*) Why did you send Zan to Baltimore?

REGINA. Why? Because I wanted you home. You can't make anything suspicious out of that, can you?

HORACE. I didn't mean to make anything suspicious about it. (*Hesitantly, taking her hand*) Zan said you wanted me to come home. I was so pleased at that and touched it made me feel good.

REGINA (*taking away her hand, turns*). Touched that I should want you home?

HORACE (*sighs*). I'm saying all the wrong things as usual. Let's try to get along better. There isn't so much more time. Regina, what's all this crazy talk I've been hearing about Zan and Leo? Zan and Leo marrying?

REGINA (*turning to him, sharply*). Who gossips so much around here?

HORACE (*shocked*). Regina!

REGINA (*annoyed, anxious to quiet him*). It's some foolishness that Oscar thought up. I'll explain later. I have no intention of allowing any such arrangement. It was simply a way of keeping Oscar quiet in all this business I've been writing you about—

HORACE (*carefully*). What has Zan to do with any business of Oscar's? Whatever it is, you had better put it out of Oscar's head immediately. You know what I think of Leo.

REGINA. But there's no need to talk about it now.

HORACE. There is no need to talk about it ever. Not as

long as I live. (HORACE *stops, slowly turns to look at her*) As long as I live. I've been in a hospital for five months. Yet since I've been here you have not once asked me about—about my health. (*Then gently*) Well, I suppose they've written you. I can't live very long.

REGINA (*coldly*). I've never understood why people have to talk about this kind of thing.

HORACE (*there is a silence. Then he looks up at her, his face cold*). You misunderstand. I don't intend to gossip about my sickness. I thought it was only fair to tell you. I was not asking for your sympathy.

REGINA (*sharply, turns to him*). What do the doctors think caused your bad heart?

HORACE. What do you mean?

REGINA. They didn't think it possible, did they, that your fancy women may have—

HORACE (*smiles unpleasantly*). Caused my heart to be bad? I don't think that's the best scientific theory. You don't catch heart trouble in bed.

REGINA (*angrily*). I didn't think you did. I only thought you might catch a bad conscience—in bed, as you say.

HORACE. I didn't tell them about my bad conscience. Or about my fancy women. Nor did I tell them that my wife has not wanted me in bed with her for— (*Sharply*) How long is it, Regina? (REGINA *turns to him*) Ten years? Did you bring me home for this, to make me feel guilty again? That means you want something. But you'll not make me feel guilty any more. My "thinking" has made a difference.

REGINA. I see that it has. (*She looks toward dining-room door. Then comes to him, her manner warm and friendly*) It's foolish for us to fight this way. I didn't mean to be unpleasant. I was stupid.

HORACE (*wearily*). God knows I didn't either. I came home wanting so much not to fight, and then all of a sudden there we were. I got hurt and—

REGINA (*hastily*). It's all my fault. I didn't ask about—about your illness because I didn't want to remind you of it. Anyway I never believe doctors when they talk about— (*Brightly*) when they talk like that.

HORACE (*not looking at her*). Well, we'll try our best with each other. (*He rises.*)

REGINA (*quickly*). I'll try. Honestly, I will. Horace, Horace, I know you're tired but, but—couldn't you stay down here a few minutes longer? I want Ben to tell you something.

HORACE. Tomorrow.

REGINA. I'd like to now. It's very important to me. It's very important to all of us. (*Gaily, as she moves toward dining room*) Important to your beloved daughter. She'll be a very great heiress—

HORACE. Will she? That's nice.

REGINA (*opens doors*). Ben, are you finished breakfast?

HORACE. Is this the mill business I've had so many letters about?

REGINA (*to* BEN). Horace would like to talk to you now.

HORACE. Horace would not like to talk to you now. I am very tired, Regina—

REGINA (*comes to him*). Please. You've said we'll try our best with each other. I'll try. Really, I will. Please do this for me now. You will see what I've done while you've been away. How I watched your interests. (*Laughs gaily*) And I've done very well too. But things can't be delayed any longer. Everything must be settled this week— (HORACE *sits down.* BEN *enters.* OSCAR *has stayed in the dining room, his head turned to watch them.* LEO *is pretending to read the newspaper*) Now you must tell Horace all about it. Only be quick because he is very tired and must go to bed. (HORACE *is looking up at her. His face hardens as she speaks*) But I think your news will be better for him than all the medicine in the world.

BEN (*looking at* HORACE). It could wait. Horace may not feel like talking today.

REGINA. What an old faker you are! You know it can't wait. You know it must be finished this week. You've been just as anxious for Horace to get here as I've been.

BEN (*very jovial*). I suppose I have been. And why not? Horace has done Hubbard Sons many a good turn. Why shouldn't I be anxious to help him now?

REGINA (*laughs*). Help him! Help him when you need him, that's what you mean.

BEN. What a woman you married, Horace. (*Laughs awkwardly when* HORACE *does not answer*) Well, then I'll make it quick. You know what I've been telling you for years. How I've always said that every one of us little Southern businessmen had great things— (*Extends his arm*)—right beyond our finger tips. It's been my dream: my dream to make those fingers grow longer. I'm a lucky man, Horace, a lucky man. To dream and to live to get what you've dreamed of. That's *my* idea of a lucky man. (*Looks at his fingers as his arm drops slowly*) For thirty years I've cried bring the cotton mills to the cotton. (HORACE *opens medicine bottle*) Well, finally I got up nerve to go to Marshall Company in Chicago.

HORACE. I know all this. (*He takes the medicine.* REGINA *rises, steps to him.*)

BEN. Can I get you something?

HORACE. Some water, please.

REGINA (*turns quickly*). Oh, I'm sorry. Let me. (*Brings him a glass of water. He drinks as they wait in silence*) You feel all right now?

HORACE. Yes. You wrote me. I know all that.

(OSCAR *enters from dining room.*)

REGINA (*triumphantly*). But you don't know that in the last few days Ben has agreed to give us—you, I mean— a much larger share.

HORACE. Really? That's very generous of him.

BEN (*laughs*). It wasn't so generous of me. It was smart of Regina.

REGINA (*as if she were signaling* HORACE). I explained to Ben that perhaps you hadn't answered his letters because you didn't think he was offering you enough, and that the time was getting short and you could guess how much he needed you—

HORACE (*smiles at her, nods*). And I could guess that he wants to keep control in the family.

REGINA (*to* BEN, *triumphantly*). Exactly. (*To* HORACE) So I did a little bargaining for you and convinced my brothers they weren't the only Hubbards who had a business sense.

HORACE. Did you have to convince them of that? How little people know about each other! (*Laughs*) But you'll know better about Regina next time, eh, Ben? (BEN, REGINA, HORACE *laugh together.* OSCAR's *face is angry*) Now let's see. We're getting a bigger share. (*Looking at* OSCAR) Who's getting less?

BEN. Oscar.

HORACE. Well, Oscar, you've grown very unselfish. What's happened to you?

(LEO *enters from dining room.*)

BEN (*quickly, before* OSCAR *can answer*). Oscar doesn't mind. Not worth fighting about now, eh, Oscar?

OSCAR (*angrily*). I'll get mine in the end. You can be sure of that. I've got my son's future to think about.

HORACE (*sharply*). Leo? Oh, I see. (*Puts his head back, laughs.* REGINA *looks at him nervously*) I am beginning to see. Everybody will get theirs.

BEN. I knew you'd see it. Seventy-five thousand, and that seventy-five thousand will make you a million.

REGINA (*steps to table, leaning forward*). It will, Horace, it will.

HORACE. I believe you. (*After a second*) Now I can understand Oscar's self-sacrifice, but what did you have to promise Marshall Company besides the money you're putting up?

BEN. They wouldn't take promises. They wanted guarantees.

HORACE. Of what?

BEN (*nods*). Water power. Free and plenty of it.

HORACE. You got them that, of course.

BEN. Cheap. You'd think the Governor of a great state would make his price a little higher. From pride, you know. (HORACE *smiles*. BEN *smiles*) Cheap wages. "What do you mean by cheap wages?" I say to Marshall. "Less than Massachusetts," he says to me, "and that averages eight a week." "Eight a week! By God," I tell him, "*I'd* work for eight a week myself." Why, there ain't a mountain white or a town nigger but wouldn't give his right arm for three silver dollars every week, eh, Horace?

HORACE. Sure. And they'll take less than that when you get around to playing them off against each other. You can save a little money that way, Ben. (*Angrily*) And make them hate each other just a little more than they do now.

REGINA. What's all this about?

BEN (*laughs*). There'll be no trouble from anybody, white or black. Marshall said that to me. "What about strikes? That's all we've had in Massachusetts for the last three years." I say to him, "What's a strike? I never heard of one. Come South, Marshall. We got good folks and we don't stand for any fancy fooling."

HORACE. You're right. (*Slowly*) Well, it looks like you made a good deal for yourselves, and for Marshall, too. (*To* BEN) Your father used to say he made the thousands and you boys would make the millions. I think he was right. (*Rises.*)

REGINA (*they are all looking at* HORACE. *She laughs nervously*). Millions for *us*, too.

HORACE. Us? You and me? I don't think so. We've got enough money, Regina. We'll just sit by and watch the boys grow rich. (*They watch* HORACE *tensely as he begins to move toward the staircase. He passes* LEO, *looks at him for a second*) How's everything at the bank, Leo?

LEO. Fine, sir. Everything is fine.

HORACE. How are all the ladies in Mobile? (HORACE *turns to* REGINA, *sharply*) Whatever made you think I'd let Zan marry—

REGINA. Do you mean that you are turning this down? Is it possible that's what you mean?

BEN. No, that's not what he means. Turning down a fortune. Horace is tired. He'd rather talk about it tomorrow—

REGINA. We can't keep putting it off this way. Oscar must be in Chicago by the end of the week with the money and contracts.

OSCAR (*giggles, pleased*). Yes, sir. Got to be there end of the week. No sense going without the money.

REGINA (*tensely*). I've waited long enough for your answer. I'm not going to wait any longer.

HORACE (*very deliberately*). I'm very tired now, Regina.

BEN (*hastily*). Now, Horace probably has his reasons. Things he'd like explained. Tomorrow will do. I can—

REGINA (*turns to* BEN, *sharply*). I want to know his reasons now! (*Turns back to* HORACE.)

HORACE (*as he climbs the steps*). I don't know them all myself. Let's leave it at that.

REGINA. We shall not leave it at that! We have waited for you here like children. Waited for you to come home.

HORACE. So that you could invest my money. So that is why you wanted me home? Well, I had hoped— (*Quietly*) If you are disappointed, Regina, I'm sorry. But I must do what I think best. We'll talk about it another day.

REGINA. We'll talk about it now. Just you and me.

HORACE (*looks down at her. His voice is tense*). Please, Regina, it's been a hard trip. I don't feel well. Please leave me alone now.

REGINA (*quietly*). I want to talk to you, Horace. I'm coming up. (*He looks at her for a minute, then moves on again out of sight. She begins to climb the stairs.*)

BEN (*softly.* REGINA *turns to him as he speaks*). Sometimes it is better to wait for the sun to rise again. (*She does not answer*) And sometimes, as our mother used to tell you, (REGINA *starts up stairs*) it's unwise for a good-looking woman to frown. (BEN *rises, moves toward stairs*) Softness and a smile do more to the heart of men — (*She disappears.* BEN *stands looking up the stairs. There is a long silence. Then, suddenly,* OSCAR *giggles.*)

OSCAR. Let us hope she'll change his mind. Let us hope (*After a second* BEN *crosses to table, picks up his newspaper.* OSCAR *looks at* BEN. *The silence makes* LEO *uncomfortable.*)

LEO. The paper says twenty-seven cases of yellow fever in New Orleans. Guess the flood-waters caused it. (*Nobody pays attention*) Thought they were building the levees high enough. Like the niggers always say: a man born of woman can't build nothing high enough for the Mississippi. (*Gets no answer. Gives an embarrassed laugh.*)

(*Upstairs there is the sound of voices. The voices are not loud, but* BEN, OSCAR, LEO *become conscious of them.* LEO *crosses to landing, looks up, listens.*)

OSCAR (*pointing up*). Now just suppose she don't change his mind? Just suppose he keeps on refusing?

BEN (*without conviction*). He's tired. It was a mistake to talk to him today. He's a sick man, but he isn't a crazy one.

OSCAR (*giggles*). But just suppose he is crazy. What then?

BEN (*puts down his paper, peers at* OSCAR). Then we'll g

outside for the money. There's plenty who would give it.

OSCAR. And plenty who will want a lot for what they give. The ones who are rich enough to give will be smart enough to want. That means we'd be working for them, don't it, Ben?

BEN. You don't have to tell me the things I told you six months ago.

OSCAR. Oh, you're right not to worry. She'll change his mind. She always has. (*There is a silence. Suddenly* REGINA's *voice becomes louder and sharper. All of them begin to listen now. Slowly* BEN *rises, goes to listen by the staircase.* OSCAR, *watching him, smiles. As they listen* REGINA's *voice becomes very loud.* HORACE's *voice is no longer heard*) Maybe. But I don't believe it. I never did believe he was going in with us.

BEN (*turning on him*). What the hell do you expect me to do?

OSCAR (*mildly*). Nothing. You done your almighty best. Nobody could blame you if the whole thing just dripped away right through our fingers. You can't do a thing. But there may be something I could do for us. (OSCAR *rises*) Or, I might better say, Leo could do for us. (BEN *stops, turns, looks at* OSCAR. LEO *is staring at* OSCAR) Ain't that true, son? Ain't it true you might be able to help your own kinfolks?

LEO (*nervously taking a step to him*). Papa, I—

BEN (*slowly*). How would he help us, Oscar?

OSCAR. Leo's got a friend. Leo's friend owns eighty-eight thousand dollars in Union Pacific bonds. (BEN *turns to look at* LEO) Leo's friend don't look at the bonds much —not for five or six months at a time.

BEN (*after a pause*). Union Pacific. Uh, huh. Let me understand. Leo's friend would—would lend him these bonds and he—

OSCAR (*nods*). Would be kind enough to lend them to us.

BEN. Leo.

LEO (*excited, comes to him*). Yes, sir?

BEN. When would your friend be wanting the bonds back?

LEO (*very nervous*). I don't know. I—well, I—

OSCAR (*sharply. Steps to him*). You told me he won't look at them until Fall—

LEO. Oh, that's right. But I—not till Fall. Uncle Horace never—

BEN (*sharply*). Be still.

OSCAR (*smiles at* LEO). Your uncle doesn't wish to know your friend's name.

LEO (*starts to laugh*). That's a good one. Not know his name—

OSCAR. Shut up, Leo! (LEO *turns away slowly, moves to table.* BEN *turns to* OSCAR) He won't look at them again until September. That gives us five months. Leo will return the bonds in three months. And we'll have no trouble raising the money once the mills are going up. Will Marshall accept bonds?

(BEN *stops to listen to sudden sharp voices from above. The voices are now very angry and very loud.*)

BEN (*smiling*). Why not? Why not? (*Laughs*) Good. We are lucky. We'll take the loan from Leo's friend—I think he will make a safer partner than our sister. (*Nods toward stairs. Turns to* LEO) How soon can you get them?

LEO. Today. Right now. They're in the safe-deposit box and—

BEN (*sharply*). I don't want to know where they are.

OSCAR (*laughs*). We will keep it secret from you. (*Pats* BEN'*s arm.*)

BEN (*smiles*). Good. Draw a check for our part. You can take the night train for Chicago. Well, Oscar (*Holds out his hand*), good luck to us.

OSCAR. Leo will be taken care of?

LEO. I'm entitled to Uncle Horace's share. I'd enjoy being a partner—

BEN (*turns to stare at him*). You would? You can go to hell, you little— (*Starts toward* LEO.)

OSCAR (*nervously*). Now, now. He didn't mean that. I only want to be sure he'll get something out of all this.

BEN. Of course. We'll take care of him. We won't have any trouble about that. I'll see you at the store.

OSCAR (*nods*). That's settled then. Come on, son. (*Starts for door.*)

LEO (*puts out his hand*) I was only going to say what a great day this was for me and— (BEN *ignores his hand.*)

BEN. Go on.

(LEO *looks at him, turns, follows* OSCAR *out.* BEN *stands where he is, thinking. Again the voices upstairs can be heard.* REGINA'S *voice is high and furious.* BEN *looks up, smiles, winces at the noise.*)

ALEXANDRA (*upstairs*). Mama—Mama—don't . . . (*The noise of running footsteps is heard and* ALEXANDRA *comes running down the steps, speaking as she comes*) Uncle Ben! Uncle Ben! Please go up. Please make Mama stop. Uncle Ben, he's sick, he's so sick. How can Mama talk to him like that—please, make her stop. She'll—

BEN. Alexandra, you have a tender heart.

ALEXANDRA (*crying*). Go on up, Uncle Ben, please—

(*Suddenly the voices stop. A second later there is the sound of a door being slammed.*)

BEN. Now you see. Everything is over. Don't worry. (*He starts for the door*) Alexandra, I want you to tell your mother how sorry I am that I had to leave. And don't worry so, my dear. Married folk frequently raise their voices, unfortunately. (*He starts to put on his hat and coat as* REGINA *appears on the stairs.*)

ALEXANDRA (*furiously*). How can you treat Papa like this? He's sick. He's very sick. Don't you know that? I won't let you.

REGINA. Mind your business, Alexandra. (*To* BEN. *Her*

voice is cold and calm) How much longer can you wait for the money?

BEN (*putting on his coat*). He has refused? My, that's too bad.

REGINA. He will change his mind. I'll find a way to make him. What's the longest you can wait now?

BEN. I could wait until next week. But I can't wait until next week. (*He giggles, pleased at the joke*) I could but I can't. Could and can't. Well, I must go now. I'm very late—

REGINA (*coming downstairs toward him*). You're not going. I want to talk to you.

BEN. I was about to give Alexandra a message for you. I wanted to tell you that Oscar is going to Chicago tonight, so we can't be here for our usual Friday supper.

REGINA (*tensely*). Oscar is going to Chi— (*Softly*) What do you mean?

BEN. Just that. Everything is settled. He's going on to deliver to Marshall—

REGINA (*taking a step to him*). I demand to know what— You are lying. You are trying to scare me. *You haven't got the money.* How could you have it? You can't have— (BEN *laughs*) You will wait until I—

(HORACE *comes into view on the landing.*)

BEN. You are getting out of hand. Since when do I take orders from you?

REGINA. Wait, you— (BEN *stops*) How *can* he go to Chicago? Did a ghost arrive with the money? (BEN *starts for the hall*) I don't believe you. Come back here. (REGINA *starts after him*) Come back here, you— (*The door slams. She stops in the doorway, staring, her fists clenched. After a pause she turns slowly.*)

HORACE (*very quietly*). It's a great day when you and Ben cross swords. I've been waiting for it for years.

ALEXANDRA. Papa, Papa, please go back! You will—

HORACE. And so they don't need you, and so you will not have your millions, after all.

REGINA (*turns slowly*). You hate to see anybody live now, don't you? You hate to think that I'm going to be alive and have what I want.

HORACE. I should have known you'd think that was the reason.

REGINA. Because you're going to die and you know you're going to die.

ALEXANDRA (*shrilly*). Mama! Don't— Don't listen, Papa. Just don't listen. Go away—

HORACE. Not to keep you from getting what you want. Not even partly that. (*Holding to the rail*) I'm sick of you, sick of this house, sick of my life here. I'm sick of your brothers and their dirty tricks to make a dime. There must be better ways of getting rich than cheating niggers on a pound of bacon. Why should I give you the money? (*Very angrily*) To pound the bones of this town to make dividends for you to spend? You wreck the town, you and your brothers, *you* wreck the town and live on it. Not me. Maybe it's easy for the dying to be honest. But it's not my fault I'm dying. (ADDIE *enters, stands at door quietly*) I'll do no more harm now. I've done enough. I'll die my own way. And I'll do it without making the world any worse. I leave that to you.

REGINA (*looks up at him slowly, calmly*). I hope you die. I hope you die soon. (*Smiles*) I'll be waiting for you to die.

ALEXANDRA (*shrieking*). Papa! Don't— Don't listen— Don't—

ADDIE. Come here, Zan. Come out of this room.

(ALEXANDRA *runs quickly to* ADDIE, *who holds her.* HORACE *turns slowly and starts upstairs.*)

Curtain

ACT THREE

SCENE: *Same as Act One. Two weeks later. It is late afternoon and it is raining.*

AT RISE: HORACE *is sitting near the window in a wheel chair. On the table next to him is a safe-deposit box, and a small bottle of medicine.* BIRDIE *and* ALEXANDRA *are playing the piano. On a chair is a large sewing basket.*

BIRDIE (*counting for* ALEXANDRA). One and two and three and four. One and two and three and four. (*Nods— turns to* HORACE) We once played together, Horace. Remember?

HORACE (*has been looking out of the window*). What, Birdie?

BIRDIE. We played together. You and me.

ALEXANDRA. *Papa* used to play?

BIRDIE. Indeed he did. (ADDIE *appears at the door in a large kitchen apron. She is wiping her hands on a towel*) He played the fiddle and very well, too.

ALEXANDRA (*turns to smile at* HORACE). I never knew—

ADDIE. Where's your mama?

ALEXANDRA. Gone to Miss Safronia's to fit her dresses.

(ADDIE *nods, starts to exit.*)

HORACE. Addie.

ADDIE. Yes, Mr. Horace.

HORACE (*speaks as if he had made a sudden decision*). Tell Cal to get on his things. I want him to go an errand.

(ADDIE *nods, exits.* HORACE *moves nervously in his chair, looks out of the window.*)

ALEXANDRA (*who has been watching him*). It's too bad it's been raining all day, Papa. But you can go out in the yard tomorrow. Don't be restless.

HORACE. I'm not restless, darling.

BIRDIE. I remember so well the time we played together, your papa and me. It was the first time Oscar brought me here to supper. I had never seen all the Hubbards together before, and you know what a ninny I am and how shy. (*Turns to look at* HORACE) You said you could play the fiddle and you'd be much obliged if I'd play with you. *I* was obliged to *you*, all right, all right. (*Laughs when he does not answer her*) Horace, you haven't heard a word I've said.

HORACE. Birdie, when did Oscar get back from Chicago?

BIRDIE. Yesterday. Hasn't he been here yet?

ALEXANDRA (*stops playing*). No. Neither has Uncle Ben since—since that day.

BIRDIE. Oh, I didn't know it was *that* bad. Oscar never tells me anything—

HORACE (*smiles, nods*). The Hubbards have had their great quarrel. I knew it would come some day. (*Laughs*) It came.

ALEXANDRA. It came. It certainly came all right.

BIRDIE (*amazed*). But Oscar was in such a good humor when he got home, I didn't—

HORACE. Yes, I can understand that.

(ADDIE *enters carrying a large tray with glasses, a carafe of elderberry wine and a plate of cookies, which she puts on the table.*)

ALEXANDRA. Addie! A party! What for?

ADDIE. Nothing for. I had the fresh butter, so I made the cakes, and a little elderberry does the stomach good in the rain.

BIRDIE. Isn't this nice! A party just for us. Let's play party music, Zan.

(ALEXANDRA *begins to play a gay piece.*)

ADDIE (*to* HORACE, *wheeling his chair to center*). Come over here, Mr. Horace, and don't be thinking so much. A glass of elderberry will do more good.

(ALEXANDRA *reaches for a cake.* BIRDIE *pours herself a glass of wine.*)

ALEXANDRA. Good cakes, Addie. It's nice here. Just us. Be nice if it could always be this way.

BIRDIE (*nods happily*). Quiet and restful.

ADDIE. Well, it won't be that way long. Little while now, even sitting here, you'll hear the red bricks going into place. The next day the smoke'll be pushing out the chimneys and by church time that Sunday every human born of woman will be living on chicken. That's how Mr. Ben's been telling the story.

HORACE (*looks at her*). They believe it that way?

ADDIE. Believe it? They use to believing what Mr. Ben orders. There ain't been so much talk around here since Sherman's army didn't come near.

HORACE (*softly*). They are fools.

ADDIE (*nods, sits down with the sewing basket*). You ain't born in the South unless you're a fool.

BIRDIE (*has drunk another glass of wine*). But we didn't play together after that night. Oscar said he didn't like me to play on the piano. (*Turns to* ALEXANDRA) You know what he said that night?

ALEXANDRA. Who?

BIRDIE. Oscar. He said that music made him nervous. He said he just sat and waited for the next note. (ALEXANDRA *laughs*) He wasn't poking fun. He meant it. Ah well— (*She finishes her glass, shakes her head.* HORACE *looks at her, smiles*) Your papa don't like to admit it but he's been mighty kind to me all these years. (*Running the back of her hand along his sleeve*) Often he'd step in when somebody said something and once— (*She stops, turns away, her face still*) Once he stopped Oscar from— (*She stops, turns. Quickly*) I'm sorry said that. Why, here I am so happy and yet I think about bad things. (*Laughs nervously*) That's not right, now, is it? (*She pours a drink.* CAL *appears in the door. He has on an old coat and is carrying a torn umbrella.*)

ALEXANDRA. Have a cake, Cal.

CAL (*comes in, takes a cake*). Yes'm. You want me, Mr. Horace?

HORACE. What time is it, Cal?

CAL. 'Bout ten minutes before it's five.

HORACE. All right. Now you walk yourself down to the bank.

CAL. It'll be closed. Nobody'll be there but Mr. Manders, Mr. Joe Horns, Mr. Leo—

HORACE. Go in the back way. They'll be at the table, going over the day's business. (*Points to the deposit box*) See that box?

CAL (*nods*). Yes, sir.

HORACE. You tell Mr. Manders that Mr. Horace says he's much obliged to him for bringing the box, it arrived all right.

CAL (*bewildered*). He know you got the box. He bring it himself Wednesday. I opened the door to him and he say, "Hello, Cal, coming on to summer weather."

HORACE. You say just what I tell you. Understand?

(BIRDIE *pours another drink, stands at table.*)

CAL. No, sir. I ain't going to say I understand. I'm going down and tell a man he give you something he already know he give you, and you say "understand."

HORACE. Now, Cal.

CAL. Yes, sir. I just going to say you obliged for the box coming all right. I ain't going to understand it, but I'm going to say it.

HORACE. And tell him I want him to come over here after supper, and to bring Mr. Sol Fowler with him.

CAL (*nods*). He's to come after supper and bring Mr. Sol Fowler, your attorney-*at*-law, with him.

HORACE (*smiles*). That's right. Just walk right in the back room and say your piece. (*Slowly*) In front of everybody.

CAL. Yes, sir. (*Mumbles to himself as he exits.*)

ALEXANDRA (*who has been watching* HORACE). Is anything the matter, Papa?

HORACE. Oh, no. Nothing.

ADDIE. Miss Birdie, that elderberry going to give you a headache spell.

BIRDIE (*beginning to be drunk. Gaily*). Oh, I don't think so. I don't think it will.

ALEXANDRA (*as* HORACE *puts his hand to his throat*). Do you want your medicine, Papa?

HORACE. No, no. I'm all right, darling.

BIRDIE. Mama used to give me elderberry wine when I was a little girl. For hiccoughs. (*Laughs*) You know, I don't think people get hiccoughs any more. Isn't that funny? (BIRDIE *laughs.* HORACE *and* ALEXANDRA *laugh*) I used to get hiccoughs just when I shouldn't have.

ADDIE (*nods*). And nobody gets growing pains no more. That is funny. Just as if there was some style in what you get. One year an ailment's stylish and the next year it ain't.

BIRDIE (*turns*). I remember. It was my first big party, at Lionnet I mean, and I was so excited, and there I was with hiccoughs and Mama laughing. (*Softly. Looking at carafe*) Mama always laughed. (*Picks up carafe*) A big party, a lovely dress from Mr. Worth in Paris, France, and hiccoughs. (*Pours drink*) My brother pounding me on the back and Mama with the elderberry bottle, laughing at me. Everybody was on their way to come, and I was such a ninny, hiccoughing away. (*Drinks*) You know, that was the first day I ever saw Oscar Hubbard. The Ballongs were selling their horses and he was going there to buy. He passed and

lifted his hat—we could see him from the window—
and my brother, to tease Mama, said maybe we should
have invited the Hubbards to the party. He said Mama
didn't like them because they kept a store, and he said
that was old-fashioned of her. (*Her face lights up*) And
then, and *then,* I saw Mama angry for the first time in
my life. She said that wasn't the reason. She said she
was old-fashioned, but not that way. She said she was
old-fashioned enough not to like people who killed
animals they couldn't use, and who made their money
charging awful interest to poor, ignorant niggers and
cheating them on what they bought. She was very
angry, Mama was. I had never seen her face like that.
And then suddenly she laughed and said, "Look, I've
frightened Birdie out of the hiccoughs." (*Her head
drops. Then softly*) And so she had. They were all gone.
(*Moves to sofa, sits.*)

ADDIE. Yeah, they got mighty well off cheating niggers.
Well, there are people who eat the earth and eat all
the people on it like in the Bible with the locusts. Then
there are people who stand around and watch them eat
it. (*Softly*) Sometimes I think it ain't right to stand and
watch them do it.

BIRDIE (*thoughtfully*). Like I say, if we could only go
back to Lionnet. Everybody'd be better there. They'd
be good and kind. I like people to be kind. (*Pours
drink*) Don't you, Horace; don't you like people to be
kind?

HORACE. Yes, Birdie.

BIRDIE (*very drunk now*). Yes, that was the first day I
ever saw Oscar. Who would have thought— (*Quickly*)
You all want to know something? Well, I don't like Leo.
My very own son, and I don't like him. (*Laughs, gaily*)
My, I guess I even like Oscar more.

ALEXANDRA. Why did you marry Uncle Oscar?

ADDIE (*sharply*). That's no question for you to be asking.

HORACE (*sharply*). Why not? She's heard enough around here to ask anything.

ALEXANDRA. Aunt Birdie, why did you marry Uncle Oscar?

BIRDIE. I don't know. I thought I liked him. He was kind to me and I thought it was because he liked me too. But that wasn't the reason— (*Wheels on* ALEXANDRA) Ask why *he* married *me*. I can tell you that: he's told it to me often enough.

ADDIE (*leaning forward*). Miss Birdie, don't—

BIRDIE (*speaking very rapidly, tensely*). My family was good and the cotton on Lionnet's fields was better. Ben Hubbard wanted the cotton and (*Rises*) Oscar Hubbard married it for him. He was kind to me, then. He used to smile at me. He hasn't smiled at me since. Everybody knew that's what he married me for. (ADDIE *rises*) Everybody but me. Stupid, stupid me.

ALEXANDRA (*to* HORACE, *holding his hand, softly*). I see. (*Hesitates*) Papa, I mean—when you feel better couldn't we go away? I mean, by ourselves. Couldn't we find a way to go—

HORACE. Yes, I know what you mean. We'll try to find a way. I promise you, darling.

ADDIE (*moves to* BIRDIE). Rest a bit, Miss Birdie. You get talking like this you'll get a headache and—

BIRDIE (*sharply, turning to her*). I've never had a headache in my life. (*Begins to cry hysterically*) You know it as well as I do. (*Turns to* ALEXANDRA) I never had a headache, Zan. That's a lie they tell for me. I drink. All by myself, in my own room, by myself, I drink. Then, when they want to hide it, they say, "Birdie's got a headache again"—

ALEXANDRA (*comes to her quickly*). Aunt Birdie.

BIRDIE (*turning away*). Even you won't like me now. You won't like me any more.

ALEXANDRA. I love you. I'll always love you.

BIRDIE (*furiously*). Well, don't. Don't love me. Because in twenty years you'll just be like me. They'll do all the same things to you. (*Begins to laugh hysterically*) You know what? In twenty-two years I haven't had a whole day of happiness. Oh, a little, like today with you all. But never a single, whole day. I say to myself, if only I had one more *whole* day, then— (*The laugh stops*) And that's the way you'll be. And you'll trail after them, just like me, hoping they won't be so mean that day or say something to make you feel so bad—only you'll be worse off because you haven't got my Mama to remember— (*Turns away, her head drops. She stands quietly, swaying a little, holding to the sofa.* ALEXANDRA *leans down, puts her cheek on* BIRDIE's *arm.*)

ALEXANDRA (*to* BIRDIE). I guess we were all trying to make a happy day. You know, we sit around and try to pretend nothing's happened. We try to pretend we are not here. We make believe we are just by ourselves, some place else, and it doesn't seem to work. (*Kisses* BIRDIE's *hand*) Come now, Aunt Birdie, I'll walk you home. You and me. (*She takes* BIRDIE's *arm. They move slowly out.*)

BIRDIE (*softly as they exit*). You and me.

ADDIE (*after a minute*). Well. First time I ever heard Miss Birdie say a word. (HORACE *looks at her*) Maybe it's good for her. I'm just sorry Zan had to hear it. (HORACE *moves his head as if he were uncomfortable*) You feel bad, don't you? (*He shrugs.*)

HORACE. So you didn't want Zan to hear? It would be nice to let her stay innocent, like Birdie at her age. Let her listen now. Let her see everything. How else is she going to know that she's got to get away? I'm trying to show her that. I'm trying, but I've only got a little time left. She can even hate me when I'm dead, if she'll only learn to hate and fear this.

ADDIE. Mr. Horace—

HORACE. Pretty soon there'll be nobody to help her but you.

ADDIE (*crossing to him*). What can I do?

HORACE. Take her away.

ADDIE. How can I do that? Do you think they'd let me just go away with her?

HORACE. I'll fix it so they can't stop you when you're ready to go. You'll go, Addie?

ADDIE (*after a second, softly*). Yes, sir. I promise. (*He touches her arm, nods.*)

HORACE (*quietly*). I'm going to have Sol Fowler make me a new will. They'll make trouble, but you make Zan stand firm and Fowler'll do the rest. Addie, I'd like to leave you something for yourself. I always wanted to.

ADDIE (*laughs*). Don't you do that, Mr. Horace. A nigger woman in a white man's will! I'd never get it nohow.

HORACE. I know. But upstairs in the armoire drawer there's seventeen hundred dollar bills. It's money left from my trip. It's in an envelope with your name. It's for you.

ADDIE. Seventeen hundred dollar bills! My God, Mr. Horace, I won't know how to count up that high. (*Shyly*) It's mighty kind and good of you. I don't know what to say for thanks—

CAL (*appears in doorway*). I'm back. (*No answer*) I'm back.

ADDIE. So we see.

HORACE. Well?

CAL. Nothing. I just went down and spoke my piece. Just like you told me. I say, "Mr. Horace he thank you mightily for the safe box arriving in good shape and he say you come right after supper to his house and bring Mr. Attorney-at-law Sol Fowler with you." Then I wipe my hands on my coat. Every time I ever told a lie in my whole life, I wipe my hands right after. Can't help doing it. Well, while I'm wiping my hands, Mr. Leo jump up and say to me, "What box? What you talking about?"

HORACE (*smiles*). Did he?

CAL. And Mr. Leo say he got to leave a little early cause he got something to do. And then Mr. Manders say Mr. Leo should sit right down and finish up his work and stop acting like somebody made him Mr. President. So he sit down. Now, just like I told you, Mr. Manders was mighty surprised with the message because he knows right well he brought the box— (*Points to box, sighs*) But he took it all right. Some men take everything easy and some do not.

HORACE (*puts his head back, laughs*). Mr. Leo was telling the truth; he *has* got something to do. I hope Manders don't keep him too long. (*Outside there is the sound of voices.* CAL *exits.* ADDIE *crosses quickly to* HORACE, *puts basket on table, begins to wheel his chair toward the stairs. Sharply*) No. Leave me where I am.

ADDIE. But that's Miss Regina coming back.

HORACE (*nods, looking at door*). Go away, Addie.

ADDIE (*hesitates*). Mr. Horace. Don't talk no more today. You don't feel well and it won't do no good—

HORACE (*as he hears footsteps in the hall*). Go on. (*She looks at him for a second, then picks up her sewing from table and exits as* REGINA *comes in from hall.* HORACE's *chair is now so placed that he is in front of the table with the medicine.* REGINA *stands in the hall, shakes umbrella, stands it in the corner, takes off her cloak and throws it over the banister. She stares at* HORACE.)

REGINA (*as she takes off her gloves*). We had agreed that you were to stay in your part of this house and I in mine. This room is *my* part of the house. Please don't come down here again.

HORACE. I won't.

REGINA (*crosses toward bell-cord*). I'll get Cal to take you upstairs.

HORACE (*smiles*). Before you do I want to tell you that after all, we have invested our money in Hubbard Sons and Marshall, Cotton Manufacturers.

REGINA (*stops, turns, stares at him*). What are you talking about? You haven't seen Ben— When did you change your mind?

HORACE. I didn't change my mind. *I* didn't invest the money. (*Smiles*) It was invested for me.

REGINA (*angrily*). What—?

HORACE. I had eighty-eight thousand dollars' worth of Union Pacific bonds in that safe-deposit box. They are not there now. Go and look. (*As she stares at him, he points to the box*) Go and look, Regina. (*She crosses quickly to the box, opens it*) Those bonds are as negotiable as money.

REGINA (*turns back to him*). What kind of joke are you playing now? Is this for my benefit?

HORACE. I don't look in that box very often, but three days ago, on Wednesday it was, because I had made a decision—

REGINA. I want to know what you are talking about.

HORACE (*sharply*). Don't interrupt me again. Because I had made a decision, I sent for the box. The bonds were gone. Eighty-eight thousand dollars gone. (*He smiles at her.*)

REGINA (*after a moment's silence, quietly*). Do you think I'm crazy enough to believe what you're saying?

HORACE (*shrugs*). Believe anything you like.

REGINA (*stares at him, slowly*). Where did they go to?

HORACE. They are in Chicago. With Mr. Marshall, I should guess.

REGINA. What did they do? Walk to Chicago? Have you really gone crazy?

HORACE. Leo took the bonds.

REGINA (*turns sharply then speaks softly, without conviction*). I don't believe it.

HORACE (*leans forward*). I wasn't there but I can guess what happened. This fine gentleman, to whom you were willing to marry your daughter, took the keys and opened the box. You remember that the day of the fight Oscar went to Chicago? Well, he went with my bonds that his son Leo had stolen for him. (*Pleasantly*) And for Ben, of course, too.

REGINA (*slowly, nods*). When did you find out the bonds were gone?

HORACE. Wednesday night.

REGINA. I thought that's what you said. Why have you waited three days to do anything? (*Suddenly laughs*) This *will* make a fine story.

HORACE (*nods*). Couldn't it?

REGINA (*still laughing*). A fine story to hold over their heads. How could they be such fools? (*Turns to him.*)

HORACE. But I'm not going to hold it over their heads.

REGINA (*the laugh stops*). What?

HORACE (*turns his chair to face her*). I'm going to let them keep the bonds—as a loan from you. An eighty-eight-thousand-dollar loan; they should be grateful to you. They will be, I think.

REGINA (*slowly, smiles*). I see. You are punishing me. But I won't let you punish me. If you won't do anything, I will. Now. (*She starts for door.*)

HORACE. You won't do anything. Because you can't. (*REGINA stops*) It won't do you any good to make trouble because I shall simply say that I lent them the bonds.

REGINA (*slowly*). You would do that?

HORACE. Yes. For once in your life I am tying your hands. There is nothing for you to do. (*There is silence. Then she sits down.*)

REGINA. I see. You are going to lend them the bonds and let them keep all the profit they make on them, and there is nothing I can do about it. Is that right?

HORACE. Yes.

REGINA (*softly*). Why did you say that I was making this gift?

HORACE. I was coming to that. I am going to make a new will, Regina, leaving you eighty-eight thousand dollars in Union Pacific bonds. The rest will go to Zan. It's true that your brothers have borrowed your share for a little while. After my death I advise you to talk to Ben and Oscar. They won't admit anything and Ben, I think, will be smart enough to see that he's safe. Because I knew about the theft and said nothing. Nor will I say anything as long as I live. Is that clear to you?

REGINA (*nods, softly, without looking at him*). You will not say anything as long as you live.

HORACE. That's right. And by that time they will probably have replaced your bonds, and then they'll belong to you and nobody but us will ever know what happened. (*Stops, smiles*) They'll be around any minute to see what I am going to do. I took good care to see that word reached Leo. They'll be mighty relieved to know I'm going to do nothing and Ben will think it all a capital joke on you. And that will be the end of that. There's nothing you can do to them, nothing you can do to me.

REGINA. You hate me very much.

HORACE. No.

REGINA. Oh, I think you do. (*Puts her head back, sighs*) Well, we haven't been very good together. Anyway, I don't hate you either. I have only contempt for you. I've always had.

HORACE. From the very first?

REGINA. I think so.

HORACE. I was in love with *you*. But why did *you* marry *me*?

REGINA. I was lonely when I was young.

HORACE. *You* were lonely?

REGINA. Not the way people usually mean. Lonely for all

the things I wasn't going to get. Everybody in this house was so busy and there was so little place for what I wanted. I wanted the world. Then, and then— (*Smiles*) Papa died and left the money to Ben and Oscar.

HORACE. And you married me?

REGINA. Yes, I thought— But I was wrong. You were a small-town clerk then. You haven't changed.

HORACE (*nods, smiles*). And that wasn't what you wanted.

REGINA. No. No, it wasn't what I wanted. (*Pauses, leans back, pleasantly*) It took me a little while to find out I had made a mistake. As for you—I don't know. It was almost as if I couldn't stand the kind of man you were— (*Smiles, softly*) I used to lie there at night, praying you wouldn't come near—

HORACE. Really? It was as bad as that?

REGINA (*nods*). Remember when I went to Doctor Sloan and I told you he said there was something the matter with me and that you shouldn't touch me any more?

HORACE. I remember.

REGINA. But you believed it. I couldn't understand that. I couldn't understand that anybody could be such a soft fool. That was when I began to despise you.

HORACE (*puts his hand to his throat, looks at the bottle of medicine on table*). Why didn't you leave me?

REGINA. I told you I married you for something. It turned out it was only for this. (*Carefully*) This wasn't what I wanted, but it was something. I never thought about it much but if I had (HORACE *puts his hand to his throat*) I'd have known that you would die before I would. But I couldn't have known that you would get heart trouble so early and so bad. I'm lucky, Horace. I've always been lucky. (HORACE *turns slowly to the medicine*) I'll be lucky again. (HORACE *looks at her. Then he puts his hand to his throat. Because he cannot reach the bottle he moves the chair closer. He reaches for the medicine, takes out the cork, picks up the spoon. The bottle slips and smashes on the table. He draws in his breath, gasps.*)

HORACE. Please. Tell Addie— The other bottle is upstairs. (REGINA *has not moved. She does not move now. He stares at her. Then, suddenly as if he understood, he raises his voice. It is a panic-stricken whisper, too small to be heard outside the room*) Addie! Addie! Come— (*Stops as he hears the softness of his voice. He makes a sudden, furious spring from the chair to the stairs, taking the first few steps as if he were a desperate runner. On the fourth step he slips, gasps, grasps the rail, makes a great effort to reach the landing. When he reaches the landing, he is on his knees. His knees give way, he falls on the landing, out of view.* REGINA *has not turned during his climb up the stairs. Now she waits a second. Then she goes below the landing, speaks up.*)

REGINA. Horace. Horace. (*When there is no answer, she turns, calls*) Addie! Cal! Come in here. (*She starts up the steps.* ADDIE *and* CAL *appear. Both run toward the stairs*) He's had an attack. Come up here. (*They run up the steps quickly.*)

CAL. My God. Mr. Horace—

(*They cannot be seen now.*)

REGINA (*her voice comes from the head of the stairs*). Be still, Cal. Bring him in here.

(*Before the footsteps and the voices have completely died away,* ALEXANDRA *appears in the hall door, in her rain-cloak and hood. She comes into the room, begins to unfasten the cloak, suddenly looks around, sees the empty wheel chair, stares, begins to move swiftly as if to look in the dining room. At the same moment* ADDIE *runs down the stairs.* ALEXANDRA *turns and stares up at* ADDIE.)

ALEXANDRA. Addie! What?

ADDIE (*takes* ALEXANDRA *by the shoulders*). I'm going for

the doctor. Go upstairs. (ALEXANDRA *looks at her, then quickly breaks away and runs up the steps.* ADDIE *exits. The stage is empty for a minute. Then the front door bell begins to ring. When there is no answer, it rings again. A second later* LEO *appears in the hall, talking as he comes in.*)

LEO (*very nervous*). Hello. (*Irritably*) Never saw any use ringing a bell when a door was open. If you are going to ring a bell, then somebody should answer it. (*Gets in the room, looks around, puzzled, listens, hears no sound*) Aunt Regina. (*He moves around restlessly*) Addie. (*Waits*) Where the hell— (*Crosses to the bell cord, rings it impatiently, waits, gets no answer, calls*) Cal! Cal! (CAL *appears on the stair landing.*)

CAL (*his voice is soft, shaken*). Mr. Leo. Miss Regina says you stop that screaming noise.

LEO (*angrily*). Where is everybody?

CAL. Mr. Horace he got an attack. He's bad. Miss Regina says you stop that noise.

LEO. Uncle Horace— What— What happened? (CAL *starts down the stairs, shakes his head, begins to move swiftly off.* LEO *looks around wildly*) But when— You seen Mr. Oscar or Mr. Ben? (CAL *shakes his head. Moves on.* LEO *grabs him by the arm*) Answer me, will you?

CAL. No, I ain't seen 'em. I ain't got time to answer you. I got to get things. (CAL *runs off.*)

LEO. But what's the matter with him? When did this happen— (*Calling after* CAL) You'd think Papa'd be some place where you could find him. I been chasing him all afternoon.

(OSCAR *and* BEN *come quickly into the room.*)

LEO. Papa, I've been looking all over town for you and Uncle Ben—

BEN. Where is he?

OSCAR. Addie just told us it was a sudden attack, and—

BEN (*to* LEO). Where is he? When did it happen?

LEO. Upstairs. Will you listen to me, please? I been looking for you for—

OSCAR (*to* BEN). You think we should go up? (BEN, *looking up the steps, shakes his head.*)

BEN. I don't know. I don't know.

OSCAR (*shakes his head*). But he was all right—

LEO (*yelling*). *Will you listen to me?*

OSCAR (*sharply*). What is the matter with you?

LEO. I been trying to tell you. I been trying to find you for an hour—

OSCAR. Tell me what?

LEO. Uncle Horace knows about the bonds. He knows about them. He's had the box since Wednesday—

BEN (*sharply*). Stop shouting! What the hell are you talking about?

LEO (*furiously*). I'm telling you he knows about the bonds. Ain't that clear enough—

OSCAR (*grabbing* LEO's *arm*). You God-damn fool! Stop screaming!

BEN. Now what happened? Talk quietly.

LEO. You heard me. Uncle Horace knows about the bonds. He's known since Wednesday.

BEN (*after a second*). How do you know that?

LEO. Because Cal comes down to Manders and says the box came O.K. and—

OSCAR (*trembling*). That might not mean a thing—

LEO (*angrily*). No? It might not, huh? Then he says Manders should come here tonight and bring Sol Fowler with him. I guess that don't mean a thing either.

OSCAR (*to* BEN). Ben— What— Do you think he's seen the—

BEN (*motions to the box*). There's the box. (*Both* OSCAR *and* LEO *turn sharply.* LEO *makes a leap to the box*) You ass. Put it down. What are you going to do with it, eat it?

LEO. I'm going to— (*Starts.*)

BEN (*furiously*). Put it down. Don't touch it again. Now sit down and shut up for a minute.

OSCAR. Since Wednesday. (*To* LEO) You said he had it since Wednesday. Why didn't he say something— (*To* BEN) I don't understand—

LEO (*taking a step*). I can put it back. I can put it back before anybody knows.

BEN (*who is standing at the table, softly*). He's had it since Wednesday. Yet he hasn't said a word to us.

OSCAR. *Why? Why?*

LEO. What's the difference why? He was getting ready to say plenty. He was going to say it to Fowler tonight—

OSCAR (*angrily*). Be still. (*Turns to* BEN, *looks at him, waits.*)

BEN (*after a minute*). I don't believe that.

LEO (*wildly*). *You* don't believe it? What do I care what *you* believe? I do the dirty work and then—

BEN (*turning his head sharply to* LEO). I'm remembering that. I'm remembering that, Leo.

OSCAR. What do you mean?

LEO. You—

BEN (*to* OSCAR). If you don't shut that little fool up, I'll show you what I mean. For some reason he knows, but he don't say a word.

OSCAR. Maybe he didn't know that *we*—

BEN (*quickly*). That *Leo*— He's no fool. Does Manders know the bonds are missing?

LEO. How could I tell? I was half crazy. I don't think so. Because Manders seemed kind of puzzled and—

OSCAR. But we got to find out— (*He breaks off as* CAL *comes into the room carrying a kettle of hot water.*)

BEN. How is he, Cal?

CAL. I don't know, Mr. Ben. He was bad. (*Going toward stairs.*)

OSCAR. But when did it happen?

CAL (*shrugs*). He wasn't feeling bad early. (ADDIE *comes in quickly from the hall*) Then there he is next thing on the landing, fallen over, his eyes tight—

ADDIE (*to* CAL). Dr. Sloan's over at the Ballongs. Hitch the buggy and go get him. (*She takes the kettle and cloths from him, pushes him, runs up the stairs*) Go on. (*She disappears.* CAL *exits.*)

BEN. Never seen Sloan anywhere when you need him.

OSCAR (*softly*). Sounds bad.

LEO. He would have told *her* about it. Aunt Regina. He would have told his own wife—

BEN (*turning to* LEO). Yes, he might have told her. But they weren't on such pretty terms and maybe he didn't. Maybe he didn't. (*Goes quickly to* LEO) Now, listen to me. If she doesn't know, it may work out all right. If she does know, you're to say he lent you the bonds.

LEO. Lent them to me! Who's going to believe that?

BEN. Nobody.

OSCAR (*to* LEO). Don't you understand? It can't do no harm to say it—

LEO. Why should I say he lent them to me? Why not to you? (*Carefully*) Why not to Uncle Ben?

BEN (*smiles*). Just because he didn't lend them to me. Remember that.

LEO. But all he has to do is say he didn't lend them to me—

BEN (*furiously*). But for some reason, he doesn't seem to be talking, does he?

(*There are footsteps above. They all stand looking at the stairs.* REGINA *begins to come slowly down.*)

BEN. What happened?

REGINA. He's had a bad attack.

OSCAR. Too bad. I'm sorry we weren't here when—when Horace needed us.

BEN. When *you* needed us.

REGINA (*looks at him*). Yes.

BEN. How is he? Can we—can we go up?

REGINA (*shakes her head*). He's not conscious.

OSCAR (*pacing around*). It's that—it's that bad? Wouldn't you think Sloan could be found quickly, just once, just once?

REGINA. I don't think there is much for him to do.

BEN. Oh, don't talk like that. He's come through attacks before. He will now.

(REGINA *sits down. After a second she speaks softly.*)

REGINA. Well. We haven't seen each other since the day of our fight.

BEN (*tenderly*). That was nothing. Why, you and Oscar and I used to fight when we were kids.

OSCAR (*hurriedly*). Don't you think we should go up? Is there anything we can do for Horace—

BEN. You don't feel well. Ah—

REGINA (*without looking at them*). No, I don't. (*Slight pause*) Horace told me about the bonds this afternoon. (*There is an immediate shocked silence.*)

LEO. The bonds. What do you mean? What bonds? What—

BEN (*looks at him furiously. Then to* REGINA). The Union Pacific bonds? *Horace's* Union Pacific bonds?

REGINA. Yes.

OSCAR (*steps to her, very nervously*). Well. Well what— what about them? What—what could he say?

REGINA. He said that Leo had stolen the bonds and given them to you.

OSCAR (*aghast, very loudly*). That's ridiculous, Regina, absolutely—

LEO. I don't know what you're talking about. What would I— Why—

REGINA (*wearily to* BEN). Isn't it enough that he stole them from me? Do I have to listen to this in the bargain?

OSCAR. You are talking—

LEO. I didn't steal anything. I don't know why—

REGINA (*to* BEN). Would you ask them to stop that, please? (*There is silence for a minute.* BEN *glowers at* OSCAR *and* LEO.)

BEN. Aren't we starting at the wrong end, Regina? What did Horace tell you?

REGINA (*smiles at him*). He told me that Leo had stolen the bonds.

LEO. I didn't steal—

REGINA. Please. Let me finish. Then he told me that he was going to pretend that he had lent them to you (LEO *turns sharply to* REGINA, *then looks at* OSCAR, *then looks back at* REGINA) as a present from me—to my brothers. He said there was nothing I could do about it. He said the rest of his money would go to Alexandra. That is all. (*There is a silence.* OSCAR *coughs,* LEO *smiles slyly.*)

LEO (*taking a step to her*). I told you he had lent them— I could have told you—

REGINA (*ignores him, smiles sadly at* BEN). So I'm very badly off, you see. (*Carefully*) But Horace said there was nothing I could do about it as long as he was alive to say he had lent you the bonds.

BEN. You shouldn't feel that way. It can all be explained, all be adjusted. It isn't as bad—

REGINA. So you, at least, are willing to admit that the bonds were stolen?

BEN (OSCAR *laughs nervously*). I admit no such thing. It's possible that Horace made up that part of the story to tease you— (*Looks at her*) Or perhaps to punish you. Punish you.

REGINA (*sadly*). It's not a pleasant story. I feel bad, Ben, naturally. I hadn't thought—

BEN. Now you shall have the bonds safely back. That was the understanding, wasn't it, Oscar?

OSCAR. Yes.

REGINA. I'm glad to know that. (*Smiles*) Ah, I had greater hopes—

BEN. Don't talk that way. That's foolish. (*Looks at his watch*) I think we ought to drive out for Sloan ourselves. If we can't find him we'll go over to Senateville for Doctor Morris. And don't think I'm dismissing this other business. I'm not. We'll have it all out on a more appropriate day.

REGINA (*looks up, quietly*). I don't think you had better go yet. I think you had better stay and sit down.

BEN. We'll be back with Sloan.

REGINA. Cal has gone for him. I don't want you to go.

BEN. Now don't worry and—

REGINA. You will come back in this room and sit down. I have something more to say.

BEN (*turns, comes toward her*). Since when do I take orders from you?

REGINA (*smiles*). You don't—yet. (*Sharply*) Come back, Oscar. You too, Leo.

OSCAR (*sure of himself, laughs*). My dear Regina—

BEN (*softly, pats her hand*). Horace has already clipped your wings and very wittily. Do I have to clip them, too? (*Smiles at her*) You'd get farther with a smile, Regina. I'm a soft man for a woman's smile.

REGINA. I'm smiling, Ben. I'm smiling because you are quite safe while Horace lives. But I don't think Horace will live. And if he doesn't live I shall want seventy-five per cent in exchange for the bonds.

BEN (*steps back, whistles, laughs*). Greedy! What a greedy girl you are! You want so much of everything.

REGINA. Yes. And if I don't get what I want I am going to put all three of you in jail.

OSCAR (*furiously*). You're mighty crazy. Having just admitted—

BEN. And on what evidence would you put Oscar and Leo in jail?

REGINA (*laughs, gaily*). Oscar, listen to him. He's getting ready to swear that it was you and Leo! What do you say to that? (OSCAR *turns furiously toward* BEN) Oh, don't be angry, Oscar. I'm going to see that he goes in with you.

BEN. Try anything you like, Regina. (*Sharply*) And now we can stop all this and say good-bye to you. (ALEXANDRA *comes slowly down the steps*) It's his money and he's obviously willing to let us borrow it. (*More pleasantly*) Learn to make threats when you can carry them through. For how many years have I told you a good-looking woman gets more by being soft and appealing? Mama used to tell you that. (*Looks at his watch*) Where the hell is Sloan? (*To* OSCAR) Take the buggy and— (*As* BEN *turns to* OSCAR, *he sees* ALEXANDRA. *She walks stiffly. She goes slowly to the lower window, her head bent. They all turn to look at her.*)

OSCAR (*after a second, moving toward her*). What? Alexandra— (*She does not answer. After a second,* ADDIE *comes slowly down the stairs, moving as if she were very tired. At foot of steps, she looks at* ALEXANDRA, *then turns and slowly crosses to door and exits.* REGINA *rises.* BEN *looks nervously at* ALEXANDRA, *at* REGINA.)

OSCAR (*as* ADDIE *passes him, irritably to* ALEXANDRA). Well, what is— (*Turns into room—sees* ADDIE *at foot of steps*) —what's? (BEN *puts up a hand, shakes his head*) My God, I didn't know—who *could* have known—I didn't know he was that sick. Well, well—I— (REGINA *stands quietly, her back to them.*)

BEN (*softly, sincerely*). Seems like yesterday when he first came here.

OSCAR (*sincerely, nervously*). Yes, that's true. (*Turns to* BEN) The whole town loved him and respected him.

ALEXANDRA (*turns*). Did you love him, Uncle Oscar?

OSCAR. Certainly, I— What a strange thing to ask! I—

ALEXANDRA. Did you love him, Uncle Ben?

BEN (*simply*). He had—

ALEXANDRA (*suddenly starts to laugh very loudly*). And you, Mama, did you love him, too?

REGINA. I know what you feel, Alexandra, but please try to control yourself.

ALEXANDRA (*still laughing*). I'm trying, Mama. I'm trying very hard.

BEN. Grief makes some people laugh and some people cry. It's better to cry, Alexandra.

ALEXANDRA (*the laugh has stopped. Tensely moves toward* REGINA). What was Papa doing on the staircase?

(BEN *turns to look at* ALEXANDRA.)

REGINA. Please go and lie down, my dear. We all need time to get over shocks like this. (ALEXANDRA *does not move.* REGINA's *voice becomes softer, more insistent*) Please go, Alexandra.

ALEXANDRA. No, Mama. I'll wait. I've got to talk to you.

REGINA. Later. Go and rest now.

ALEXANDRA (*quietly*). I'll wait, Mama. I've plenty of time.

REGINA (*hesitates, stares, makes a half shrug, turns back to* BEN). As I was saying. Tomorrow morning I am going up to Judge Simmes. I shall tell him about Leo.

BEN (*motioning toward* ALEXANDRA). Not in front of the child, Regina. I—

REGINA (*turns to him. Sharply*). I didn't ask her to stay. Tomorrow morning I go to Judge Simmes—

OSCAR. And what proof? What proof of all this—

REGINA (*turns sharply*). None. I won't need any. The bonds are missing and they are with Marshall. That will be enough. If it isn't, I'll add what's necessary.

BEN. I'm sure of that.

REGINA (*turns to* BEN). You can be quite sure.

OSCAR. We'll deny—

REGINA. Deny your heads off. You couldn't find a jury that wouldn't weep for a woman whose brothers steal from her. And you couldn't find twelve men in this state you haven't cheated and who hate you for it.

OSCAR. What kind of talk is this? You couldn't do anything like that! We're your own brothers. (*Points upstairs*) How can you talk that way when upstairs not five minutes ago—

REGINA (*slowly*). There are people who can't go back, who must finish what they start. I am one of those people, Oscar. (*After a slight pause*) Where was I? (*Smiles at* BEN) Well, they'll convict you. But I won't care much if they don't. (*Leans forward, pleasantly*) Because by that time you'll be ruined. I shall also tell my story to Mr. Marshall, who likes me, I think, and who will not want to be involved in your scandal. A respectable firm like Marshall and Company. The deal would be off in an hour. (*Turns to them angrily*) And you know it. Now I don't want to hear any more from any of you. *You'll do no more bargaining in this house.* I'll take my seventy-five per cent and we'll forget the story forever. That's one way of doing it, and the way I prefer. You know me well enough to know that I don't mind taking the other way.

BEN (*after a second, slowly*). None of us has ever known you well enough, Regina.

REGINA. You're getting old, Ben. Your tricks aren't as smart as they used to be. (*There is no answer. She waits, then smiles*) All right. I take it that's settled and I get what I asked for.

OSCAR (*furiously to* BEN). Are you going to let her do this—

BEN (*turns to look at him, slowly*). You have a suggestion?

REGINA (*puts her arms above her head, stretches, laughs*). No, he hasn't. All right. Now, Leo, I have forgotten that you ever saw the bonds. (*Archly, to* BEN *and* OSCAR) And as long as you boys both behave yourselves, I've forgotten that we ever talked about them. You can draw up the necessary papers tomorrow. (BEN *laughs.* LEO *stares at him, starts for door. Exits.* OSCAR *moves toward door angrily.* REGINA *looks at* BEN, *nods, laughs with him. For a second,* OSCAR *stands in the door, looking back at them. Then he exits.*)

REGINA. You're a good loser, Ben. I like that.

BEN (*he picks up his coat, then turns to her*). Well, I say to myself, what's the good? You and I aren't like Oscar. We're not sour people. I think that comes from a good digestion. Then, too, one loses today and wins tomorrow. I say to myself, years of planning and I get what I want. Then I don't get it. But I'm not discouraged. The century's turning, the world is open. Open for people like you and me. Ready for us, waiting for us. After all this is just the beginning. There are hundreds of Hubbards sitting in rooms like this throughout the country. All their names aren't Hubbard, but they are all Hubbards and they will own this country some day. We'll get along.

REGINA (*smiles*). I think so.

BEN. Then, too, I say to myself, things may change. (*Looks at* ALEXANDRA) I agree with Alexandra. What is a man in a wheel chair doing on a staircase? I ask myself that.

REGINA (*looks up at him*). And what do you answer?

BEN. I have no answer. But maybe some day I will. Maybe never, but maybe some day. (*Smiles. Pats her arm*) When I do, I'll let you know. (*Goes toward hall.*)

REGINA. When you do, write me. I will be in Chicago. (*Gaily*) Ah, Ben, if Papa had only left me his money.

BEN. I'll see you tomorrow.

REGINA. Oh, yes. Certainly. You'll be sort of working for me now.

BEN (*as he passes* ALEXANDRA, *smiles*). Alexandra, you're turning out to be a right interesting girl. (*Looks at* REGINA) Well, good night all. (*He exits.*)

REGINA (*Sits quietly for a second, stretches, turns to look at* ALEXANDRA). What do you want to talk to me about, Alexandra?

ALEXANDRA (*slowly*). I've changed my mind. I don't want to talk. There's nothing to talk about now.

REGINA. You're acting very strange. Not like yourself. You've had a bad shock today. I know that. And you loved Papa, but you must have expected this to come some day. You knew how sick he was.

ALEXANDRA. I knew. We all knew.

REGINA. It will be good for you to get away from here. Good for me, too. Time heals most wounds, Alexandra. You're young, you shall have all the things I wanted. I'll make the world for you the way I wanted it to be for me. (*Uncomfortably*) Don't sit there staring. You've been around Birdie so much you're getting just like her.

ALEXANDRA (*nods*). Funny. That's what Aunt Birdie said today.

REGINA (*nods*). Be good for you to get away from all this. (ADDIE *enters.*)

ADDIE. Cal is back, Miss Regina. He says Dr. Sloan will be coming in a few minutes.

REGINA. We'll go in a few weeks. A few weeks! That means two or three Saturdays, two or three Sundays. (*Sighs*) Well, I'm very tired. I shall go to bed. I don't want any supper. Put the lights out and lock up. (ADDIE *moves to the piano lamp, turns it out*) You go to your room, Alexandra. Addie will bring you something hot. You look very tired. (*Rises. To* ADDIE) Call me when Dr. Sloan gets here. I don't want to see anybody else. I don't want any condolence calls tonight. The whole town will be over.

ALEXANDRA. Mama, I'm not coming with you. I'm not going to Chicago.

REGINA (*turns to her*). You're very upset, Alexandra.

ALEXANDRA (*quietly*). I mean what I say. With all my heart.

REGINA. We'll talk about it tomorrow. The morning will make a difference.

ALEXANDRA. It won't make any difference. And there isn't anything to talk about. I am going away from you. Because I want to. Because I know Papa would want me to.

REGINA (*puzzled, careful, polite*). You *know* your papa wanted you to go away from me?

ALEXANDRA. Yes.

REGINA (*softly*). And if I say no?

ALEXANDRA (*looks at her*). Say it Mama, say it. And see what happens.

REGINA (*softly, after a pause*). And if I make you stay?

ALEXANDRA. That would be foolish. It wouldn't work in the end.

REGINA. You're very serious about it, aren't you? (*Crosses to stairs*) Well, you'll change your mind in a few days.

ALEXANDRA. You only change your mind when you want to. And I won't want to.

REGINA (*going up the steps*). Alexandra, I've come to the end of my rope. Somewhere there has to be what I want, too. Life goes too fast. Do what you want; think what you want; go where you want. I'd like to keep you with me, but I won't make you stay. Too many people used to make me do too many things. No, I won't make you stay.

ALEXANDRA. You couldn't, Mama, because I want to leave here. As I've never wanted anything in my life before. Because now I understand what Papa was trying to tell me. (*Pause*) All in one day: Addie said there were people who ate the earth and other people who stood around and watched them do it. And just now Uncle Ben said the same thing. Really, he said the same thing (*Tensely*) Well, tell him for me, Mama, I'm not going to stand around and watch you do it. Tell him I'll be fighting as hard as he'll be fighting (*Rises*) some place where people don't just stand around and watch.

REGINA. Well, you have spirit, after all. I used to think

you were all sugar water. We don't have to be bad friends. I don't want us to be bad friends, Alexandra. (*Starts, stops, turns to* ALEXANDRA) Would you like to come and talk to me, Alexandra? Would you—would you like to sleep in my room tonight?

ALEXANDRA (*takes a step toward her*) Are you afraid, Mama? (REGINA *does not answer. She moves slowly out of sight.* ADDIE *comes to* ALEXANDRA, *presses her arm.*)

The Curtain Falls

WATCH ON THE RHINE

FOR

HERMAN SHUMLIN

THANKS AND AFFECTION

Watch on the Rhine was first produced at the Martin Beck Theatre, New York City, on April 1, 1941, with the following cast:

(In the order of their appearance)

ANISE	EDA HEINEMANN
JOSEPH	FRANK WILSON
FANNY FARRELLY	LUCILE WATSON
DAVID FARRELLY	JOHN LODGE
MARTHE DE BRANCOVIS	HELEN TRENHOLME
TECK DE BRANCOVIS	GEORGE COULOURIS
SARA MÜLLER	MADY CHRISTIANS
JOSHUA MÜLLER	PETER FERNANDEZ
BODO MÜLLER	ERIC ROBERTS
BABETTE MÜLLER	ANNE BLYTH
KURT MÜLLER	PAUL LUKAS

Produced and staged by HERMAN SHUMLIN

Setting designed by JO MIELZINER

Costumes designed by HELENE PONS

SCENE

The scene of the play is the living room of the Farrelly country house, about twenty miles from Washington. The time is late spring, 1940.

ACT ONE

Early on a Wednesday morning.

ACT TWO

Ten days later.

ACT THREE

A half hour later.

ACT ONE

SCENE: *The living room of the Farrelly house, about twenty miles from Washington, D. C., on a warm spring morning.*

Center stage are large French doors leading to an elevated open terrace. On the terrace are chairs, tables, a large table for dining. Some of this furniture we can see; most of it is on the left side of the terrace, beyond our sight. Left stage is an arched entrance, leading to the oval reception hall. We can see the main staircase as it goes off to the back of the hall. Right stage is a door leading to a library. The Farrelly house was built in the early nineteenth century. It has space, simplicity, style. The living room is large. Up stage right is a piano; down stage left, a couch; down stage right, a couch and chairs; up stage a few smaller chairs. Four or five generations have furnished this room and they have all been people of taste. There are no styles, no periods; the room has never been refurnished. Each careless aristocrat has thrown into the room what he or she liked as a child, what he or she brought home when grown up. Therefore the furniture is of many periods: the desk is English, the couch is Victorian, some of the pictures are modern, some of the ornaments French. The room has too many things in it: vases, clocks, miniatures, boxes, china animals. On the right wall is a large portrait of a big kind-faced man in an evening suit of 1900. On another wall is a large, very ugly landscape. The room is crowded. But it is cool and clean and its fabrics and woods are in soft colors.

AT RISE: ANISE, *a thin Frenchwoman of about sixty, in a dark housekeeper's dress, is standing at a table sorting mail. She takes the mail from a small basket, holds each letter to the light, reads each postal card, then places them in piles. On the terrace,* JOSEPH, *a tall, middle-aged Negro butler, wheels a breakfast wagon. As he appears,* FANNY FARRELLY *comes in from the hall. She is a handsome woman of about sixty-three. She has on a fancy, good-looking dressing-gown.*
Left and right are the audience's left and right.

FANNY (*stops to watch* ANISE. *Sees* JOSEPH *moving about on terrace. Calls*). Joseph! (*To* ANISE) Morning.

ANISE (*continues examining mail*). Good morning, Madame.

JOSEPH (*comes to terrace door*). Yes'm?

FANNY. Everybody down?

JOSEPH. No'm. Nobody. I'll get your tea. (*He returns to breakfast wagon on terrace.*)

FANNY. Mr. David isn't down yet? But he knows he is to meet the train.

JOSEPH (*comes in from the terrace with the cup of tea*). He's got plenty of time, Miss Fanny. The train ain't in till noon.

FANNY. Breakfast is at nine o'clock in this house and will be until the day after I die. Ring the bell.

JOSEPH. It ain't nine yet, Miss Fanny. It's eight-thirty.

FANNY. Well, put the clocks up to nine and ring the bell.

JOSEPH. Mr. David told me not to ring it any more. He says it's got too mean a ring, that bell. It disturbs folks.

FANNY. That's what it was put there for. I like to disturb folks.

JOSEPH. Yes'm.

FANNY. You slept well, Anise. You were asleep before I could dismantle myself.

ANISE. I woke several times during the night.

FANNY. Did you? Then you were careful not to stop snoring. We must finally get around to rearranging your room. (ANISE *hands her three or four letters*) Even when you don't snore, it irritates me. (FANNY *opens a letter, begins to read it. After a minute*) What time is it?

ANISE. It is about eight-thirty. Joseph just told you.

FANNY. I didn't hear him. I'm nervous. Naturally. My mail looks dull. (*Reading the letter*) Jenny always tell you a piece of gossip three times, as if it grew fresher with the telling. Did you put flowers in their rooms?

ANISE. Certainly.

FANNY. David ought to get to the station by eleven-thirty.

ANISE (*patiently*). The train does not draw in until ten minutes past noon.

FANNY. But it might come in early. It's been known.

ANISE. Never. Not in the Union Station in Washington, the District of Columbia.

FANNY (*irritably*). But it might. It might. Don't argue with me about everything. What time is it?

ANISE. It's now twenty-seven minutes before nine. It will be impossible to continue telling you the time every three minutes from now until Miss Sara arrives. I think you are having a nervous breakdown. Compose yourself.

FANNY. It's been twenty years. Any mother would be nervous. If your daughter were coming home and you hadn't seen her, and a husband, *and* grandchildren—

ANISE. I do not say that it is wrong to be nervous. I, too, am nervous. I say only that you are.

FANNY. Very well. I heard you. *I* say that I am. (*She goes back to reading her letter. Looks up*) Jenny's still in California. She's lost her lavallière again. Birdie Chase's daughter is still faire l'amouring with that actor. Tawdry, Jenny says it is. An actor. Fashions in sin change. In my day, it was Englishmen. I don't understand infidelity. If you love a man, then why? If you don't love him, then why stay with him? (*Without turning, she points over her head to Joshua Farrelly's portrait)* Thank God, I was in love. I thought about Joshua last night. Three grandchildren. He would have liked that. I hope I will. (*Points to other letters*) Anything in anybody else's mail?

ANISE. Advertisements for Mr. David and legal things. For our Count and Countess, there is nothing but what seems an invitation to a lower-class embassy tea and letters asking for bills to get paid.

FANNY. That's every morning. (*Thoughtfully*) In the six weeks the Balkan nobility have been with us, they seem to have run up a great many bills.

ANISE. Yes. *I* told you that. Then there was a night-letter for Mr. David.

(*A very loud, very unpleasant bell begins to ring.*)

FANNY (*through the noise*). Really? From whom?

ANISE. From her. I took it on the telephone, and—

(*Bell drowns out her voice.*)

FANNY. Who is "her"? (*Bell becomes very loud*) Go tell him to stop that noise—

ANISE (*goes toward terrace, calling*). Joseph! Stop that bell. Miss Fanny says to stop it.

JOSEPH (*calls*). Miss Fanny said to start it.

FANNY (*shouts out to him*). I didn't tell you to hang yourself with it.

JOSEPH (*appears on terrace*). I ain't hung. Your breakfast is ready. (*Disappears.*)

FANNY (*to* ANISE). Who is "her"?

ANISE. That Carter woman from Lansing, Michigan.

FANNY. Oh, my. Is she back in Washington again? What did the telegram say?

ANISE. It said the long sickness of her dear Papa had terminated in full recovery.

FANNY. That's too bad.

ANISE. She was returning, and would Mr. David come for dinner a week from Thursday? "Love," it said, "to you and your charming mother." (*To* FANNY) That's you. I think Miss Carter from Lansing, Michigan, was unwise in attending the illness of her Papa.

FANNY. I hope so. Why?

ANISE (*shrugs*). There is much winking of the eyes going on between our Countess and Mr. David.

FANNY (*eagerly*). I know that. Anything new happen?

ANISE (*too innocently*). Happen? I don't know what you mean?

FANNY. You know damn well what I mean.

ANISE. *That?* Oh, no, I don't think that.

JOSEPH (*appears in the door*). The sausage cakes is shrinking.

FANNY (*rises. To* ANISE). I want everybody down here immediately. Is the car ready? (ANISE *nods*) Did you order a good dinner? (*Shrieks*) David! Oh.

(DAVID FARRELLY, *a pleasant-looking man of thirty-nine, comes in from the entrance hall, almost bumps into* FANNY.)

DAVID. Good morning, everybody.

ANISE (*to* FANNY). Everything is excellent. You have been asking the same questions for a week. You have made the kitchen very nervous.

DAVID (*to* JOSEPH). Why did you ring that air-raid alarm again?

JOSEPH. Ain't me, Mr. David. I don't like no noise. Miss Fanny told me.

FANNY. Good morning, David.

DAVID (*to* JOSEPH). Tell Fred to leave the car. I'll drive to the station.

JOSEPH (*nods*). Yes, sir. (*Exits.*)

DAVID (*to* FANNY, *half amused, half annoyed, as he begins to read his mail*). Mama, I think we'll fix up the chicken-house for you as a playroom. We'll hang the room with bells and you can go into your second childhood in the proper privacy.

FANNY. I find it very interesting. You sleep soundly, you rise at your usual hour—although your sister, whom you haven't seen in years, is waiting at the station—

DAVID. She is not waiting at the station. (*Laughs*) The train does not come in until ten minutes past twelve.

FANNY (*airily*). It's almost that now.

ANISE (*turns to look at her*). Really, Miss Fanny, contain yourself. It is twenty minutes before nine.

DAVID. And I have *not* slept soundly. And I've been up since six o'clock.

FANNY. The Balkans aren't down yet. Where are they?

DAVID. I don't know.

ANISE. There's nothing in your mail, Mr. David. Only the usual advertisements.

DAVID. And for me, that is all that is ever likely to come—here.

ANISE (*haughtily, as she starts toward hall*). I cannot, of course, speak for Miss Fanny. *I* have never opened a letter in my life.

DAVID. I know. You don't have to. For you they fly open.

FANNY (*giggles*). It's true. You're a snooper, Anise. (ANISE *exits.* FANNY *talks as* ANISE *moves out*) I rather admire it. It shows an interest in life. (*She looks up at Joshua's portrait*) You know, I've been lying awake most of the night wondering what Papa would have thought about Sara. He'd have been very pleased, wouldn't he? I always find myself wondering what Joshua would have felt.

DAVID. Yes. But maybe it would be just as well if you didn't expect me to be wondering about it, too. I wasn't married to him, Mama. He was just my father.

FANNY. My. You got up on the wrong side of the bed. (*She moves past him. Points to the mail which he is still opening*) The bills are for our noble guests. Interesting, how many there are every morning. How much longer are they going to be with us?

DAVID (*without looking at her*). I don't know.

FANNY. It's been six weeks. Now that Sara and her family are coming, even this house might be a little crowded— (*He looks up at her. Quickly*) Yes. I know I invited them. I felt sorry for Marthe, and Teck rather amused me. He plays good cribbage, and he tells good jokes. But that's not enough for a lifetime guest. If you've been urging her to stay, I wish you'd stop it. They haven't any money; all right, lend them some—

DAVID. I have been urging them to stay?

FANNY. I'm not so old I don't recognize flirting when I see it.

DAVID. But you're old enough not to be silly.

FANNY. I'm not silly. I'm charming.

(MARTHE DE BRANCOVIS, *an attractive woman of thirty-one or thirty-two, enters.*)

MARTHE. Good morning, Fanny. Morning, David.

FANNY. Good morning, Marthe.

DAVID (*warmly*). Good morning.

MARTHE. Fanny, darling, couldn't you persuade yourself to let me have a tray in bed and some cotton for my ears?

DAVID. Certainly not. My father ate breakfast at nine; and whatever my father did . . .

FANNY (*carefully, to* DAVID). There was a night-letter for you from that Carter woman in Lansing, Michigan. She is returning and you are to come to dinner next Thursday. (*As she exits on terrace*) C-A-R-T-E-R. (*Pronounces it carefully*) Lansing, Michigan.

DAVID (*laughs*). I know how to spell Carter, but thank you. (FANNY *exits.* DAVID *looks up at* MARTHE) Do you understand my mother?

MARTHE. Sometimes.

DAVID. Miss Carter was done for your benefit.

MARTHE (*smiles*). That means she has guessed that I would be jealous. And she has guessed right.

DAVID (*looks at her*). Jealous?

MARTHE. I know I've no right to be, but I am. And Fanny knows it.

DAVID (*carelessly*). Don't pay any attention to Mama. She has a sure instinct for the women I like, and she begins to hammer away early. Marthe— (*Goes to decanter on side-table*) I'm going to have a drink. I haven't had a drink before breakfast since the day I took my bar examination. (*Pours himself a drink, gulps it down*) What's it going to be like to stand on a station platform and see your sister after all these years? I'm afraid, I guess.

MARTHE. Why?

DAVID. I don't know. Afraid she won't like me— (*Shrugs*) We were very fond of each other, but it's been a long time.

MARTHE. I remember Sara. Mama brought me one day when your father was stationed in Paris. I was about six and Sara about fifteen and you were—

DAVID. You were a pretty little girl.

MARTHE. Do you really remember me? You never told me before.

FANNY (*yelling from the terrace*). David! Come to breakfast.

DAVID (*as if he had not been listening*). You know, I've never met Sara's husband. Mama did. I think the first day Sara met him, in Munich. Mama didn't like the marriage much in those days—and Sara didn't care, and Mama didn't like Sara not caring. Mama cut up about it, bad.

MARTHE. Why?

DAVID. Probably because they didn't let her arrange it. Why does Mama ever act badly? She doesn't remember ten minutes later.

MARTHE. Wasn't Mr. Müller poor?

DAVID. Oh, Mama wouldn't have minded that. If they'd

only come home and let her fix their lives for them— (*Smiles*) But Sara didn't want it that way.

MARTHE. You'll have a house full of refugees—us and—

DAVID. Are you and Teck refugees? I'm not sure I know what you're refugees from.

MARTHE. From Europe.

DAVID. From what Europe?

MARTHE (*smiles, shrugs*). I don't know. I don't know myself, really. Just Europe. (*Quickly, comes to him*) Sara will like you. I like you. (*Laughs*) That doesn't make sense, does it?

(*On her speech,* TECK DE BRANCOVIS *appears in the hall. He is a good-looking man of about forty-five. She stops quickly.*)

TECK (*to* MARTHE *and* DAVID). Good morning.

(*The bell gives an enormous ring.*)

DAVID (*goes to terrace*). Good morning, Teck. For years I've been thinking they were coming for Mama with a net. I'm giving up hope. I may try catching her myself. (*Disappears, calling*) Mama! Stop that noise.

TECK. I wonder if science has a name for women who enjoy noise? (*Goes to table, picks up his mail*) Many mistaken people, Marthe, seem to have given you many charge accounts.

MARTHE. The Countess de Brancovis. That still does it. It would be nice to be able to pay bills again—

TECK. Do not act as if I refused to pay them. I did not sleep well last night. I was worried. We have eighty-seven dollars in American Express checks. (*Pleasantly, looking at her*) That's all we have, Marthe.

MARTHE (*shrugs*). Maybe something will turn up. It's due.

TECK (*carefully*). David? (*Then, as she turns to look at him*) The other relatives will arrive this morning?

MARTHE. Yes.

TECK (*points to porch*). I think Madame Fanny and Mr

David may grow weary of accents and charity guests. Or is the husband of the sister a rich one?

MARTHE. No. He's poor. He had to leave Germany in '33.

TECK. A Jew?

MARTHE. No. I don't think so.

TECK. Why did he have to leave Germany?

MARTHE (*still reading*). Oh, I don't know, Teck. He's an anti-Nazi.

TECK. A political?

MARTHE. No, I don't think so. He was an engineer. I don't know. I don't know much about him.

TECK. Did you sleep well?

MARTHE. Yes. Why not?

TECK. Money does not worry you?

MARTHE. It worries me very much. But I just lie still now and hope. I'm glad to be here. (*Shrugs*) Maybe something good will happen. We've come to the end of a road. That's been true for a long time. Things will have to go one way or the other. Maybe they'll go well, for a change.

TECK. I have not come to the end of any road.

MARTHE (*looks at him*). No? I admire you.

TECK. I'm going into Washington tonight. Phili has a poker game every Wednesday evening. He has arranged for me to join it.

MARTHE (*after a pause*). Have you been seeing Phili?

TECK. Once or twice. Why not? Phili and I are old friends. He may be useful. I do not want to stay in this country forever.

MARTHE. You can't leave them alone. Your favorite dream, isn't it, Teck? That they will let you play with them again? I don't think they will, and I don't think you should be seeing Phili, or that you should be seen at the Embassy.

TECK (*smiles*). You have political convictions now?

MARTHE. I don't know what I have. I've never liked Nazis,

as you know, and you should have had enough of them. They seem to have had enough of you, God knows. It would be just as well to admit they are smarter than you are and let them alone.

TECK (*looking at her carefully, after a minute*). That is interesting.

MARTHE. What is interesting?

TECK. I think you are trying to say something to me. What is it?

MARTHE. That you ought not to be at the Embassy, and that it's insane to play cards in a game with Von Seitz with eighty-seven dollars in your pocket. I don't think he'd like your not being able to pay up. Suppose you lose?

TECK. I shall try not to lose.

MARTHE. But if you do lose and can't pay, it will be all over Washington in an hour. (*Points to terrace*) They'll find out about it, and we'll be out of here when they do.

TECK. I think I want to be out of here. I find that I do not like the picture of you and our host.

MARTHE (*carefully*). There is no picture, as you put it, to like or dislike.

TECK. Not yet? I am glad to hear that. (*Comes toward her slowly*) Marthe, you understand that I am not really a fool? You understand that it is unwise to calculate me that way?

MARTHE (*slowly, as if it were an effort*). Yes, I understand that. And I understand that I am getting tired. Just plain tired. The whole thing's too much for me. I've always meant to ask you, since you played on so many sides, why we didn't come out any better. I've always wanted to ask you what happened. (*Sharply*) I'm tired, see? And I just want to sit down. Just to sit down in a chair and stay.

TECK (*carefully*). Here?

MARTHE. I don't know. Any place—

TECK. You have thus arranged it with David?

MARTHE. I've arranged nothing.

TECK. But you are trying, eh? (*He comes close to her*) I think not. I would not like that. Do not make any arrangements, Marthe. I may not allow you to carry them through. (*Smiles*) Come to breakfast now. (*He passes her, disappears on the terrace. She stands still and thoughtful. Then she, too, moves to the terrace, disappears.* JOSEPH *appears on the terrace, carrying a tray toward the unseen breakfast table. The stage is empty. After a minute, there are sounds of footsteps in the hall.* SARA MÜLLER *appears in the doorway, comes toward the middle of the room as if expecting to find somebody, stops, looks around, begins to smile. Behind her in the doorway, are three children; behind them,* KURT MÜLLER. *They stand waiting, watching* SARA. SARA *is forty-one or forty-two, a good-looking woman, with a well-bred, serious face. She is very badly dressed. Her dress is too long, her shoes were bought a long time ago and have no relation to the dress, and the belt of her dress has become untied and is hanging down. She looks clean and dowdy. As she looks around the room, her face is gay and surprised. Smiling, without turning, absently, she motions to the children and* KURT. *Slowly, the children come in.* BODO MÜLLER, *a boy of nine, comes first. He is carrying coats. Behind him, carrying two cheap valises, is* JOSHUA MÜLLER, *a boy of fourteen. Behind him is* BABETTE MÜLLER, *a pretty little girl of twelve. They are dressed for a much colder climate. They come forward, look at their mother, then move to a couch. Behind them is* KURT MÜLLER, *a large, powerful, German-looking man of about forty-seven. He is carrying a shabby valise and a brief-case. He stands watching* SARA. JOSHUA *puts down the valises, goes to his father, takes the valise from* KURT, *puts it neatly near his, and*

. *puts the brief-case near* KURT. BABETTE *goes to* SARA, *takes a package from her, places it near the valise. Then she turns to* BODO, *takes the coats he is carrying, puts them neatly on top of the valises. After a second,* KURT *sits down. As he does so, we see that his movements are slow and careful, as if they are made with effort.*)

BABETTE (*points to a couch near which they are standing She has a slight accent*). Is it allowed?

KURT (*smiles. He has an accent*). Yes. It is allowed. (BAB-ETTE *and* BODO *sit stiffly on the couch.*)

JOSHUA (*nervously. He has a slight accent*). But we did not sound the bell—

SARA (*idly, as she wanders around the room, her face excited*). The door isn't locked. It never was. Never since I can remember.

BODO (*softly, puzzled*). The entrance of the home is never locked. So.

KURT (*looks at him*). You find it curious to believe there are people who live and do not need to watch, eh, Bodo?

BODO. Yes, Papa.

KURT (*smiles*). You and I.

JOSHUA (*smiles*). It is strange. But it must be good, I think.

KURT. Yes.

SARA. Sit back. Be comfortable. I—I wonder where Mama and David— (*Delighted, sees portrait of Joshua Farrelly, points to it*) And that was my Papa. That was the famous Joshua Farrelly. (*They all look up at it. She wanders around the room*) My goodness, isn't it a fine room? I'd almost forgotten— (*Picks up a picture from the table*) And this was my grandmother. (*Very nervously*) Shall I go and say we're here? They'd be having breakfast, I think. Always on the side terrace in nice weather. I don't know. Maybe— (*Picks up another picture*) "To Joshua and Fanny Farrelly. With admiration. Alfonso, May 7, 1910." I had an ermine boa and a pink coat. I was angry because it was too warm in Madrid to wear it.

BODO. Alfons von Spanien? Der hat immer Bilder von sich verschenkt. Ein schlectes Zeichen für einen Mann.

JOSHUA. Mama told you it is good manners to speak the language of the country you visit. Therefore, speak in English.

BODO. I said he seemed always to give his photograph. I said that is a bad flag on a man. Grow fat on the poor people and give pictures of the face. (JOSHUA *sits down.*)

SARA. I remember a big party and cakes and a glass of champagne for me. I was ten, I guess— (*Suddenly laughs*) That was when Mama said the first time a king got shot at, he was a romantic, but the fifth time he was a comedian. And when my father gave his lecture in Madrid, he repeated it—right in Madrid. It was a great scandal. You know, Alfonso was always getting shot at or bombed.

BODO (*shrugs*). Certainement.

JOSHUA. Certainement? As-tu perdu la tête?

BABETTE. Speak in English, please.

KURT (*without turning*). You are a terrorist, Bodo?

BODO (*slowly*). No.

JOSHUA. Then since when has it become *natural* to shoot upon people?

BODO. Do not give me lessons. It is neither right nor natural to shoot upon people. I know that.

SARA (*looks at* BABETTE, *thoughtfully*). An ermine boa. A boa is a scarf. I should like to have one for you, Babbie. Once, in Prague, I saw a pretty one. I wanted to buy it for you. But we had to pay our rent. (*Laughs*) But I almost bought it.

BABETTE. Yes, Mama. Thank you. Tie your sash, Mama.

SARA (*thoughtfully*). Almost twenty years.

BODO. You were born here, Mama?

SARA. Upstairs. And I lived here until I went to live with your father. (*Looks out beyond terrace*) Your Uncle David and I used to have a garden, behind the terrace. I wonder if it's still there. I like a garden. I've always hoped we'd have a house some day and settle down— (*Stops, nervously, turns to stare at* KURT, *who is looking at her*) I am talking so foolish. Sentimental. At my age. Gardens and ermine boas. I haven't wanted anything—

KURT (*comes toward her, takes her hand*). Sara. Stop it. This is a fine room. A fine place to be. Everything is so pleasant and full of comfort. This will be a good piano on which to play again. And it is all so clean. I like that. Now, you shall not be a baby. You must enjoy your house, and not be afraid that you hurt me with it. Yes?

BABETTE. Papa, tie Mama's sash, please.

SARA (*shyly smiles at him as he leans down to tie the belt*). Yes, of course. It's strange, that's all. We've never been in a place like this together—

KURT. That does not mean, and should not mean, that we do not remember how to enjoy what comes our way. We are on a holiday.

JOSHUA. A holiday? But for how long? And what plans afterward?

KURT (*quietly*). We will have plans when the hour arrives to make them. (ANISE *appears from the hall. She starts into the room, stops, bewildered. The* MÜLLERS *have not seen her. Then, as* SARA *turns,* ANISE *speaks. As she speaks, the children rise.*)

ANISE. What? What?

SARA (*softly*). Anise. It's me. It's Sara.

ANISE (*coming forward slowly*). What? (*Then as she approaches* SARA, *she begins to run toward her*) Miss Sara! Miss Sara! (*They reach each other, both laugh happily.* SARA *kisses* ANISE) I would have known you. Yes, I would. I would have known— (*Excited, bewildered,*

nervous, she looks toward KURT) How do you do, sir?
How do you do? (*Turns toward the children*) How do
you do?

JOSHUA. Thank you, Miss Anise. We are in good health.

SARA (*very happily*). You look the same. I think you look
the same. Just the way I've always remembered. (*To the
others*) This is the Anise I have told you about. She was
here before I was born.

ANISE. But how— Did you just come in? What a way to
come home! And after all the plans we've made! But you
were to come on the twelve o'clock train, and Mr. David
was to meet you—

BABETTE. The twelve o'clock train was most expensive.
We could not have come with that train. We liked the
train we came on. It was most luxurious.

ANISE (*very nervously, very rattled*). But Madame Fanny
will have a fit. I will call her— She will not be able to
contain herself. She—

SARA (*softly*). I wanted a few minutes. I'm nervous about
coming home, I guess.

BODO (*conversationally*). You are French, Madame Anise?

ANISE. Yes, I am from the Bas Rhin. (*She looks past* SARA,
and bobs her head idiotically at KURT) Sara's husband.
That is nice. That is nice.

BODO. Yes. Your accent is from the North. That is fine country. We were in hiding there once. (BABETTE *quickly
pokes him.*)

ANISE. Hiding? You— (*Turns nervously to* KURT) But here
we stand and talk. You have not had your breakfast, sir!

BABETTE (*simply, eagerly*). It would be nice to have breakfast.

ANISE. Yes, of course— I will go and order it.

SARA (*to the children*). What would you like for breakfast?

BABETTE (*surprised*). What would we like? Why, Mama,

we will have anything that can be spared. If eggs are not too rare or too expensive—

ANISE (*amazed*). Rare? Why— Oh, I—I must call Miss Fanny now. It is of a necessity. (*Excited, rushing toward terrace, calling*) Miss Fanny. Miss Fanny. (*Back to* SARA) Have you forgotten your Mama's nature? She cannot bear not knowing things. Miss Fanny! What a way to come home! After twenty years and nobody at the station—

FANNY'S VOICE. Don't yell at me. What is the matter with you?

ANISE (*excitedly, as* FANNY *draws near*). She's here. They're here. Miss Sara. She's here, I tell you. (FANNY *comes up to her, stares at her, then looks slowly around until she sees* SARA.)

SARA (*softly*). Hello, Mama.

FANNY (*after a long pause, softly, coming toward her*) Sara. Sara, darling. You're here. You're really here. (*She reaches her, takes her arms, stares at her, smiles*) Welcome. Welcome. Welcome to your house. (*Slowly*) You're not young, Sara.

SARA (*smiles*). No, Mama. I'm forty-one.

FANNY (*softly*). Forty-one. Of course. (*Presses her arms again*) Oh, Sara, I'm— (*Then quickly*) You look more like Papa now. That's good. The years have helped you. (*Turns to look at* KURT) Welcome to this house, sir.

KURT (*warmly*). Thank you, Madame.

FANNY (*turns to look at* SARA *again, nervously pats her arm. Nods, turns again to stare at* KURT. *She is nervous and chatty*). You are a good-looking man, for a German. I didn't remember you that way. I like a good-looking man. I always have.

KURT (*smiles*). I like a good-looking woman. I always have.

FANNY. Good. That's the way it should be.

BODO (*to* SARA). Ist das Grossmama?

FANNY (*looks down*). Yes. I am your grandmother. Also, I speak German, so do not talk about me. I speak languages very well. But there is no longer anybody to speak with. Anise has half forgotten her French, which was always bad; and I have nobody with whom to speak my Italian or German or—Sara, it's very good to have you home. I'm chattering away, I—

JOSHUA. Now you have us, Madame. We speak ignorantly, but fluently, in German, French, Italian, Spanish—

KURT. And boastfully in English.

BODO. There is never a need for boasting. If we are to fight for the good of all men, it is to be accepted that we must be among the most advanced.

ANISE. My God.

FANNY (*to* SARA). Are these your *children?* Or are they dressed up midgets?

SARA (*laughs*). These are my children, Mama. This, Babette. (BABETTE *bows*) This, Joshua. (JOSHUA *bows*) This is Bodo. (BODO *bows.*)

FANNY. Joshua was named for Papa. You wrote me. (*Indicates picture of Joshua Farrelly*) You bear a great name, young man.

JOSHUA (*smiles, indicates his father*). My name is Müller.

FANNY (*looks at him, laughs*). Yes. You look a little like your grandfather. (*To* BABETTE) And so do you. You are a nice-looking girl. (*To* BODO) You look like nobody.

BODO (*proudly*). I am not beautiful.

FANNY (*laughs*). Well, Sara, well. Three children. You have done well. (*To* KURT) You, too, sir, of course. Are you quite recovered? Sara wrote that you were in Spain and—

BODO. Did Mama write that Papa was a great hero? He was brave, he was calm, he was expert, he was resourceful, he was—

KURT (*laughs*). My biographer. And as unprejudiced as most of them.

SARA. Where is David? I am so anxious— Has he changed much? Does he . . .

FANNY (*to* ANISE). Don't stand there. Go and get him right away. Go get David. (*As* ANISE *exits*) He's out having breakfast with the titled folk. Do you remember Marthe Randolph? I mean, do you remember Hortie Randolph, her mother, who was my friend? Can you follow what I'm saying? I'm not speaking well today.

SARA (*laughs*). Of course I remember Marthe and Hortie. You and she used to scream at each other.

FANNY. Well, Martha, her daughter, married Teck de Brancovis. *Count* de Brancovis. He was fancy when she married him. Not so fancy now, I suspect. Although still chic and tired. You know what I mean, the way they are in Europe. Well, they're here.

SARA. What's David like now? I—

FANNY. Like? Like? I don't know. He's a lawyer. You know that. Papa's firm. He's never married. You know that, too—

SARA. Why hasn't he married?

FANNY. Really, I don't know. I don't think he likes his own taste. Which is very discriminating of him. He's had a lot of girls, of course, one more ignorant and silly than the other— (*Goes toward terrace, begins to scream*) And where is he? David! David!

ANISE'S VOICE. He's coming, Miss Fanny. He's coming. Contain yourself. He was down at the garage getting ready to leave—

FANNY. I don't care where he is. Tell him to come.— David! (*Suddenly points to picture of Joshua*) That's my Joshua. Handsome, eh? We were very much in love. Hard to believe of people nowadays, isn't it?

SARA. Kurt and I love each other.

FANNY. Oh. You do? I daresay. But there are ways and ways of loving.

SARA. How dare you, Mama—

KURT (*laughs*). Ladies, ladies.

SARA (*giggles*). Why, I almost got mad then. You know, I don't think I've been mad since I last saw you.

BODO. My! You and Mama must not get angry. Anger is protest. And so you must direction it to the proper channels and then harness it for the good of other men. That is correct, Papa?

FANNY (*peers down at him*). If you grow up to talk like that, and stay as ugly as you are, you are going to have one of those successful careers on the lecture platform. (JOSHUA *and* BABETTE *laugh.*)

JOSHUA (*to* BODO). Ah. It is a great pleasure to hear Grandma talk with you.

BODO (*to* FANNY, *tenderly*). We will not like each other. (KURT *has wandered to the piano. Standing, he touches the keys in the first bars of a Mozart Rondo.*)

FANNY. You are wrong. I think we are rather alike; if that is so, let us at least remember to admire each other. (DAVID *comes running in from the entrance hall. At the door he stops, stares at* SARA.)

DAVID (*to* SARA). Sara. Darling—

SARA (*wheels, goes running toward him. She moves into his arms. He leans down, kisses her with great affection*). David. David.

DAVID (*softly*). It's been a long, long time. I got to thinking it would never happen. (*He leans down, kisses her hair. After a minute, he smiles, presses her arm.*)

SARA (*excited*). David, I'm excited. Isn't it strange? To be here, to see each other— But I am forgetting. This is my husband. These are my children. Babette, Joshua, Bodo. (*They all three advance, stand in line to shake hands.*)

BODO (*shaking hand*). How do you do, Uncle David?

DAVID. How do you do, Bodo? (DAVID *shakes hands with*

JOSHUA) Boys can shake hands. But so pretty a girl must be kissed. (*He kisses* BABETTE. *She smiles, very pleased, and crosses to the side of* SARA.)

BABETTE. Thank you. Fix your hairpin, Mama. (SARA *shoves back a falling hairpin.*)

DAVID (*crossing to* KURT). I'm happy to meet you, sir, and to have you here.

KURT. Thank you. Sara has told me so much from you. You have a devoted sister.

DAVID (*very pleased*). Have I? Still? That's mighty good to hear. (ANISE *comes in from the library.*)

ANISE. Your breakfast is coming. Shall I wash the children, Miss Sara?

JOSHUA (*amazed*). Wash us? Do people wash each other?

SARA. No, but the washing is a good idea. Go along now, and hurry. (*All three start for the hall*) And then we'll all have a fine, big breakfast again. (*The children exit.*)

FANNY. Again? Don't you usually have a good breakfast?

KURT (*smiles*). No, Madame. Only sometimes.

SARA (*laughs*). Oh, we do all right, usually. (*Very happily, very gaily*) Ah, it's good to be here. (*Puts her arm in* DAVID'S) We were kids. Now we're all grown up! I've got children, you're a lawyer, and a fine one, I bet—

FANNY. The name of Farrelly on the door didn't, of course, hurt David's career.

DAVID (*smiles*). Sara, you might as well know Mama thinks of me only as a monument to Papa and a not very well-made monument at that. I am not the man Papa was.

SARA (*to* FANNY, *smiles*). How do you know he's not?

FANNY (*carefully*). I beg your pardon. That is the second time you have spoken disrespectfully of your father. (SARA *and* DAVID *laugh.* FANNY *turns to* KURT) I hope you will like me.

KURT. I hope so.

SARA (*pulls him to the couch, sits down with him*). Now I want to hear about you— (*Looks at him, laughs*) I'm awfully nervous about seeing you. Are you, about me?

DAVID. Yes. I certainly am.

SARA (*looks around*). I'm like an idiot. I want to see everything right away. The lake, and my old room—and I want to talk and ask questions . . .

KURT (*laughs*). More slow, Sara. It is most difficult to have twenty years in a few minutes.

SARA. Yes, I know, but— Oh, well. Kurt's right. We'll say it all slowly. It's just nice being back. Haven't I fine children?

DAVID. Very fine. You're lucky. I wish I had them.

FANNY. How could you have them? All the women you like are too draughty, if you know what I mean. I'm sure that girl from Lansing, Michigan, would be sterile. Which is as God in his wisdom would have it.

SARA. Oh. So you have a girl?

DAVID. I have no girl. This amuses Mama.

FANNY. He's very attractive to some women. (*To* KURT) Both my children are attractive, whatever else they're not. Don't you think so? (*Points to* DAVID) He's flirting with our Countess now, Sara. You will see for yourself.

DAVID (*sharply*). You are making nervous jokes this morning, Mama. And they're not very good ones.

FANNY (*gaily*). I tell the truth. If it turns out to be a joke, all the better.

SARA (*affectionately*). Ah, Mama hasn't changed. And that's good, too.

FANNY. Don't mind me, Sara. I, too, am nervous about seeing you. (*To* KURT) You'll like it here. You are an engineer?

KURT. Yes.

FANNY. Do you remember the day we met in München? The day Sara brought you to lunch? I thought you were rather a clod and that Sara would have a miserable life. I think I was wrong. (*To* DAVID) You see? I always admit when I'm wrong.

DAVID. You are a woman who is noble in all things, at all times.

FANNY. Oh, you're mad at me. (*To* KURT) As I say, you'll like it here. I've already made some plans. The new wing will be for you and Sara. The old turkey-house we'll fix up for the children. A nice, new bathroom, and we'll put in their own kitchen, and Anise will move in with them—

SARA. That's kind of you, Mama. But—but—we won't make any plans for a while— (*Very quietly*) A good, long vacation; God knows Kurt needs it—

FANNY. A vacation? You'll be staying here, of course. You don't have to worry about work—engineers can always get jobs, David says, and he's already begun to inquire—

KURT. I have not worked as an engineer since many years, Madame.

DAVID. Haven't you? I thought— Didn't you work for Dornier?

KURT. Yes. Before '33.

FANNY. But you have worked in other places. A great many other places, I should say. Every letter of Sara's seemed to have a new postmark.

KURT (*smiles*). We move most often.

DAVID. You gave up engineering?

KURT. I gave it up? (*Shrugs*) One could say it that way.

FANNY. What do you do?

SARA. Mama, we—

KURT. It is difficult to explain.

DAVID (*after a slight pause*). If you'd rather not.

FANNY. No, I—I'm trying to find out something. (*To* KURT) May I ask it, sir?

KURT. Let me help you, Madame. You wish to know whether not being an engineer buys adequate breakfasts for my family. It does not. I have no wish to make a mystery of what I have been doing; it is only that it is awkward to place neatly. (*Smiles, motions with his hand*) It sounds so big: it is so small. I am an Anti-Fascist. And that does not pay well.

FANNY. Do you mind questions?

SARA. Yes.

KURT (*sharply*). Sara. (*To* FANNY) Perhaps I shall not answer them. But I shall try.

FANNY. Are you a radical?

KURT. You would have to tell me what that word means to you, Madame.

FANNY (*after a slight pause*). That is just. Perhaps we all have private definitions. We all are Anti-Fascists, for example—

SARA. Yes. But Kurt works at it.

FANNY. What kind of work?

KURT. Any kind. Anywhere.

FANNY (*sharply*). I will stop asking questions.

SARA (*very sharply*). That would be sensible, Mama.

DAVID. Darling, don't be angry. We've been worried about you, naturally. We knew so little, except that you were having a bad time.

SARA. I didn't have a bad time. We never—

KURT. Do not lie for me, Sara.

SARA. I'm not lying. I didn't have a bad time, the way they mean. I—

FANNY (*slowly*). You had a bad time just trying to live, didn't you? That's obvious, Sara, and foolish to pretend it isn't. Why wouldn't you take money from us? What kind of nonsense—

SARA (*slowly*). We've lived the way we wanted to live. I don't know the language of rooms like this any more. And I don't want to learn it again.

KURT. Do not bristle about it.

SARA. I'm not bristling. (*To* FANNY) I married because I fell in love. You can understand that.

FANNY (*slowly*). Yes.

SARA. For almost twelve years, Kurt went to work every

morning and came home every night, and we lived modestly, and happily— (*Sharply*) As happily as people could in a starved Germany that was going to pieces—

KURT. Sara, please. You are angry. I do not like it that way. I will try to find a way to tell you with quickness. Yes. (SARA *turns, looks at him, starts to speak, stops*) I was born in a town called Fürth. (*Pauses. Looks up, smiles*) There is a holiday in my town. We call it Kirchweih. It was a gay holiday with games and music and a hot white sausage to eat with the wine. I grow up, I move away—to school, to work—but always I come back for Kirchweih. It is for me, the great day of the year. (*Slowly*) But after the war, that day begins to change. The sausage is made from bad stuff, the peasants come in without shoes, the children are too sick— (*Carefully*) It is bad for my people, those years, but always I have hope. In the festival of August, 1931, more than a year before the storm, I give up that hope. On that day, I see twenty-seven men murdered in a Nazi street fight. I cannot stay by now and watch. My time has come to move. I say with Luther, "Here I stand. I can do nothing else. God help me. Amen."

SARA. It doesn't pay well to fight for what we believe in. But I wanted it the way Kurt wanted it. (*Shrugs*) They don't like us in Europe; I guess they never did. So Kurt brought us home. You've always said you wanted us. If you don't, I will understand.

DAVID. Darling, of course we want you—

FANNY (*rises*). I am old. And made of dry cork. And bad-mannered. Please forgive me.

SARA (*goes quickly to* FANNY). Shut up, Mama. We're all acting like fools. I'm glad to be home. That's all I know. So damned glad.

DAVID. And we're damned glad to have you. Come on. Let's walk to the lake. We've made it bigger and planted the island with blackberries— (*She smiles and goes to him. Together they move out the hall entrance.*)

FANNY (*after a silence*). They've always liked each other. We're going to have Zwetschgen-Knoedel for dinner. You like them?

KURT. Indeed.

FANNY. I hope you like decent food.

KURT. I do.

FANNY. That's a good sign in a man.

MARTHE (*coming in from the terrace. Stops in the doorway*). Oh, I'm sorry, Fanny. We were waiting. I didn't want to interrupt the family reunion. I—

FANNY. This is my son-in-law, Herr Müller. The Countess de Brancovis.

KURT AND MARTHE (*together*). How do you do?

MARTHE. And how is Sara, Herr Müller? I haven't seen her since I was a little girl. She probably doesn't remember me at all. (TECK *comes in from the hall. She turns*) This is my husband, Herr Müller.

KURT. How do you do?

TECK. How do you do, sir? (KURT *bows. They shake hands*) Would it be impertinent for one European to make welcome another?

KURT (*smiles*). I do not think so. It would be friendly.

BODO (*appears at the hall door*). Papa— (*Sees* TECK *and* MARTHE, *bows*) Oh, good morning. Miss Anise says you are the Count and Countess. Once before we met a Count and Countess. They had a small room bordering on ours in Copenhagen. They were more older than you, and more poor. We shared with them our newspaper.

MARTHE (*laughs*). It wasn't us, but it might have been. What's your name?

TECK (*laughs*). We hope you will be as kind to us.

BODO. My name is Bodo. It's a strange name. No? (*To* KURT) Papa, this is the house of great wonders. Each has his bed, each has his bathroom. The arrangement of it, that is splendorous.

FANNY (*laughs*). You are a fancy talker, Bodo.

KURT. Oh, yes. In many languages.

BODO (*to* FANNY). Please to correct me when I am wrong. Papa, the plumbing is such as you have never seen. Each implement is placed on the floor, and all are simultaneous in the same room. You will therefore see that being placed most solidly on the floor allows of no rats, rodents or crawlers, and is most sanitary. (*To the others*) Papa will be most interested. He likes to know how each thing of everything is put together. And he is so fond of being clean—

KURT (*laughs. To* FANNY). I am a hero to my children. It bores everybody but me.

TECK. It is most interesting, Herr Müller. I thought I had a good ear for the accents of your country. But yours is most difficult to place. It is Bayrisch? Or is it—

BODO. That's because Papa has worked in so many—

KURT (*quickly*). German accents are the most difficult to identify. I, myself, when I try, am usually incorrect. It would be particularly difficult with me because I speak other languages. Yours would be Roumanian?

MARTHE (*laughs*). My God, is it that bad?

KURT (*smiles*). I am showing off. I know the Count de Brancovis is Roumanian.

TECK (*heartily*). So? We have met before? I thought so, but I cannot remember—

KURT. No, sir. We have not met before. I read your name in the newspapers.

TECK (*to* KURT). Strange. I was sure I had met you. I was in the Paris Legation for many years, and I thought perhaps—

KURT. Oh, no. If it is possible to believe, I am the exile who is not famous. (*To* FANNY) I have been thinking with pleasure, Madame Fanny, of breakfast on your porch. (*He points to the picture of Joshua Farrelly*) Your husband once wrote: "I am getting older now and Europe seems far away. Fanny and I will have an early breakfast on the porch and then I shall drive the bays into Washington." (*Remembering*) And then he goes on: "Henry Adams tells me he has been reading Karl Marx. I shall have to tell him my father made me read Marx many years ago and that, since he proposes to exhibit himself to impress me, will spoil Henry's Sunday."

FANNY (*laughs, delighted. Takes* KURT's *arm*). And so it did. I had forgotten that. I am pleased with you. I shall come and serve your food myself. I had forgotten Joshua ever wrote it. (*They start out of the terrace doors together, followed by* BODO.)

KURT (*as they disappear*). I try to impress you. I learned it last night. (FANNY *laughs. They disappear.*)

TECK (*smiles*). He is a clever man. A quotation from Joshua Farrelly is a sure road to Fanny's heart. Where did you say Herr Müller was from?

MARTHE. Germany.

TECK. I know that. (*Goes to a valise. He leans over, stares at it, looks at the labels, pushes the lock. The lock opens; he closes it. Then he turns and, as he speaks, picks up the brief-case*) What part of Germany?

MARTHE. I don't know. And I never knew you were an expert on accents.

TECK. I never knew it either. Are you driving into Washington with David this morning?

MARTHE. I was going to. But he may not be going to the office, now that Sara's here. I was to have lunch with Sally Tyne. (TECK *puts down the brief-case*) What are you doing?

TECK. Wondering why luggage is unlocked and a shabby brief-case is so carefully locked.

MARTHE. You're very curious about Mr. Müller.

TECK. Yes. And I do not know why. Something far away
. . . I am curious about a daughter of the Farrellys' who
marries a German who has bullet scars on his face and
broken bones in his hands.

MARTHE (*sharply*). Has he? There are many of them now,
I guess.

TECK. So there are. But this one is in this house. (*He goes
to the bell cord, pulls it. She watches him nervously.*)

MARTHE. Is it—is he any business of yours?

TECK. What is my business? Anything might be my business now.

MARTHE. Yes—unfortunately. You might inquire from your
friend Von Seitz. They always know their nationals.

TECK. (*pleasantly, ignoring the sharpness with which she
has spoken*). Oh, yes, I will do that, of course. But I do
not like to ask questions without knowing the value of
the answers.

MARTHE. Teck. This man is a little German Sara married
years ago. I remember Mama talking about it. He was
nothing then and he isn't now. They've had a tough
enough time already without—

TECK. Have you— Have you been sleeping with David?

MARTHE (*stops, stares at him, then simply*). No. I have
not been. And that hasn't been your business for a good
many years now.

TECK. You like him?

MARTHE (*nervously*). What's this for, Teck?

TECK. Answer me, please.

MARTHE. I— (*She stops.*)

TECK. Yes? Answer me.

MARTHE. I do like him.

TECK. What does he feel about you?

MARTHE. I don't know.

TECK. But you are trying to find out. You have made plans
with him?

MARTHE. Of course not. I—

TECK. But you will try to make him have plans. I have recognized it. Well, we have been together a long— (JOSEPH *enters.* TECK *stops*) Joseph, Miss Fanny wishes you to take the baggage upstairs.

JOSEPH. Yes, sir. I was going to. (*He begins to pick up the baggage.* MARTHE *has turned sharply and is staring at* TECK. *Then she rises, watches* JOSEPH *pick up the baggage, turns again to look at* TECK.)

TECK. As I was saying. It is perhaps best that we had this talk.

MARTHE (*she stops, waits for* JOSEPH *to move off. He exits, carrying the valises*). Why did you do that? Why did you tell Joseph that Fanny wanted him to take the baggage upstairs?

TECK. Obviously it is more comfortable to look at baggage behind closed doors.

MARTHE (*very sharply*). What kind of silliness is this now? Leave these people alone— (*As he starts to exit*) I won't let you—

TECK. What? (*As he moves again, she comes after him.*)

MARTHE. I said I won't let you. You are not—

TECK. How many times have you seen me angry? (MARTHE *looks up, startled*) You will not wish to see another. Run along now and have lunch with something you call Sally Tyne. But do not make plans with David. You will not be able to carry them out. You will go with me, when I am ready to go. You understand. (*He exits during his speech. The last words come as he goes through the door, and as the curtain falls.*)

ACT TWO

SCENE: *The same as Act One, about ten days later. During the act it will begin to grow dark; but the evening is warm and the terrace doors are open.*

AT RISE: SARA *is sitting on the couch, crocheting.* FANNY *and* TECK *are sitting at a small table playing cribbage.* BODO *is sitting near them, at a large table, working on a heating pad. The cord is torn from the bag, the bag is ripped open.* ANISE *sits next to him, anxiously watching him. Outside on the terrace,* JOSHUA *is going through baseball motions, coached by* JOSEPH. *From time to time they move out of sight, reappear, move off again.*

FANNY (*playing a card*). One.

BODO (*after a minute, to* TECK). The arrangement of this heating pad grows more complex.

TECK (*smiles, moves on the cribbage board*). And the more wires you remove, the more complex it will grow.

BODO (*points to bag*). Man has learned to make man comfortable. Yet all cannot have the comforts. (*To* ANISE) How much did this cost you?

ANISE. It cost me ten dollars. And you have made a ruin of it.

BODO. That is not yet completely true. (*To* FANNY) Did I not install for you a twenty-five-cent button-push for your radio?

TECK (*playing a card*). Two and two. (*Moves pegs on the cribbage board.*)

FANNY. Yes, you're quite an installer.

BODO (*to* TECK). As I was wishing to tell you, Count de

Brancovis, comfort and plenty exist. Yet all cannot have them it. Why?

TECK. I do not know. It has worried many men. Why?

ANISE (*to* BODO). Yes, why?

BODO (*takes a deep breath, raises his finger as if about to lecture*). Why? (*Considers a moment, then deflates himself*) I am not as yet sure.

ANISE. I thought not.

FANNY (*turns to look at* JOSHUA *and* JOSEPH *on the terrace*). Would you mind doing that dancing some place else?

JOSEPH (*looking in.*) Yes'm. That ain't dancing. I'm teaching Josh baseball.

FANNY. Then maybe he'd teach you how to clean the silver.

JOSEPH. I'm a good silver-cleaner, Miss Fanny.

FANNY. But you're getting out of practice.

JOSEPH (*after a moment's thought*). Yes'm. I see what you mean. (*He exits.*)

FANNY (*playing a card*). Three.

JOSHUA. It is my fault. I'm crazy about baseball.

BODO. Baseball players are among the most exploited people in this country. I read about it.

FANNY. You never should have learned to read.

BODO. Their exploited condition is foundationed on the fact that—

JOSHUA (*bored*). All right, all right. I still like baseball.

SARA. Founded, Bodo, not foundationed.

JOSHUA. He does it always. He likes long words. In all languages.

TECK. How many languages do you children speak?

BODO. Oh, we do not really know any very well, except German and English. We speak bad French and—

SARA. And bad Danish and bad Czech.

TECK. You seem to have stayed close to the borders of Germany. Did Herr Müller have hopes, as so many did, that National Socialism would be overthrown on every tomorrow?

SARA. We have not given up that hope. Have you, Count de Brancovis?

TECK. I never had it.

JOSHUA (*pleasantly*). Then it must be most difficult for you to sleep.

TECK. I beg your pardon?

SARA. Schweig doch, Joshua!

FANNY (*to* TECK). Sara told Joshua to shut up. (*Playing a card*) Twelve.

TECK. I have offended you, Mrs. Müller. I am most sorry.

SARA (*pleasantly*). No, sir, you haven't offended me. I just don't like polite political conversations any more.

TECK (*nods*). All of us, in Europe, had too many of them.

SARA. Yes. Too much talk. By this time all of us must know where we are and what we have to do. It's an indulgence to sit in a room and discuss your beliefs as if they were a juicy piece of gossip.

FANNY. You know, Sara, I find it very pleasant that Kurt, considering his history, doesn't make platform speeches. He hasn't tried to convince anybody of anything.

SARA (*smiles*). Why should he, Mama? You are quite old enough to have your own convictions—or Papa's.

FANNY (*turns to look at her*). I am proud to have Papa's convictions.

SARA. Of course. But it might be well to have a few new ones, now and then.

FANNY (*peers over at her*). Are you criticizing me?

SARA (*smiles*). Certainly not.

BABETTE (*comes running in from the right entrance door. She has on an apron and she is carrying a plate. She goes to* FANNY). Eat it while it's hot, Grandma.

(FANNY *peers down, takes the fork, begins to eat.* ANISE *and* BODO *both rise, move to* FANNY, *inspect the plate.*)

FANNY (*to them*). Go away.

ANISE. It is a potato pancake.

FANNY. And the first good one I've eaten in many, many years. I love a good potato pancake.

BODO. I likewise.

BABETTE. I am making a great number for dinner. Move away, Bodo.

TECK (*playing a card*). Fifteen and two.

ANSIE (*who has followed* BODO *back to the table, leans over to look at the heating pad*). You've ruined it! I shall sue you.

JOSHUA. I told you not to let him touch it.

SARA (*laughs*). I remember you were always saying that, Anise—that you were going to sue. That's very French. I was sick once in Paris, and Babbie stayed up for a whole night and day and finished a dress I was making for a woman in the Rue Jacob. I told her to tell the woman she'd done it—I thought perhaps the woman would give her a candy or something—and anyway, I was very proud of her work. But no. The woman admitted the dress was well done, but said she was going to sue because I hadn't done it myself. Fancy that.

FANNY (*slowly*). You sewed for a living?

SARA. Not a very good one. But Babbie and I made a little something now and then. Didn't we, darling?

FANNY (*sharply*). Really, Sara, were these—these things necessary? Why couldn't you have written?

SARA (*laughs*). You've asked me that a hundred times in the last week.

JOSHUA (*gently*). I think it is only that Grandma feels sorry for us. Grandma has not seen much of the world.

FANNY. Don't you start giving me lectures, Joshua. I'm fond of you. And of you, Babbie. (*To* ANISE) Are there two desserts for dinner? And are they sweet?

ANISE. Yes.

FANNY (*turns to* BODO). I wish I were fond of you.

BODO. You are. (*Happily*) You are very fond of me.

FANNY (*playing a card*). Twenty-five.

BABETTE. This is for you, Grandma. I'm making a bed-jacket. It is nice lace. Papa brought it to me from Spain and I mean for you to have it.

FANNY (*kisses* BABETTE). Thank you, darling. A sequence and three. A pair and five. (*To* TECK, *as they finish the cribbage game*) There. That's two dollars off. I owe you eight-fifty.

TECK. Let us carry it until tomorrow. You shall give it to me as a going-away token.

FANNY (*too pleased*). You're going away?

TECK (*laughs*). Ah, Madame Fanny. Do not sound *that* happy.

FANNY. Did I? That's rude of me. When are you going?

TECK. In a few days, I think. (*Turns to look at* SARA) We're too many refugees, eh, Mrs. Müller?

SARA (*pleasantly*). Perhaps.

TECK. Will you be leaving, also?

SARA. I beg your pardon?

TECK. I thought perhaps you, too, would be moving on. Herr Müller does not give me the feeling of a man who settles down. Men who have done his work, seldom leave it. Not for a quiet country house.

(*All three children look up.*)

SARA (*very quietly*). What work do you think my husband has done, Count de Brancovis?

TECK. Engineering?

SARA (*slowly*). Yes. Engineering.

FANNY (*very deliberately to* TECK). I don't know what you're saying. They shall certainly not be leaving—ever. Is that understood, Sara?

SARA. Well, Mama—

FANNY. There are no wells about it. You've come home to see me die and you will wait until I'm ready.

SARA (*laughs*). Really, Mama, that isn't the reason I came home.

FANNY. It's a good enough reason. I shall do a fine death. I intend to be a great deal of trouble to everybody.

ANISE. I daresay.

FANNY. I shall take to my bed early and stay for years. In great pain.

ANISE. I am sure of it. You will duplicate the disgrace of the birth of Miss Sara.

SARA (*laughs*). Was I born in disgrace?

ANISE. It was not your fault. But it was disgusting. Three weeks before you were to come—all was excellent, of course, in so healthy a woman as Madame Fanny—a great dinner was given here and, most unexpectedly, attended by a beautiful lady from England.

FANNY. Do be still. You are dull and fanciful—

ANISE. Mr. Joshua made the great error of waltzing the beauty for two dances, Madame Fanny being unfitted for the waltz and under no circumstances being the most graceful of dancers.

FANNY (*her voice rising*). Are you crazy? I danced magnificently.

ANISE. It is well you thought so. A minute did not elapse between the second of the waltzes and a scream from Madame Fanny. She was in labor. Two hundred people, and if we had left her alone, she would have remained in the ballroom—

FANNY. How you invent! How you invent!

ANISE. Do not call to me that I am a liar. For three weeks you are in the utmost agony—

FANNY. And so I was. I remember it to this day—

ANISE (*to* SARA, *angrily*). Not a pain. Not a single pain. She would lie up there in state, stealing candy from herself. Then, when your Papa would rest himself for a minute at the dinner or with a book, a scream would dismantle the house—it was revolting. (*Spitefully to* FANNY) And now the years have passed I may disclose to you that Mr. Joshua knew you were going through the play-acting—

FANNY (*rises*). He did not. You are a malicious—

ANISE. Once he said to me, "Anise, it is well that I am in love. This is of a great strain and her great-uncle Freddie was not right in the head, neither."

FANNY (*screaming*). You will leave this house— You are a liar, a woman of—

SARA. Mama, sit down.

ANISE. I will certainly leave this house. I will—

SARA (*sharply*). Both of you. Sit down. And be still.

ANISE. She has intimated that I lie—

FANNY (*screaming*). Intimated! Is that what I was doing— (ANISE *begins to leave the room*) All right. I beg your pardon. I apologize.

(ANISE *turns.*)

SARA. Both of you. You are acting like children.

BODO. Really, Mama. You insult us.

ANISE. I accept your apology. Seat yourself.

(*They both sit down.*)

FANNY (*after a silence*). I am unloved.

BABETTE. I love you, Grandma.

FANNY. Do you, Babbie?

JOSHUA. And I.

FANNY (*nods, very pleased. To* BODO). And you?

BODO. *I* loved you the primary second I saw you.

FANNY. You are a charlatan.

ANISE. As for me, I am fond of all the living creatures. It is true that the children cause me greater work, which in turn more greatly inconveniences the feet. However, I do not complain. I believe in children.

FANNY. Rather like believing in the weather, isn't it? (DAVID *and* KURT *come in from the terrace. Both are in work clothes, their sleeves rolled up*) Where have you been?

DAVID. Oh, we've been helping Mr. Chabeuf spray the fruit trees.

ANISE. Mr. Chabeuf says that Herr Müller has the makings of a good farmer. From a Frenchman that is a large thing to say.

KURT (*who has looked around the room, looked at* TECK, *strolled over to* BODO). Mr. Chabeuf and I have an excellent time exchanging misinformation. My father was a farmer. I have a wide knowledge of farmer's misinformation.

FANNY. This is good farm land. Perhaps, in time—

DAVID (*laughs*). Mama would give you the place, Kurt, if you guaranteed that your great-grandchildren would die here.

KURT (*smiles*). I would like to so guarantee.

TECK. A farmer. That is very interesting. Abandon your ideals, Herr Müller?

KURT. Ideals? (*Carefully*) Sara, heisst das auf deutsch "Ideale"?

SARA. Yes.

KURT. Is that what I have now? I do not like the word. It gives to me the picture of a small, pale man at a seaside resort. (*To* BODO) What are you doing?

BODO. Preparing an elderly electric pad for Miss Anise. I am confused.

KURT (*wanders toward the piano*). So it seems.

BODO. Something has gone wrong with the principle on which I have been working. It is probably that I will ask your assistance.

KURT (*bows to him*). Thank you. Whenever you are ready. (*Begins to pick out notes with one hand.*)

FANNY. We shall have a little concert tomorrow evening. In honor of Babbie's birthday. (*To* KURT) Kurt, you and I will play "The Clock Symphony." Then Joshua and I will play the duet we've learned, and Babbie will sing. And I shall finish with a Chopin Nocturne.

DAVID (*laughs*). I thought you'd be the last on the program.

TECK. Where is Marthe?

FANNY. She'll be back soon. She went into town to do an errand for me. (*To* DAVID) Did you buy presents for everybody?

DAVID. I did.

SARA (*smiles, to* BABETTE). We always did that here. If somebody had a birthday, we all got presents. Nice, isn't it?

DAVID (*to* ANISE). I shall buy you an electric pad. You will need it.

ANISE. Indeed.

FANNY. Did you buy me a good present?

DAVID. Pretty good. (*Pats* BABETTE's *head*) The best present goes to Babbie; it's *her* birthday.

FANNY. Jewelry?

DAVID. No, not jewelry.

FANNY. Oh. Not jewelry.

DAVID. Why?

FANNY (*too casually*). I just asked you.

TECK (*gets up*). It was a natural mistake, David. You see, Mrs. Mellie Sewell told your mother that she had seen you and Marthe in Barstow's. And your mother said you were probably buying her a present, or one for Babbie.

DAVID (*too sharply*). Yes.

TECK (*laughs*). Yes what?

DAVID (*slowly*). Just yes.

FANNY (*too hurriedly*). Mellie gets everything wrong. She's very anxious to meet Marthe because she used to know Francie Cabot, her aunt. Marthe's aunt, I mean, not Mellie's.

SARA (*too hurriedly*). She really came to inspect Kurt and me. But I saw her first. (*She looks anxiously at* DAVID, *who has turned his back on the room and is facing the terrace*) You were lucky to be out, David.

DAVID. Oh, she calls every Saturday afternoon, to bring Mama all the Washington gossip of the preceding week. She gets it all wrong, you understand, but that doesn't make any difference to either Mama or her. Mama then augments it, wits it up, Papa used to say—

FANNY. Certainly. I sharpen it a little. Mellie has no sense of humor.

DAVID. So Mama sharpens it a little, and delivers it to-morrow afternoon to old lady Marcy down the road. Old lady Marcy hasn't heard a word in ten years, so she unsharpens it again, and changes the names. By Wednesday afternoon—

TECK (*smiles*). By Wednesday afternoon it will not be you who were in Barstow's, and it will be a large diamond pin with four sapphires delivered to Gaby Deslys.

DAVID (*turns, looks at him*). Exactly.

FANNY (*very nervously*). Francie Cabot, Marthe's aunt, you understand— (*To* KURT) Did you ever know Paul von Seitz, a German?

KURT. I have heard of him.

FANNY (*speaking very rapidly*). Certainly. He was your Ambassador to somewhere, I've forgotten. Well, Francie Cabot married him. I could have. Any American, not crippled, whose father had money— He was crazy about me. I was better-looking than Francie. Well, years later when he was your Ambassador—my father was, too, as you probably know—not your Ambassador, of course, ours—but I am talking about Von Seitz.

DAVID (*laughs to* KURT). You can understand how it goes. Old lady Marcy is not entirely to blame.

FANNY. Somebody asked me if I didn't regret not marrying him. I said, "Madame, je le regrette tous les jours et j'en suis heureuse chaque soir." (FANNY *turns to* DAVID) That means I regret it every day and am happy about it every night. You understand what I meant, by *night?* Styles in wit change so.

DAVID. I understood it, Mama.

JOSHUA. We, too, Grandma.

BABETTE (*approvingly*). It was most witty.

BODO. I do not know that I understood. You will explain to me, Grandma?

SARA. Later.

FANNY (*turns to look at* TECK). You remember the old Paul von Seitz?

TECK (*nods*). He was stationed in Paris when I first was there.

FANNY. Of course. I always forget you were a diplomat.

TECK. It is just as well.

FANNY. There's something insane about a Roumanian diplomat. Pure insane. I knew another one, once. He wanted to marry me, too.

SARA (*laughs*). All of Europe.

FANNY. Not all. Some. Naturally. I was rich, I was witty, my family was of the best. I was handsome, unaffected—

DAVID. And noble and virtuous and kind and elegant and fashionable and simple—it's hard to remember everything you were. I've often thought it must have been boring for Papa to have owned such perfection.

FANNY (*shrieks*). What! Your father bored with me! Not for a second of our life—

DAVID (*laughs*). Oh God, when will I learn?

BODO. Do not shriek, Grandma. It is an unpleasant sound for the ear.

FANNY. Where was I? Oh, yes. What I started out to say was— (*She turns, speaks carefully to* TECK) Mellie Sewell told me, when you left the room, that she had heard from Louis Chandler's child's governess that you had won quite a bit of money in a poker game with Sam Chandler and some Germans at the Embassy. (KURT, *who has been playing the piano, stops playing very abruptly.* TECK *turns to look at him*) That's how

I thought of Von Seitz. His nephew Philip was in on the game.

DAVID (*looks at* TECK). It must have been a big game. Sam Chandler plays in big games.

TECK. Not big enough.

DAVID. Have you known Sam long?

TECK. For years. Every Embassy in Europe knew him.

DAVID (*sharply*). Sam and Nazis must make an unpleasant poker game.

(KURT *begins to play a new melody.*)

TECK (*who has not looked away from* KURT). I do not play poker to be amused.

DAVID (*irritably*). What's Sam selling now?

TECK. Bootleg munitions. He always has.

DAVID. You don't mind?

TECK. Mind? I have not thought about it.

FANNY. Well, you ought to think about it. Sam Chandler has always been a scoundrel. All the Chandlers are. They're cousins of mine. Mama used to say they never should have learned to walk on two feet. They would have been more comfortable on four.

TECK. Do you know the young Von Seitz, Herr Müller? He was your military attaché in Spain.

KURT. He was the German government attaché in Spain. I know his name, of course. He is a famous artillery expert. But the side on which I fought was not where he was stationed, Count de Brancovis.

ANISE (BABETTE *and* JOSHUA *begin to hum the song* KURT *is playing.* SARA *begins to hum*). It is time for the bath and the change of clothes. I will give you five more minutes—

FANNY. What is the song?

TECK. It was a German soldier's song. They sang it as they straggled back in '18. I remember hearing it in Berlin. Were you there then, Herr Müller?

KURT (*the playing and the humming continue*). I was not in Berlin.

TECK. But you were in the war, of course?

KURT. Yes. I was in the war.

FANNY. You didn't think then you'd live to see another war.

KURT. Many of us were afraid we would.

FANNY. What are the words?

SARA. The Germans in Spain, in Kurt's Brigade, wrote new words for the song.

KURT. This was what you heard in Berlin, in 1918. (*Begins to sing.*)

> "Wir zieh'n Heim, wir zieh'n Heim,
> Mancher kommt nicht mit,
> Mancher ging verschütt,
> Aber Freunde sind wir stets."
>   (*In English.*)
> "We come home. We come home.
> Some of us are gone, and some of us are lost, but
>   we are friends:
> Our blood is on the earth together.
> Some day. Some day we shall meet again.
> Farewell."

(*Stops singing*) At a quarter before six on the morning of November 7th, 1936, eighteen years later, five hundred Germans walked through the Madrid streets on their way to defend the Manzanares River. We felt good that morning. You know how it is to be good when it is needed to be good? So we had need of new words to say that. I translate with awkwardness, you understand. (*Begins to sing.*)

> "And so we have met again.
> The blood did not have time to dry.
> We lived to stand and fight again.
> This time we fight for people.
> This time the bastards will keep their hands away.

Those who sell the blood of other men, this time,
They keep their hands away.
For us to stand.
For us to fight.
This time no farewell, no farewell."

(*Music dies out. There is silence for a minute*) We did not win. (*Looks up, gently*) It would have been a different world if we had.

SARA. Papa said so years ago. Do you remember, Mama? "For every man who lives without freedom, the rest of us must face the guilt."

FANNY. Yes. "We are liable in the conscience-balance for the tailor in Lodz, the black man in our South, the peasant in—" (*Turns to* TECK. *Unpleasantly*) Your country, I think.

ANISE (*rises*). Come. Baths for everybody. (*To* BODO) Gather the wires. You have wrecked my cure.

BODO. If you would allow me a few minutes more—

ANISE. Come along. I have been duped for long enough. Come Joshua. Babette. Baths.

JOSHUA (*starts out after* ANISE. BABETTE *begins to gather up her sewing*) My tub is a thing of glory. But I do not like it so prepared for me and so announced by Miss Anise. (*He exits.*)

BODO (*to* ANISE). You are angry about this. I do not blame you with my heart or my head. I admit I have failed. But Papa will repair it, Anise. Will you not, Papa? In a few minutes—

TECK (*to* BODO). Your father is an expert electrician?

BODO. Oh yes, sir.

TECK. And as good with radio—

(BODO *begins to nod.*)

KURT (*sharply*). Count de Brancovis. Make your questions to me, please. Not to my children.

(*The others look up, surprised.*)

TECK (*pleasantly*). Very well, Herr Müller.

ANISE (*as she exits with* BODO). Nobody can fix it. You have made a pudding of it.

BODO (*as he follows her*). Do not worry. In five minutes tonight, you will have a pad far better— (*As* BODO *reaches the door he bumps into* MARTHE *who is carrying large dress boxes*) Oh. Your pardon. Oh, hello. (*He disappears.*)

MARTHE (*gaily*). Hello. (*To* FANNY) I waited for them. I was afraid they wouldn't deliver this late in the day. (*To* SARA) Come on, Sara. I can't wait to see them.

SARA. What?

MARTHE. Dresses. From Fanny. A tan linen, and a dark green with wonderful buttons, a white net for Babbie, and a suit for you, and play dresses for Babbie, and a dinner dress in gray to wear for Babbie's birthday— gray should be good for you, Sara—all from Savitt's. We sneaked the measurements, Anise and I—

SARA (*she goes toward* FANNY). How nice of you, Mama. How very kind of you. And of you, Marthe, to take so much trouble— (*She leans down, kisses* FANNY) You're a sweet woman, Mama.

DAVID. That's the first time Mama's ever heard that word. (*He takes the boxes from* MARTHE, *puts them near the staircase.* MARTHE *smiles at him, touches his hand, as* TECK *watches them.*)

FANNY (*giggles*). I have a bottom sweetness, if you understand what I mean.

DAVID. I have been too close to the bottom to see it.

FANNY. That should be witty. I don't know why it isn't.

(BABETTE *goes over to stare at the boxes.*)

SARA. From Savitt's. Extravagant of you. They had such lovely clothes. I remember my coming-out dress—. (*Goes to* KURT) Do you remember the black suit with the braid, and the Milan hat? Not the *first* day we met, but the picnic day? (*He smiles up at her*) Well, they were from Savitt's. That was over twenty years ago—

I've known you a long time. Me, in an evening dress. Now you'll have to take me into Washington. I want to show off. Next week, and we'll dance, maybe— (*Sees that he is not looking at her*) What's the matter, darling? (*No answer. Slowly he turns to look at her*) What's the matter, Kurt? (*Takes his arms, very unhappily*) What have I done? It isn't that dresses have ever mattered to me, it's just that—

KURT. Of course, they have mattered to you. As they should. I do not think of the dresses. (*Draws her to him*) How many years have I loved that face?

SARA (*her face very happy*). So?

KURT. So. (*He leans down, kisses her, as if it were important.*)

SARA (*pleased, unembarrassed*). There are other people here.

MARTHE (*slowly*). And good for us to see.

TECK. Nostalgia?

MARTHE. No. Nostalgia is for something you have known. (*FANNY coughs.*)

BABETTE (*comes to FANNY*). Grandma, is it allowed to look at my dresses?

FANNY. Of course, child. Run along.

BABETTE (*picks up the boxes, goes toward the hall entrance, stops near FANNY*). I love dresses, I have a great fondness for materials and colors. Thank you, Grandma. (*She runs out of the room.*)

(JOSEPH *appears in the doorway.*)

(JOSEPH. There is a long-distance operator with a long-distance call for Mr. Müller. She wants to talk with him on the long-distance phone.

KURT. Oh— Excuse me, please—

(KURT *rises quickly.* SARA *turns sharply to look at him.* TECK *looks up.* KURT *goes quickly out.* TECK *watches him go.* SARA *stands staring after him.*)

MARTHE (*laughs*). I feel the same way as Babbie. Come on, Sara. Let's try them on.

(SARA *does not turn.*)

TECK. You also have a new dress?

MARTHE (*looks at him*). Yes. Fanny was kind to me, too.

TECK. You are a very generous woman, Madame Fanny. Did you also give her a sapphire bracelet from Barstow's?

FANNY. I beg your—

DAVID (*slowly*). No. I gave Marthe the bracelet. And I understand that it is not any business of yours.

(FANNY *rises.* SARA *turns.*)

FANNY. Really, David—

DAVID. Be still, Mama.

TECK (*after a second*). Did you tell him that, Marthe?

MARTHE. Yes.

TECK (*looks up at her*). I shall not forgive you for that. (*Looks at* DAVID) It is a statement which no man likes to hear from another man. You understand that? (*Playfully*) That is the type of thing about which we used to play at duels in Europe.

DAVID (*comes toward him*). We are not so musical comedy here. And you are not in Europe.

TECK. Even if I were, I would not suggest any such action. I would have reasons for not wishing it.

DAVID. It would be well for you not to suggest *any* action. And the reason for *that* is you might get hurt.

TECK (*slowly*). That would not be my reason. (*To* MARTHE) Your affair has gone far enough—

MARTHE (*sharply*). It is not an affair—

TECK. I do not care what it is. The time has come to leave here. Go upstairs and pack your things. (*She does not move.* DAVID *turns toward her*) Go on, Marthe.

MARTHE (*to* DAVID). I am not going with him. I told you that.

DAVID. I don't want you to go with him.

FANNY (*carefully*). Really, David, aren't you interfering in all this a good deal—

DAVID (*carefully*). Yes, Mama. I am.

TECK (*to* MARTHE). When you are speaking to me, please say what you have to say to me.

MARTHE (*comes to him*). You are trying to frighten me. But you are not going to frighten me any more. I will say it to you: I am not going with you. I am never going with you again.

TECK (*softly*). If you do not fully mean what you say, or if you might change your mind, you are talking unwisely, Marthe.

MARTHE. I know that.

TECK. Shall we talk about it alone?

MARTHE. You can't make me go, can you, Teck?

TECK. No, I can't make you.

MARTHE. Then there's no sense talking about it.

TECK. Are you in love with him?

MARTHE. Yes.

FANNY (*sharply*). Marthe! What is all this?

MARTHE (*sharply*). I'll tell *you* about it in a minute.

DAVID. You don't have to explain anything to anybody.

TECK (*ignores him*). Is he in love with you?

MARTHE. I don't think so. You won't believe it, because you can't believe anything that hasn't got tricks to it, but David hasn't much to do with this. I told you I would leave some day, and I remember where I said it—(*Slowly*)— and why I said it.

TECK. I also remember. But I did not believe you. I have not had much to offer you these last years. But if now we had some money and could go back—

MARTHE. No. I don't like you, Teck. I never have.

TECK. And I have always known it.

FANNY (*stiffly*). I think your lack of affections should be discussed with more privacy. Perhaps—

DAVID. Mama—

MARTHE. There is nothing to discuss. Strange. I've talked to myself about this scene for almost fifteen years. I knew a lot of things to say to you and I used to lie awake at night or walk along the street and say them. Now I don't want to. I guess you only want to talk that way, when you're not sure what you can do. When you're sure, then what's the sense of saying it? "This is why and this is why and this—" (*Very happily*) But when you know you can do it, you don't have to say anything; you can just go. And I'm going. There is nothing you can do. I would like you to believe that now.

TECK. Very well, Marthe. I think I made a mistake. I should not have brought you here. I believe you now.

MARTHE (*after a pause, she looks at* DAVID). I'll move into Washington, and—

DAVID. Yes. Later. But I'd like you to stay here for a while, with us, if you wouldn't mind.

SARA. It would be better for you, Marthe—

FANNY. It's very interesting that I am not being consulted about this. (*To* MARTHE) I have nothing against you, Marthe. I am sorry for you, but I don't think—

MARTHE. Thank you, Sara, David. But I'd rather move in now. (*Turns, comes toward* FANNY) But perhaps I have something against you. Do you remember my wedding?

FANNY. Yes.

MARTHE. Do you remember how pleased Mama was with herself? Brilliant Mama, handsome Mama—everybody thought so, didn't they? A seventeen-year-old daughter, marrying a pretty good title, about to secure herself in a world that Mama liked—she didn't ask me what I liked. And the one time I tried to tell her, she frightened me— (*Looks up*) Maybe I've always been frightened. All my life.

TECK. Of course.

MARTHE (*to* FANNY, *as if she had not heard* TECK). I remember Mama's face at the wedding—it was *her* wedding, really, not mine.

FANNY (*sharply*). You are very hard on your mother.

MARTHE. Nineteen hundred and twenty-five. No, I'm not hard on her. I only tell the truth. She wanted a life for me, I suppose. It just wasn't the life I wanted for myself. (*Sharply*) And that's what you have tried to do. With your children. In another way. Only Sara got away. And that made you angry—until so many years went by that you forgot.

FANNY. I don't usually mind people saying anything they think, but I find that—

MARTHE. I don't care what you mind or don't mind. I'm in love with your son—

FANNY (*very sharply*). That's unfortunate—

MARTHE. And I'm sick of watching you try to make him into his father. I don't think you even know you do it any more and I don't think he knows it any more, either. And that's what's most dangerous about it.

FANNY (*very angrily*). I don't know what you are talking about.

DAVID. I think you do. (*Smiles*) You shouldn't mind hearing the truth—and neither should I.

FANNY (*worried, sharply*). David! What does all this nonsense mean? I—

MARTHE (*to* FANNY). Look. That pretty world Mama got me into was a tough world, see? I'm used to trouble. So don't try to interfere with me, because I won't let you. (*She goes to* DAVID) Let's just have a good time. (*He leans down, takes both her hands, kisses them. Then slowly, she turns away, starts to exit. To* TECK) You will also be going today?

TECK. Yes.

MARTHE. Then let us make sure we go in different directions, and do not meet again. Good-bye, Teck.

TECK. Good-bye, Marthe. You will not believe me, but I tried my best, and I am now most sorry to lose you.

MARTHE. Yes. I believe you. (*She moves out. There is silence for a minute.*)

FANNY. Well, a great many things have been said in the last few minutes.

DAVID (*crosses to bell cord. To* TECK). I will get Joseph to pack for you.

TECK. Thank you. Do not bother. I will ring for him when I am ready. (KURT *comes in from the study door.* SARA *turns, stares at him, waits. He does not look at her*) It will not take me very long. (*He starts for the door, looking at* KURT.)

SARA. What is it, Kurt?

KURT. It is nothing of importance, darling— (*He looks quickly at* TECK, *who is moving very slowly.*)

SARA. Don't tell me it's nothing. I know the way you look when—

KURT (*sharply*). I said it was of no importance. I must get to California for a few weeks. That is all.

SARA. I—

TECK (*turns*). It is in the afternoon newspaper, Herr Müller. (*Points to paper on table*) I was waiting to find the proper moment to call it to your attention. (*He moves toward the table, as they all turn to watch him. He picks up the paper, turns it over, begins to read*) "Zurich, Switzerland: The Zurich papers today reprinted a despatch from the *Berliner Tageblatt* on the capture of Colonel Max Freidank. Freidank is said—(SARA *begins to move toward him*)—to be the chief of the Anti-Nazi Underground Movement. Colonel Freidank has long been an almost legendary figure. The son of the famous General Freidank, he was a World War officer and a distinguished physicist before the advent of Hitler." That is all.

SARA. Max—

KURT. Be still, Sara.

TECK. They told me of it at the Embassy last night. They also told me that with him they had taken a man who called himself Ebber, and a man who called himself Triste. They could not find a man called Gotter. (*He starts again toward the door*) I shall be a lonely man without Marthe. I am also a very poor one. I should like to have ten thousand dollars before I go.

DAVID (*carefully*) You will make no loans in this house.

TECK. I was not speaking of a loan.

FANNY (*carefully*). God made you not only a scoundrel but a fool. That is a dangerous combination.

DAVID (*suddenly leaps toward* TECK). Damn you, you—

KURT (*suddenly pounds on the top of the piano, as* DAVID *almost reaches* TECK). Leave him alone. (*Moves quickly to stop* DAVID) Leave him alone! *David! Leave him alone!*

DAVID (*angrily to* KURT). Keep out of it. (*Starts toward* TECK *again*) I'm beginning to see what Marthe meant. Blackmailing with your wife— You—

KURT (*very sharply*). He is not speaking of his wife. Or you. He means me. (*Looks at* TECK) Is that correct?

(SARA *moves toward* KURT. DAVID *draws back, bewildered.*)

TECK. Good. It was necessary for me to hear you say it. You understand that?

KURT. I understand it.

SARA. (*frightened, softly*). Kurt—

DAVID. What is all this about? What the hell are you talking about?

TECK (*sharply for the first time*). Be still. (*To* KURT) At your convenience. Your hands are shaking, Herr Müller.

KURT (*quietly*). My hands were broken: they are bad when I have fear.

TECK. I am sorry. I can understand that. It is not pleasant. (*Motions toward* FANNY *and* DAVID) Perhaps you would

like a little time to— I will go and pack, and be ready
to leave. We will all find that more comfortable, I think.
You should get yourself a smaller gun, Herr Müller.
That pistol you have been carrying is big and awkward.

KURT. You saw the pistol when you examined our bags?

TECK. You knew that?

KURT. Oh, yes. I have the careful eye, through many years
of needing it. And then you have not the careful eye.
The pistol was lying to the left of a paper package and
when you leave, it is to the right of the package.

SARA. Kurt! Do you mean that—

KURT (*sharply*). Please, darling, do not do that.

TECK. It is a German Army Luger?

KURT. Yes.

TECK. Keep it in your pocket, Herr Müller. You will have
no need to use it. And, in any case, I am not afraid of it.
You understand that?

KURT (*slowly*). I understand that you are not a man of
fears. That is strange to me, because I am a man who
has so many fears.

TECK (*laughs, as he exits*). Are you? That is most interesting. (*He exits.*)

DAVID (*softly*). What is this about, Kurt?

KURT. He knows who I am and what I do and what I
carry with me.

SARA (*carefully*). What about Max?

KURT. The telephone was from Mexico. Ilse received a
cable. Early on the morning of Monday, they caught
Ebber and Triste. An hour after they took Max in Berlin. (*She looks up at him, begins to shake her head. He
presses her arm*) Yes. It is hard.

FANNY (*softly*). You said he knew who you were and
what you carried with you. I don't understand.

KURT. I am going to tell you: I am an outlaw. I work with
many others in an illegal organization. I have so worked

for seven years. I am on what is called a desired list. But I did not know I was worth ten thousand dollars. My price has risen.

DAVID (*slowly*). And what do you carry with you?

KURT. Twenty-three thousand dollars. It has been gathered from the pennies and the nickels of the poor who do not like Fascism, and who believe in the work we do. I came here to bring Sara home and to get the money. I had hopes to rest here for a while, and then—

SARA (*slowly*). And I had hopes someone else would take it back and you would stay with us— (*Shakes her head, then*) Max is not dead?

KURT. No. The left side of his face is dead. (*Softly*) It was a good face.

SARA (*to* FANNY *and* DAVID, *as if she were going to cry*). It was a very good face. He and Kurt—in the old days— (*To* KURT) After so many years. If Max got caught, then nobody's got a chance. Nobody. (*She suddenly sits down.*)

DAVID (*points upstairs*). He wants to sell what he knows to you? Is that right?

KURT. Yes.

FANNY. Wasn't it careless of you to leave twenty-three thousand dollars lying around to be seen?

KURT. No, it was not careless of me. It is in a locked brief-case. I have thus carried money for many years. There seemed no safer place than Sara's home. It was careless of you to have in your house a man who opens baggage and blackmails.

DAVID (*sharply*). Yes. It was very careless.

FANNY. But you said you knew he'd seen it—

KURT. Yes. I knew it the first day we were here. What was I to do about it? He is not a man who steals. This is a safer method. I knew that it would come some other way. I have been waiting to see what the way would be. That is all I could do.

DAVID (*to* FANNY). What's the difference? It's been done. (*To* KURT) If he wants to sell to you, he must have another buyer. Who?

KURT. The Embassy. Von Seitz, I think.

DAVID. You mean he has told Von Seitz about you and—

KURT. No. I do not think he has told him anything. As yet. It would be foolish of him. He has probably only asked most guarded questions.

DAVID. But you're here. You're in this country. They can't do anything to you. They wouldn't be crazy enough to try it. Is your passport all right?

KURT. Not quite.

FANNY. Why not? Why isn't it?

KURT (*wearily, as if he were bored*). Because people like me are not given visas with such ease. And I was in a hurry to bring my wife and my children to safety. (*Sharply*) Madame Fanny, you must come to understand it is no longer the world you once knew.

DAVID. It doesn't matter. You're a political refugee. We don't turn back people like you. People who are in danger. You will give me your passport and tomorrow morning I'll see Barens. We'll tell him the truth— (*Points to the door*) Tell de Brancovis to go to hell. There's not a damn thing he or anybody else can do.

SARA (*looks up at* KURT, *who is staring at her*). You don't understand, David.

DAVID. There's a great deal I don't understand. But there's nothing to worry about.

SARA. Not much to worry about as long as Kurt is in this house. But he's not going to—

KURT. The Count has made the guess that—

SARA. That you will go back to get Ebber and Triste and Max. Is that right, Kurt? Is that right?

KURT. Yes, darling, I will try. They were taken to Sonnenburg. Guards can be bribed— It has been done once before at Sonnenburg. We will try for it again. I must go back, Sara. I must start.

SARA. Of course, you must go back. I guess I was trying to think it wouldn't come. But— (*To* FANNY *and* DAVID) Kurt's got to go back. He's got to go home. He's got to buy them out. He'll do it, too. You'll see. (*She stops, breathes*) It's hard enough to get back. Very hard. But if they knew he was coming— They want Kurt bad. Almost as much as they wanted Max— And then there are hundreds of others, too— (*She gets up, comes to him. He holds her, puts his face in her hair. She stands holding him, trying to speak without crying. She puts her face down on his head*) Don't be scared, darling. You'll get back. You'll see. You've done it before— you'll do it again. Don't be scared. You'll get Max out all right. (*Gasps*) And then you'll do his work, won't you? That's good. That's fine. You'll do a good job, the way you've always done. (*She is crying very hard. To* FANNY) Kurt doesn't feel well. He was wounded and he gets tired— (*To* KURT) You don't feel well, do you? (*Slowly. She is crying too hard now to be heard clearly*) Don't be scared, darling. You'll get home. Don't worry, you'll get home. Yes, you will.

(*The curtain falls.*)

ACT THREE

SCENE: *The same. A half hour later.*

AT RISE: FANNY *is sitting in a chair.* KURT *is at the piano, his head resting on one hand. He is playing softly with the other hand.* SARA *is sitting very quietly on the couch.* DAVID *is pacing on the terrace.*

FANNY (*to* DAVID). David, would you stop that pacing, please? (DAVID *comes in*) And would you stop that one-hand piano playing? Either play, or get up.

(KURT *gets up, crosses to the couch, sits.* SARA *looks at him, gets up, crosses to the decanters, begins to make a drink.*)

SARA (*to* DAVID). A drink?

DAVID. What? Yes, please. (*To* KURT) Do you intend to buy your friends out of jail?

KURT. I intend to try.

FANNY. It's all very strange to me. I thought things were so well run that bribery and—

KURT (*smiles*). What a magnificent work Fascists have done in convincing the world that they are men from legends.

DAVID. They have done very well for themselves—unfortunately.

KURT. Yes. But not by themselves. Does it make us all uncomfortable to remember that they came in on the shoulders of the most powerful men in the world? Of course. And so we would prefer to believe they are men from the planets. They are not. Let me reassure you. They are smart, they are sick, and they are cruel. But given

309

men who know what they fight for— (*Shrugs*) I will console you. A year ago last month, at three o'clock in the morning, Freidank and I, with two elderly pistols, raided the home of the Gestapo chief in Konstanz, got what we wanted, and the following morning Friedank was eating his breakfast three blocks away, and I was over the Swiss border.

FANNY (*slowly*). You are brave men.

KURT. *I* do not tell you the story to prove we are remarkable, but to prove they are *not*.

(SARA *brings him a drink. Gives one to* DAVID.)

SARA (*softly, touching* KURT's *shoulder*). Kurt loves Max.

KURT. Always since I came here I have a dream: that he will come into this room some day. How he would like it here, eh, Sara? He loves good food and wine, and you have books— (*Laughs happily*) He is fifty-nine years of age. And when he was fifty-seven, he carried me on his back, seven miles across the border. I had been hurt— That takes a man, does it not?

FANNY (*to* KURT). You look like a sick man to me.

KURT. No. I'm only tired. I do not like to wait. It will go. It is the waiting that is always most bad for me.

DAVID (*points upstairs*). Damn him! He's doing it deliberately.

KURT. It is then the corruption begins. Once in Spain I waited for two days until the planes would exhaust themselves. I think then why must our side fight always with naked hands. The spirit and the hands. All is against us but ourselves.

SARA. You will not think that when the time comes. It will go.

KURT. Of a certainty.

FANNY. But does it have to go on being your hands?

KURT. For each man, his own hands. He has to sleep with them.

DAVID (*uncomfortably, as if he did not like to say it*). That's right. I guess it's the way all of us should feel. But—but you have a family. Isn't there somebody else who hasn't a wife and children—

KURT. Each could have his own excuse. Some love for the first time, some have bullet holes, some have fear of the camps, some are sick, many are getting older. (*Shrugs*) Each could find a reason. And many find it. My children are not the only children in the world, even to me.

FANNY. That's noble of you, of course. But they are your children, nevertheless. And Sara, she—

SARA. Mama—

KURT (*after a slight pause*). One means always in English to insult with that word noble?

FANNY. Of course not, I—

KURT. It is not noble. It is the way I must live. Good or bad, it is what I am. (*Turns deliberately to look at* FANNY) And what I am is not what you wanted for your daughter, twenty years ago or now.

FANNY. You are misunderstanding me.

KURT (*smiles*). For our girl, too, we want a safe and happy life. And it is thus I try to make it for her. We each have our way. I do not convert you to mine.

DAVID. You are very certain of your way.

KURT (*smiles*). I seem so to you? Good.

(JOSEPH *appears in the hall doorway. He is carrying valises and overcoats.*)

JOSEPH. What'll I do with these, Miss Fanny?

FANNY. They're too large for eating, aren't they? What were you thinking of doing with them?

JOSEPH. I mean, it's Fred's day off.

DAVID. All right. You drive him into town.

JOSEPH. Then who's going to serve at dinner?

FANNY (*impatiently*). Belle can do it alone tonight.

JOSEPH. No she can't. Belle's upstairs packing with Miss

Marthe. My, there's quite a lot of departing, ain't there?

FANNY (*very impatiently*). All right, then cook can bring in dinner.

JOSEPH. I wouldn't ask her to do that, if I were you. She's mighty mad: the sink pipe is leaking again. You just better wait for your dinner till I get back from Washington.

FANNY (*shouting*). We are not cripples and we were eating dinner in this house before you arrived to show us how to use the knife and fork. (JOSEPH *laughs*) Go on. Put his things in the car. I'll ring for you when he's ready.

JOSEPH. You told me the next time you screamed to remind you to ask my pardon.

FANNY. You call that screaming?

JOSEPH. Yes'm.

FANNY. Very well. I ask your pardon. (*Waves him away*) Go on!

JOSEPH. Yes'm. (*Exits.*)

(TECK *appears in the door. He is carrying his hat and the brief-case we have seen in Act One.* SARA, *seeing the brief-case, looks startled, looks quickly at* KURT. KURT *watches* TECK *as he comes toward him.* TECK *throws his hat on a chair, comes to the table at which* KURT *is sitting, puts the brief-case on the table.* KURT *puts out his hand, puts it on the brief-case, leaves it there.*)

TECK (*smiles at the gesture*). Nothing has been touched, Herr Müller. I brought it from your room, for your convenience.

FANNY (*angrily*). Why didn't you steal it? Since you do not seem to—

TECK. That would have been very foolish of me, Madame Fanny.

KURT. Very.

TECK. I hope I have not kept you waiting too long. I

wanted to give you an opportunity to make any explanations—

DAVID (*angrily*). Does your price include listening to this tony conversation?

TECK (*turns to look at him*). My price will rise if I have to spend the next few minutes being interrupted by your temper. I will do my business with Herr Müller. And you will understand, I will take from you no interruptions, no exclamations, no lectures, no opinions of what I am or what I am doing.

KURT (*quietly*). You will not be interrupted.

TECK (*sits down at table with* KURT). I have been curious about you, Herr Müller. Even before you came here. Because Fanny and David either knew very little about you, which was strange, or wouldn't talk about you, which was just as strange. Have you ever had come to you one of those insistent half-memories of some person or some place?

KURT (*quietly, without looking up*). You had such a half-memory of me?

TECK. Not even a memory, but something. The curiosity of one European for another, perhaps.

KURT. A most sharp curiosity. You lost no time examining—(*Pats the case*)—this. You are an expert with locks?

TECK. No, indeed. Only when I wish to be.

FANNY (*angrily, to* TECK). I would like you out of this house as quickly as—

TECK (*turns to her*). Madame Fanny, I have just asked Mr. David not to do that. I must now ask you. (*Leans forward to* KURT) Herr Müller, I got one of the desired lists from Von Seitz, without, of course, revealing anything to him. As you probably know, they are quite easy to get. I simply told him that we refugees move in small circles and I might come across somebody on it. If, however, I have to listen to any more of this from any of you, I shall go immediately to him.

KURT (*to* DAVID *and* FANNY). Please allow the Count to do this in his own way. It will be best.

TECK (*takes a sheet of paper from his pocket*). There are sixty-three names on this list. I read them carefully, I narrow the possibilities and under "G" I find Gotter. (*Begins to read*) "Age, forty to forty-five. About six feet. One hundred seventy pounds. Birthplace unknown to us. Original occupation unknown to us, although he seems to know Munich and Dresden. Schooling unknown to us. Family unknown to us. No known political connections. No known trade-union connections. Many descriptions, few of them in agreement and none of them of great reliability. Equally unreliable, though often asked for, were Paris, Copenhagen, Brussels police descriptions. Only points on which there is agreement: married to a foreign woman, either American or English; three children; has used name of Gotter, Thomas Bodmer, Karl Francis. Thought to have left Germany in 1933, and to have joined Max Freidank shortly after. Worked closely with Freidank, perhaps directly under his orders. Known to have crossed border in 1934—February, May, June, October. Known to have again crossed border with Max Freidank in 1935—August, twice in October, November, January—"

KURT (*smiles*). The report is unreliable. It would have been impossible for God to have crossed the border that often.

TECK (*looks up, laughs. Then looks back at list*). "In 1934, outlaw radio station announcing itself as Radio European, begins to be heard. Station was located in Düsseldorf: the house of a restaurant waiter was searched, and nothing was found. Radio heard during most of 1934 and 1935. In an attempt to locate it, two probable

Communists killed in the tool-house of a farm near Bonn. In three of the broadcasts, Gotter known to have crossed border immediately before and after. Radio again became active in early part of 1936. Active attempt made to locate Freidank. Gotter believed to have then appeared in Spain with Madrid Government army, in one of the German brigades, and to have been a brigade commander under previously used name of Bodmer. Known to have stayed in France the first months of 1938. Again crossed German border some time during week when Hitler's Hamburg radio speech interrupted and went off the air." (*Looks up*) That was a daring deed, Herr Müller. It caused a great scandal. I remember. It amused me.

KURT. It was not done for that reason.

TECK. "Early in 1939, informer in Konstanz reported Gotter's entry, carrying money which had been exchanged in Paris and Brussels. Following day, home of Konstanz Gestapo chief raided for spy list by two men—" (KURT *turns to look at* FANNY *and* DAVID, *smiles*) My God, Herr Müller, that job took two good men.

SARA (*angrily*). Even you admire them.

TECK. Even I. Now I conclude a week ago that you are Gotter, Karl Francis—

KURT. Please. Do not describe me to myself again.

TECK. And that you will be traveling home—(*Points to brief-case*)—with this. But you seem in no hurry, and so I must wait. Last night when I hear that Freidank has been taken, I guess that you will now be leaving. Not for California. I will tell you free of charge, Herr Müller, that they have got no information from Freidank or the others.

KURT. Thank you. But I was sure they would not. I know all three most well. They will take what will be given them.

TECK (*looks down. Softly*). There is a deep sickness in the German character, Herr Müller. A pain-love, a death-love—

DAVID (*very angrily*). Oh, for God's sake, spare us *your* moral judgments.

FANNY (*very sharply*). Yes. They are sickening. Get on!

KURT. Fanny and David are Americans and they do not understand our world—as yet. (*Turns to* DAVID *and* FANNY) All Fascists are not of one mind, one stripe. There are those who give the orders, those who carry out the orders, those who watch the orders being carried out. Then there are those who are half in, half hoping to come in. They are made to do the dishes and clean the boots. Frequently they come in high places and wish now only to survive. They came late: some because they did not jump in time, some because they were stupid, some because they were shocked at the crudity of the *German* evil, and preferred their own evils, and some because they were fastidious men. For those last, we may well some day have pity. They are lost men, their spoils are small, their day is gone. (*To* TECK) Yes?

TECK (*slowly*). Yes. You have the understanding heart. It will get in your way some day.

KURT (*smiles*). I will watch it.

TECK. We are both men in trouble, Herr Müller. The world, ungratefully, seems to like your kind even less than it does mine. (*Leans forward*) Now. Let us do business. You will not get back if Von Seitz knows you are going.

KURT. You are wrong. Instead of crawling a hundred feet an hour in deep night, I will walk across the border with as little trouble as if I were a boy again on a summer walking trip. There are many men they would like to have. I would be allowed to walk directly to them—until they had all the names and all the addresses.

(*Laughs, points his finger at* TECK) *Roumanians* would pick me up ahead of time. *Germans* would not.

TECK (*smiles*). Still the national pride?

KURT. Why not? For that which is good.

FANNY (*comes over, very angrily, to* TECK). I have not often in my life felt what I feel now. Whatever you are, and however you became it, the picture of a man selling the lives of other men—

TECK. Is very ugly, Madame Fanny. I do not do it without some shame, and therefore I must sink my shame in large money. (*Puts his hand on the brief-case*) The money is here. For ten thousand, you go back to save your friends, nobody will know that you go, and I will give you my good wishes. (*Slowly, deliberately,* KURT *begins to shake his head.* TECK *waits, then carefully*) No?

KURT. This money is going home with me. It was not given to me to save my life, and I shall not so use it. It is to save the lives and further the work of more than I. It is important to me to carry on that work and to save the lives of three valuable men, and to do that with all speed. But— (*Sharply*) Count de Brancovis, the first morning we arrived in this house, my children wanted their breakfast with great haste. That is because the evening before we had been able only to buy milk and buns for them. If I would not touch this money for them, I would not touch it for you. (*Very sharply*) It goes back with me. The way it is. And if it does not get back, it is because I will not get back.

(*There is a long pause.* SARA *gets up, turns away.*)

TECK. Then I do not think you will get back. You are a brave one, Herr Müller, but you will not get back.

KURT (*as if he were very tired*). I will send to you a postal card and tell you about my bravery.

DAVID (*coming toward* KURT). Is it true that if this swine talks, you and the others will be—

SARA (*very softly*). Caught and killed. Of course. If they're lucky enough to get killed quickly. (*Quietly, points to the table*) You should have seen his hands in 1935.

FANNY (*violently, to* DAVID). We'll give him the money. For God's sake, let's give it to him and get him out of here.

DAVID (*to* SARA). Do you want Kurt to go back?

SARA. Yes. I do.

DAVID. All right. (*Goes to her, lifts her face*) You're a good girl.

KURT. That is true. Brave and good, my Sara. She is everything. She is handsome and gay and— (*Puts his hand over his eyes.* SARA *turns away.*)

DAVID (*after a second, comes to stand near* TECK). If we give you the money, what is to keep you from selling to Von Seitz?

TECK. I do not like your thinking I would do that. But—

DAVID (*tensely*). Look here. I'm sick of what you'd like or wouldn't like. And I'm sick of your talk. We'll get this over with now, without any more fancy talk from you, or as far as I am concerned, you can get out of here without my money and sell to any buyer you can find. I can't take much more of you at any cost.

TECK (*smiles*). It is your anger which delays us. I was about to say that I understood your fear that I would go to Von Seitz, and I would suggest that you give me a small amount of cash now and a check dated a month from now. In a month, Herr Müller should be nearing home, and he can let you know. And if you should not honor the check because Herr Müller is already in Germany, Von Seitz will pay a little something for a reliable description. I will take my chance on that. You will now say that I could do that in any case—and that is the chance you will take.

DAVID (*looks at* KURT, *who does not look up*). Is a month enough? For you to get back?

KURT (*shrugs*). I do not know.

DAVID (*to* TECK). Two months from today. How do you want the cash and how do you want the check?

TECK. *One month from today.* That I will not discuss. One month. Please decide now.

DAVID (*sharply*). All right. (*To* TECK) How do you want it?

TECK. Seventy-five hundred dollars in a check. Twenty-five hundred in cash.

DAVID. I haven't anywhere near that much cash in the house. Leave your address and I'll send it to you in the morning.

TECK (*laughs*). Address? I have no address, and I wish it now. Madame Fanny has cash in her sitting-room safe.

FANNY. Have you investigated that, too?

TECK (*laughs*). No. You once told me you always kept money in the house.

DAVID (*to* FANNY). How much have you got upstairs?

FANNY. I don't know. About fifteen or sixteen hundred.

TECK. Very well. That will do. Make the rest in the check.

DAVID. Get it, Mama, please. (*He starts toward the library door.* FANNY *starts for the hall exit.*)

FANNY (*turns, looks carefully at* TECK). Years ago, I heard somebody say that being Roumanian was not a nationality, but a profession. The years have brought no change.

KURT (*softly*). Being a Roumanian aristocrat is a profession.

(FANNY *exits. After her exit, there is silence.* KURT *does not look up,* SARA *does not move.*)

TECK (*awkwardly*). The new world has left the room. (*Looks up at them*) I feel less discomfort with you. We are Europeans, born to trouble and understanding it.

KURT. My wife is not a European.

TECK. Almost. (*Points upstairs*) They are young. The world has gone well for most of them. For us— (*Smiles*) The three of us—we are like peasants watching the big frost. Work, trouble, ruin— (*Shrugs*) But no need to call curses at the frost. There it is, it will be again, always—for us.

SARA (*gets up, moves to the window, looks out*). You mean my husband and I do not have angry words for you. What for? We know how many there are of you. They don't, yet. My mother and brother feel shocked that you are in their house. For us—we have seen you in so many houses.

TECK. I do not say you *want* to understand me, Mrs. Müller. I say only that you do.

SARA. Yes. You are not difficult to understand.

KURT (*slowly gets up, stands stiffly. Then he moves toward the decanter table*). A whiskey?

TECK. No, thank you. (*He turns his head to watch* KURT *move. He turns back.*)

KURT. Sherry?

TECK (*nods*). Thank you, I will.

KURT (*as he pours*). You, too, wish to go back to Europe.

TECK. Yes.

KURT. But they do not much want you. Not since the Budapest oil deal of '31.

TECK. You seem as well informed about me as I am about you.

KURT. That must have been a conference of high comedy, that one. Everybody trying to guess whether Kessler was working for Fritz Thyssen, and what Thyssen *really* wanted—and whether this "National Socialism" was a smart blind of Thyssen's, and where was Wolff—I should like to have seen you and your friends. It is too bad: you guessed an inch off, eh?

TECK. More than an inch.

KURT. And Kessler has a memory? (*Almost playfully*) I do not think Von Seitz would pay you money for a description of a man who has a month to travel. But I think he would pay you in a visa and a cable to Kessler.

think you want a visa almost as much as you want money. Therefore, I conclude you will try for the money here, and the visa from Von Seitz. (*He comes toward the table carrying the sherry glass*) I cannot get anywhere near Germany in a month and you know it. (*He is about to place the glass on the table*) I have been bored with this talk of paying you money. If they are willing to try you on this fantasy, I am not. Whatever made you think I would take such a chance? Or *any* chance? You are a gambler. But you should not gamble with your life. (TECK *has turned to stare at him, made a half motion as if to rise. As he does so, and on the words, "gamble with your life,"* KURT *drops the glass, hits* TECK *in the face. Struggling,* TECK *makes a violent effort to rise.* KURT *throws himself on* TECK, *knocking him to the floor. As* TECK *falls to the floor,* KURT *hits him on the side of the head. At the fourth blow,* TECK *does not move.* KURT *rises, takes the gun from his pocket, begins to lift* TECK *from the floor. As he does so,* JOSHUA *appears in the hall entrance. He is washed and ready for dinner. As he reaches the door, he stops, sees the scene, stands quietly as if he were waiting for orders.* KURT *begins to balance* TECK, *to balance himself. To* JOSHUA) Hilf mir. (JOSHUA *comes quickly to* KURT) Mach die Tür auf! (JOSHUA *runs toward the doors, opens them, stands waiting*) Bleib da! Mach die Tür zu! (KURT *begins to move out through the terrace. When he is outside the doors,* JOSHUA *closes them quickly, stands looking at his mother.*)

SARA. There's trouble.

JOSHUA. Do not worry. I will go up now. I will pack. In ten minutes all will be ready. I will say nothing. I will get the children ready— (*He starts quickly for the hall, turns for a second to look toward the terrace doors. Then almost with a sob*) This was a nice house.

SARA (*softly*). We're not going this time, darling. There's no need to pack.

JOSHUA (*stares at her, puzzled*). But Papa—

SARA. Go upstairs, Joshua. Take Babbie and Bodo in your room, and close the door. Stay there until I call you. (*He looks at her,* SARA *sits down*) There's nothing to be frightened of, darling. Papa is all right. (*Then very softly*) Papa is going home.

JOSHUA. To Germany?

SARA. Yes.

JOSHUA. Oh. Alone?

SARA. Alone. (*Very softly*) Don't say anything to the children. He will tell them himself.

JOSHUA. I won't.

SARA (*as he hesitates*). I'm all right. Go upstairs now. (*He moves slowly out, she watches him, he disappears. For a minute she sits quietly. Then she gets up, moves to the terrace doors, stands with her hands pressed against them. Then she crosses, picks up the overturned chair, places it by the table, picks up the glass, puts it on the table. As if without knowing what she is doing, she wipes the table with her handkerchief.*)

(FANNY *comes in from hall. After a second,* DAVID *comes in from library. Stops, looks around room.*)

DAVID. Where is he? Upstairs?

SARA. No. They went outside.

FANNY. Outside? They went outside. What are they doing, picking a bouquet together?

SARA (*without turning*). They just went outside.

DAVID (*looks at her*). What's the matter, Sara?

(SARA *shakes her head. Goes to the desk, opens the telephone book, looks at a number, begins to dial the telephone.*)

FANNY. Eleven hundred, eleven hundred and fifty, twelve, twelve-fifty—

DAVID. For God's sake, stop counting that money.

FANNY. All right. I'm nervous. And I don't like to think of giving him too much.

SARA. It's very nice of you and Mama. All that money— (*Into the telephone*) Hello. What time is your next plane? Oh. To— South. To El Paso, or—Brownsville. Yes.

DAVID (*to* FANNY). Is Joseph ready?

FANNY. I don't know. I told him I'd call him.

SARA. To Brownsville? Yes. Yes. That's all right. At what time? Yes. No. The ticket will be picked up at the airport. (DAVID *begins to cross to the bell cord. She looks up*) No. David. Don't call Joseph. *David! Please!* (*He draws back, stares at her. Looking at him, she goes on with the conversation*) Ritter. R-I-T-T-E-R. From Chicago. Yes. Yes. (*She hangs up, walks away.*)

DAVID. Sara! What's happening? What is all this? (*She does not answer*) Where is Kurt? What— (*He starts for the terrace door.*)

SARA. David. *Don't go out.*

FANNY (*rises*). Sara! What's happening—

SARA. For seven years now, day in, day out, men have crossed the German border. They are always in danger. They always may be going in to die. Did you ever see the face of a man who never knows if this day will be the last day? (*Softly*) Don't go out on the terrace, David. Leave Kurt alone.

FANNY (*softly*). Sara! What is—

SARA (*quietly*). For them, it may be torture, and it may be death. Some day, when it's all over, maybe there'll be a few of them left to celebrate. There aren't many of Kurt's age left. He couldn't take a chance on them. They wouldn't have liked it. (*Suddenly, violently*) He'd have had a bad time trying to explain to them that because of this house and this nice town and my mother and my brother, he took chances with their work and with their lives. (*Quietly*) Sit down, Mama. I think it's all over

now. (*To* DAVID) There's nothing you can do about it.
It's the way it had to be.

DAVID. Sara—

FANNY. Do you mean what I think you— (*She sits down.*)

SARA (*she turns, looks out toward the doors. After a pause*).
He's going away tonight and he's never coming back any
more. (*In a sing-song*) Never, never, never. (*She looks
down at her hands, as if she were very interested in
them*) I don't like to be alone at night. I guess everybody in the world's got a time they don't like. Me, it's
right before I go to sleep. And now it's going to be for
always. All the rest of my life. (*She looks up as* KURT
comes in from the terrace) I've told them. There is an
eight-thirty plane going as far south as Brownsville. I've
made you a reservation. In the name of Ritter.

KURT (*stands looking at her*). Liebe Sara! (*Then he goes
to the table at which* FANNY *is sitting. To* FANNY) It is
hard for you, eh? (*He pats her hand*) I am sorry.

FANNY (*without knowing why, she takes her hand away*).
Hard? I don't know. I— I don't— I don't know what I
want to say.

KURT (*looks at the hand she has touched, then turns to
look at* DAVID). Before I come in, I stand and think. I
say, I will make Fanny and David understand. I say,
how can I? Does one understand a killing? No. To
hell with it, I say. I do what must be done. I have long
sickened of words when I see the men who live by
them. What do you wish to make them understand, I
ask myself. Wait. Stand here. Just stand here. What are
you thinking? Say it to them just as it comes to you.
And this is what came to me. When you kill in a war,
it is not so lonely; and I remember a cousin I have not
seen for many years; and a melody comes back and I
begin to make it with my fingers; a staircase in a house
in Bonn years ago; an old dog who used to live in our

town; Sara in a hundred places— Shame on us. Thousands of years and we cannot yet make a world. Like a child I am. I have stopped a man's life. (*Points to the place on the couch where he had been sitting opposite* TECK) I sit here. I listen to him. You will not believe— but I pray that I will not have to touch him. Then I know I will have to. I know that if I do not, it is only that I pamper myself, and risk the lives of others. I want you from the room. I know what I must do. (*Loudly*) All right. Do I now pretend sorrow? Do I now pretend it is not I who act thus? No. I do it. I have done it. I will do it again. And I will keep my hope that we may make a world in which all men can die in bed. I have a great hate for the violent. They are the sick of the world. (*Softly*) Maybe I am sick now, too.

SARA. You aren't sick. Stop that. It's late. You must go soon.

KURT (*he puts out his hands, she touches them*). I am going to say good-bye now to my children. Then I am going to take your car— (*Motions with his head*) I will take him with me. After that, it is up to you. Two ways: You can let me go and keep silent. I believe I can hide him and the car. At the end of two days, if they have not been found, you will tell as much of the truth as is safe for you to say. Tell them the last time you saw us we were on our way to Washington. You did not worry at the absence, we might have rested there. Two crazy foreigners fight, one gets killed, you know nothing of the reason. I will have left the gun, there will be no doubt who did the killing. If you will give me those two days, I think I will be far enough away from here. If the car is found before then—(*Shrugs*) I will still try to move with speed. And all that will make you, for yourselves, part of a murder. For the world, I do not think you will be in bad trouble. (*He pauses*) There is another way. You can call your police. You can tell them the truth. I will not get home. (*To* SARA) I wish to see the children now. (*She goes out into the hall and up the stairs. There is silence.*)

FANNY. What are you thinking, David?

DAVID. I don't know. What are you thinking?

FANNY. Me? Oh, I was thinking about my Joshua. I was thinking that a few months before he died, we were sitting out there. (*Points to terrace*) He said, "Fanny, the Renaissance American is dying, the Renaissance man is dying." I said what do you mean, although I knew what he meant, I always knew. "A Renaissance man," he said, "is a man who wants to know. He wants to know how fast a bird will fly, how thick is the crust of the earth, what made Iago evil, how to plow a field. He knows there is no dignity to a mountain, if there is no dignity to man. You can't put that in a man, but when it's *really* there, and he will fight for it, put your trust in him."

DAVID (*gets up, smiles, looks at* FANNY). You're a smart woman sometimes. (SARA *enters with* JOSHUA. *To* KURT) Don't worry about things here. My soul doesn't have to be so nice and clean. I'll take care of it. You'll have your two days. And good luck to you.

FANNY. You go with my blessing, too. I like you. (BODO *enters.*)

SARA. See? I come from good stock. (KURT *looks at* DAVID. *Then he begins to smile. Nods to* DAVID. *Turns, smiles at* FANNY.)

FANNY. Do you like me?

KURT. I like you, Madame, very much.

FANNY. Would you be able to cash that check?

KURT (*laughs*). Oh, no.

FANNY. Then take the cash. I, too, would like to contribute to your work.

KURT (*slowly*). All right. Thank you. (*He takes the money from the table, puts it in his pocket.*)

BODO (*to* KURT). You like Grandma? I thought you would, with time. I like her, too. Sometimes she dilates with screaming, but— Dilates is correct? (BABETTE *enters.* JOSHUA *stands away from the others, looking at his father.* KURT *turns to look at him.*)

JOSHUA. Alles in Ordnung?

KURT. Alles in Ordnung.

BODO. What? What does that mean, all is well? (*There is an awkward silence.*)

BABETTE (*as if she sensed it*). We are all clean for dinner. But nobody else is clean. And I have on Grandma's dress to me—

FANNY (*very nervously*). Of course. And you look very pretty. You're a pretty little girl, Babbie.

BODO (*looks around the room*). What is the matter? Everybody is acting like such a ninny. I got that word from Grandma.

KURT. Come here. (*They look at him. Then slowly* BABETTE *comes toward him, followed by* BODO. JOSHUA *comes more slowly, to stand at the side of* KURT's *chair*) We have said many good-byes to each other, eh? We must now say another. (*As they stare at him, he smiles, slowly, as if it were difficult*) This time, I leave you with good people to whom I believe you also will be good. (*Half playfully*) Would you allow me to give away my share in you, until I come back?

BABETTE (*slowly*). If you would like it.

KURT. Good. To your mother, her share. My share, to Fanny and David. It is all I have to give. (*Laughs*) There. I have made a will, eh? Now. We will not joke. I have something to say to you. It is important for me to say it.

JOSHUA (*softly*). You are talking to us as if we were children.

KURT (*turns to look at him*). Am I, Joshua? I wish you were children. I wish I could say love your mother, do not eat too many sweets, clean your teeth— (*Draws* BODO *to him*) I cannot say these things. You are not children. I took it all away from you.

BABETTE. We have had a most enjoyable life, Papa.

KURT (*smiles*). You are a gallant little liar. And I thank you for it. I have done something bad today—

FANNY (*shocked, sharply*). Kurt—

SARA. Don't, Mama. (BODO *and* BABETTE *have looked at* FANNY *and* SARA, *puzzled. Then they have turned again to look at* KURT.)

KURT. It is not to frighten you. In a few days, your mother and David will tell you.

BODO. You could not do a bad thing.

BABETTE (*proudly*). You could not.

KURT (*shakes his head*). Now let us get straight together. The four of us. Do you remember when we read "Les Misérables"? Do you remember that we talked about it afterward and Bodo got candy on Mama's bed?

BODO. I remember.

KURT. Well. He stole bread. The world is out of shape we said, when there are hungry men. And until it gets in shape, men will steal and lie and—(*A little more slowly*) —kill. But for whatever reason it is done, and whoever does it—you understand me—it is all bad. I want you to remember that. Whoever does it, it is bad. (*Then very gaily*) But you will live to see the day when it will not have to be. All over the world, in every place and every town, there are men who are going to make sure it will not have to be. They want what I want: a childhood for every child. For my children, and I for theirs. (*He picks* BODO *up, rises*) Think of that. It will make you happy. In every town and every village and every mud hut in the world, there is always a man who loves children and who will fight to make a good world for them. And now good-bye. Wait for me. I shall try to come back for you. (*He moves toward the hall, fol-*

lowed by BABETTE, *and more slowly, by* JOSHUA) Or you shall come to me. At Hamburg, the boat will come in. It will be a fine, safe land— I will be waiting on the dock. And there will be the three of you and Mama and Fanny and David. And I will have ordered an extra big dinner and we will show them what our Germany can be like— (*He has put* BODO *down. He leans down, presses his face in* BABETTE's *hair. Tenderly, as her mother has done earlier, she touches his hair.*)

JOSHUA. Of course. That is the way it will be. Of course. But—but if you should find yourself delayed— (*Very slowly*) Then I will come to you. Mama.

SARA (*she has turned away*). I heard you, Joshua.

KURT (*he kisses* BABETTE). Gute Nacht, Liebling!

BABETTE. Gute Nacht, Papa. Mach's gut!

KURT (*leans to kiss* BODO). Good night, baby.

BODO. Good night, Papa. Mach's gut! (BABETTE *runs up the steps. Slowly* BODO *follows her.*)

KURT (*kisses* JOSHUA). Good night, son.

JOSHUA. Good night, Papa. Mach's gut! (*He begins to climb the steps.* KURT *stands watching them, smiling. When they disappear, he turns to* DAVID.)

KURT. Good-bye, and thank you.

DAVID. Good-bye, and good luck.

KURT (*he moves to* FANNY). Good-bye. I have good children, eh?

FANNY. Yes, you have. (KURT *kisses her hand.*)

KURT (*slowly, he turns toward* SARA). Men who wish to live have the best chance to live. I wish to live. I wish to live with you. (*She comes toward him.*)

SARA. For twenty years. It is as much for me today— (*Takes his arms*) Just once, and for all my life. (*He pulls her toward him*) Come back for me, darling. If you can. (*Takes brief case from table and gives it to him.*)

KURT (*simply*). I will try. (*He turns*) Good-bye, to you all. (*He exits. After a second, there is the sound of a car starting. They sit listening to it. Gradually the noise begins to go off into the distance. A second later,* JOSHUA *appears.*)

JOSHUA. Mama— (*She looks up. He is very tense*) Bodo cries. Babette looks very queer. I think you should come.

SARA (*gets up, slowly*). I'm coming.

JOSHUA (*to* FANNY *and* DAVID. *Still very tense*). Bodo talks so fancy, we forget sometimes he is a baby. (*He waits for* SARA *to come up to him. When she reaches him, she takes his hand, goes up the steps, disappears.* FANNY *and* DAVID *watch them.*)

FANNY (*after a minute*). Well, here we are. We're shaken out of the magnolias, eh?

DAVID. Yes. So we are.

FANNY. Tomorrow will be a hard day. But we'll have Babbie's birthday dinner. And we'll have music afterward. You can be the audience. I think you'd better go up to Marthe now. Be as careful as you can. She'd better stay here for a while. I daresay I can stand it.

DAVID (*turns, smiles*). Even your graciousness is ungracious, Mama.

FANNY. I do my best. Well, I think I shall go and talk to Anise. I like Anise best when I don't feel well. (*She begins to move off.*)

DAVID. Mama. (*She turns*) We are going to be in for trouble. You understand that?

FANNY. I understand it very well. We will manage. You and I. I'm not put together with flour paste. And neither are you—I am happy to learn.

DAVID. Good night, Mama. (*As she moves out, the curtain falls.*)

ANOTHER PART OF THE FOREST

FOR

MY GOOD FRIEND

GREGORY ZILBOORG

Kermit Bloomgarden presents Lillian Hellman's New Play
Another Part of the Forest

CAST

(In order of their appearance)

REGINA HUBBARD	PATRICIA NEAL
JOHN BAGTRY	BARTLETT ROBINSON
LAVINIA HUBBARD	MILDRED DUNNOCK
CORALEE	BEATRICE THOMPSON
MARCUS HUBBARD	PERCY WARAM
BENJAMIN HUBBARD	LEO GENN
JACOB	STANLEY GREENE
OSCAR HUBBARD	SCOTT MCKAY
SIMON ISHAM	OWEN COLL
BIRDIE BAGTRY	MARGARET PHILLIPS
HAROLD PENNIMAN	PAUL FORD
GILBERT JUGGER	GENE O'DONNELL
LAURETTE SINCEE	JEAN HAGEN

The play was directed by MISS HELLMAN.

The settings were designed by JO MIELZINER.

Opened at the Fulton Theatre on the night of November 20, 1946.

SCENE

ACT ONE

A Sunday morning in June, 1880, the Alabama town of Bowden, the side portico of the Hubbard house.

ACT TWO

The next evening, the living room of the Hubbard house.

ACT THREE

Early the next morning, the side portico of the Hubbard house.

Throughout the play, in the stage directions, left and right mean audience's left and right.

ANOTHER PART OF THE FOREST

ACT ONE

SCENE: *The side portico of the Hubbard house, a Sunday morning in the summer of 1880 in the Alabama town of Bowden. The portico leads into the living room by back center French doors. On the right side of the portico is an old wing of the house. An exterior staircase to this wing leads to an upper porch off which are the bedrooms of the house and behind the staircase are the back gardens and the kitchen quarters. Under the second-story porch is a door leading to the dining room of the house, and a back door leading to the kitchen. The other side of the portico leads to a lawn which faces the town's main street. The main part of the house, built in the 1850's, is Southern Greek. It is not a great mansion but it is a good house built by a man of taste from whom* MARCUS HUBBARD *bought it after the Civil War. There is not much furniture on the portico: two chairs and a table at one end, one comfortable chair and a table at the other end. Twin heads of Aristotle are on high pedestals. There is something too austere, too pretended Greek about the portico, as if it followed one man's eccentric taste and was not designed to be comfortable for anyone else.*

As the curtain rises, REGINA HUBBARD, *a handsome girl of twenty, is standing looking down at* JOHN BAGTRY. REGINA *has on a pretty negligee thrown over a nightgown. Her hair is pinned high, as if she had pinned it up*

quickly. JOHN BAGTRY *is a man of thirty-six with a sad,*
worn face. He is dressed in shabby riding shirt and Con-
federate Cavalry pants.

REGINA (*after a long silence*). Where were you going?
JOHN (*he has a soft, easy voice*). And what you doing
awake so early?
REGINA. Watching for you. But you tried not to hear me
when I called you. I called you three times before you
turned.
JOHN. I didn't think this was the place or the hour for us
to be meeting together. (*Looks around nervously*) We'll
be waking your folks. You out here in your wrapper!
That would make a pretty scandal, honey—
REGINA (*impatiently*). Nobody's awake. And I don't care.
Why didn't you—
JOHN (*quickly, gaily*). Oh, your Mama's up all right. I
saw her and your Coralee going into nigger church. I
bowed to her—
REGINA (*softly*). Why didn't you meet me last night?
JOHN (*after a second*). I couldn't. And I didn't know how
to send word.
REGINA. Why couldn't you? Plantation folks giving balls
again? Or fancy dress parties?
JOHN (*smiles*). I haven't been to a party since I was sixteen years old, Regina. The Bacons gave the last ball I
ever remember, to celebrate the opening of the war and
say good-bye to us—
REGINA. You've told me about it. Why couldn't you come
last night?
JOHN. I couldn't leave Aunt Clara and Cousin Birdie. They
wanted to sit out and talk after supper, and I couldn't.
REGINA (*slowly*). They wanted to talk? And so they made
you stay?
JOHN. No, they didn't *make* me. They're lonely, Regina,
and I'm not with them much, since you and I—

REGINA. Why should you be with them? When I want to meet you, I go and do it.

JOHN. Things are different with us. Everything is bad. This summer is the worst, I guess, in all the years. They are lonely—

REGINA. It's not the first time you didn't come. And you think I shouldn't be angry, and take you back the next day. It would be better if you lied to me where you were. This way it's just insulting to me. Better if you lied.

JOHN. Lie? Why would I lie?

REGINA. Better if you said you were with another woman. But not meeting me because of those two mummies—

JOHN (*softly*). I like them, Regina. And they don't go around raising their voices in anger on an early Sunday day.

REGINA. I don't want you to tell me about the differences in your family and mine.

JOHN (*stares at her*). I've never done that. Never.

REGINA. That's what you always mean when you say I'm screaming.

JOHN (*sharply*). I mean no such thing. I said only that I stayed with Aunt Clara and Cousin Birdie last night. And I'll do it again. (*Desperately*) Look, honey, I didn't mean not to come to meet you. But I've lived on them for fifteen years. They're good to me. They share with me the little they got, and I don't give back anything to them—

REGINA (*tensely*). I'm getting sick of them. They've got to know about you and me some day soon. I think I'm going to sashay right up to that sacred plantation grass and tell them the war's over, the old times are finished, and so are they. I'm going to tell them to stay out of my way—

JOHN (*sharply*). They've never mentioned you, Regina.

REGINA. That's good breeding: to know about something and not talk about it?

JOHN. I don't know about good breeding.

REGINA (*turns to him*). They think they do. Your Cousin Birdie's never done more than say good morning in all these years—when she knows full well who I am and who Papa is. Knows full well he could buy and sell Lionnet on the same morning, its cotton and its women with it—

JOHN. I would not like to hear anybody talk that way again. No, I wouldn't.

REGINA (*pleadingly, softly*). I'm sorry, I'm sorry, I'm sorry. I give you my apology. I'm sorry, darling.

JOHN. We shouldn't be—

REGINA (*runs to him, takes his arm*). I'm never going to be mean again, never going to talk mean— Look, honey, I was mad about last night because I wanted to tell you about my plan. I've been thinking about it for months, and I've got Papa almost ready for it. But I can't tell it to you tonight because Papa makes me read to him every Sunday. But late tomorrow night, after Papa's music—it's over early—please, darling, tomorrow night— tomorrow night— (*She clings to him.*)

JOHN (*turns to her*). Regina, we mustn't. We mustn't any more. It's not right for you, honey, we're a scandal now. I'm no good for you. I'm too old, I'm—

REGINA (*clinging to him, impatient*). Why do you say that? A man at thirty-six talking that way? It comes from hanging around this town and your kinfolk.

JOHN. I was only good once—in a war. Some men shouldn't ever come home from a war. You know something? It's the only time I was happy.

REGINA (*draws away from him, wearily*). Oh, don't tell me that again. You and your damn war. Wasn't it silly to be happy when you knew you were going to lose?

JOHN. You think it is silly? You think we all were? Of

course you do. In this house you couldn't think anything else. (*She draws back*) And now *I'm* sorry. That was most rude. It's late, honey.

REGINA (*quickly*). You haven't even asked me about my plan.

JOHN. I have a plan, too. I have a letter from Cod Carter. He's in Brazil. He's fighting down there, he says—

(LAVINIA HUBBARD *and* CORALEE *appear from around the portico, as if coming from street.* JOHN *stares at them, draws back nervously.* REGINA *watches him, amused.* LAVINIA HUBBARD *is a woman of about fifty-eight, stooped, thin, delicate-looking. She has a sweet, high voice and a distracted, nervous way of speaking.* CORALEE *is a sturdy Negro woman of about forty-five. She is holding a parasol over* LAVINIA. JOHN *steps forward.* CORALEE *folds parasol, stares at* REGINA'S *costume, exits under porch to kitchen.*)

LAVINIA (*as if this were an ordinary morning scene*). Morning, Captain Bagtry. Been for a nice little stroll?

JOHN (*quickly*). Morning, Mrs. Hubbard. No, ma'am. I was just riding by and glimpsed Miss Regina—

LAVINIA (*nods*). That's nice. Coralee and I been to our church. The colored folks said a prayer for me and a little song. It's my birthday.

JOHN. Congratulations, ma'am. I sure give you my good wishes.

LAVINIA. Thank you, sir. And later I'm going back to the second service. And I know a secret: they're going to give me a cake. Ain't that lovely of them, and me undeserving? (*Looks up at him*) I always go to the colored church. I ain't been to a white church in years. Most people don't like my doing it, I'm sure, but I got my good reasons—

REGINA. All right, Mama.

LAVINIA. There's got to be one little thing you do that you want to do, all by yourself you want to do it.

REGINA (*sharply*). All right, Mama.

LAVINIA (*hurries toward the doors of the living room*). Oh. Sorry. (*At the door of living room, looks back at* JOHN) I remember you and your cousins the day you left town for war. I blew you a kiss. Course we were living in our little house then and you didn't know. But I blew you all a kiss.

JOHN (*very pleased*). I'm glad to know it, ma'am. It was a great day. A hot day— You know something, ma'am? It was my birthday, too, that day. I was sixteen, and my cousins not much older. My birthday. Isn't that a coincidence, ma'am?

REGINA. Why?

JOHN (*lamely*). Because it's your Mama's birthday today.

LAVINIA. And you know something else, Captain Bagtry? Tomorrow's my wedding anniversary day. Your birthday, my birthday, and a wedding anniversary day.

REGINA (*very sharply*). All right, Mama.

(MARCUS HUBBARD *opens the door of his bedroom and appears on the upper porch. He is a strong-looking man of sixty-three, with a soft voice of tone and depth. He speaks slowly, as if he put value on the words.*)

MARCUS. Who's speaking on the porch?

(*At the sound of his voice* LAVINIA *hurries into the house.* JOHN *draws back into the living-room doors.* REGINA *comes forward.*)

REGINA. I'm down here, Papa.

MARCUS. Morning, darling. Waiting for me?

REGINA. Er. Mama's just been to church.

MARCUS. Of course—where else would she go? Wait. Have your first coffee with me. (*He exits into his room.*)

REGINA (*amused at* JOHN's *nervous movements, takes his arm*). I want you to meet Papa. Not now. But soon.

JOHN. I know your Papa. I'm in and out of your store—

REGINA. I want you to come *here*. I guess no Bagtry ever been inside our house. But would your Aunt Clara and your Cousin Birdie allow you to come, do you reckon?

JOHN. Allow me? I didn't think that was the way it was. I thought your Papa didn't want anybody here—

REGINA. He doesn't. But I'll find a way. Will you meet me tomorrow night, same place? Darling, darling, please. Please. (*She pulls him toward her. He hesitates for a second. Then he takes her in his arms, kisses her with great feeling. She smiles.*) Meet me?

JOHN (*softly*). I always do. No matter what I say or think, I always do.

(*He kisses her again. Then he runs off. She stands for a minute staring after him. Then, from the street side of the lawn,* BENJAMIN HUBBARD *appears. He is followed by* JACOB *carrying a small valise and three boxes.* JACOB *is a tall, thin Negro of about thirty.* BEN *is thirty-five: a powerful, calm man with a quiet manner.*)

REGINA (*amused*). Morning, Ben. Have a good trip?

BEN. Was that Bagtry?

REGINA. He said that was his name.

BEN. What you doing having men on the porch, you in your wrapper?

REGINA (*gaily*). Isn't it a pretty wrapper? Came from Chicago.

BEN (*pointing to boxes*). And so did these, on the mail train. They got your name on 'em. Belong to you?

REGINA (*giggling*). Writing can't lie. Specially writing in ink.

MARCUS (*reappears on balcony, calls down*). Coffee ready for me, darling?

REGINA (*gaily, smiling at* BEN). Going in to brew it myself, honey.

(*She disappears into house.* MARCUS *comes forward on the porch, sees* BEN *and* JAKE.)

MARCUS (*stares at* JAKE). Jake, take the boxes in. (JAKE *starts in*) And put Mr. Benjamin's valise out of your hand. (JAKE *hesitates, looks puzzled.* BEN *stares up at*

MARCUS. *Then* JAKE *puts valise down, exits*) How was the world of fashion, Benjamin?

BEN. I was only in it for twenty-four hours.

MARCUS. Ah. That isn't long enough.

BEN. You ordered me back.

MARCUS. What for?

BEN (*looks up, smiles*). The pleasure of it, I think.

MARCUS (*giggles*). Certainly. But what did I call the pleasure?

BEN. You said the books needed checking, and I was to be back to do them today.

MARCUS (*thinks*). Books? I wouldn't let you touch the books in my library, Benjamin. Certainly you know that.

BEN (*annoyed*). Books for the store. *Store. Bookkeeping. Accounts.*

MARCUS. Oh. But why today?

BEN. I don't know, Papa. I'd like to have stayed in Mobile. I had some business—

MARCUS (*clucks*). But I brought you back on a Sunday to look at store books. Now why did I do that? I must have had some reason. I'll think of it later. (*He looks down, realizes* BEN *isn't going to answer*) What business did you have, Ben?

BEN. I wanted to invest two thousand dollars in Birmingham Coal, Incorporated. It will bring fifty thousand some day. There's coal there, and they're sending down men from the North with money for it— But I couldn't raise it. And you wouldn't lend it to me.

MARCUS. That why you went? That foolish old scheme of yours? I had hoped you went to Mobile for a lady.

BEN. No, sir. I have no lady.

MARCUS. I believe you. But certainly you went to the concert last night?

BEN. No, I didn't. I told you: I was trying to borrow the two thousand you wouldn't let me have.

MARCUS. Well, you must hear a good concert before you die.

(LAVINIA *and* CORALEE *enter from kitchen door.*)

MARCUS (*starts into his room*). Carry in your own valise, son. It is not seemly for a man to load his goods on other men, black or white.

(BEN *looks up, half annoyed, half amused. He picks up his valise, starts toward door as* CORALEE *appears, carrying breakfast tray.* LAVINIA *follows her.* BEN *watches them as* CORALEE *puts tray on table.* LAVINIA, *knowing that* MARCUS *is on the balcony, but not knowing whether she should speak to him, helps* CORALEE *by aimlessly fussing about with the tray.*)

LAVINIA (*to* BEN). Morning, son.

BEN. Morning, Mama.

LAVINIA. Pleasant trip?

BEN. No, unsuccessful.

LAVINIA. That's good, I'm sure. I mean— Morning, Marcus.

MARCUS. Coralee. I'll be right down. Lavinia, send everybody else to the dining room for breakfast. Go on, Lavinia.

(*He disappears.* LAVINIA *spills coffee.*)

CORALEE (*quickly*). All right, Miss Viney. No harm. Go on in and have your breakfast before there's trouble.

LAVINIA. I was only trying—

(LAVINIA *goes into living room as* MARCUS *comes downstairs carrying a book. He goes immediately to table.* CORALEE *pours coffee.*)

MARCUS. Who is down for breakfast?

CORALEE. I don't know.

LAVINIA (*reappears in living-room doorway*). Oh, Marcus, Colonel Isham is calling. Can he come out?

MARCUS. If he is capable of walking.

(COLONEL ISHAM, *a man of sixty-five appears in the doorway.*)

MARCUS. Colonel Isham.

ISHAM. You will forgive this too early visit?

MARCUS. You're in town for church?

ISHAM. I've come to see you. I was asked to come to see you.

MARCUS. To talk about bad cotton?

ISHAM. No sir. I don't mix with a man's Sunday breakfast, to talk about cotton. I come to talk about your son Oscar.

MARCUS. Then you will need coffee.

ISHAM. Thank you, no. Two nights ago—

MARCUS. People like you don't drink coffee with people like me?

ISHAM. I've had coffee. Now, Mr. Hubbard—

MARCUS. Then come again when you haven't had it.

(*There is a pause. Slowly* ISHAM *comes to the table.* MARCUS *smiles, pours a cup of coffee, hands it to* ISHAM, *who takes it and sits down.*)

ISHAM. Thank you. I have come here for your sake, Mr. Hubbard. There is dangerous feeling up in my town this morning—

MARCUS. Colonel, I hate conversations for my sake. Sunday is my day of study. I don't wish to sound rude but please say quickly what you have come about.

ISHAM (*smiles*). Mr. Hubbard, I'm too old to frighten.

MARCUS (*smiles*). And I should be a daring man to try it. You, one of our great heroes. Commanding the first Alabama troops at—

ISHAM (*sharply*). I am not interested in talking to you about the War Between the States, or about your personal war on the people of this state— Now, please listen to me. Two nights ago Sam Taylor in Roseville was badly beaten up. Last night fourteen people identified the night riders as the Cross boys, from over the line, and your son Oscar.

MARCUS (*shouts into the house*). Benjamin. Rope Oscar and bring him out here immediately. I told you fifteen years ago you were damn fools to let Klansmen ride around, carrying guns—

ISHAM. Were you frightened of our riding on you? I came here to tell you to make your son quit. He can thank me he's not swinging from a rope this minute. You have good reason to know there's not a man in this county wouldn't like to swing up anybody called Hubbard. I stopped my friends last night but I may not be able to stop them again. Tell him what patriots do is our business. But he's got no right to be riding down on anybody—

(BEN, *followed by* OSCAR, *appears in the dining-room door-way.* OSCAR *looks frightened, decides to be cute.*)

OSCAR. *Rope* me out. I can stand up, Papa. Never felt my Saturday night liquor that bad—

ISHAM (*ignoring* OSCAR, *to* MARCUS). Taylor is a good man. He's got no money for treatment, got no job now, won't get one again.

MARCUS (*to* OSCAR). Colonel Isham has just saved you from a lynching party. Should I thank him?

OSCAR (*terrified*). Lynching! What did— Colonel Isham —I—

ISHAM. I don't want to speak with you.

MARCUS. Who does?

OSCAR. But what did I—

MARCUS. Do I have to tell you that if you ever put on those robes again, or take a gun to any man— (*Takes roll of bills from his pocket, throws it to* BENJAMIN) Count out five hundred dollars, Benjamin.

OSCAR (*very nervous*). You mean Taylor? I wasn't riding with the Klan boys. No, I wasn't. I was thinking about it, but—

BEN. No, he couldn't have been with them. He took me to the Mobile train, and the train was late, so we sat talking. He couldn't have got up to Roseville.

ISHAM. You say you're willing to swear to that, Mr. Benjamin? You sure you're willing to go against fourteen people identifying your brother—?

BEN. Oh, Oscar looks like anybody.

MARCUS (*smiles*). Give the money to Colonel Isham, Benjamin. Go away, Oscar. (*Oscar exits through dining-room door*) Please use the money for Taylor.

ISHAM. We'll take care of him, Hubbard. Good day, sir.

MARCUS. You won't take care of him, because you can't. Learn to be poor, Isham, it has more dignity. Tell Taylor there will be a check each month. Tell him that my other son, Benjamin, wishes to make amends. Ben has a most charitable nature.

(ISHAM *hesitates, decides, takes the money, looks at it.*)

ISHAM. There is no need for so much. A hundred would be more proper.

MARCUS. Good day, Colonel. Don't give me lectures on propriety.

(ISHAM *starts to speak, changes his mind, exits left toward street. There is a pause.* BEN *looks at* MARCUS, *drops the roll of money on* MARCUS's *table.*)

BEN (*smiles*). You didn't like my story about Oscar?

MARCUS. Not much. Very loyal of you, however.

BEN. I like it.

MARCUS. Good. It's yours. Keep it. You must have one of your usual involved reasons for wanting it.

BEN. Five hundred dollars is a lot of money to a man who allows himself six dollars for a trip to Mobile.

MARCUS. Perhaps you're stingy.

BEN. You can't be much else on a salary of twenty dollars a week.

MARCUS. Is that all I pay you? Ah, well, you'll be better off when I—if and when I die. But I may not die; did I tell you, Benjamin?

(REGINA, OSCAR *and* LAVINIA *appear from the living room.* REGINA *hurries to* MARCUS.)

REGINA. Forgive me, darling. I forgot your coffee.

(OSCAR *is carrying a cup of coffee and a roll.* LAVINIA, *who never sees anything, bumps into him.* OSCAR *turns on her angrily.*)

OSCAR. Goodness sake, Mama. Watch where you going.

REGINA. Oscar's in a bad humor this morning. Oscar's got one of those faces shows everything.

LAVINIA (*to everybody—nobody pays any attention*). I'm sorry. I'm sure I didn't mean to—

MARCUS. Oscar has good reason for being in a bad humor. He owes me five hundred dollars.

(OSCAR's *hand begins to shake on the cup. He rattles the spoon and saucer.*)

BEN. For God's sake sit down and stop rattling that cup.

OSCAR. Papa, you can't mean that— Ben told you where I was. I wasn't even—

MARCUS (*to* REGINA). You look charming. New?

REGINA. No. But I *did* buy a few new dresses.

MARCUS. A few? I saw the boxes coming in.

OSCAR. Seven dresses. Seven, I counted them.

REGINA. Can you count up to seven now? And more coming next week, Papa.

MARCUS. What are you going to do with them, honey?

REGINA (*hesitates, then gaily*). Could we go for a walk?

BEN. You buying these clothes out of your allowance?

REGINA (*laughs*). Aren't you silly? How could I? There's a fur piece and a muff that cost three hundred dollars alone. They're charming, Papa, wait till you see them—

OSCAR (*delighted at the diversion in the conversation*). You really gone crazy? Nobody's ever worn furs in this climate since old lady Somers put that bear rug around her and jumped out the porch.

REGINA. I won't jump out the porch.

BEN. I will have to O.K. the bills, so would you tell me how much you've spent?

REGINA (*airily*). I don't know. I didn't even ask.

OSCAR (*shrilly*). Didn't even ask? Didn't even ask? You

gone real crazy, acting like Miss Vanderbilt, whatever her name is—rich people up North don't act that way. They watch their money, and their fathers' money.

REGINA. Oh, that's not true. Those people in Chicago, just the other day, gave their daughter a hundred-thousand-dollar check for a trousseau—

BEN (*looks at her*). A trousseau? So that's what you're buying? I saw Horace Giddens in Mobile last evening, and he was mighty disappointed you haven't answered his letter about coming up for another visit here.

OSCAR. Hey, he wouldn't be bad for you, Regina—

BEN. He's in love with you. That was obvious when he was here. It's good society, that family, and rich. Solid, quiet rich.

OSCAR. And you'd get to like him. A lot of people get married not liking each other. Then, after marriage, they still don't like each other much, I guess—

BEN (*sharply*). Are you still drunk?

LAVINIA (*comes to life*). A wedding? That would be nice. I hope you make your plans right quick, Regina, because—

MARCUS (*very slowly*). What is all this, Regina?

LAVINIA. I didn't say anything. I was twisting my handkerchief—

REGINA. It's nothing, Papa, nothing. You know Ben. You know he wants me to marry money for him. I'm not even thinking about Giddens. I don't like him.

BEN. Certainly I want you to marry money. More than that— (*She wheels around to stare at him*) You're twenty years old. You ought to be settled down. You been worrying us. (*Pleased at the nervousness* REGINA *is showing*) Isn't that so, Mama? Hasn't Regina been worrying you?

LAVINIA. I really don't know, son. I really couldn't say.

OSCAR. Well, I could say she's been worrying me. Many's

the time I thought of taking action. Sashaying around as open as—

REGINA (*to* OSCAR). Oh, shut up. (*To* MARCUS) Papa. You can't blame me if Ben thinks up one of his plans to annoy you, and Oscar chimes in like he always does. I bought the clothes because I—because I want to take a little trip. That's all, Papa.

MARCUS. A trip?

REGINA. All right. I'll send back the dresses. I don't know what all this talk's about. (*Comes to him*) Spoiling your Sunday. Come on, darling. Let's take our lunch and go on a picnic, just you and me. We haven't done that in a long time.

MARCUS. No, not for a long time. (*To* BEN) Something amuses you?

BEN. Yes. You and Regina.

MARCUS (*to* BEN *and* OSCAR). The two of you have contrived to give me a bad morning. (*To* OSCAR) And you have cost me five hundred dollars. How much you drawing at the store?

OSCAR (*nervous but determined*). I was going to talk to you about that, Papa. I'm drawing sixteen a week. It ain't enough, Papa, because, well, I'm getting on and I want a little life of my own. I was going to ask you if you couldn't sort of make a little advance against a little raise—

MARCUS. You'll get eleven a week hereafter. Five dollars will go to repay me for the five hundred.

OSCAR. My God, Papa. You can't— Eleven a week! My God, Papa— That wasn't what I meant. You misunderstood me 'cause I wasn't talking clear. I wanted a little *raise*, not a—

MARCUS (*to* BEN, *sharply*). Put aside your plans for your sister's future. Spend with profit your time today going over the store books. (*Then amused*) You'll find we are short of cash. Call in some cotton loans or mortgages. (*giggles*) Then go to church.

LAVINIA (*delighted*). Want to come with me, Benjamin? I'm going to my church, because they're saying a prayer for my birthday. (*To* MARCUS) It's my birthday, Marcus.

MARCUS. Congratulations, Lavinia.

LAVINIA. Thank you. (*Comes to* MARCUS) We were going to talk today. You promised, Marcus—

MARCUS. I promised to talk? Talk about what?

LAVINIA (*amazed, worried*). Talk about what? You know, Marcus. You promised last year, on my last birthday. You said you were too busy that day, but this year you said—

MARCUS. I'm still busy, my dear. Now you run and tell Belle to make us up a fine picnic basket. (*To* REGINA) And a good bottle of wine. I'll get it myself.

LAVINIA. But, Marcus, I been waiting since last year—

MARCUS. Get the lunch now. (*She hesitates, looks frightened, goes toward kitchen door. To* REGINA) I'll bring my Aristotle. You'll read in English, I'll follow you in Greek. Shall we walk or drive?

REGINA (*smiling*). Let's walk. You get the wine and your books. I'll change my clothes— (*He nods, smiles, goes into house. She stops to look at* BEN, *smiles*) You never going to learn, Ben. Been living with Papa for thirty-five years, and never going to learn.

OSCAR. Regina, you got a few hundred dollars to lend me? Wouldn't take me long to pay it back—

BEN. Learn what, honey?

OSCAR. Papa's sure hard on me. It's unnatural. If a stranger came in he'd think Papa didn't like me, his own son.

REGINA (*turns to* OSCAR). You want some money? If you had any sense, you'd know how to get it: just tell Papa Ben don't want you to have it. You'll get it. (*To* BEN) You ain't smart for a man who wants to get somewhere.

You should have figured out long ago that Papa's going to do just whatever you tell him not to do, unless *I* tell him to do it. (*Pats his shoulder*) Goodness gracious, that's been working for the whole twenty years I been on earth.

BEN (*to* REGINA). You are right, and you're smart. You must give me a full lecture on Papa some day; tell me why he's so good to you, how you manage, and so on.

REGINA (*laughs*). I'm busy now, taking him on a picnic.

BEN. Oh, not now. Too hot for lectures. We'll wait for a winter night. Before the fire. I'll sit opposite you and you'll talk and I'll listen. And I'll think many things, like how you used to be a beauty but at fifty years your face got worn and sour. Papa'll still be living, and he'll interrupt us, the way he does even now: he'll call from upstairs to have you come and put him to bed. And you'll get up to go, wondering how the years went by— (*Sharply*) Because, as you say, he's most devoted to you, and he's going to keep you right here with him, all his long life.

REGINA (*angrily*). He's not going to keep me here. And don't you think he is. I'm going away. I'm going to Chicago— (BEN *gets up, stares at her*. OSCAR *looks up. She catches herself*) Oh, well, I guess you'd have to know. But I wanted him to promise before you began any interfering— I'm going for a trip, and a nice long trip. So you're wrong, honey.

BEN (*slowly*). He's consented to the trip?

REGINA (*giggles*). No. But he will by the time the picnic's over.

OSCAR. Chicago? You sure got Mama's blood. Little while now, and you're going to be just as crazy as Mama.

REGINA (*to* BEN). And the trip's going to cost a lot of money. I got books from hotels, and I know. But you'll be working hard in the store and sending it on to me—

BEN. You could always come home occasionally and go

on another picnic. (*Comes up to her*) This time I don't think so. Papa didn't just get mad about you and Horace Giddens. Papa got mad about you and any man, or any place that ain't near him. I wouldn't like to be in the house, for example, the day he ever hears the gossip about you and Bagtry— (*Sharply*) Or is Bagtry going to Chicago—

REGINA (*tensely, softly*). Be still, Ben.

OSCAR. And everybody sure is gossiping. Laurette even heard it up in Roseville. I said there's nothing between you. I wouldn't believe it. But if ever I thought there was I'd ride over to Lionnet, carrying a gun. I sure would—

REGINA (*carefully*). And the day you do I'll be right behind you. It'll be your last ride, darling.

OSCAR (*backing away*). All right, all right, I was joking. Everybody's talking so wild today—

REGINA (*turns back to* BEN). Look, Ben, don't start anything. I'll get you in trouble if you do.

BEN. I believe you.

REGINA. Wish me luck. I got a hard day's work ahead. (*She goes up steps to upper porch and into her room.*)

OSCAR (*yawns*). Where she going?

BEN. Try to keep awake. Why did you beat up Sam Taylor?

OSCAR (*after a second, sulkily*). He's a no-good carpetbagger.

BEN (*wearily*). All right. Let's try again. Why did you beat up Sam Taylor?

OSCAR. He tried to make evening appointments with Laurette. He tried it twice. I told him the first time, and I told her too.

BEN. Is Laurette the little whore you've been courting?

OSCAR (*slowly, tensely*). Take that back, Ben. Take back that word. (BEN *laughs.* OSCAR *advances toward him, very angry*) I don't let any man—

BEN. Now listen to me, you clown. You put away your

gun and keep it away. If those fools in your Klan want to beat up niggers and carpetbaggers, you let 'em do it. But you're not going to make this country dangerous to me, or dangerous to the business. We had a hard enough time making them forget Papa made too much money out of the war, and I ain't ever been sure they forgot it.

OSCAR. Course they haven't forgot it. Every time anybody has two drinks, or you call up another loan, there's plenty of talk, and plenty of hints I don't understand. (*Rises*) If I had been old enough to fight in the war, you just bet I'd been right there, and not like you, bought off. I'm a Southerner. And when I see an old carpetbagger or upstart nigger, why, I feel like taking revenge.

BEN. For what? Because Papa got rich on them? (*Very sharply*) Put away that gun, sonny, and keep it put away, you hear me?

OSCAR (*frightened*). All right, all right. I want to thank you. I forgot. For saying that I was talking to you on the train. Thanks, Ben.

BEN. I wasn't lying for you. I was trying to save five hundred dollars.

OSCAR (*hurt*). Oh. Guess I should have known. (*Sighs*) How'm I ever going to pay it back? I'm in a mess. I— Ben, help me, will you? I'm deeply and sincerely in love.

BEN. Go give yourself a cooling sponge bath.

OSCAR. I want to marry Laurette. I was going to ask Papa to advance me a little money, so we could ship on down to New Orleans. He's going to leave money when he dies, plenty of it. I just want a little of mine now, and I'll go away—

BEN. He won't leave much. Not at this rate. He's spent forty thousand on nothing in the last six months.

OSCAR. My God, forty thousand and us slaving away in the store! And that's the way it's always going to be. I'm telling you: I'm taking Laurette and I'm going. Laurette's a fine girl. Hasn't looked at another man for a year.

BEN. Well, she better take them up again if you're going away. *You* can't earn a living.

(*Jake appears from the living room.*)

JAKE. Mr. Ben, a lady who says she doesn't want to say her name, she would like to speak with you. She's in the front hall, waiting.

BEN. Who? Who is it?

JAKE. Miss Birdie Bagtry.

(BEN *and* OSCAR *turn in surprise.*)

BEN (*after a minute*). Wants to see *me?* (JAKE *nods vigorously*) Bring her out.

(JAKE *exits.*)

OSCAR. Now what do you think of that? What's she want to come here for? To see *you?* (*Giggles*) What you been up to, boy?

BEN. Maybe she's come to look at you. Didn't you tell me she once gave you a glass of lemonade?

OSCAR. Did she?

BEN. I don't know. I only know that you told me so.

OSCAR. Then I guess it happened.

BEN. That doesn't necessarily follow.

OSCAR. Well, it was true. I was pushing a lame horse past Lionnet. I was lame myself from something or other—

BEN. Laurette Sincee?

OSCAR. I told you once, stop that. I am in love with Laurette, deeply and sincerely.

BEN. Better you'd stayed for the lemonade and fallen in love with Lionnet's cotton-fields.

OSCAR: Oh, this girl's supposed to be awfully silly. Melty-mush-silly. (*Smiles*) That's what Laurette calls people like that. Melty-mush-silly.

BEN. She's witty, Laurette, eh? (JAKE *appears in the living-room door followed by a slight, pretty, faded-looking girl of twenty. Her clothes are seedy, her face is worn and frightened*) Good morning, ma'am.

OSCAR (*with charm*). Well, hello there, Miss Birdie!

BIRDIE (*bows*). Mr. Benjamin. And morning to you. Mr. Oscar. (*Nervously*) We haven't seen you in many a long day. You haven't been hunting lately?

OSCAR. Oh, my time's been taken up with so many things, haven't had much chance.

BIRDIE (*nods*). I know, you gentlemen in business. Please, you all, forgive my coming to your house, particularly on this day of privacy. I'll just take a few minutes and—

OSCAR. Excuse me, Miss Birdie. Hope you'll come again. (*He starts toward room.*)

BEN. Wait inside, Oscar. (OSCAR *turns to stare at him, then shrugs, disappears. To* BIRDIE) Please.

BIRDIE (*sits down*). Yes, sir. Thank you.

BEN. Can I get you coffee?

BIRDIE. No, sir. Thank you. You see, I only got a few minutes before Mama begins wondering. I'm sorry to worry you here, but I couldn't come to see you in the store, because then the whole town would know, wouldn't they? And my Mama and Cousin John would just about— (*Giggles nervously*) Isn't that so, Mr. Benjamin?

BEN. Isn't what so?

BIRDIE (*very nervous*). About knowing. I must apologize for disturbing— Oh, I said that before. It's not good manners to take up all your time saying how sorry I am to take up all your time, now is it? (*Giggles*) Oh, and I'm doing that again, too. Mama says I say everything in a question. Oh.

BEN. What do you want to talk to me about, Miss Birdie?

BIRDIE. Yes. (*Rises. Desperately*) Mr. Benjamin, we're having a mighty bad time. It can't go on. It got so bad that last month Mama didn't want to do it, but she did it, and it was just awful for her.

BEN (*after a second, politely*). Did what?

BIRDIE. Went all the way to Natchez, just to keep from going to our kinfolk in Mobile. Course they're so poor now they couldn't have done anything anyway, but just to keep them from knowing she went all the way to Natchez.

BEN. Really?

BIRDIE. Yes, sir, all the way by herself. But they said they just couldn't. They said they'd like to, for Papa's dead sake and Grandpapa's, but they just couldn't. Mama said she didn't want it for anybody's sake, not like that, not for those reasons—well, you know Mama, Mr. Benjamin.

BEN. No, I don't.

BIRDIE. Oh. Well, I don't blame her, although . . . No, when everything else is gone, Mama says you at least got pride left. She did it to save me, Mr. Benjamin, the trip, I mean. I was such a ninny, being born when I did, and growing up in the wrong time. I'm much younger than my brothers. I mean I am younger, if they were living. But it didn't do any good.

BEN. I beg your pardon?

BIRDIE. The trip to Natchez. It didn't do any good.

BEN. What kind of good didn't it do? (*She looks puzzled*) Why did your Mama make the trip?

BIRDIE. To borrow money on the cotton. Or on the land— (*softly*)—or even to sell the pictures, or the silver. But they said they couldn't: that everybody was raising cotton that nobody else wanted. I don't understand that. I thought people always wanted cotton.

BEN. They will again in fifty years.

BIRDIE (*after a pause*). Oh. Fifty years. (*Smiles sadly*) Well, I guess we can't wait that long. The truth is, we can't pay or support our people, Mr. Benjamin, we can't— Well, it's just killing my Mama. And my Cousin John, he wants to go away.

BEN. Where does he want to go?

BIRDIE. Away from here. (*Tense, very frightened*) Forgive

me. Would you, I mean your father and you, would you lend money on our cotton, or land, or—

BEN. Your Cousin John, does he want to go to New York or Chicago, perhaps? Has he spoken of going to Chicago?

BIRDIE. Oh dear, no. There's no war going on in Chicago.

BEN. I beg your pardon?

BIRDIE. A war. He wants to go back to war. Mama says she can even understand that. She says there isn't any life for our boys any more.

BEN. I see. Where will Captain Bagtry find a war?

BIRDIE. There's something going on in Brazil, John says. He looked it up in the paper, and he's got a map.

BEN. Brazil. Is there a nice war going on in Brazil?

BIRDIE. Yes. I think so. (*Eagerly*) You see, that was one of the things Mama was going to do with the money. Pay all our people and give John the carfare. He can earn a lot in Brazil, he can be a general. (*Pauses, breathes*) Now about the loan, Mr. Benjamin—

BEN. You will inherit Lionnet?

BIRDIE. Me? Er. Yes. You mean if Mama were to— You mustn't believe those old stories. Mama's not so sick that a little good care and— (*Very embarrassed*) I'm sorry.

BEN. You don't want your Mama to know you've come here?

BIRDIE. Oh, no, no. She'd never forgive me, rather die—

BEN (*laughs*). To think you had come to us.

BIRDIE. I didn't mean that. I am so sorry. I didn't—

BEN. You have not offended me, ma'am. I only ask because as I understand it you don't own Lionnet, your Mama does. But you don't want her to know about the loan. And so who would sign for it?

BIRDIE (*stares at him*). I would. Oh. You mean you can't sign for what you don't own. Oh. I see. I hadn't thought of that. Oh. That's how much of a ninny I am. Forgive me for bothering you. I shouldn't have. I'm sorry I just ruined your Sunday morning. Good day, sir.

BEN (*goes to dining-room door*). Oscar, Oscar, I know you want to walk Miss Bagtry home.

BIRDIE. Oh, no. Thank you. I—

OSCAR (*calling, offstage*). I have an appointment. I'm late.

BIRDIE (*embarrassed*). Please, sir—

BEN (*to* BIRDIE). How much of a loan were you thinking about?

BIRDIE. Five thousand dollars. It would take that much to pay our people and buy seed and pay debts and— But I guess I was as foolish about that as—

BEN. You know, of course, that all loans from our company are made by my father. I only work for him. Yours is good cotton and good land. But you don't own it. That makes it hard. It's very unusual, but perhaps I could think of some way to accommodate you. A promise from you, in a letter—

BIRDIE (*delighted*). Oh. Oh. Of course, I'd make the promise.

BEN. Why don't you talk to my father yourself? I'll tell him what it's all about, and you come back this afternoon—

BIRDIE (*backing away*). Oh, no. I couldn't say all that to-day again. I just couldn't— (*Softly*) That's silly. Of course I could. What time will I come?

BEN. I have a pleasanter idea. Come tomorrow evening. Once a month my father has a music evening with musicians from Mobile to play on the violin, and flatter him. He's always in a good humor after his music. Come in then, Miss Birdie, and please invite Captain Bagtry to escort you.

BIRDIE. You really think there's any chance? Your Papa would— And my Mama wouldn't ever have to find out?

BEN (*bows*). I will do my best for you before you come.

BIRDIE (*after a second, with determination*). Thank you very much. I will be most pleased to come. Imagine having a concert right in your own house! I just love music. (OSCAR *appears in the door, stares angrily at* BEN) Thank you for your courtesy in offering to walk me back, Mr. Oscar. And thank you, Mr. Benjamin. (BIRDIE *smiles happily, moves quickly off.*)

OSCAR (*comes close to* BEN, *softly, very angry*). What the hell's the matter with you? Bossing me around, ruining my day?

BEN (*softly*). Be nice to the girl. You hear me?

OSCAR. I'm taking her home. That's enough. Damned little ninny.

BEN. I was thinking of trying to do you a favor. I was thinking if something works right for me, I'd lend you the five hundred to pay Papa back.

OSCAR. Squee, Ben! If you only could. What would you be doing it for?

BEN. Because I want you to be nice to this girl. Flatter her, talk nice. She's kind of pretty.

OSCAR. Pretty? I can't stand 'em like that.

BEN. I know. Virtue in woman offends you. Now go on. Be charming. Five hundred possible dollars' charming.

OSCAR (*smiles*). All right.

(*He runs off. After a minute* MARCUS, *carrying three books and a bottle of wine, appears on the porch.*)

MARCUS (*reading*). "The customary branches of education number four. Reading and writing." You know *those*, Benjamin, I think. "Gymnastic exercise"—(MARCUS *laughs*)—"and music." Aristotle. *You* don't know any music, Benjamin.

BEN. I've been too busy, Papa.

MARCUS. At what?

BEN. Working all my life for you. Doing a lot of dirty jobs. And then watching you have a wild time throwing the money around. But when I ask you to lend me a little . . .

MARCUS. You're a free man, Benjamin. A free man. You

don't like what I do, you don't stay with me. (*Holding up the book*) I do wish you would read a little Aristotle, take your mind off money.

(REGINA *comes down the steps, in a new dress, carrying a parasol and a steamer rug.*)

BEN (*looks at her*). Oh. Before I forget. I invited Miss Birdie Bagtry and her cousin to come here tomorrow night.

MARCUS. To come here? What do you mean?

BEN. I thought you'd like having the quality folk here. (*Smiles*) Come here to beg a favor of you.

MARCUS (*stares at him, giggles*). You teasing me?

BEN. No. The girl just left here. She wants us to lend money on the cotton. Her Mama didn't know, and mustn't know. But Miss Birdie doesn't own the place—

MARCUS. Then what kind of nonsense is that?

BEN. Maybe it's not nonsense. Take a note from her. If she dies before her mother—

MARCUS (*sharply*). Who said anything about dying? You're very concerned with people dying, aren't you?

BEN (*Laughs*). You hate that word. (*Quickly*) Her mother could get out of it legally, maybe, but I don't think she would. Anyway, the old lady is sick, and it's worth a chance. Make it a short loan, call it in a few years. They've wrecked the place and the money won't do 'em much good. I think the time would come when you'd own the plantation for almost nothing— (*Looks up at* REGINA) A loan would make them happy and make us money. Make the Bagtrys grateful to us—

REGINA (*softly*). Course I don't know anything about business, Papa, but could I say something, please? I've been kind of lonely here with nobody nice having much to do with us. I'd sort of like to know people of my own age, a girl my own age, I mean—

MARCUS (*to* BEN). How much does she want?

BEN (*hesitates for a minute*). Ten thousand.

MARCUS. On Lionnet? Ten thousand is cheap. She's a fool.

BEN (*smiles*). Yes, I think she's a fool.

MARCUS (*giggles*). Well, the one thing I never doubted was your making a good business deal. Kind of cute of you to think of their coming here to get it, too. Bagtrys in this house, begging. Might be amusing for an hour.

REGINA (*quickly*). Can't invite 'em for an hour. Papa. And we've got to be nice to them. Otherwise I just wouldn't want to see him come unless we'd be awful nice and polite.

MARCUS. They'll think we're nice and polite for ten thousand.

REGINA (*laughs, in a high good humor*). I guess. But you be pleasant to them—

MARCUS. Why, Regina? Why are you so anxious?

REGINA. Papa, I told you. I been a little lonesome. No people my age ever coming here— I do think people like that sort of want to forgive you, and be nice to us—

MARCUS (*sharply, angrily*). Forgive me?

REGINA (*turns away, little-girl tearful*). I'm mighty sorry. What have I done? Just said I'd like to have a few people to listen to your old music. Is that so awful to want?

MARCUS (*quickly, pleadingly*). Come on, darling. (*Shouts*) Lavinia, *where* is the basket? Lavinia! Coralee! (*To* REGINA) Come on now, honey. It's been a long time since you been willing to spend a Sunday with me. If I was sharp, I'm sorry. Don't you worry. I'll be charming to the visiting gentry.

BEN. Miss Birdie got a fear of asking you for the loan and of her cousin, John, knowing about it. Might be better if you just gave your consent, Papa, and didn't make her tell the story all over again. I can do the details.

(LAVINIA *appears with a basket.* MARCUS *takes it from her, peers in it.*)

MARCUS (*to* REGINA). That's mighty nice-looking. We'll have a good lunch. (*To* BEN) I don't want to hear the

woes of Lionnet and Mistress Birdie. Most certainly you
will do the details. Be kind of pleasant owning Lionnet.
It's a beautiful house. Very light in motive, very well
conceived—

LAVINIA. You going now, Marcus? Marcus! You promised
you'd talk to me. Today—

MARCUS. I'm talking to you, Lavinia.

LAVINIA. Last year this morning, you promised me it would
be today—

MARCUS (*gently*). I'm going out now, Lavinia.

LAVINIA. I've fixed you a mighty nice lunch, Marcus, the
way you like it. I boiled up some crabs right fast, and—

MARCUS. I'm sure. Thank you. (*He starts to move off.*)

LAVINIA (*comes running to him*). Please, Marcus, I won't
take up five minutes. Or when you come back? When
you come back, Marcus?

MARCUS. Another day, my dear.

LAVINIA. It can't be another day, Marcus. It was to be on
my birthday, this year. When you sat right in that chair,
and I brought my Bible and you swore—

MARCUS. Another day.

LAVINIA. It ought to be today. If you swear to a day, it's
got to be that day— (*Very frightened*) Tomorrow then.
Tomorrow wouldn't hurt so much, because tomorrow is
just after today— I've *got* to go this week, because I had
a letter from the Reverend—

REGINA. Oh, Mama. Are you talking that way again?

LAVINIA (*shaking, wildly*). Tomorrow, Marcus? Tomorrow, tomorrow.

MARCUS (*to Ben*). Ben, get Coralee.

LAVINIA. Tomorrow— (BEN *exits. She grabs* MARCUS's *arm*)
Promise me tomorrow, Marcus. Promise me. I'll go get
my Bible and you promise me—

MARCUS (*very sharply*). Stop that nonsense. Get hold of
yourself. I've had enough of that! I want no more.

LAVINIA (*crying*). I'm not making any trouble. You know that, Marcus. Just promise me tomorrow.

MARCUS. Stop it! I've had enough. Try to act like you're not crazy. Get your self in hand. (*He exits.*)

REGINA (*as Coralee appears*). Never mind, Mama. Maybe you'll be coming away with me. Would you like that? There are lots of churches in Chicago—

CORALEE. All right, Miss Regina. Don't tease her now.

REGINA (*gaily, as she goes off*). I'm not teasing.

(*After a pause,* LAVINIA *sits down.*)

LAVINIA. Now I'm going to pretend. You ready?

CORALEE (*as if this had happened a thousand times before*). All right.

LAVINIA. He didn't say any of those things. He said he would speak with me sure thing— (*Her voice rises*) No man breaks a Bible promise, and you can't tell me they do. You know I got my correspondence with the Reverend. He wants me to come and I got my mission and my carfare. In his last letter, the Reverend said if I was coming I should come, or should write him and say I couldn't ever come. "Couldn't ever come—" Why did he write that?

CORALEE. I don't know.

LAVINIA. Your people are my people. I got to do a little humble service. I lived in sin these thirty-seven years, Coralee. (*Rocks herself*) Such sin I couldn't even tell you.

CORALEE. You told me.

LAVINIA. Now I got to finish with the sin. Now I got to do my mission. And I'll be— I'll do it nice, you know I will. I'll gather the little black children round, and I'll teach them good things. I'll teach them how to read and write, and sing the music notes and—

CORALEE (*wearily*). Oh, Miss Viney. Maybe it's just as well. Maybe they'd be scared of a white teacher coming among them.

LAVINIA (*after a pause*). Scared of me?

CORALEE (*turns*). No, ma'am. You're right. News of you has gone ahead.

LAVINIA. Course they could have many a better teacher. I know mighty little, but I'm going to try to remember better. (*Quietly*) And the first thing I'm going to remember is to speak to Marcus tomorrow. Tomorrow. (*Turns pleadingly to* CORALEE) I was silly to speak to-day. And I did it wrong. Anyway, he didn't say I *couldn't* go, he just said— (*Stops suddenly*) My goodness, it's such a little thing to want. Just to go back where you were born and help little colored children to grow up knowing how to read books and— (*Giggles*) You'll be proud of me. I'll remember things to teach them. You remember things when you're happy. And I'm going to be happy. You get to be fifty-nine, you don't be happy then, well, you got to find it. I'm going to be a very happy, happy, happy, happy— I'm going, Coralee. (*She suddenly stops, looks down in her lap.*)

CORALEE. Nice and cool in your room. Want to lie down? (LAVINIA *doesn't answer*) Want to play a little on the piano? Nobody's inside. (*No answer. She waits, then very gently*) All right, if you don't want to. I tell you what. Come on in the kitchen and rest yourself with us. (LAVINIA *gets up*, CORALEE *takes her arm, they start out as*

Curtain Falls

ACT TWO

SCENE: *The living room of the* HUBBARD *house. This is the room we have seen through the French doors of the first act, and now we are looking at the room as if we were standing in the French doors of the portico. A large bay window is center stage, leading to a porch that faces the first-act portico. Right stage is a door leading to the dining room. Left stage is an open arch leading to the entrance hall and main staircase. The furniture is from the previous owner but* MARCUS *has cleared the room of the ornaments and the ornamented. Right stage is a round table and three chairs. Left stage is a sofa and chair. Right, upstage, is a desk. Left, upstage, is a piano. Right, upstage, is a long table. Center of the room, before the columns of the porch, are a table and chairs. The room is simpler, more severe, than many rooms of the 1880's. A Greek vase, glass-enclosed, stands on a pedestal; a Greek statue sits on the table; Greek battle scenes are hung on the walls.*

As the curtain rises, BEN *and* OSCAR *are sitting at table, stage right. They each have a glass of port and the port decanter is in front of them.* MARCUS, PENNIMAN *and* JUGGER *are standing at a music stand, looking down at a music score.* PENNIMAN *is a tall, fattish man.* JUGGER *looks like everybody.* PENNIMAN *looks up from the score, hums, drains his glass, looks at the empty glass, and crosses to* BEN *and* OSCAR. MARCUS *is intent on the score.*

PENNIMAN (*meaning the score*). Very interesting. Harmonically fresh, eh, Mr. Benjamin?
BEN. I know nothing of music.

JUGGER. Why do people always sound so proud when they announce they know nothing of music?

PENNIMAN (*quickly, as* OSCAR *fills his glass*). A fine port, and a mighty good supper. I always look forward to our evening here. I tell my wife Mrs. Hubbard is a rare housekeeper.

BEN. You like good port, Mr. Penniman?

PENNIMAN. Yes, sir, and don't trust the man who don't.

(OSCAR *goes off into gales of laughter. This pleases* PEN-NIMAN *and he claps* OSCAR *on the shoulder.* MARCUS *looks up, annoyed, taps bow on music stand.* PENNIMAN *and* OSCAR *stop laughing,* PENNIMAN *winks at* OSCAR, *carries his glass back to music stand.* JAKE *comes from the hall entrance carrying two chairs, a lamp, and passes through to porch.* LAVINIA *hurries in from the dining room. Her hair is mussy, her dress spotted. She looks around the room, smiles at everybody. When nobody notices her, she crosses to* MARCUS, *leans over to examine the score, nods at what she reads.*)

LAVINIA. Oh, it's nice, Marcus. Just as nice as anybody could have. It's going to be a cold collation. Is that all right?

MARCUS (*who is in a good humor*). Yes, certainly. What's that?

LAVINIA. A cold collation? That's what you call food when you have guests. A cold collation.

PENNIMAN (*looks toward the dining room, delighted*). More food? After that fine supper—

LAVINIA. This is a special night. Guests. Isn't that pleasant? My, we haven't had guests— I don't think I remember the last time we had guests—

MARCUS (*looks at her*). All right, Lavinia.

LAVINIA. There'll be a dish of crabs, of course. And a dish of crawfish boiled in white wine, the way Belle does. And a chicken salad, and a fine strong ham we've been saving. (*Stops*) Oh. I'm worrying you gentlemen—

PENNIMAN (*lifting his glass*). Worrying us? You, the honor of Rose County, and the redeemer of this family.

(JUGGER *and* MARCUS *look up sharply.* BEN *laughs.* MARCUS *reaches over and takes* PENNIMAN'S *glass, carries it to table.*)

MARCUS. I am awaiting your opinion.

PENNIMAN (*who has the quick dignity of a man with too much port*). The judgment of music, like the inspiration for it, must come slow and measured, if it comes with truth.

OSCAR (*to* BEN). Talks like a Christmas tree, don't he?

LAVINIA. It's your third composition, isn't it, Marcus? Oh, I'm sure it's lovely. Just lovely.

MARCUS (*looks at her—softly*). How would you know, Lavinia?

LAVINIA (*hurt*). I can read notes, Marcus. Why, I taught you how to read music. Don't you remember, Marcus? (*She goes toward* BEN *and* OSCAR) I did. Yes, I did.

BEN (*amused*). Of course you did.

PENNIMAN (*hurriedly*). I would say this: It is done as the Greeks might have imposed the violin upon the lute. (*Hums*) Right here. Close to Buxtehude— (*Inspiration*) Or, the Netherland Contrapuntalists. Excellent.

(OSCAR *pours himself another port,* LAVINIA *has wandered to the piano, mumbling to herself.*)

MARCUS (*very pleased, to* PENNIMAN). You like it?

PENNIMAN. I like it very much. And if you would allow us, I would like to introduce it in Mobile during the season. Play it first at the school, say, then, *possibly*—

MARCUS. That would make me very happy. And what do you think of it, Mr. Jugger?

JUGGER (*slowly*). Penniman speaks for me. He always does.

PENNIMAN (*quickly*). Come. We'll try it for you. I am most anxious to hear it. (*Points to* MARCUS'S *violin, coyly*) I daresay you know the solo part you have written for yourself?

MARCUS. Well, I—yes. (*Very pleased*) I had hoped you would want to try it tonight. I— (JUGGER *picks up his violin, starts for portico.* MARCUS *turns to him*) Mr. Jugger. Would *you* like to try it now?

JUGGER (*turns, looks at* MARCUS, *seems about to say something, changes his mind*). I would like to try.

PENNIMAN. But where *is* my cello? Goodness God—

JUGGER (*sharply, at door of portico*). It's out here. When will you learn that it's hard to mislay a cello? (PENNIMAN *giggles, trips out to porch.*)

LAVINIA (*suddenly plays a few notes on the piano*). See? I told you, Marcus. *That's* it. I told you I could read music just as good as I used to—

MARCUS. Is there something disturbing you this evening, Lavinia? More than usual?

(REGINA *enters for the hall. She is dressed up, very handsome. They all turn to stare at her. She smiles, goes to* MARCUS.)

MARCUS (*softly*). You're a beautiful girl.

OSCAR. Looks like the decorated pig at the county fair.

REGINA (*wheels around for* MARCUS). It's my Chicago dress. *One* of my Chicago dresses. (REGINA *notices* LAVINIA) Oh, Mama, it's late. Do go and get dressed.

LAVINIA. I'm dressed, Regina.

REGINA. You can't look like that. Put on a nice silk—

LAVINIA. I only have what I have—

REGINA. Put on your nice dress, Mama. It will do for tonight. We must order you new things. You can't go to Chicago looking like a tired old country lady—

LAVINIA (*wheels around*). *Chicago?* I'm not going to Chicago. Where I'm going I don't need clothes or things of the world. I'm going to the poor, and it wouldn't be proper to parade in silk— Marcus! You tell Regina where I'm going. *Tell her where I'm going.* You tell her right now. You—

REGINA. All right, Mama. Now don't you fret. Go upstairs and get dressed up for the high-toned guests. (*She leads* LAVINIA *to the hall*) Don't you worry now. Go on up, honey. Coralee's waiting for you. (*She comes back into room. To* MARCUS) Whew! I'm sorry. I should have known. I hope she isn't going to act queer the rest of the evening.

MARCUS. There's always that chance.

REGINA. Well, don't let's worry. (*Gaily*) I'll see to everything. I'd better have a look in the kitchen, and more chairs— Let's have the very good champagne, Papa?

PENNIMAN (*from portico*). Mr. Hubbard—

MARCUS (*takes keys from his pocket, throws them to* BEN). Wine as good as Regina's dress. And count the bottles used. I don't want to find that Oscar has sold them again.

BEN (*to* REGINA). So your picnic was successful? When do you leave for Chicago?

REGINA (*gaily*). In ten days, two weeks. (*Comes to him*) Going to miss me?

BEN. Yes. Very much.

MARCUS. What's the matter? What's the matter, Regina?

REGINA (*gaily, leaving* BEN). Matter? Nothing. (*Calls into dining room as she exits*) Two more chairs, Jake—

OSCAR. Now just tell me how I'm going to get word to Laurette that I can't meet her till later tonight, just somebody tell me that.

MARCUS (*very sharply to* BEN). I told you to get the wine.

(BEN *looks at him, smiles as if he understood why* MARCUS *was angry, exits through dining-room door.* MARCUS *stands staring at him. Then goes to piano, looks through scores.* OSCAR *moves nervously toward* MARCUS.)

OSCAR (*desperately*). Papa, I'm in trouble. You see, I had an appointment with a lady from out of town, Roseville, I mean.

MARCUS. What were they doing?

OSCAR. Who?

MARCUS. Regina and Ben when they were standing together— (*Breaks off, turns sharply away.*)

OSCAR. Oh, you know Ben. Always up to something. Yesterday, trying to marry off Regina, tonight trying to press
me on the Bagtry girl.

MARCUS (*looks up*). Oh, come. Ben's not a fool. You and a
Bagtry is a very comic idea.

OSCAR. I know, but Ben's figured they're so hard up for
money they might even have me. It all fits in with this
mortgage you're giving them, or something. He's got his
eye on the cotton— (*Giggles*) And Ben's eye goes in a
lot of directions, mostly around corners. It's true, Papa.
He made me take the girl home yesterday—

MARCUS (*looks at* OSCAR). The mortgage, and then the girl
and you. Interesting man, Benjamin.

OSCAR (*pleadingly*). Papa, like I say. I've got a friend who's
waiting for me right now. I want you to meet her. You
see, I'm deeply and sincerely in love. Deeply and sincerely. She's a fine girl. But *Ben* cries her down. *Ben*
don't want me to be happy.

MARCUS. Isn't that too bad. Your own brother. It's a shame.

OSCAR. Course she's of the lower classes, and that doesn't
fit in with Ben's plans for us to marry money for him.
But the lower classes don't matter to me; I always say
it's not how people were born but what they are—

MARCUS. You always say that, eh? Well, some people are
democrats by choice, and some by necessity. You, by
necessity.

OSCAR. Could I go fetch her here—(*desperately*) tonight?
Could I, Papa?

MARCUS. What is this, a night at the circus?

OSCAR (*slyly, as a last chance*). I think it would just about
finish Mr. Ben to have a member of the lower classes,
sort of, mixing with the gentry, here. I thought it would

sort of, sort of amuse you, and well, you could meet her at the same time. Be a good joke on Ben, sort of—

MARCUS (*slowly*). Is this Laurette that, that little, er— little thing from Roseville you been steaming about?

OSCAR. She's not, Papa. Oh, maybe she was a little wild before I met her, but— She was left an orphan and she didn't know what else to do, starving and cold, friendless.

MARCUS (*shudders*). Oh God, shut up. (*Hesitates, then laughs*) All right, go and get her, if you like. Er. Does she come dressed? I wouldn't like her here, er, unrobed.

OSCAR (*hurt but happy*). Aw, she's a fine woman, Papa, don't talk like that. And she loves music. She wants to learn just about everything—

MARCUS. Don't bring her as a student, Oscar.

OSCAR. Oh, no. No, I wouldn't. She won't say a word. She admires you, Papa—

MARCUS. For what?

OSCAR. Well, just about, well, just for everything, I guess— (MARCUS *makes a dismissive gesture, goes on porch as* REGINA *comes into room.* OSCAR *sees* REGINA, *smiles*) I'll be back in a few minutes. Going across the square to get Laurette, bring her here.

REGINA (*starts toward him, as* BEN *comes in carrying champagne bottles*). Here? That girl—What's the matter with you? You're doing nothing of the kind. Come back here. You can't bring that—

OSCAR. Can't I? Well, just ask Papa. *He* wants her to meet my folks.

REGINA (*turns to* BEN). Ben, stop him. He can't bring her here tonight— Stop him! (*But* OSCAR *has disappeared*) Get him, Ben!

BEN. What am I supposed to do, shoot him? I'm too old to run down streets after men in love.

REGINA. He *can't* bring her here. You know what John will

think. I saw him this afternoon: I had to beg him to come tonight. He doesn't know why Birdie wants him to come, but— Ben, he'll think we meant to do it, planned to insult them—

BEN. Yes, I'm sure he will.

(*The music on the porch beings.*)

REGINA. What's the matter with Papa? Why did he let Oscar—

BEN (*smiles*). *You're* going to learn some day about Papa. It's not as easy as you think, Regina. (*They stand looking out to the porch, listening to the music*) He gave those clowns five thousand last month for something they call their music school. Now that they are playing his composition he should be good for another five thousand—

REGINA (*turns, softly, amazed*). Did he? Really? (*Shakes her head*) Well, anyway, he's promised me plently for—

BEN. To marry Bagtry? Enough to support you the rest of your life, you and your husband? I'm taking a vacation the day he finds out about your marriage plans.

REGINA (*angrily, nervous*). I don't know what you're talking about. Marry— What are you saying—? I— (*Turns to him, tensely*) Leave me alone, Ben. Leave me alone. Stop making trouble. If you dare say *anything* to Papa about John, I'll—

BEN (*very sharply*). Don't threaten me. I'm sick of threats.

REGINA (*angry*). You'll be much sicker of them if you— (*Then, softly*) Ben, don't. I'm in love with John.

BEN (*softly*). But he's not in love with you.

(LAVINIA *comes into room, followed by* CORALEE *who is pulling at her, trying to button her dress.* REGINA *turns away from* BEN.)

LAVINIA. Don't bother with the lower buttons. (*Timidly*) Am I proper now, daughter? (REGINA *doesn't answer her.* LAVINIA *points out to porch, meaning the music*) You know, I've made myself cheer up. I know you were just teasing about Chicago, Regina, and I know full well I've never been good about teasing. What do people do now, curtsy or shake hands? I guess it's just about the first guests we had since the suspicion on your Papa.

REGINA. Now, Mama. Please don't talk about any of that tonight. Don't talk at all about the war, or anything that happened. Please remember, Mama. Do you hear?

CORALEE (*quickly*). She won't. You all have been teasing her, and she's tired.

(CORALEE *goes to* BEN, *takes the champagne bottles from the table.* JAKE *comes in from the dining room carrying a tray of glasses and a punch bowl.*)

LAVINIA. Could I try the nice punch, Coralee?

CORALEE. You certainly can. (JAKE *exits.* BEN *starts to the table. As if such courtesy were unusual,* CORALEE *stares at him*) Thank you, Mr. Ben.

(CORALEE *exits.* BEN *pours three glasses of punch.*)

LAVINIA. Regina, when you don't frown you look like my Grandmama—(*as* BEN *brings her a glass of punch, and moves on to* REGINA)—the one who taught me to read and write. And 'twas mighty unusual, a lady to know how to read and write, up in the piney woods.

BEN (*laughs*). Now, that's a safer subject, Mama. Tell the Bagtrys about our kinfolk in the piney woods. (*He lifts his glass to* REGINA) To you, honey.

REGINA (*smiles*). And to you, *honey*.

(*On the porch the music comes to an end.* REGINA *who has not, of course, been paying any attention, starts to applaud. She turns to* LAVINIA, *indicates* MARCUS *on porch.*)

LAVINIA. But I didn't hear it. I wasn't paying any attention.

(MARCUS *comes into room.*)

REGINA (*goes to him*). It's brilliant of you, Papa.

MARCUS. I'm glad you liked it. Come along. We're about to start—(*laughs*)—the better-known classics.

BEN. Won't you wait for our guests?

MARCUS. Certainly not, I resent their thinking they can stroll in late on my music.

REGINA (*placatingly*). You're right, darling. *We'll* come out.

(MARCUS *goes to porch.* REGINA *follows.* BEN *follows her.* LAVINIA *puts down her glass, follows* BEN. REGINA *and* BEN *sit down,* LAVINIA *sits down. The musicians tune up.* MARCUS, PENNIMAN, *and* JUGGER *begin to play a divertimento by Leopold Mozart, a trio for violin, viola, and cello. Then the hall door opens and closes. On the porch,* REGINA *and* BEN *both turn, turn back again. After a second,* OSCAR *appears in the living room pulling* LAURETTE SINCEE. LAURETTE *is about twenty, pig-face cute, a little too fashionably dressed. She stands in the door, admiring the room.*)

LAURETTE. Squee!

OSCAR (*proud and excited*). Not bad, eh? (*Looks toward portico*) We got to talk soft.

LAURETTE. This *is* nice. You born here, Oskie?

OSCAR. No. Like I told you. Right after the war Papa bought—(*giggles*)—or something, this house from old man Reed. Like it?

LAURETTE. Squee. Who wouldn't?

OSCAR. Well, maybe, some day—

LAURETTE. Ah, go on, Oskie. Go on.

OSCAR. You just wait and see.

LAURETTE (*points to portico*). What's that?

OSCAR. What?

LAURETTE. The noise?

OSCAR. That's music, honey.

LAURETTE. Oh.

OSCAR. When you speak to Papa, tell him how much you like music. Tell him how fine he plays.

LAURETTE. What's he playing?

OSCAR. The violin.

LAURETTE. Ain't that a coincidence? I had a beau who said

he played the violin. A Frenchman, much older than me. Had to leave his very own country because of the revolution.

OSCAR (*winces*). I don't like to hear about him, Laurette, him or any other men. I am deeply and sincerely in love with you.

LAURETTE (*pleasantly, but without too much interest*). Are you really, Oskie?

OSCAR. Laurette, I'm going to ask Papa for a loan. Then we'll go on down to New Orleans. Would you, Laurette—

LAURETTE. You've asked me the same question for the last year, twenty times. But you never yet asked your Papa for the loan.

OSCAR. I've been wating for the right opportunity. I want you to be my *wife*, honey. I am deeply and—

LAURETTE. We can't eat on deeply and sincerely.

OSCAR. No, I know. But this is the big night, don't you see? (*Laughs happily*) I never thought he'd let you come here. I mean—I mean a chance like this. And he's in a good humor about something. Now, darling, be very very—well, er. I tell you: you speak with him about what *he* likes. Tell him how much you think of music, not new music, mind you, but—and tell him how you stay awake reading.

LAURETTE. I've always been a reader. But I can't talk about it. What's there to say?

OSCAR. And he's fond of Mozart. Talk about Mozart.

LAURETTE. I can't do that.

OSCAR. Well, just try to please him. So much depends on it. We could have our own little place in New Orleans—

LAURETTE. What kind of place?

OSCAR. I'd find a job. You bet I would, and with you behind me to encourage and love me, with you to fight for, I'd forge ahead.

LAURETTE (*looks at him, puzzled*). Oh. Well, I'd certainly

like to go to New Orleans. I know a girl there. She has an embroidery shop on Royal Street. I'm good at embroidery. It's what I always wanted to do. Did I ever tell you that? Always wanted to do embroidery.

OSCAR. Did you?

LAURETTE. Yep. Instead of whoring. I just wanted to do fancy embroidery.

OSCAR (*loudly, in a hurt cry*). Don't Laurette, don't talk that way! (BEN *and* REGINA, *on the porch, look into room.* REGINA *coughs loudly*) We better go out now.

LAURETTE. Why did your papa let me come tonight?

OSCAR. Don't let him worry you, honey. Just take it nice and easy. Pretend nobody knows anything about you, pretend you're just as good as them—

LAURETTE (*stares at him*). Pretend? Pretend I'm as good as anybody called Hubbard? Why, my Pa died at Vicksburg. He didn't stay home bleeding the whole state of Alabama with money tricks, and suspected of worse. You think I been worried for that reason?

OSCAR (*desperately*). No, no. I— For God's sake don't talk like that—

LAURETTE. You may be the rich of this county, but everybody knows how. Why, the Frenchman, I used to eat dinner with, and his sister, the Countess. What you mean, boy, your folks—?

OSCAR. I didn't mean anything bad. Haven't I just said I wanted to *marry* you? I think you're better than anybody.

LAURETTE. I'm not better than anybody, but I'm as good as piney wood crooks.

OSCAR (*puts his hand over her mouth, looks toward porch*). Stop, *please*. We've got to go outside. *Please*—

LAURETTE (*good-natured again*). Sometimes you bring out the worst in my nature, Oskie, and make me talk foolish. Squee, it's the truth—I am a little twitchy about coming

here and meeting your folks. That's why I'm talking so
brave. I ain't been in a place like this before. . . . (*Pats
him*) All right, I'll be very good and nice. I would like
to go to New Orleans.

(OSCAR *takes her in his arms. The front bell rings, but they
don't hear it.*)

OSCAR. Course you would, with me. You love me, honey?
(*He leans down to kiss her.*) Tell me you love me.

LAURETTE. Now, Oskie, you know this ain't the place or
the time for mush—

(BEN *rises at the sound of the bell. As* BEN *comes from
the porch,* JAKE *brings in the* BAGTRYS. *As they enter,*
OSCAR *is kissing* LAURETTE, *she is giggling, trying to
push him away. The* BAGTRYS *stop in the doorway as
they see the scene.* BEN *comes to meet them, crosses
stage. As he passes* OSCAR *and* LAURETTE, *he shoves*
OSCAR.)

BEN. Excuse me. (*As* LAURETTE *jumps away,* REGINA *comes
in from porch, tapping* LAVINIA *on the arm as she
comes.* BEN *speaks to* BIRDIE) My apologies. We don't always arrange this scene for our guests.

(BIRDIE *smiles nervously.* JOHN *stares at* LAURETTE.)

OSCAR. We were just, I was, we were—

REGINA (*sharply*). All right. (*Goes quickly to* BIRDIE) I am
happy to have you here, Miss Birdie.

(BIRDIE *curtsies, puts out her hand, smiles warmly.*
LAVINIA *enters room.*)

JOHN (*bows to* REGINA, BEN, OSCAR, *then speaks to* LAU-
RETTE). Hello, Laurette.

LAURETTE. Hello, John.

JOHN (*turns to* BIRDIE). Birdie, this is Miss Sincee.

LAURETTE. Finely, thank you.

(BIRDIE *bows.*)

LAVINIA (*hears* LAURETTE *speak and so hurries to her*). An
honor to have you here, Miss Birdie—

REGINA (*sharply*). *This* is Miss Birdie, Mama.

LAVINIA (*who is shaking hands with* LAURETTE, *looks bewildered*). Oh. Sorry. I—

(OSCAR *bumps into* LAVINIA, *who is coming toward* BIRDIE.)

BIRDIE. I'm sorry we're late. I just couldn't seem to get dressed—

REGINA. Do come out now for the music.

(*They move out together.* LAVINIA *speaks to* BIRDIE.)

LAVINIA. Come, ma'am. And you, Miss— (*Brightly, to* BIRDIE.) Is the other lady your sister?

LAURETTE (*annoyed, shoves* OSCAR). What's the matter with you?

OSCAR. Oh. Mama, this is Miss Laurette Sincee. She's a visitor in town.

LAVINIA. Who's she visiting?

BEN. Us.

(BEN *reaches the porch door, stands aside to let* LAVINIA *pass him. She looks puzzled, passes on to porch.* LAURETTE, OSCAR, REGINA, JOHN, *are now seated on the porch.* LAVINIA *sits near them.* BIRDIE *and* BEN *stand for a minute listening to the music.*)

BIRDIE. Nice. To have a special night, just to play music— I've heard your father is a very cultured gentleman. Have you been able, did he, speak of the matter that I—

BEN. Yes. We will make the loan.

BIRDIE (*turns radiant—softly*). Oh, what fine news! You can't imagine how worried I've been. I am very grateful to you, sir—

BEN. You don't have to be. It is a good loan for Hubbard Company, or my father wouldn't be taking it. We'll meet tomorrow, you and I, and work out the details.

BIRDIE. Oh, you won't have any trouble with me, Mr. Ben.

BEN. You wanted five thousand dollars, Miss Birdie. I have asked my father to lend you ten thousand.

BIRDIE (*puzzled—worried*). Oh. Mr. Ben, I don't need—

BEN (*quickly*). You can take five now, but if you should happen to need more, it will be there for you.

BIRDIE. But I won't need ten thousand dollars. No, indeed I won't. It's very kind of you, but—

BEN (*carefully*). You will only get five. I will keep the rest waiting for you. That's the way these things are done—(*smiles*)—sometimes.

BIRDIE. But it's bad enough to owe five thousand, not less ten—

BEN. *You will only owe five.* Now don't worry about it. Will you take my advice now about something else? Don't speak to my father about the loan. It is all arranged. And he's a man of such culture, as you say, that talk of money would disturb him on his music night.

BIRDIE (*gently*). Oh, of course. After all, it's a party, and as worried and pushing as I am, I wouldn't ever have talked business with him at a party.

BEN (*smiles down at her*). Good breeding is very useful. Thank you, Miss Birdie.

BIRDIE (*gently*). No, sir. It is I who must thank you.

(*He bows, stands aside, indicates porch. She moves to it, sits down.* BEN *stands in the doorway. The music continues. After a minute we see* OSCAR *trying to move into the room. He leans over, bends down, moves rapidly into room, passes* BEN. LAURETTE *turns and* OSCAR *beckons to her to come into room.*)

OSCAR. Papa going to play all night? (*Crosses to get a drink.*) Laurette's getting restless, sitting there.

BEN. She's not accustomed to a sitting position? Have another drink. I got a feeling you're going to need it.

LAURETTE (*enters the room from the porch*). Squee. I don't like this punch. It don't mean anything.

BEN. Can I put in a little brandy? I think that would make it mean more.

(MARCUS *appears on the porch, comes up the aisle of*

chairs. He bows to BIRDIE *and to* JOHN, *comes into room.*
OSCAR *rushes to get him a drink of punch.*)

OSCAR. Papa, this is Miss Sincee.

MARCUS (*finishes drink, hands glass to* OSCAR). How do you do?

LAURETTE. Finely, thank you. (MARCUS *stares at her. She becomes very nervous.*) I love music, Mr. Hubbard. I had an uncle who played. *He* taught me to love music.

OSCAR (*too brightly*). Did he play the violin, like Papa?

LAURETTE. Er. Er. No. He had a little drum.

OSCAR (*very fast*). He liked Mozart. You told me, remember?

LAURETTE. Yeah. Sure did.

(REGINA *and* BIRDIE, *followed by* JOHN *and* LAVINIA, *come in from the porch.*)

MARCUS. Miss Sincee pleases me. Her uncle played Mozart on a little drum. Have you ever heard of that, Miss Bagtry?

BIRDIE. Oh. Well, *I* haven't, but I'm sure there must be such an arrangement.

MARCUS (*looks at her with interest*). That's very kind of you, to be so sure. Do you play any instrument, Miss Bagtry? Not the little drum?

BIRDIE. Yes, sir. Not well. The piano.

MARCUS. Then you would oblige me—(*she smiles, moves toward the piano, quickly*)—some other night, very soon.

BIRDIE (*very flustered*). Yes. Yes, sir.

OSCAR. It's a coincidence, ain't it, that Laurette's Papa liked Mozart?

REGINA (*to* LAURETTE). I thought it was your uncle? Was your Papa the same as your uncle?

LAURETTE. What do you mean? Do you mean mon père was on one side of my family, and mon oncle on the other? I can understand *that*.

BEN (*fills her glass from the brandy decanter*). Your family were French?

LAURETTE. No. I learned that from a French gentleman who came from France. I don't know where he is now. I liked him.

BEN. Perhaps we could locate him for you.

LAURETTE. No. He married money.

REGINA. Oh, dear. All foreigners do, I guess. Light wines and light money.

LAURETTE. I never blamed him. I figured, well— (*Looks at* REGINA) You've had some bad experiences with Frenchmen?

(REGINA, BEN, *and* MARCUS *laugh*.)

BIRDIE (*to* MARCUS—*making conversation*). John's been to Europe, you know.

MARCUS. I didn't know.

BIRDIE. Yes, he was. Just a few months before the war. Paris, France; London, England; St. Petersburg, Russia; Florence, Italy; Lake Como, Switzerland—

MARCUS. Your geography is remarkable.

BIRDIE. Oh, I only know because John kept a book. Pictures and notes and menus—if the war hadn't come, and my Papa had lived, I would have gone to Europe. It was planned for me to study water color.

MARCUS. Water color?

BIRDIE. Small water color. I like small water color.

MARCUS. Is that very different from large water color?

LAURETTE (*belligerently*). She means she likes small water color. What's the matter with that?

BIRDIE (*smiles at her*). Yes. (*To* MARCUS) You've been to Europe, Mr. Hubbard?

MARCUS (*laughs*). No, but I'm going. Might even settle down there. Yes, Regina?

REGINA (*looks at* JOHN, *nervously*). Maybe some day, Papa. Chicago first.

MARCUS. Of course, we'll take our residence in Greece, but some place gayer, for Regina, at first. Perhaps you'd advise us, Captain Bagtry?

JOHN. I'd like to, sir. But I have no memory of Europe.

MARCUS (*turns elaborately in his chair*). Something unpleasant took it from your mind?

JOHN. No, sir. I just don't remember. It's as if I had never been there.

LAVINIA. I used to have a good memory. (*Quickly*) I still have. Most of the time.

MARCUS (*very politely, to* JOHN). Captain Bagtry, does anything stay in your memory, anything at all?

JOHN (*looks at* MARCUS, *but the tone has been polite*). The war.

REGINA (*softly*). Only the war?

LAVINIA (*to* JOHN, *motherly*). Well, I just bet. That's natural: you rode off so young.

JOHN (*turns to her*). Yes, ma'am. I can't remember the years before, and the years after have just passed like a wasted day. But the morning I rode off, and for three years, three months, and eight days after, well, I guess I remember every soldier, every gun, every meal, even every dream I had at night—

(BEN *is pouring* LAURETTE *another drink.* OSCAR *is trying to keep her from having it. She pushes* OSCAR's *hand.*)

LAURETTE. I wouldn't ever name a boy Oscar. It's silly.

REGINA. Well?

(MARCUS *and* BEN *laugh. The others look embarrassed.* OSCAR *makes an angry move, decides not to speak.*)

LAVINIA. I can't remember why we chose the name. Can you, Marcus?

MARCUS (*to* LAVINIA). Your father's name was Oscar.

LAVINIA (*worried, crushed*). Oh, goodness, yes.

BIRDIE (*embarrassed, speaks quickly*). John's just wonderful about the war, Mr. Hubbard. Just as good as having a history book. He was everywhere: Vicksburg, Chattanooga, Atlanta.

MARCUS. And he remembers it *all?* What now seems to you the most important of your battles, Captain Bagtry?

JOHN (*annoyed*). I don't know. But there's no need for us to talk about the war, sir.

MARCUS. Oh, I'm interested. I know more of the Greek wars than I do of our own.

LAURETTE. Bet you anything there's a good reason for that. There's a good reason for everything in this vale of tears.

(MARCUS *turns to stare at her.*)

BIRDIE. John, Mr. Hubbard says he's interested. Bet he'd like to hear about Vicksburg, just the way you always tell it to Mama and me.

(JAKE *appears at the door.*)

JAKE. Supper's laid out, waiting.

MARCUS (*to* JOHN). People remember what made them happy, and you were happy in the war, weren't you?

JOHN. Yes, sir. I was happy. I thought we would win.

MARCUS. I never did. Never, from the first foolish talk to the last foolish day. (JOHN *sharply turns away*) I have disturbed you. I'm most sorry. I speak the truth— whenever I can.

BIRDIE (*hastily*). Oh, John doesn't mind. He means—well, you see, it's hard for us to understand anybody who thought we'd lose—

JOHN (*sharply*). It's still hard for a soldier to understand.

BIRDIE (*quickly*). John means once a soldier, always a soldier. He wants to go to Brazil right now. Of course you know, Mr. Hubbard, the radical people down there are trying to abolish slavery, and ruin the country. John wants to fight for his ideals.

MARCUS. Why don't you choose the other side? Every man needs to win once in his life.

JOHN (*angrily*). I don't like that way of saying it. I don't necessarily fight for slavery, I fight for a way of life.

MARCUS. Supper, Captain. (*Turns, calls to the porch*) Put away the music, gentlemen, and have a little more to eat. (*Turns back to* REGINA) What is disturbing you, Regina?

(LAVINIA, BIRDIE, OSCAR, *and* LAURETTE *exit to dining room.*)

REGINA (*sharply*). Nothing.

(BEN *exits.*)

MARCUS (*looks at* JOHN). You disapprove of me, Captain?

JOHN. I am in your house, sir, and you forced me into this kind of talk.

(PENNIMAN *and* JUGGER *come through the room, go into the dining room.*

MARCUS. Well, I disapprove of you. Your people deserved to lose their war and their world. It was a backward world, getting in the way of history. Appalling that you still don't realize it. Really, people should read more books.

REGINA (*angrily*). Papa, I didn't ask John here to listen to you lecture and be nasty and insulting.

MARCUS. *You* asked him here? You asked *John?* (*Sharply*) Come in to supper, Regina.

REGINA (*very sharply*). When I'm ready, Papa. (MARCUS *looks at her, hesitates for a second, then goes into dining room. There is a pause. She goes to* JOHN) I am so sorry.

JOHN. Why should you be sorry? It's the way you feel, too.

REGINA (*impatiently*). All that damn war nonsense— Don't worry about Papa. I'll take care of him. You didn't give me a chance to tell you about Chicago—

JOHN. You didn't give me a chance to tell you about Brazil.

REGINA. Will you stop that foolish joke—

JOHN. It may not be a joke. Birdie has a plan. She won't

tell me about it. Anyway, she says there's going to be money to run Lionnet and enough for me to borrow a little. I'll go on down to Brazil right away. Cod Carter says there's no trick in getting a commission with good pay. The planters there are looking for Confederate officers. I want to be with fighting men again. I'm lonely for them.

REGINA. Now you stop frightening me. I'm going to Chicago, and a month later you're coming and we'll get married. When Papa finds out he'll have a fit. Then we'll come on home for a while, and I'll talk him out of his fit—

JOHN (*gently, smiles*). Now you're joking. Don't talk silly, honey.

REGINA (*softly*). You don't want to come with me? You don't want to marry me?

JOHN (*after a second*). You don't ask that seriously.

REGINA (*softly*). Answer me, please.

JOHN. No. I don't. I never said I did. (*Comes to her*) I don't want to talk this way, but I don't want to lie, either. Honey, I like you so much, but—I shouldn't have let us get like this. You're not in love with me. I'm no good for you—

REGINA. I am in love with you. I've never loved before, and I won't love again.

JOHN. My darling child, everybody thinks that, the first time. You're a lonely girl and I'm the first man you've liked. You can have anybody you want—

REGINA. John. Come away with me. We'll be alone. And after a while, if you still don't want me, then— (*Softly*) I've never pleaded for anything in my life before. I might hold it against you.

JOHN. Oh, Regina, don't speak of pleading. You go away. By the time you come back, you'll be in love with somebody else, and I'll be gone.

REGINA (*stares at him*). Where did you say Miss Birdie

was getting this money, this money for you to travel
with?

JOHN. I don't know where: she won't tell me. But she
says we'll have five thousand dollars this week.

REGINA (*after a second*). Five thousand?

JOHN (*nods*). I'd guess she's arranged something about
the Gilbert Stuart or the West. We haven't anything
but the portraits—

REGINA. Is that what you'd guess? Well, I'd guess different.
So she's planning to get you away from me?

JOHN. Nobody's *planning* anything. Oh, look, honey. This
isn't any good. We'll go home now—

REGINA (*quickly, looking toward dining room*). Papa's
coming. Please go into supper now. It will be bad for
me if you make any fuss or left now— (*Softly*) We'll
talk tomorrow. I love you. Go in to supper.

(MARCUS *appears in the dining-room door.*)

JOHN (*who has his back to the door*). I'm sorry, honey,
if— (*He turns, moves across room, passes* MARCUS *in the
doorway, disappears into the dining room*)

(MARCUS *stares at* REGINA; *she does not look at him.*)

MARCUS. Who is sillier, who is more dead, the captain or
his cousin? (*She doesn't answer him*) You have a reason for not joining us at supper?

REGINA. I wanted to talk to—to Captain Bagtry.

MARCUS. Can he talk of anything but war?

REGINA. Have you agreed to make Ben's loan on Lionnet?

MARCUS. Ben's loan? Of course I'll make it. It is good for
me, and bad for them. Got nothing to do with Ben.

REGINA. No? Have you asked yourself why Ben wants it
so much?

MARCUS. I am not interested in Ben's motives. As long as
they benefit me, he is welcome to them.

REGINA. How much money did he say Miss Birdie had
asked for?

MARCUS. Ten thousand. (REGINA *smiles*) Why does this interest you?

REGINA (*rises*). Don't make the loan, Papa. I don't like the girl. I think she's come here tonight to make fun of us. She's snubbing all of us, laughing up her sleeve. Why should you pay her to do it?

MARCUS (*stares at her*). That's not true and I don't think you think it is. You're lying to me about something. Stop it. It hurts me. Tell me why you were talking to that man, why he called you honey—

REGINA (*carefully*). Ben is sometimes smarter than you are, and you are so sure he isn't, that you get careless about him. (*Nods toward dining room*) Bagtry doesn't know about *your* loan on Lionnet, but the girl told him she was getting five thousand dollars this week. *Five thousand dollars, not ten.* I'd like to bet the extra five is meant for Ben to keep. (*Carefully, as he stares at her*) You're getting older, Papa, and maybe you're getting tired and don't think as fast. I guess that happens to everybody. You'll have to start watching Ben even more—

MARCUS (*sharply*). All right, Regina.

(PENNIMAN *and* JUGGER *come in from the dining room. They stand awkwardly, not knowing what to do.* REGINA *goes into dining room.*)

PENNIMAN (*hesitates*). Shall we—would you like us to continue the music?

MARCUS. As soon as you have finished overeating.

(PENNIMAN *coughs, embarrassed.* JUGGER *starts forward angrily, then stops, follows* PENNIMAN *out to the porch.* LAVINIA *comes in from the dining room.*)

LAVINIA. I think that Miss Laurette has a touch of heart trouble. I asked the poor child what she was doing for it. She said she was trying to see if good, strong drinks would help. I've never heard that, although Ben says it's a good cure. She's a nice little thing.

MARCUS. You've always been a good judge of people, Lavinia, but that's true of all the pure in heart, isn't it?

(LAURETTE, *followed by* OSCAR, *comes into the room. She is steady, but the liquor has blinded her a little, and she bumps into things.* OSCAR *follows her, very nervous, staring at* MARCUS, *who does not turn around.*)

LAVINIA (*speaks to* LAURETTE *only because she is nervous*). Hello.

(LAURETTE *now finds herself near the piano. She strikes a note. Pleased, she presses her right hand on the keyboard. Delighted, she presses both hands.* OSCAR *jumps toward her.*)

LAURETTE. Hello . . . I never had opportunities . . . (OSCAR *grabs both her hands, she pulls them away, pounds again, grins, indicates* MARCUS) Your Papa likes music, she says.

MARCUS (*to* OSCAR). Is there any effective way of stopping that?

(LAURETTE *throws off* OSCAR, *comes over to* MARCUS.)

LAURETTE. Oskie says he wants to marry little old Laurette.

MARCUS. Does little old Laurette think that fortunate?

LAURETTE (*laughs—puts her hand through his arm*). Sometimes yes, sometimes no. We're going on down to New Orleans.

(BEN *and* BIRDIE *come in from the dining room.*)

MARCUS (*takes* LAURETTE's *hand from his arm*). This will sound very rude but I have a nervous dislike of being grabbed.

LAURETTE. Oh, sure. Me, too. Can't stand people pressing me unless I know about it, I mean. (*Glares at* OSCAR) Don't you ever press me, Oskie, unless I know about it.

MARCUS. That reminds me. I'm told you work for a living. That is good: Oscar is not a rich man.

LAURETTE (*laughs*). Rich? How could he be, on that stinking slave salary you pay him? That's why you're sure to repent and help us, Oskie says. When you die you're going to leave it to him anyway, so why not now, Oskie says?

MARCUS (*softly*). Oscar is a liar. Always has been. (BIRDIE *moves toward porch*) And he steals a little. Nothing much, not enough to be respectable. But you know all that, of course.

LAVINIA. Oh, Marcus. (*Turns to* BIRDIE) My husband makes little jokes. All the time—

OSCAR (*very loudly, to* MARCUS). It's not true. It's just not true—

MARCUS (*to* BIRDIE). Miss Bagtry, don't you find that people always think you're joking when you speak the truth in a soft voice?

BIRDIE (*very embarrassed*). No, sir. I—

MARCUS (*back to* LAURETTE). If you want him, Miss Laurette, do have him.

OSCAR (*with dignity*). Come on, Laurette. I'll settle this later.

(MARCUS *laughs.*)

LAURETTE. Well, I'll just about say you will. A Papa talking about his son! No animal would talk about their own son that way. I heard tales about you ever since I was born, but—

OSCAR (*frantic*). Come on, Laurette.

LAURETTE. You old bastard.

(MARCUS *slowly rises.*)

LAVINIA (*to* LAURETTE). Dear child—

LAURETTE (*to* MARCUS). Everybody in this country knows how you got rich, bringing in salt and making poor, dying people give up everything for it. Right in the middle of the war, men dying for you, and you making their kinfolk give you all their goods and money—and I heard how they suspected you of worse, and you only just got out of a hanging rope. (*Points to* OSCAR) Why, the first night he slept with me, I didn't even want to speak to him because of you and your doings. My uncle used to tell me about—

BEN. Go on, Oscar. Get out.

(JOHN *and* REGINA *come in from dining room.*)

MARCUS (*to* OSCAR). Take that girl out of here. Then come back. And come back quickly.

(OSCAR *stares at him, starts to speak, changes his mind. Then he hurries to* LAURETTE, *takes her arm, moves her out.* JOHN *crosses to* BIRDIE.)

LAVINIA (*in an odd tone*). Why, Marcus. The girl only told the truth. Salt is just a word, it's in the Bible quite a lot. And that other matter, why, death, is also just a word. And—

MARCUS. You grow daring, Lavinia. (*Moves toward her*) Now stop that prattling or go to your room—

BEN (*moves in front of him*). We have guests.

JOHN (*takes* BIRDIE's *arm, comes forward*). Good night and thank you, Mrs. Hubbard. (*Coldly, to others*) Good night.

MARCUS. You came to beg a favor, and you stayed to be amused. Good night.

BIRDIE (*scared*). Mr. Hubbard, please . . .

JOHN. Came to ask a favor? From you? Who in this county would be so dishonored? If you were not an old man, Mr. Hubbard, I—

MARCUS. There is never so great a hero as the man who fought on a losing side.

BIRDIE (*goes to* JOHN—*desperate*). Stop it, John. Go outside. Wait for me in the carriage.

JOHN. I don't want you here. Come on, Birdie—

BIRDIE (*firmly*). I want to stay for a few minutes. Please go outside. *Please. Please.*

(*He stares at her, then he turns, moves quickly out of the room.* MARCUS *is watching* REGINA. REGINA *looks at* MARCUS, *then turns and moves quickly after* JOHN. MARCUS *wheels around as if to stop* REGINA.)

BIRDIE. Mr. Hubbard, I am sorry. John is upset. You know that his twin brother was killed that night in the massacre, and any mention of it—

MARCUS (*sharply*). What night do you speak of, Miss Birdie, and what massacre?

BIRDIE (*desperately*). Oh, I don't know. I—I'm just so sorry it has been unpleasant. I was hoping we could all be nice friends. Your family and mine—

MARCUS (*smiles*). Your mother hasn't bowed to me in the forty years I've lived in this town. Does she wish to be my nice friend now?

BIRDIE (*desperate*). Mama is old-fashioned. I'll speak to her and after a bit— (*Pauses, looks down*) Oh. I've said the wrong thing again. I don't know how to— (*Turns to him, simply*) I guess I just better say it simple, the way it comes to me. I didn't only come tonight for the loan. I *wanted* to come. I was frightened, of course, but, well, it was a big holiday for me, and I tried to get all dressed up in Mama's old things, and that was why we were late because I haven't had a new dress, and I've never had a party dress since I was four years old, and I had to get the dress without Mama's knowing why or where we were going, and I had to sew—

MARCUS. Then it *is* too bad you troubled yourself, because I have bad news for you: I have decided not to make the loan.

(BIRDIE *draws back, turns to* BEN, *starts to speak, puts her hands to her face.*)

BEN (*slowly*). Why? Why? You said yourself—

BIRDIE (*moves toward him*). Oh, please, Mr. Hubbard. Please. I went around all day telling our people they might be paid and—I'll give more, whatever you want—

MARCUS. That is unjust of you. I am not bargaining.

BEN (*angrily, to* MARCUS). I want to know why you have changed your mind.

MARCUS. I will tell you, in time. (*Turns to* BIRDIE) I am

sorry to disappoint you. Please come another night, without a motive, just for the music.

BIRDIE. Yes, I had a motive. Why shouldn't I have? It was why I was asked here— Oh, I mustn't talk proud. I have no right to. Look, Mr. Hubbard, I'll do anything. I'm sure you like good pictures: we have a Stuart and a West, and a little silver left. Couldn't I give—couldn't I bring them to you—

MARCUS (*gently, hurt*). Miss Birdie, Miss Birdie, please spare us both.

BIRDIE (*softly*). I was going to use the first money to buy molasses and sugar. All that land and cotton and we're starving. It sounds crazy, to need even molasses—

MARCUS. Everybody with cotton is starving.

BIRDIE (*angrily*). That's just a way of using a word. That isn't what I mean. I mean starving. (*She looks up him, her voice changes, sighs*) I should have known I couldn't do anything right. I never have. I'm sorry to have told you such things about us. You lose your manners when you're poor. (*Goes to* LAVINIA) Thank you, ma'am.

LAVINIA (*smiles gently, takes her hand*). Good night, child. You ride over and see me, or come down by the river and we'll read together.

BIRDIE (*smiles, crosses to* BEN). Thank you, Mr. Ben. I know you acted as my good friend.

MARCUS (*laughs*). Good night.

(*She nods, runs out.*)

LAVINIA (*after a second*). Goodness, Marcus. Couldn't you have—it's pig mean, being poor. Takes away your dignity.

MARCUS. That's correct, Lavinia. And a good reason for staying rich.

PENNIMAN'S VOICE. We're waiting for you, Mr. Hubbard.

MARCUS (*calling out*). That will be all for tonight.

(REGINA *appears from the hall.*)

REGINA (*to* MARCUS). I didn't intend you to insult them and make enemies of them.

MARCUS. Why are you so disturbed about the Bagtrys? (BEN *laughs*) You are amused?

BEN. Yes. I am amused.

MARCUS. All right. Enjoy yourself—for a few minutes. (PENNIMAN *and* JUGGER *appear carrying their instruments.* MARCUS *turns to them*) The Mozart was carelessly performed. The carriage is waiting to take you to the station. Good night.

JUGGER. "Carelessly performed." What do you know about music? Nothing, and we're just here to pretend you do. Glad to make a little money once a month— (*Angrily*) I won't do it any more, do you hear me?

MARCUS. Very well. Good night.

(JUGGER *moves quickly out.* PENNIMAN *comes forward, nervously.*)

PENNIMAN. He didn't mean—Gil is tired— Why, we're just as happy to come here— (*No answer. Desperately*) Well, see you next month, sir. Just as usual. Huh?

(*When* MARCUS *doesn't answer,* PENNIMAN *sighs, exits as* OSCAR *appears from porch.*)

OSCAR (*rushes toward* BEN). Trying to ruin my life, are you? Pouring liquor down her. Come on outside and fight it out like a man. I'll beat you up for it, the way you deserve—

LAVINIA (*as if she had come out of a doze*). Oh, goodness! The blood of brothers. (*To* BEN) You in trouble, Ben? (*Sees* OSCAR) Oh, *you're* in trouble, Oscar.

OSCAR. Come on—

BEN. Oh, shut up.

(MARCUS *laughs.*)

OSCAR (*turns on* MARCUS, *angrily*). You laugh. I told you he had his eye on Birdie and Lionnet, and me getting it for him. So I fool him by bringing Laurette here. And then *he* fools *you:* gets Laurette drunk, and you get mad. That's just what he wanted you to do. And you did it for him. I think the joke's kind of on you.

REGINA. You must have told the truth once before in your life, Oscar, but I can't remember it.

MARCUS (*to* BEN). You're full of tricks these days. Did you get the girl drunk?

BEN. Just as good for Oscar to marry a silly girl who owns cotton, as a silly girl who doesn't even own the mattress on which she—

(OSCAR *springs toward* BEN, *grabs his shoulder.*)

MARCUS (*to* OSCAR). Will you stop running about and pulling at people? Go outside and shoot a passing nigger if your blood is throwing clots into your head.

OSCAR. I'm going to kill Ben if he doesn't stop—

MARCUS. Are you denying the girl makes use of a mattress, or do you expect to go through life killing every man who knows she does?

OSCAR (*screaming*). Papa, stop it! I am deeply and sincerely in love.

MARCUS. In one minute I shall put you out of the room. (*Looks at* BEN) So that was the way it was supposed to work? Or better than that: the girl was to borrow ten thousand from me and you were to keep five of it, and take your chances on her being a fool, and nobody finding out.

BEN (*slowly*). I understand now. (*Softly to* REGINA) Bagtry told *you*. Yes? (REGINA *nods, and smiles, sits down.*)

MARCUS. Your tricks are getting nasty and they bore me. I don't like to be bored: I've told you that before.

BEN (*shrugs*). I want something for myself. I shouldn't think you were the man to blame me for that.

MARCUS. I wouldn't have, if you hadn't always been such a failure at getting it. (*Goes to* BEN) I'm tired of your games, do you hear me? You're a clerk in my store and that you'll remain. You won't get the chance to try anything like this again. But in case you anger me once more, there won't be the job in the store, and you won't be here. Is that clear?

BEN (*slowly*). Very clear.

OSCAR (*who has been thinking*). Papa, you couldn't condemn a woman for a past that was filled with loathing for what society forced upon her; a woman of inner purity made to lead a life of outward shame?

MARCUS. What are you talking about?

REGINA. He's read a book.

MARCUS (*softly*). At nine years old I was carrying water for two bits a week. I took the first dollar I ever had and went to the paying library to buy a card. When I was twelve I was working out in the fields, and that same year I taught myself Latin and French. At fourteen I was driving mules all day and most of the night, but that was the year I learned my Greek, read my classics, taught myself— Think what I must have wanted for sons. And then think what I got. One unsuccessful trickster, one proud illiterate. No, I don't think Oscar's ever read a book.

LAVINIA. He did, Marcus. I used to read my Bible to him.

MARCUS (*to* OSCAR). If you want to go away with this girl, what's detaining you?

OSCAR (*eagerly*). Your permission, sir.

MARCUS. Talk sense. Do you mean money?

OSCAR. Just a loan. Then we'd ship on down to New Orleans—

MARCUS. How much?

OSCAR. Could invest in a little business Laurette knows about— (REGINA *laughs loudly*) Ten thousand could start me off fine, Papa—

MARCUS. There will be a thousand dollars for you, in an envelope, on that table by six in the morning. Get on the early train. Send a Christmas card each year to an aging man who now wishes you to go upstairs.

OSCAR (*starts to protest, changes his mind*). Well, thank you. Seems kind of strange to be saying good-bye after twenty-five years—

REGINA (*gaily*). Oh, don't think of it that way. We'll be coming to see you some day. You'll have ten children, and five of the leaner ones may be yours.

LAVINIA. Good-bye, son. I'm sorry if— I'm sorry.

OSCAR. I'll write you, Mama. (*To* BEN, *sharply*) You've bullied me since the day I was born. But before I leave— (*fiercely*)—you're going to do what I tell you. You're going to be on the station platform tomorrow morning. You're going to be there to apologize to Laurette.

MARCUS. Goodness, what a thousand dollars won't do!

OSCAR. And if you're not ready on time—(*takes a pistol from his pocket*)—I'll get you out of bed with this. And then you won't apologize to her standing up, but on your knees—

MARCUS (*violently, turning around*). Put that gun away. How dare you, in this house—

BEN (*smiles*). You've always been frightened of guns, Papa. Ever since that night, wasn't it?

LAVINIA. That's true, ever since that night.

MARCUS (*very angry*). *Put that gun away. And get upstairs. Immediately.*

OSCAR (*to* BEN). See you at the station. (*He crosses room, exits.*)

BEN (*after a second*). No need to be so nervous. I could have taken the gun away from him.

LAVINIA. And they had hot tar and clubs and ropes that night—

MARCUS. *Stop your crazy talk, Lavinia.*

LAVINIA (*softly*). I don't like that word, Marcus. No, I don't. I think you use it just to hurt my feelings.

BEN (*smiles*). He's upset, Mama. Old fears come back, strong.

MARCUS (*slowly, to* BEN). You're wearing me thin.

REGINA (*yawns*). Oh, don't you and Ben start again. (*She pats* BEN *on the arm*) You know Papa always wins. But maybe you'll have your time some day. Try to get along, both of you. After Mama and I leave you'll be here alone together.

MARCUS. I don't know, darling. I'm going to miss you. I think I may join you.

REGINA (*turns, hesitantly*). Join me? But—

BEN. That would spoil the plan.

MARCUS (*to* REGINA). I'll let you and Lavinia go ahead. Then I'll come and get you and we'll take a turn in New York. And then Regina and I will go on to Europe and you'll come back here, Lavinia.

LAVINIA. Oh, Marcus, you just can't have been listening to me. I been telling you since yesterday, and for years before *that*—

MARCUS (*looks at* REGINA). You want me to come, darling?

REGINA (*nervously*). Of course. When were you thinking of coming, Papa? Soon or—

BEN (*to* REGINA—*laughs*). I'm dying to see you get out of this one, honey.

MARCUS (*angrily, to* BEN). What are you talking about?

BEN. I'm going to be sorry to miss the sight of your face when Regina produces the secret bridegroom. (MARCUS *wheels to stare at* REGINA) Oh, you know about it. You guessed tonight. Captain Bagtry. I don't think he wants to marry her. I don't think he even wants to sleep with her any more. But he's a weak man and— (MARCUS *is advancing toward him*) That won't do any good. I'm going to finish. Yesterday, if you remember, Regina wanted you to make the loan to the girl. Tonight, when she found out John Bagtry wanted to use a little of the money to leave here, and her, she talked you out of it.

REGINA. *Ben, be still.* Ben— (*Goes swiftly to* MARCUS)

Don't listen, Papa. I have seen John, I told you that. I like him, yes. But don't you see what Ben is doing? He wanted to marry me off to money, he's angry—

BEN (*to* MARCUS). I'm telling the truth. The whole town's known it for a year.

LAVINIA. Don't, Benjamin, don't! Marcus, you look so bad—

BEN. You do look bad. Go up to him, Regina, put your arms around him. Tell him you've never really loved anybody else, and never will. Lie to him, just for tonight. Tell him you'll never get in bed with anybody ever again—

(MARCUS *slaps* BEN *sharply across the face.*)

LAVINIA (*desperately*). God help us! Marcus! Ben!

BEN (*softly*). I won't forget that. As long as I live.

MARCUS. Lock your door tonight, and be out of here before I am down in the morning. Wherever you decide to go, be sure it's far away. Get yourself a modest job, because wherever you are, I'll see to it that you never get any other.

BEN. I spent twenty years lying and cheating to help make you rich. I was trying to outwait you, Papa, but I guess I couldn't do it. (*He exits.*)

LAVINIA. Twenty years, he said. Then it would be my fault, my sin, too— (*She starts for hall door, calling*) Benjamin! I want to talk to you, son. You're my first-born, going away—

(*She disappears. There is a long pause.* MARCUS *sits down.*)

MARCUS. How could you let him touch you? When did it happen? How could you— *Answer me.*

REGINA (*wearily*). Are they questions that can be answered?

MARCUS. A dead man, a foolish man, an empty man from an idiot world. A man who wants nothing but war, any war, just a war. A man who believes in nothing, and never will. A man in space—

REGINA (*softly—comes to him*). All right, Papa. That's all

true, and I know it. And I'm in love with him, and I want to marry him. (*He puts his hands over his face. She speaks coldly*) Now don't take on so. It just won't do. You let me go away, as we planned. I'll get married. After a while we'll come home and we'll live right here—

MARCUS. *Are you crazy?* Do you think I'd stay in this house with you and—

REGINA. Otherwise, I'll go away. I say I will, and you know I will. I'm not frightened to go. But if I go that way I won't ever see you again. And you don't want that: I don't think you could stand that. My way, we can be together. You'll get used to it, and John won't worry us. There'll always be you and me— (*Puts her hand on his shoulder*) You must have known I'd marry some day, Papa. Why, I've never seen you cry before. It'll just be like going for a little visit, and before you know it I'll be home again, and it will all be over. You know? Maybe next year, or the year after, you and I'll make that trip to Greece, just the two of us. (*Smiles*) Now it's all settled. Kiss me good night, darling. (*She kisses him, he does not move. Then she moves toward door as* LAVINIA *comes in.*)

LAVINIA. Ben won't let me talk to him. He'd feel better if he talked, if he spoke out— I'm his Mama and I got to take my responsibility for what—

REGINA. Mama, I think we'll be leaving for Chicago sooner than we thought. We'll start getting ready tomorrow morning. Good night. (*She exits.*)

LAVINIA (*softly, after a minute*). Did you forget to tell her that I can't go with her? Didn't you tell them all where I'm going? I think you better do that, Marcus—

MARCUS (*softly—very tired*). I don't feel well. Please stop jabbering, Lavinia.

LAVINIA. You tell Regina tomorrow. You tell her how you

promised me. (*Desperately*) Marcus. It's all I've lived for. And it can't wait now. I'm getting old, and I've got to go and do my work.

MARCUS (*wearily*). It isn't easy to live with you, Lavinia. It really isn't. Leave me alone.

LAVINIA (*gently*). I know. We weren't ever meant to be together. You see, being here gives me—well, I won't use bad words, but it's always made me feel like I sinned. And God wants you to make good your sins before you die. That's why I got to go now.

MARCUS. I've stood enough of that. Please don't ever speak of it again.

LAVINIA. Ever speak of it? But you swore to me over and over again.

MARCUS. Did you ever think I meant that nonsense?

LAVINIA. But I'm going!

MARCUS. You're never going. Dr. Seckles knows how strange you've been, the whole town knows you're crazy. Now I don't want to listen to any more of that talk ever. I try to leave you alone, try to leave me alone. If you worry me any more with it, I'll have to talk to the doctor and ask him to send you away. (*Softly— crying*) Please go to bed now, and don't walk around all night again.

LAVINIA (*stares at him*). Coralee. . . . Coralee! He never ever meant me to go. He says I can't go. Coralee— (*She starts to move slowly, then she begins to run*) Coralee, are you in bed—

Curtain

ACT THREE

SCENE: *Same as Act One, early the next morning.*
At rise of curtain, LAVINIA *is moving about in the living room.*

LAVINIA (*singing*).

> Got one life, got to hold it bold
> Got one life, got to hold it bold
> Lord, my year must come.

(*She comes on the porch. She is carrying a small Bible.*)

> Got one life, got to hold it bold
> Got one life, got to hold it bold
> Lord, my year must come.

(BEN, *carrying a valise, comes from the living room.* LA-VINIA *gets up.*)

LAVINIA. All night I been waiting. You wouldn't let your Mama talk to you.

BEN. I put all my stuff in the ironing room. I'll send for it when I find a place.

LAVINIA (*softly*). Take me with you, son. As far as Alta-loosa. There I'll get off, and there I'll stay. Benjamin, he couldn't bring me back, or send me, or do, or do. He couldn't, if you'd protect me for a while and—

BEN. I, protect you? (*Smiles*) Didn't you hear him last night? Don't you know about me?

LAVINIA. I don't know. I heard so much. I get mixed. I know you're bad off now. (*She reaches up as if to touch his face*) You're my first-born, so it must be my fault some way.

BEN. Do you like me, Mama?

LAVINIA (*after a second*). Well. You've grown away from— I loved you, Benjamin.

BEN (*turns away*). Once upon a time.

403

LAVINIA. Take me with you. Take me where I can do my little good. The colored people are forgiving people. And they'll help me. You know, I should have gone after that night, but I stayed for you children. I didn't know then that none of you would ever need a Mama. Well, I'm going now. *I tell you I'm going.* (*Her voice rises*) I spoke with God this night, in prayer. He said I should go no matter. Strait are the gates, He said. Narrow is the way, Lavinia, He said—

BEN (*sharply*). Mama! You're talking loud. (*Turns to her*) Go to bed now. You've had no sleep. I'm late. (*Starts to move.*)

LAVINIA. Take me, Benjamin!

BEN (*sharply*). Now go in to Coralee before you get yourself in bad shape and trouble.

LAVINIA. You've got to take me. Last night he said he'd never ever meant me to go. Last night he said if ever, then he'd have Dr. Seckles, have him, have him— (*Turns, her fist clenched*) Take me away from here. For ten years he swore, for ten years he swore a lie to me. I told God about that last night, and God's message said, "Go, Lavinia, even if you have to tell the awful truth. If there is no other way, tell the truth."

BEN (*turns slightly*). The truth about what?

LAVINIA. I think, now, I should have told the truth that night. But you don't always know how to do things when they're happening. It's not easy to send your own husband into a hanging rope.

BEN. What do you mean?

LAVINIA. All night long I been thinking I should go right up those steps and tell him what I know. Then he'd have to let me leave or— (*Puts her hands to her face*) I've always been afraid of him, because once or twice—

BEN. Of course. But you're not afraid of me.

LAVINIA. Oh, I been afraid of you, too. I spent a life afraid. And you know that's funny, Benjamin, because way down deep I'm a woman wasn't made to be afraid. What are most people afraid of? Well, like your Papa, they're afraid to die. But I'm not afraid to die because my colored friends going to be right there to pray me in.

BEN (*carefully*). Mama, what were you talking about? Telling the truth, a hanging rope—

LAVINIA. And if you're not afraid of dying then you're not afraid of anything. (*Sniffs the air*) The river's rising. I can tell by the azalea smell.

BEN (*tensely, angrily*). For God's sake, Mama, try to remember what you were saying, if you were saying anything.

LAVINIA. I was saying a lot. I could walk up those steps and tell him I could still send him into a hanging rope unless he lets me go: I could say I saw him that night, and I'll just go and tell everybody I did see him—

BEN. *What night?*

LAVINIA. The night of the massacre, of course.

BEN (*tensely, sharply*). Where did you see him, how—

LAVINIA. You being sharp with me now. And I never been sharp with you. Never—

BEN (*carefully*). Mama. Now listen to me. It's late and there isn't much time. I'm in trouble, bad trouble, and you're in bad trouble. Tell me fast what you're talking about. Maybe I can get us both out of trouble. Maybe. But only if you tell me now. *Now.* And tell me quick and straight. You can go away and I—

LAVINIA (*rises*). I saw him, like I told you, the night of the massacre, on the well-house roof.

BEN. All right. I understand what you mean. All right. But there's a lot I don't know or understand.

LAVINIA (*as if she hadn't heard him*). One time last night, I thought of getting his envelope of money, bringing it out here, tearing it up, and watching his face when he saw it at breakfast time. But it's not nice to see people grovel on the ground for money—

BEN. The envelope of money? The little envelope of money or the big envelope?

LAVINIA. I could get it, tear it up.

BEN (*carefully*). Why not? Get it now and just tear it up.

LAVINIA. And I thought too about giving it to the poor. But it's evil money and not worthy of the poor.

BEN. No, the poor don't want evil money. That's not the way.

LAVINIA (*turns to him*). Oh, I am glad to hear you say that, but you can see how I have been tempted when I thought what the money could do for my little school. I want my colored children to have many things.

BEN (*desperately*). You can have everything for them if—

LAVINIA. Oh, nobody should have everything. All I want is a nice school place, warm in winter, and a piano, and books and a good meal every day, hot and fattening.

BEN (*comes to her, stands in front of her*). Get up, Mama. Come here. He'll be awake soon. (LAVINIA *rises, he takes her by the arms*) Papa will be awake soon.

LAVINIA (*looks at him, nods*). First part of the war I was so ill I thought it was brave of your Papa to run the blockade, even though I knew he was dealing with the enemy to do it. People were dying for salt and I thought it was good to bring it to them. I didn't know he was getting eight dollars a bag for it, Benjamin, a little bag, Imagine taking money for other people's misery.

BEN (*softly*). Yes, I know all that, Mama. Everybody does now.

LAVINIA (*puzzled*). But I can't tell what you know, Benjamin. You were away in New Orleans in school and it's hard for me to put in place what you know and— (BEN *moves impatiently*) So—well, there was the camp where our boys were being mobilized. It was up the river, across the swamp fork, back behind the old delta fields.

BEN. Yes, I know where it was. And I know that Union troops crossed the river and killed the twenty-seven boys who were training there. And I know that Papa was on one of his salt-running trips that day and that every man in the county figured Union troops couldn't have found the camp unless they were led through to it, and I know they figured Papa was the man who did the leading.

LAVINIA. He didn't lead them to the camp. Not on purpose. No, Benjamin, I am sure of that.

BEN. I agree with you. It wouldn't have paid him enough, and he doesn't like danger. So he didn't do it. And he proved to them he wasn't here so he couldn't have done it. (*Turns to her*) So now where are we?

LAVINIA. They were murder mad the night they found the poor dead boys. They came with hot tar and guns to find your Papa.

BEN (*softly*). But they didn't find him.

LAVINIA. But I found him. (*She opens the Bible, holds it up, peers at it. BEN comes toward her*) At four-thirty o'clock Coralee and I saw him and heard him, on the well-house roof. We knew he kept money and papers there, and so we guessed right away where to look, and there he was.

BEN (*looks at her, smiles, softly*). And there he was.

LAVINIA. So you see I hadn't told a lie, Benjamin. He wasn't ever in the *house*. But maybe half a lie is worse than a real lie.

BEN (*quickly*). Yes, yes. Now how did he get away, and how did he prove to them—

LAVINIA. Coralee and I sat on the wet ground, watching him. Oh, it was a terrible thing for me. It was a wet night and Coralee caught cold. I had to nurse her for days afterward, with—

BEN (*looks up at balcony*). *Mama!* It's got to be quick now. Shall I tell you why? I've got to go unless— Now tell me how did he get away, and how did he prove to them that all the time he had been down Mobile road?

LAVINIA (*opens her Bible*). Twenty minutes to six he climbed down from the roof, unlocked the well-house door, got some money from the envelope, and went on down through the back pines. Coralee and I ran back to the house, shivering and frightened. I didn't know what was going to happen, so we locked all the doors and all the windows and Coralee coughed, and sneezed, and ran a fever.

BEN (*angrily*). I don't give a damn about Coralee's health.

LAVINIA (*gently*). That's the trouble with you, Benjamin. You don't ever care about other folks.

(*There is the sound of a door closing inside the house.*)

BEN (*quietly*). *There is not much time left now. Try, Mama, try hard.* Tell me how he managed.

LAVINIA (*looks down at the Bible*). Well, three days later, no, two days later, the morning of April 5, 1864, at exactly ten-five—

BEN (*sharply*). What are you reading?

LAVINIA. He rode back into town, coming up Mobile road. They were waiting for him and they roped him and searched him. But he had two passes proving he had ridden through Confederate lines the day before the massacre, and didn't leave till after it. The passes were signed by—(*looks at Bible*)—Captain Virgil E. McMullen of the 5th Tennessee from Memphis. They were stamped passes, they were good passes, and they had to let him go. But he had no money when he came home. So Coralee and I just knew he paid Captain Virgil E. McMullen to write those passes. (*Looks down at book*) Virgil E. McMullen, Captain in the 5th Tennessee—

BEN (*tensely—points to Bible*). It's written down there?

LAVINIA. Coralee and I were half wild with what was the right thing to do and the wrong. So we wrote it all down here in my Bible and we each put our hand on the Book and swore to it. That made us feel better—

BEN. I'm sure of it. Give me the Bible, Mama—

LAVINIA. I think there's one in your room, at least there used to be—

BEN. Oh, Mama. For God's sake. I need it. It's the only proof we've got, and even then he'll—

LAVINIA. You don't need half this proof. That's the trouble with your kind of thinking, Benjamin. My, I could just walk down the street, tell the story to the first people I met. They'd believe me, and they'd believe Coralee. We're religious women and everybody knows it. (*Smiles*) And then they'd want to believe us, nothing would give them so much pleasure as, as, as, well, calling on your Papa. I think people always believe what they want to believe, don't you? I don't think I'd have any trouble, if you stood behind me, and gave me courage to do the right talking.

BEN (*laughs*). I'll be behind you. But I'd like the Bible behind me. Come, Mama, give it to me now. I need it for us. (*Slowly she hands the Bible to him*) All right. Now I'd like to have that envelope.

LAVINIA. But what has the money got to do with—I don't understand why the envelope—I'm trying hard to understand everything, but I can't see what it has—

BEN. I can't either. So let's put it this way: it would make me feel better to have it. There's nothing makes you feel better at this hour of the morning than an envelope of money.

LAVINIA (*thinks*). Oh. Well. (*Points into living room*) It's in the small upper left-hand drawer of your Papa's desk. But I don't know where he keeps the key.

BEN (*laughs*). That's very negligent of you. We won't need the key. (*Takes her hand, takes her under balcony*) Now call Papa. I'll be back in a minute.

LAVINIA. Oh, I couldn't do that. I never have—

BEN (*softly*). You're going to do a lot of things you've never done before. Now I want you to do what I tell you, and trust me from now on, will you?

LAVINIA. I'm going to do what you tell me.

BEN (*goes into living room*). All right. Now go ahead. (JAKE *appears. He is carrying a mop and a pail.*)

JAKE. You all up specially early, or me, am I late?

LAVINIA (*calling*). Marcus. Marcus. (*To* JAKE) What do you think of that, Jake?

JAKE (*takes a nervous step toward her—softly*). I don't think well of it. Please, Miss Viney, don't be doing—

LAVINIA. Marcus! Marcus! I want—we want to speak to you. (*To* JAKE) Hear what I did? (*Nervously*) Everything's different—Marcus!

(MARCUS *appears on the porch. He has been dressing; he is now in shirtsleeves. He peers down at* LAVINIA.)

MARCUS. Are you shouting at me? What's the matter with you now, Lavinia?

LAVINIA. Well, I just—

MARCUS. You are up early to give your blessings to your departing sons?

LAVINIA. I haven't seen Oscar.

MARCUS. Benjamin has gone?

LAVINIA (*looks into drawing room*). No, Marcus. He hasn't gone. He's inside knocking off the locks on your desk. My, he's doing it with a pistol. The other end of the pistol, I mean.

(*During her speech, we hear three rapid, powerful blows.* MARCUS *grips the rail of the porch.* BEN *comes onto the porch, the pistol in one hand, a large envelope in the other. He looks up at* MARCUS. *There is a long pause.*)

MARCUS. Put the gun on the table. Bring me that envelope.

LAVINIA. Same old envelope. Like I said, I used to dream about tearing up that money. You could do it, Benjamin, right now. Make you feel better and cleaner, too.

BEN. I feel fine. (*To* MARCUS) I like you better up there.

So stay there. *Stay there.* (BEN *turns to* JAKE, *takes another envelope from his pocket, puts in money from first envelope*) Take this over to Lionnet. Ask for Miss Birdie Bagtry and talk to nobody else. Give her this and ask her to forget about last night.

MARCUS. Take that envelope from him, Lavinia, and bring it to me quickly.

LAVINIA. I can't walk as fast as I used to, Marcus, I'm getting old—

BEN (*to* JAKE). Tell Miss Birdie I'll call on her in the next few days and we'll attend to the details then. Go on, be quick—

MARCUS (*to* JAKE). Come back here! (*To* BEN) How dare you touch—

BEN. Well, come and get it from me. (*Turns again to* JAKE) And tell her I wish Captain Bagtry good luck. And stop at the wharf and buy two tickets on the sugar boat.

LAVINIA. Thank you, son. (*There is a long pause. She is puzzled by it*) Well. Why doesn't somebody say something?

BEN. We're thinking.

MARCUS. Yes. Shall I tell you what I'm thinking? That I'm going to be sorry for the scandal of a son in jail.

BEN. What would you put me in jail for?

MARCUS. For stealing forty thousand dollars.

BEN (*looking at the envelope, smiles*). That much? I haven't had time to count it. I always said there wasn't a Southerner, born before the war, who ever had sense enough to trust a bank. Now do you want to know what *I'm* thinking?

MARCUS. Yes, I'm puzzled. This piece of insanity isn't like you. In the years to come, when I do think about you, I would like to know why you walked yourself into a jail cell.

BEN. In the years to come, when you think about me, do it this way. (*Sharply*) You had been buying salt from the Union garrison across the river. On the morning of April 2nd you rode over to get it. Early evening of April 3rd you started back with it—

MARCUS. Are you writing a book about me? I would not have chosen you as my recorder.

BEN. You were followed back—which is exactly what Union officers had been waiting for—at eleven o'clock that night—

LAVINIA. Marcus didn't *mean* to lead them back. I explained that to you, Benjamin—

MARCUS (*sharply*). *You* explained it to him? What—

BEN. Eleven o'clock that night twenty-seven boys in the swamp camp were killed. The news reached here, and you, about an hour later.

LAVINIA. More than that. About two hours later. Or maybe more, Benjamin.

MARCUS. What the hell is this? Lavinia, I want—

BEN. And the town, guessing right, and hating you anyway, began to look for you. They didn't find you. Because you were on the well-house roof.

LAVINIA. Yes, you were, Marcus, that's just where you were. I saw you.

MARCUS (*softly*). I don't know why I'm standing here listening to this foolishness, and I won't be for long. Bring me the envelope, and you will still have plenty of time to catch the train. You come up here, Lavinia—

BEN. I'll tell you why you're standing there: you are very, very, very—as Mama would say—afraid.

MARCUS (*carefully*). What should I be afraid of, Benjamin? (*Sharply*) A bungler who leaves broken locks on a desk to prove he's stolen, and gives away money to make sure I have further proof? Or a crazy woman, who dreams she saw something sixteen years ago?

LAVINIA. Marcus, I must ask you to stop using that awful word and—

MARCUS. And I must ask you to get used to it because within an hour you'll be where they use no other word—

BEN (*as* LAVINIA *makes frightened motion*). Mama, stop it. (*To* MARCUS) And you stop interrupting me. Mama saw you on the well-house roof. Coralee saw you. They saw you take money from an envelope—

LAVINIA. The same one. My, it wore well, didn't it?

BEN. To buy the passes that saved you from a hanging. You bought them from—

MARCUS (*tensely*). Get out of here. I—

BEN. From a Captain Virgil E. McMullen. Now I'd figure it this way: by the grace of Captain McMullen you got sixteen free years. So if they swing you tonight, tell yourself sixteen years is a long time, and lynching is as good a way to die as any other.

LAVINIA. Benjamin, don't talk like that, don't, son—

MARCUS (*in a different voice*). Walk yourself down to the sheriff's office now. I'll catch up with you. If you're fool enough to believe some invention of your mother's, understand that nobody else will believe it. The whole town knows your mother's been crazy for years, and Dr. Seckles will testify to it—

BEN. Let's put it this way: they think Mama is an eccentric, and that you made her that way. And they know Seckles is a drunken crook. They know Mama is a good woman, they respect her. They'll take her word because, as she told me a little while ago, people believe what they want to believe.

MARCUS (*carefully*). Lavinia, you're a religious woman, and religious people don't lie, of course. But I know you are subject to dreams. Now, I wonder why and when you had this one. Remember, will you, that you were ill right after the incident of which you speak so incorrectly, and remember please that we took you— (*sharply, to* BEN)—not to that drunken Seckles, but to

Dr. Hammanond in Mobile. He told me then that you were— (LAVINIA *draws back*) And he is still living to remember it, if you can't.

LAVINIA (*worried, rattled*). I was ill after that night. Who wouldn't have been? It had nothing to do with, with my nerves. It was taking part in sin, your sin, that upset me, and not knowing the right and wrong of what to do—

MARCUS. She didn't tell you about that illness, did she? You think they'd believe her against Hammanond's word that she was a very sick woman at the time she speaks about? (*Very sharply*) Now stop this damned nonsense and get out of here or—

BEN. Go change your dress, Mama. Get ready for a walk.

LAVINIA. But you told Jake—you said I could go on the sugar boat.

BEN. You can still catch the boat. We won't be walking long. And if you have to stay over a few hours more, I figure you can wear the same costume to a lynching as you can on a boat. We'll walk around to old Isham first, whose youngest son got killed that night. John Bagtry will be mighty happy to remember that his twin brother also died that night. And Mrs. Mercer's oldest son and the two Sylvan boys and— We won't have to go any further because they'll be glad to fetch their kinfolk and, on their way, all the people who got nothing else to do tonight, or all the people who owe you on cotton or cane or land. Be the biggest, happiest lynching in the history of Roseville County. All right. Go change your clothes—

MARCUS (*softly, carefully*). Lavinia. I—

LAVINIA. A lynching? *I don't believe in lynching.* If you lynch a white man, it can lead right into lynching a black man. No human being's got a right to take a life, in the sight of God.

MARCUS (*to* BEN). You're losing your witness. What a clown you turned out to be. Only you would think your mother would go through with this, only you would trust her—

BEN (*sharply*). She won't have to do much. I'm taking her Bible along. (*Opens the book*) On this page, that night, she wrote it all down. The names, the dates, the hours. Then she and Coralee swore to it. Everybody will like the picture of the two lost innocents and a Bible, and if they don't, sixteen-year-old ink will be much nicer proof than your Mobile doctor. (*Softly*) Anyway, you won't have time to get him here. Want to finish now?

LAVINIA (*who has been thinking*). I never told you I was going to have anything to do with a lynching. No, I didn't.

MARCUS. Of course you wouldn't. Of course you wouldn't. Not of your husband—

LAVINIA. Not of my husband, not of anybody.

BEN. Mama, go upstairs and let me finish this—

LAVINIA. I only said I was going to tell the truth to everybody. And that I'm going to do. (*To* MARCUS) If there's any nasty talk of lynching, I'm going to plead for your life hard as I can, yes I am.

BEN (*laughs*). Now, that's merciful of you. I'm going to do the same thing. I'm going to plead with them for Papa's life.

LAVINIA. That's the least a son can do for his father.

BEN (*to* MARCUS). Better than that. I'll come tomorrow morning and cut you down from the tree, and bury you with respect. How did the Greeks bury fathers who were murdered? Tell me, and I'll see to it. You'd like that, wouldn't you?

LAVINIA. Benjamin, don't talk that way—

MARCUS. You gave him the right to talk that way. You

did, Lavinia, and I don't understand anything that's been happening. Do you mean that you actually wrote a lie in your Bible, you who—

LAVINIA (*very angry*). Don't you talk like that. Nobody can say there's a lie in my Bible— You take that back. You take it back right away. I don't tell lies, and then I don't swear to them, and I don't swear on my Bible to a false thing and neither does Coralee. You just apologize to me and then you apologize to Coralee, that's what you do—

MARCUS (*quickly*). No, no. I don't mean you knew it was a lie. Of course not, Lavinia. But let me see it, and then tell me—

LAVINIA (*puts out her hand*). Let him see it. Of course.

BEN. Tell him to come down and look at it. I'll put it here, under the gun.

LAVINIA. Bibles are there for all people. For grown people. I'm not going to have any Bibles in my school. That surprise you all? It's the only book in the world but it's just for grown people, after you know it don't mean what it says. You take Abraham: he sends in his wife, Sarah, to Pharaoh, and he lets Pharaoh think Sarah is his sister. And then Pharaoh, he, he, he. Well, he does, with Sarah. And afterward Abraham gets mad at Pharaoh because of Sarah, even though he's played that trick on Pharaoh. Now if you didn't understand, a little child could get mighty mixed up—

MARCUS (*gently*). You want to go to your school, don't you, Lavinia?

LAVINIA. Or about Jesus. The poor are always with you. Why, I wouldn't have colored people believe a thing like that: that's what's the matter now. You have to be full grown before you know what Jesus meant. Otherwise you could make it seem like people ought to be poor.

BEN. All right. Go upstairs now and start packing. You're going to be on the sugar boat.

LAVINIA. Am I? Isn't that wonderful—

MARCUS. Lavinia. (*She turns toward him*) It would be wrong of me to say ours had been a good marriage. But a marriage it was. And you took vows in church, sacred vows. If you sent me to trouble, you would be breaking your sacred vows—

BEN. Oh, shut up, Papa.

LAVINIA. I don't want trouble, for anybody. I've only wanted to go away—

MARCUS (*slowly, as he comes down from balcony*). I was wrong in keeping you.

BEN (*laughs*). Yes. That's true.

MARCUS. It was wrong, I can see it now, to have denied you your great mission. I should have let you go, helped you build you a little schoolhouse in Altaloosa.

BEN. I built it about ten minutes ago.

LAVINIA. What? Oh, about the marriage vows, Marcus. I had a message last night, and it said it was right for me to go now and do my work. Once I get a message, you know.

MARCUS. Yes. Yes, you'll want a lot of things for your colored pupils. A schoolhouse isn't enough—you'll need books and—

LAVINIA. That's absolutely true. And I want to send for a teacher— I'm getting old and I'm ignorant— I want to make a higher learning.

MARCUS. Lavinia. I'll get them for you.

LAVINIA. Thank you. But of course, it isn't just getting them, I've got to keep up the schoolhouse every year—

MARCUS. Certainly. Did your, did your messages suggest any definite figure?

LAVINIA. Why, yes, they did.

MARCUS. How much was suggested?

LAVINIA. To tell you the truth, my message said a thousand dollars a year would make my colored children happy. But I think ten thousand a year would make them happier. Altaloosa's a mighty poor little village and everybody needs help there—

MARCUS. Ten thousand wouldn't be enough. I think—

LAVINIA (*firmly*). It would be enough. I'd make it enough. Then, of course, I been forgetting about Coralee coming with me. And Coralee supports a mighty lot of kinfolk right here in town. She got a crippled little cousin, her old Mama can't take washing any more—

MARCUS. Oh, that's too bad. What could I do for them?

LAVINIA. Maybe two hundred dollars a month would take Coralee's mind from worrying.

MARCUS. I should think so. They'll be the richest family in the South. But, of course, your friends should have the best.

LAVINIA. You're being mighty nice to me, Marcus. I wish it had always been that way.

MARCUS (*quickly*). It started out that way, remember? I suppose little things happened, as they do with so many people—

LAVINIA. No, I don't really think it started out well. No, I can't say I do.

MARCUS. Oh, come now. You're forgetting. All kind of pleasant things. Remember in the little house? The piano? I saved and bought it for you and—

LAVINIA. Bought it for me? No, I don't remember it that way. I always thought you bought it for yourself.

MARCUS. But perhaps you never understood why I did anything, perhaps you were a little unforgiving with me.

BEN (*to* MARCUS). Aren't you getting ashamed of yourself?

MARCUS. For what? For trying to recall to Lavinia's mind that we were married with sacred vows, that together we had children, that she swore in a church to love, to honor—

BEN. If I wasn't in a hurry, I'd be very amused.

LAVINIA (*thoughtfully*). I did swear. That's true, I—

BEN (*quickly*). Mama, please go upstairs. Please let me finish here. You won't get on the boat any other way—

MARCUS. Indeed you will, Lavinia. And there's no need to take the boat. I'll drive you up. We can stay overnight in Mobile, look at the churches, have a nice dinner, continue on in the morning—

LAVINIA. How did you guess? I always dreamed of returning that way. Driving in, nice and slow, seeing everybody on the road, saying hello to people I knew as a little girl, stopping at the river church—church . . . (*To herself*) Every Sunday here I always saved and put a dollar in the collection box. They're going to miss the dollar. You all know, in my vanity, what I'd like to have when I'm gone to Altaloosa?

MARCUS. What, Lavinia? I am most anxious to know.

LAVINIA. A mahogany pew, with my name on it, in brass.

MARCUS. Brass! It shall be writ in gold—

LAVINIA. I don't like gold. Brass. Now, what else did I think about last night?

MARCUS. We'll be in constant communication. And if you have more practical messages from God we can take care of them later. Now bring me the envelope and the Bible, and we'll start immediately—

(*She puts her hand on the Bible, as if to pick it up.*)

BEN (*quickly takes her hand*). Do I really have to explain it to you? Do I really have to tell you that unless you go through with it, he's got to take you to the hospital? You don't really think that he's going to leave you free in Altaloosa with what you know, to tell anybody— Why do you think he took you to Dr. Hammonond in the first place? Because he thought you might have seen him, and because it wouldn't hurt to have a doctor say that you were—

MARCUS (*very sharply*). That's a lie.

BEN. Maybe it is. But then you're only sorry you didn't think of it that way.

MARCUS. Lavinia—

LAVINIA (*softly*). I don't ever want to hear such things again, or one person do or say, to another.

MARCUS. Lavinia, you'll get what you want. You know I am not a stingy man or one who—

BEN. You'll get nothing. For the very simple reason that he isn't going to have a nickel to buy it with.

LAVINIA (*wearily*). Oh. That isn't what worries me— It's that Marcus may have been saying things he didn't mean. (*Softly*) Would you really have told me you would drive me to Mobile and then you would have taken me—

MARCUS. *Of course not.* If you listen to that scoundrel— You're my wife, aren't you? I also took vows. I also stood up and swore. Would I break a solemn vow—

LAVINIA (*appalled*). Oh, now, I don't believe what you're saying. One lie, two lies, that's for all of us: but to pile lie upon lie and sin upon sin, and in the sight of God—

BEN (*sharply*). Write it to him, Mama. Or you'll miss your boat.

LAVINIA. Oh, yes. Oh, I wouldn't want to do that. (*She picks up the Bible, exits*)

MARCUS. You're a very ugly man.

BEN. Are you ready now?

MARCUS. For what?

BEN. To write a piece of paper, saying you sell me the store for a dollar.

MARCUS (*pauses*). All right. Bring me that envelope. I'll sell you the store for a dollar. Now I have had enough and that will be all.

BEN. You'll write another little slip of paper telling Shannon in Mobile to turn over to me immediately all stocks and bonds, your safe-deposit box, all liens, all mortgages, *all* assets of Marcus Hubbard, Incorporated.

MARCUS. I will certainly do no such thing. I will leave you your proper share of things in my will, or perhaps increase it, if you behave—

BEN (*angrily*). You're making fun of me again. A will? That you could change tomorrow? You've made fun of me for enough years. It's dangerous now. One more joke. So stop it now. Stop it.

MARCUS. All right. But I would like to give you a little advice—you're so new at this kind of thing. If you get greedy and take everything there's bound to be a lot of suspicion. And you shouldn't want that. Take the store, take half of everything else, half of what's in the envelope. Give me the rest. I'll go on living as I always have, and tell everybody that because you're my oldest son, I wanted you to have—

BEN. You'll tell nobody anything, because you can't, and you'll stop bargaining. You're giving me everything you've got. It that clear? If I don't have to waste any more time with you, I'll give you enough to live on, here or wherever you want to go. But if I have to talk to you any longer, you won't get that. I mean what I'm saying, and you know I do. And it's the last time I'll say it. (*There is no answer. He smiles*) All right. Now start writing things down. When you finish, bring them to me. You're waiting for something?

MARCUS (*softly, as he goes up the porch steps*). To tell you the truth, I am trying to think of some way out.

BEN. If I told you that it's been a large temptation to see you—to do it the other way, you will believe me, I know; remember the past and don't waste your time, or put yourself in further danger, or tempt me longer. Ever since you started your peculiar way of treating me, many years ago, I have had many ugly dreams. But this is better than I ever dreamed— Go in and start writing now. I consider you a lucky man: you'll die in bed.

MARCUS. You will give me enough for a clean bed?

BEN. Yes, of course.

MARCUS. Well, I daresay one could make some small bargains with you still. But I don't like small bargains. You win or you lose—

BEN. And I don't like small talk. (MARCUS *turns, goes into his room.* BEN *waits for a second, then crosses to kitchen door, calls in*) Breakfast here, please. (*As* JAKE *comes from street side of porch*) Yes? Did you find Miss Birdie?

JAKE. Yes, sir. She was mighty happy and said to thank you.

BEN. All right. Did you get the tickets?

JAKE. Sure. Boat's loading now.

BEN (*sits down at* MARCUS's *table*). Take them up to Miss Lavinia, get the carriage ready. Get me coffee first.

JAKE (*as he goes off*). Lot of running around this morning. (*The sound of knocking is heard from the hall of the second floor.*)

OSCAR's VOICE (*with the knocking*). Papa! Papa! It's me. Hey, Papa. Please. Open your door. (*After a second* OSCAR *runs in from the living room, runs up the porch steps, calls into* MARCUS's *room*) Papa. I'm all ready. (*Pounds on* MARCUS's *door.*)

BEN (*looking up at* OSCAR). Traveling clothes? You look nice.

OSCAR. What you doing there? I told you to get on down to the station to make your apologies. I ain't changed my mind.

BEN. Oh, I never thought you meant that silly talk.

OSCAR. You didn't, huh? (*Looks down, sees the gun on the table*) What's my pistol doing out?

BEN. Waiting for you.

OSCAR. You just put it back where you found it— (*Then*

as if he remembered) Papa. Please. Let me in. *Please.* Papa, I can't find it. Papa— (REGINA *appears on the balcony. She is arranging her hair. She has on a riding skirt and shirt*) Regina, go in and tell him, will you? *Please, Regina.* Laurette's waiting for me to fetch her up—

REGINA (*looks down at* BEN *on the porch. Looks at* OSCAR). Oh, God. I slept late, hoping you'd both be gone. What's the matter with you, Oscar, what are you carrying on about?

(JAKE *appears with coffee tray, brings cup to* BEN, *puts tray down, and exits.*)

OSCAR (*desperately*). The thousand dollars on the table. But it's *not* on the table. You heard him promise last night—

REGINA. Go look again. Papa certainly wouldn't stop your going.

OSCAR. I tell you it's not there. I been over the whole house. I crawled around under the table—

BEN. Come on down and crawl some more.

REGINA (*softly*). You're in Papa's chair, Ben, eating breakfast at Papa's table, on Papa's porch.

OSCAR (*softly, very puzzled*). I'm telling you that Ben is a crazy Mama's crazy son.

BEN (*looks up at* REGINA). Come on down and have breakfast with me, darling. I'm lonely for you.

REGINA. Papa told you to be out of here.

BEN (*smiles*). Come on down, honey.

REGINA. No, I'm going out before the horse-whipping starts.

BEN. Going to look for a man who needs a little persuading?

REGINA. That's right.

OSCAR. Regina. Help me. It's *not* there. (*Screaming*) Papa! *Papa!*

REGINA (*disappears into her room*). Oh, stop that screaming.

OSCAR. Papa, I got to go. The money's not there. Papa, answer me—

MARCUS (*comes out from his room*). You looking for me, son? Speak up.

OSCAR (*softly*). It's getting late. The money. You forgot to leave it. (*When he gets no answer, his voice changes to a sudden shriek*) It just ain't there.

MARCUS. A voice injured at your age is possibly never recovered. The money isn't there, Oscar, because I didn't put it there. (*To* BEN) Would you like to give him a little—some—explanation, or will I, or—

BEN (*shakes his head*). I'm eating.

(OSCAR *stares down at* BEN, *stares at* MARCUS.)

MARCUS (*to* OSCAR). An unhappy event interfered. I am thus unable to finance your first happy months in the rose-covered brothel about which you have always dreamed. I assure you I am most sorry, for many reasons, none of them having anything to do with you.

OSCAR. What the hell does all that mean? That you're *not* giving me the money to leave here—

BEN (*nods*). It means that. And it means that Papa has found a new way of postponing for a few minutes an unpleasant writing job. Go back in, Papa.

(OSCAR *stares at* MARCUS, *stares down at* BEN. *Then he suddenly runs down the steps, off the porch, going toward the street.* BEN *smiles,* MARCUS *smiles.*)

MARCUS. Where would you prefer me to have breakfast? A tray in my room, this side of the porch, or the dining room or—

BEN. Any place you like. My house is your house.

MARCUS. I eat a large breakfast, as you know. Should that continue?

BEN. Certainly. But before you eat this large breakfast,

on this large morning, I want you to finish the papers
I'm waiting for.

MARCUS. Naturally, I've been inside thinking. Is there
any chance I could get out of here and on the train
without your interfering with me?

BEN. No, I don't think so. I've thought of that. And if
you did, I feel confident I could bring you back.

MARCUS (*pleasantly*). Yes. Thank you, Benjamin.

(*He re-enters his room as* REGINA *comes on the porch.
She hears his last sentence, stares at* MARCUS. *She comes
down the steps, goes to the table, pours herself coffee,
takes a biscuit, looks curiously at* BEN *and sits down.*)

REGINA (*after a minute*). What's the matter with Papa?

BEN. He's changed. You think it's age?

REGINA (*annoyed*). Why aren't you getting on the train?

BEN. I'm going to build a new house. I never liked this
house; it wasn't meant for people like us. Too delicate,
too fancy. Papa's idea of postwar swell.

REGINA (*stares at him*). I want to know why you aren't
leaving this morning?

BEN. I can't tell you why. (*Laughs*) My lips are sealed in
honor.

REGINA. Before there's any more trouble you better go
quiet down Mama. She's *packing*. She says she's going
to her destiny. You know what that always means. And
I'm sick of fights—

BEN. But that's where she is going.

REGINA (*bewildered*). Papa said she could go?

BEN. No . . . I said so.

REGINA. And who have you become?

BEN. A man who thinks you have handled yourself very
badly. It's a shame about you, Regina: beautiful, warm
outside, and smart. That should have made a brilliant
life. Instead, at twenty, you have to start picking up
the pieces, and start mighty fast now.

REGINA (*gets up, laughs*). I like the pieces, and I'm off to pick them up.

BEN. To try to persuade the Captain by the deed of darkness to a future legal bed? So early in the morning?

REGINA (*pleasantly, as she passes him*). I'm sure something very interesting has happened here. (*Sharply. Turns to him*) But whatever it is, don't talk that way to me.

BEN. Can I talk this way? You're not going to Chicago. And for a very simple reason. Papa has no money at all —now. No money for you to travel with, or to marry with, or even to go on here with.

REGINA (*stands staring at him. Then, quietly*). *What are you talking about? What's happened?* What's he done with his money—

BEN. Given it to me.

REGINA. Do you take that new drug I've been reading about? What would make you think he had given it to you?

BEN. You mean what were his reasons? Oh, I don't know. I'm the eldest son: isn't that the way with royalty? Maybe he could find me a Greek title— Go up and talk to him. I think he's been waiting.

(*Slowly she starts for the staircase. Then the speed of her movements increases, and by the time she is near the door of* MARCUS's *room she is running. She goes into the room.* BEN *picks up his newspaper. There is low talking from* MARCUS's *room.* BEN *looks up, smiles. After a moment,* REGINA *comes slowly out of* MARCUS's *room. She crosses porch, starts downstairs.*)

REGINA (*slowly*). He says there is nothing he will tell me. He says there's nothing he can tell me. He's crying. What does all that mean?

BEN. It means there is nothing he can tell you, and that he's crying. Don't you feel sorry for him?

REGINA. Why can't he tell me? I'll make him—

BEN. He can't tell you, and I won't tell you. Just take my word: you're, er, you're not well off, shall we say?

REGINA (*tensely*). What have you been doing to Papa or—

BEN. A great deal. Whatever you think of me, honey, you know I'm not given to this kind of joke. So take it this way: what is in your room, is yours. Nothing else. And save your time on the talk. No Chicago, honey. No nothing.

REGINA. You can't stop my going, and you're not going to stop it—

BEN. Certainly not. What people want to do, they do. You go ahead, your own way. Ride over to your soldier. Stand close and talk soft: he'll marry you. But do it quickly: he was angry last night and I think he wants to get away from you as fast as he can. Catch him quick. Marry him this morning. Then come back here to pack your nice Chicago clothes, and sell your pearls.

REGINA. Do you think I'm going to take your word for what's happening, or believe I can't talk Papa out of whatever you've done to him—

BEN. Believe me, you can't. Not because your charms have failed, but because there's nothing to talk him out of. I have it now, and your charms won't work on me. Money from the pearls will be plenty to take you to Brazil, and love and war will feed you. People in love should be poor.

REGINA. Ben, tell me, what storm happened here this morning. Tell me so that I can—can find out what I think or—

BEN. Or if you don't want to go to the war in Brazil, stay here and starve with them at Lionnet. I'd love to see you in the house with those three ninnies, dying on the vine. Either way, he'd leave you soon enough and you'd find out there's never anybody nastier than a weak man. Hurry— Or have a cup of coffee.

REGINA (*softly, tensely*). I'll find out what's happened, and—

BEN. No you won't.

REGINA. And the day I do, I'll pay you back with carnival trimmings.

BEN. Good girl. I won't blame you. But in the meantime, learn to win, and learn to lose. And don't stand here all day losing, because it's my house now, and I don't like loser's talk.

REGINA. You've ruined everything I wanted, you've—

BEN. Now, look here. Write *him* a poem, will you? I've ruined nothing. You're not marrying a man who didn't love you. You can't go away, or at least not on my money, and therefore a willful girl can't have a willful way. You're not in love; I don't think anybody in this family can love. You're not a fool; stop talking like one. The sooner you do, the sooner I'll help you.

REGINA. You heard me say I'd pay you back for this?

BEN. All right. Be a fool.

(MARCUS *opens his door, comes out on the porch, comes down the steps.* REGINA *turns to look at him.* MARCUS *comes to* BEN, *hands him two pieces of paper.* BEN *takes them, reads them.* MARCUS *puts his hand out to take the newspaper.* BEN *smiles, shakes his head,* MARCUS *quickly takes his hand away.*)

REGINA (*desperately, to* MARCUS). You still won't tell me? You're willing to see—

MARCUS (*softly*). Regina, honey, I can't, I—

(OSCAR, *dejected and rumpled, appears.*)

REGINA (*to* OSCAR). Do you know what's happened here? Did you have anything to do with it?

OSCAR. What?

(REGINA *turns away from him.* OSCAR *sits down, puts his head in his hands.*)

REGINA (*after a minute*). Well, what's the matter with you then? Ben Hubbard trouble?

OSCAR. She wouldn't wait. She wouldn't even wait for a few days until Papa could give me the money again.

BEN. Again?

OSCAR. That's how much she cared for me. Wouldn't even wait. Said she was going on to New Orleans, anyway. That she'd had enough— My God, I talked and begged. I even tried to carry her off the train.

MARCUS. Oh, how unfortunate.

BEN. I think it's charming. How did you do it, Oscar?

OSCAR (*to nobody*). You know what she did? She spat in my face and screamed in front of everybody that she was glad I wasn't coming, that she had never cared for me, and had only been doing the best she could. If I didn't have the money, what the hell did she need me for?

REGINA (*sympathetic*). Spat in your face! How could she do a thing like that?

MARCUS. How does one spit in your face?

BEN. Why, I imagine the way one spits in anybody's face.

REGINA. But it's special in a railroad station. How did she do it, Oscar? You can't just up and spit—

OSCAR (*in his sorrow, spits out on the porch*). Just like that. The way you wouldn't do with a dog. And all the while yelling I was to let her alone, with everybody staring and laughing—(MARCUS, REGINA, *and* BEN *laugh.* OSCAR *rises*) So. So, making fun of me, huh?

REGINA. Now really, Oskie, can you blame us? You on a railroad station trying to carry off a spitting—girl? You'd laugh yourself, if you didn't always have indigestion.

OSCAR (*carefully*). Your love didn't laugh. Your love, looking like a statue of Robert E. Lee. Dressed up and with his old medals all over him. (REGINA *rises.* MARCUS *rises*) So you didn't know he was going on the train, huh? I thought not. So you're no better off than me, are you, with all your laughing. Sneaked out on you, did he?

REGINA. So you arranged that, too, so that I couldn't—

BEN. All right. That's enough. I'm sick of love. Both of you follow the trash you've set your hearts on, or be still about it from now on. I don't want any more of this.

OSCAR. *You* don't want any more. What the—

BEN (*to* REGINA). You, early-maturing flower, can go any place you want and find what it's like to be without Papa's money. (*To* OSCAR) And you, lover, can follow your spitting heart and get yourself a wharf job loading bananas. Or you can stay, keep your job, settle down. I got a girl picked out for you—make yourself useful.

OSCAR (*completely bewildered, turns to* MARCUS). What's he talking about, Papa? Since when—

BEN. It's not necessary to expain it to you. (*To* REGINA) Now, honey, about you, if you're staying. You're a scandal in this town. Papa's the only person didn't know you've been sleeping with the warrior.

MARCUS. Benjamin—

BEN (*laughs*). Papa, and Horace Giddens in Mobile. How soon he'll find out about it, I don't know. Before he does, we're taking you up to see him. You'll get engaged to him by next week, or sooner, and you'll get married in the first church we bump into. Giddens isn't bad off, and if you're lucky it'll be years before he hears about you and the Brazilian general. I don't say it's a brilliant future, but I don't say it's bad. You could have done a lot better, but girls who have been despoiled in this part of the country—

MARCUS (*softly*). You don't have to marry a man, Regina, just because— We can go away, you and I—

OSCAR (*goes toward kitchen door*). I certainly don't know what's happened here. I certainly don't. I'm hungry. (*Calls in*) Where's breakfast, you all?

REGINA (*sharply*). Order breakfast for me, too, selfish.

BEN (*laughs*). That's my good girl. (*Picks up the news-*

paper) Nothing for anybody to be so unhappy about. You both going to do all right. I'm going to help you. I got ideas. You'll go to Chicago some day, get everything you want— Then—

REGINA (*softly*). When I'm too old to want it.

MARCUS. Regina, you didn't hear me. We could go away, you and I— I could start over again just as I started once before.

REGINA. When you did—whatever Ben made you do, did you realize what you were doing to me? Did you care?

MARCUS (*slowly*). I cared very much.

REGINA. And what good did that do?

OSCAR. Sure must have been an earthquake here since last night. You go to bed and Papa's one kind of man, and you wake up—

BEN (*reading newspaper*). They got that ad in again, Oscar. Dr. Melgoyd's "All Cure." Two bits, now, on special sale, for gentlemen only. Sluggish blood, cure for a wild manhood, nothing to be ashamed of, it says—

REGINA. He's still got the last bottle.

(JAKE *appears with a large tray. He has on his hat and coat.*)

OSCAR (*annoyed*). I never bought that rot. Don't believe in it. Somebody gave it to me.

REGINA (*laughing*). That was tactless, wasn't it?

BEN. Big goings on all over the country. Railroads going across, oil, coal. I been telling you, Papa, for ten years. Things are opening up.

OSCAR (*who has started to eat*). That don't mean they're opening up in the South.

BEN. But they are. That's what nobody down here sees or understands. Now you take you, Papa. You were smart in your day and figured out what fools you lived among. But ever since the war you been too busy getting cultured, or getting Southern. A few more years and you'd have been just like the rest of them.

MARCUS (*to* JAKE). Bring my breakfast, Jake.

JAKE. Belle will have to do it, Mr. Marcus. Last breakfast I can bring. I got the carriage waiting to take Miss Viney. (*He exits.*)

BEN. But now we'll do a little quiet investing, nothing big, because unlike Papa I don't believe in going outside your class about anything—

OSCAR (*his mouth full*). Think we've got a chance to be big rich, Ben?

BEN. I think so. All of us. I'm going to make some for you and Regina and—

(LAVINIA *appears in the living-room door. She is carrying a purse and the Bible. Coralee is standing behind her.*)

LAVINIA. Well, I'm off on my appointed path. I brought you each a little something. (*Goes to* REGINA) This is my pin. (REGINA *gets up*, LAVINIA *kisses her*) Smile, honey, you're such a pretty girl. (*Goes to* OSCAR) Here's my prayer book, Oscar. I had it since I was five years old. (OSCAR *kisses her. She goes to* BEN) I want you to have my Papa's watch, Benjamin.

BEN. Thank you, Mama. (*He kisses her, she pats his arm.*)

LAVINIA (*goes to* MARCUS). I didn't have anything left, Marcus, except my wedding ring.

MARCUS (*gets up, smiles*). That's kind, Lavinia.

LAVINIA. Well, I guess that's all.

BEN. Mama, could I have your Bible instead of Grandpa's watch? (MARCUS *laughs*) It would make me happier, and I think—

MARCUS. Or perhaps you'd give it to me. I can't tell you how happy it would make me, Lavinia.

LAVINIA. Oh, I wouldn't like to give it up. This Bible's been in my Papa's family for a long time. I always keep it next to me, you all know that. But when I die, I'll leave it to you all. Coralee, you hear that? If I die before you, you bring it right back here.

CORALEE. Come on, Miss Viney.

LAVINIA. I'll be hearing from you, Benjamin?

BEN. You will, Mama. Every month. On time.

LAVINIA. Thank you, son. Thank you in the name of my colored children.

CORALEE. Miss Viney, it's late.

LAVINIA. Well. (*Wistfully*) Don't be seeing me off, any of you. Coralee and I'll be just fine. I'll be thinking of you, and I'll be praying for you, all of you. Everybody needs somebody to pray for them, and I'm going to pray for you all. (*Turns to* MARCUS) I hope you feel better, Marcus. We got old, you and me, and— Well, I guess I just mean it's been a long time. Good-bye.

MARCUS. Good-bye, Lavinia.

(LAVINIA *and* CORALEE *exit.* MARCUS *goes to sit by* REGINA.)

MARCUS (*softly*). Pour me a cup of coffee, darling.

(REGINA *looks at him, gets up, crosses to table, pours coffee, brings it to him.* MARCUS *pulls forward the chair next to him.* REGINA *ignores the movement, crosses to chair near* BEN, *sits down.* BEN *smiles.*)

Curtain

THE AUTUMN GARDEN

FOR DASH

CHARACTERS

(In order of their speaking)

ROSE GRIGGS	FLORENCE ELDRIDGE
MRS. MARY ELLIS	ETHEL GRIFFIES
GENERAL BENJAMIN GRIGGS	COLIN KEITH-JOHNSTON
EDWARD CROSSMAN	KENT SMITH
FREDERICK ELLIS	JAMES LIPTON
CARRIE ELLIS	MARGARET BARKER
SOPHIE TUCKERMAN	JOAN LORRING
LEON	MAXWELL GLANVILLE
CONSTANCE TUCKERMAN	CAROL GOODNER
NICHOLAS DENERY	FREDRIC MARCH
NINA DENERY	JANE WYATT
HILDA	LOIS HOLMES

The play was presented by KERMIT BLOOMGARDEN *on the night of March 7, 1951, at the Coronet Theater, New York.*

The play was directed by HAROLD CLURMAN *and the settings were designed by* HOWARD BAY.

SCENE

The time is September 1949. The place is the Tucker-man house in a summer resort on the Gulf of Mexico, about one hundred miles from New Orleans.

ACT ONE

Monday night after dinner.

ACT TWO

Scene I. The following Sunday morning.
Scene II. That night.

ACT THREE

Early the next morning.

THE AUTUMN GARDEN

ACT ONE

SCENE: *The living room of the Tuckerman house in a town on the Gulf of Mexico, a hundred miles from New Orleans. A September evening, 1949, after dinner. To the right of the living room is a side porch, separated from the room by a glass door. Upstage left is a door leading into the entrance hall of the house: through this door we can see the hall and staircase. On the porch are chairs and tables. The furniture of the living room is handsome but a little shabby. It is all inherited from another day. (Right and left are the audience's right and left.)*

ON STAGE AT RISE OF CURTAIN: GENERAL GRIGGS, *a good-looking man of fifty-three, is seated at one side of the room reading a newspaper. His wife—*

ROSE GRIGGS, *ex-pretty, soft-looking and about forty-three, is seated at a table wearing an evening dress that is much too young for her. She is chatting across the room with—*

CARRIE ELLIS, *a distinguished-looking woman of about forty-five, who is sitting on a side chair, near her son, Frederick, and her mother-in-law—*

MRS. MARY ELLIS, *in her seventies, sprightly in manner and movement when she wishes to be, broken and senile when she wishes to be broken and senile. She has piled cushions on her chair so she can read a manuscript over the shoulder of her grandson—*

FREDERICK ELLIS, *a pleasant-looking young man of around*

twenty-five. Occasionally he makes a correction in the manuscript, looks up amused and annoyed at his grandmother. On the right porch—

EDWARD CROSSMAN, *about forty-six, tired and worn-looking as if he is not in good health, is sitting alone, his back to those in the room. There is a second of silence after the curtain goes up.*

ROSE (*Gets up from her chair. She finds silence uncomfortable and breaks into song: "We stroll the lane together"*). Now where is it? Everything's been so topsy-turvy all evening. If I can't have it immediately after dinner then I just about don't want it. At home you can bet it's right waiting for us when we leave the dining room, isn't it, Ben? Too bad it's Thursday. I'd almost rather go and see him than go to the party. (*To* MRS. ELLIS) I think it's what keeps you awake, Mrs. Ellis. I mean a little is good for your heart, the doctor told me always to have a little, but my goodness the amount you have every night.

MRS. ELLIS (*Pleasantly*). Would you mind telling me what you're talking about, Mrs. Griggs? You said if it wasn't for the party you'd go and see *him*, but you thought *I* drank too much on a Thursday?

ROSE (*Giggles*). Coffee. I mean you drink too much coffee.

MRS. ELLIS. Then it is coffee you wish to go and see?

ROSE. Now, now. You're teasing. You know very well I mean Robert Taylor in that thing.

MRS. ELLIS. Believe me, I did *not* know you meant Robert Taylor in that thing. You know, General Griggs, after seven summers I have come to the conclusion that your wife considers it vulgar to mention anything by name. There's nothing particularly genteel about pronouns, my dear. Coffee is coffee and not it, Robert Taylor is Robert Taylor and not him, I suppose, and a fool is a fool and not her.

ROSE (*Pleasantly*). I know. It's a naughty habit. Ben has been telling me for years. (*She is close to* BEN.) Do you like my dress, Ben?

GRIGGS. It's nice.

ROSE. Have I too much rouge? (*To others*) Know what she used to say? (*Quickly*) Ben's mother, I mean. She used to say it before she died. (*To* CROSSMAN) Come and join us. (*To others*) She used to say that Southern women painted a triangle of rouge on their faces as if they were going out to square the hypotenuse. Ben came from Boston, and his mother was sometimes a little sharp about Southerners.

MRS. ELLIS. Who could have blamed her?

ROSE (*Calling out to* CROSSMAN). Know what she told me last winter when I met her at the Club?

CROSSMAN (*Turns, smiles*). Ben's mother?

ROSE. No. Your sister, of course. She said we see more of you here on your summer vacation than she sees all year round in New Orleans. She says you're getting to be a regular old hermit. You have to watch that as you get older. You might get to like being alone—and that's dangerous.

MRS. ELLIS. I used to like being alone. When you get old, of course, then you don't any more. But somewhere in the middle years, it's fine to be alone. A room of one's own isn't nearly enough. A house, or, best, an island of one's own. Don't you agree, General Griggs? (*Very quickly*) Happiest year of my life was when my husband died. Every month was springtime and every day I seemed to be tipsy, as if my blood had turned a lovely *vin rosé*.

CARRIE. You're lyrical, Mother.

MRS. ELLIS (*To* FREDERICK). Do you know I almost divorced your grandfather, Frederick? During the racing season in 1901.

FREDERICK (*Looks up, laughs*). You don't feel it's a little late to talk about it?

(*The phone rings.*)

MRS. ELLIS. Thought you might like to write my biography —when you're finished with regional poetry.

(*As the phone rings again,* SOPHIE *comes into the hall to answer it.*)

SOPHIE (*Into the phone*). No, sir. We do not take transient guests. No, never, sir. Only permanent guests. You might telephone to Mrs. Prescott in the village. Thank you, sir.

ROSE (*Calls into hall*). Dear Sophie, where *is* coffee?

(SOPHIE *comes to the hall door. She is a plain-looking, shy girl of about seventeen. She has a hesitant, overpolite manner and speaks with a slight accent. She has on a party dress, covered by a kitchen apron.*)

SOPHIE. Aunt Constance is most sorry for the delay. We bring it immediately.

(*She disappears.*)

ROSE. Frederick, do you know I've been giving Sophie dancing lessons, or trying to? She's a charming child, your intended, but she's never going to be a dancer.

FREDERICK (*Pleasantly*). Terrible expression, Mrs. Griggs: my intended. Sounds like my indentured. Did you tell Mrs. Griggs, Mother? I thought we agreed that since there were no definite plans as yet—

CARRIE (*A little uncomfortable*). It's natural that I should speak about my son's marriage, isn't it?

ROSE. Why, goodness, yes indeed it is. I'd have felt hurt—

GRIGGS. Don't you know that women have no honor, Frederick, when it comes to keeping secrets about marriage or cancer?

FREDERICK (*Looks at his mother*). No, sir. I didn't know. I'm too young for my age.

MRS. ELLIS (*Who has been busy reading the manuscript*). I know I'm too young to be reading Payson's book. Full of the most confused sex. I can't tell who is what. And all out of doors. Is that new, so much sex out of doors? Is it, General?

GRIGGS. I don't think it's a question of "new." I think it's a question of climate.

MRS. ELLIS (*Points to book*). But aren't sexual relations the way they used to be: between *men and women?* It's so twitched about in Mr. Payson's book. You know, I think the whole country is changing.

GRIGGS (*As if he wished to help* FREDERICK). Has Payson written a good book, Fred?

FREDERICK. It's a wonderful book. I think he's going to be the most important young writer—

CARRIE. You said the first two books were wonderful, Frederick. And they didn't sell very well.

MRS. ELLIS. I don't know why they didn't— I always thought houses of prostitution had a big lending-library trade.

(FREDERICK *gets up, as if he were angry.*)

CARRIE. Will this new book sell, Frederick?

FREDERICK. I don't know, Mother.

CARRIE. I hope it sells. Any man is better off supporting himself.

FREDERICK (*Smiles*). Mother, sometimes I think no people are quite so moral about money as those who clip coupons for a living.

MRS. ELLIS. And why not? Particularly your mother who is given the coupons already clipped by me who has the hardship of clipping them. That leaves her more time to grow moral. And then, of course, you who don't even have that much trouble are left at leisure to be moral about those who have to go to the trouble of living on unearned money.

CARRIE (*To* GENERAL GRIGGS). You mustn't look uncomfortable, General. You should know by this time that my mother-in-law enjoys discussing family matters in public. And the more uncomfortable you look, the longer she will continue.

GRIGGS. Do I look uncomfortable? I was thinking how hard it is to be young.

ROSE (*To* BEN). Won't you come to the party? (*To others*) Ben has never gone to the Carter party. I am sure they're just as insulted every year—

GRIGGS. I don't think so.

ROSE. But what will you do with yourself? Why don't you go to see Robert Taylor? It's that war picture where he does so well and you'll want to see if it's accurate.

GRIGGS. No. I don't want to see if it's accurate.

ROSE. Do you like my dress?

GRIGGS. It's nice.

MRS. ELLIS. You are a patient man. (*To* ROSE) Do you know you've asked him that five times since rising from dinner?

ROSE. Well, I feel young and gay, and I'm going to a party. I wish the Denerys would come before we leave. I like meeting new people and they sound so interesting. I thought they were supposed to arrive in time for dinner. (*To* CARRIE) Is he absolutely fascinating?

CARRIE. I don't know, Mrs. Griggs. I haven't seen him in twenty years or more.

ROSE (*Calling to* CROSSMAN). Is he fascinating, Mr. Crossman?

CROSSMAN (*Pleasantly*). You're making it a little harder than usual. Is who fascinating?

ROSE. Nicholas Denery, of course.

CROSSMAN. Of course. I don't know.

ROSE. But, goodness. Didn't you all grow up together? I mean you and Constance and Mrs. Ellis and—

CROSSMAN. I don't remember any of us as fascinating. Do you, Carrie?

(CARRIE *shakes her head, laughs.* SOPHIE, *carrying a tray with brandy and brandy glasses, comes into the room. She is followed by* LEON, *a young, colored butler, carrying coffee and coffee cups.* FREDERICK *rises and takes the tray from* SOPHIE. *She looks at him and smiles.*)

ROSE. Let's see your dress, Sophie. (SOPHIE *smiles shyly, begins to take off her apron as* LEON *pours coffee*) Oh. It's right nice. But you should wear tighter things, dear. (*Comes in back of her, begins to fool with her hair*) I'd like to try your hair again. (SOPHIE *moves to help* LEON *but is cornered by* ROSE) Now you just sit down. How's this?

(CROSSMAN *comes into the room.*)

CROSSMAN. Makes her look like everybody else. That's desirable, isn't it?

ROSE. What does Frederick think? We're out to please Frederick, after all, aren't we, dear?

FREDERICK (*Turns to look*). I like Sophie her own way.

SOPHIE (*Smiles*). I have no "way."

ROSE. But most European girls have such chic— (GENERAL GRIGGS *gets up, as if he were annoyed*) They have, Ben. You said it yourself when you came back from the Pacific, and I was jealous.

MRS. ELLIS. Pacific? I thought you fought in Europe.

GRIGGS. I did. Robert Taylor fought in the Pacific.

(*He rises, wanders off to the porch.*)

ROSE (*Holding* SOPHIE'S *hair another way*). Or is *this* better?

FREDERICK (*Smiles to* SOPHIE). Don't you mind being pulled about?

SOPHIE. No. Well. (*Gently pulls away*) I am grateful for the trouble that Mrs. Griggs— Thank you.

CROSSMAN. Sophie doesn't mind anything. All she has said all summer is thank you.

(*Through his speech the phone rings.* FREDERICK *starts for the phone. At the same time,* CONSTANCE TUCKERMAN *comes through the hall. She is a handsome woman of forty-three or forty-four. She is carrying two flower vases. She puts down one of the vases in order to answer the phone.*)

CONSTANCE. Yes. Just a minute. Frederick. Mr. Payson would like to speak to you. (*She picks up the other vase, comes into the door, as if she were in a hurry.* FREDERICK *immediately moves to the phone*) Sorry coffee was late. You all want more just ring. And do, Carrie, explain to the Carters why I can't come to their party this year—

ROSE. Any news from them, Constance?

CONSTANCE (*Carefully*). News from whom?

ROSE (*Laughs*). Oh, come now. Stop pretending. When do the Denerys arrive?

CONSTANCE. Don't wait up for them, Rose. You'll see them at breakfast.

(*She turns, goes out and goes up the stairs.*)

ROSE. My, Constance is nervous. Well, I suppose I should be if I were seeing an old beau for the first time in— But I don't believe in old beaux. Beaux should be brand-new, or just friends, don't you think? (CROSSMAN *starts out to porch, carrying his coffee and the brandy bottle.* ROSE *points outside, meaning* GENERAL GRIGGS *and* CROSSMAN) Now are you boys just going to sit here and share the bottle—

CROSSMAN. General Griggs is only being kind when he says he shares the bottle with me.

(*He goes off.* FREDERICK *comes in, starts to speak, changes his mind.*)

CARRIE (*Carefully*). Was that Mr. Payson on the phone? Is he coming to the party?

FREDERICK. How many generations do you have to summer in this joint before you're invited to the Carters'?

MRS. ELLIS. Oh, that's not true. They're very liberal lately. (*Points to* ROSE) After all, the last few years they've always included Mrs. Griggs. (*To* ROSE) And nobody can be more *nouveau riche* than your family, can they? I mean your brother during the war and all that.

ROSE (*Giggles*). My. Everybody is so jealous of Henry.

MRS. ELLIS. Well, of course we are. I wish we were *nouveau riche* again.

FREDERICK (*Sharply*). All right, Grandma.

ROSE. Oh, I don't mind. I enjoy your grandmother.

FREDERICK (*To his mother*). I'm sorry I'm not going to be able to take you to the party. I hope you'll excuse me, Sophie. Mother. Grandma.

CARRIE (*Carefully*). What has happened, Frederick?

FREDERICK. Payson had a wire from his publishers. They want the manuscript in the mail tomorrow morning. (*He goes to take the manuscript from the table*) So I'll have to proofread it with him tonight. It's a nasty job alone, almost impossible—

CARRIE (*Slowly*). I don't understand.

ROSE (*Hurriedly*). I must fix my face. As you get older your face needs arranging more often.

(*She goes off.*)

CARRIE. We're ready to leave, Frederick.

FREDERICK. Mother, I'm not going to the party, I wasn't making a joke—

CARRIE. Oh. I hoped you were. You have no obligation to us, or Sophie? An appointment broken, because Payson summons you?

FREDERICK. I am sorry, Sophie. Maybe I can pick you up later. (*Haltingly*) I am sorry.

SOPHIE. I do not mind, really. It is better this way.

CARRIE. Don't you? Why not? (*No answer*) Why don't you mind, Sophie?

SOPHIE (*Smiles*). I do not like parties. I did not want to go. Now Frederick has some important business and must leave quickly—

CARRIE. Perhaps you are going to make *too* good a wife.

FREDERICK. Suppose you let me decide that, Mother. Good night. Have a good time. See you in the morning—

CARRIE. I want to talk to you, Frederick.

FREDERICK (*Stops, smiles*). When you use that tone of voice you need two hours. Let's make it in the morning, Mother.

(SOPHIE *has turned away, gone upstage, as if she wanted to be as far away as possible.*)

CARRIE. I ask you to break your appointment with Payson. As a favor to me.

FREDERICK. There's nothing important about my being at the party and it is important to him. He wants to consult me—

CARRIE (*Sharply*). He is always consulting you. You talk like a public accountant or a landscape gardener. Why should he want to consult *you* about his work?

FREDERICK (*Hurt*). Maybe because I try to write and maybe because he thinks I know a little. I realize that's hard for you to believe—

CARRIE. I didn't mean that.

FREDERICK. I think you did. Good night.

CARRIE. You have no sense of obligation to me. (*Looks around for* SOPHIE *who is trying at this minute to leave the room*) And none to Sophie. Who evidently won't speak for herself. Do stay here, Sophie, it's your business as well as mine— (SOPHIE *stands still*) I am getting tired of Mr. Payson, Frederick, and with good reason. When he came to stay with us in town last winter, I fully understood that he was a brilliant and gifted man and I was glad for you to have such a friend. But when he followed you down here this summer—

FREDERICK (*Slowly, angrily*). He did not follow me down

here and I wouldn't like you to put it that way again. He came here for the summer and is that your business, Mother?

CARRIE. There is just too much of Mr. Payson. Every day or every evening— How often do you take Sophie with you? (*Sharply*) How often have you seen Mr. Payson this summer, Sophie? (*There is no answer*) Please answer me.

FREDERICK. And please stop using that tone to Sophie. Say what you have to say to me.

CARRIE (*Turning to* MRS. ELLIS, *who has been watching them*). Mother—

MRS. ELLIS. I've been dozing. How many hours have passed?

CARRIE (*Slowly*). You are always dozing when there is something unpleasant to face out with Frederick.

MRS. ELLIS. What better time? You all want to know something's been worrying me all day? Nobody in the South has tapeworm any more. In my day that was all you ever heard. Tapeworm, tapeworm, tapeworm. (*Gets up*) Now kiss your mother good night, boy. Otherwise she'll be most unhappy. And say you forgive her.

FREDERICK. I have nothing to forgive her for, Grandma.

MRS. ELLIS. Of course not. But even when your mother starts out being right she talks and talks until she gets around to being wrong.

(*She exits. There is silence.*)

CARRIE (*Softly*). I'm sorry if I spoke unfairly, or at the wrong time—

FREDERICK (*Comes to her, smiling*). You didn't, you didn't. Now don't feel bad. Nothing's happened. And don't let Grandma tease you.

CARRIE. I know. (*She turns to go*) You go ahead, dear. Try to join us later.

(*He kisses her. She smiles, pleased, and goes out.* FREDERICK *turns to* SOPHIE.)

FREDERICK. Sophie, Mother didn't mean to be sharp with you. But when she is, you mustn't let her. She's a little bossy from time to time, but no harm in it. You look so worried.

SOPHIE (*Very puzzled*). Your mother is not angry now?

FREDERICK. Of course not. You mustn't take these things too seriously. Mother is like that.

SOPHIE (*Smiles*). You know it is most difficult in another language. Everything in English sounds so important. I get a headache from the strain of listening.

FREDERICK (*Laughs*). Don't. It's not worth it. (*Looks at her, then slowly*) Mother is right: I have been rude and neglectful. But I haven't meant to be, Sophie.

SOPHIE. No, no. You have not been.

FREDERICK. And in two weeks Mother and I will be going off to Europe. I hope you don't mind about the European trip. It was all arranged long before you and I— (*Stares at her, smiles*) got engaged. (SOPHIE *smiles at him as if she were embarrassed, then she coughs and clears her throat*) We're an awkward pair. I like you, Sophie.

SOPHIE (*Warmly*). I like you, Frederick.

FREDERICK. Sophie, I think we'll have to sit down soon and talk about ourselves. I don't think we even know how we got engaged. We haven't said much of anything—

SOPHIE. Sometimes it is better not to say things. There is time and things will come as they come.

FREDERICK. The day we got engaged, we tried to speak as honestly as we both knew how but we didn't say very much—

SOPHIE. And I think we should not try so hard to talk. Sometimes it is wise to let things grows more roots before one blows them away with many words— (*Shyly touches his hand*) It will come better if we give it time.

FREDERICK. We will give it time. And you'll make no decisions and set no dates until you are sure about what you think and feel.

SOPHIE. Oh, I have made the decision for myself. And I am pleased.

FREDERICK (*Pleased*). And you are quite sure of your decision?

SOPHIE. You know, sometimes I have thought that with rich people— (*Very quickly*) with educated people, I mean, decisions are made only in order to speak about changing them. It happens often with Aunt Constance and with your mother, also, I think. And the others.

FREDERICK. Yes. (*Takes her hand*) We'll get along fine. I want you to know that I feel very lucky—

SOPHIE. Lucky? You will have to be patient with me. I am not a good success here.

FREDERICK. Now, you stop that. I don't want you a good success. And you're to stop thinking it. You're to stop a lot of things: letting Mother boss you about, letting Mrs. Griggs tell you what to wear, or pull your hair—

SOPHIE. Oh, I do not mind. Because I look so bad makes Mrs. Griggs think she looks so good.

FREDERICK (*Smiles*). Good night, my dear.

SOPHIE (*Smiles*). Good night.

(*He exits.* SOPHIE *begins to pick up the coffee cups, brandy glasses, etc. After a minute* ROSE GRIGGS *comes down the steps carrying a light summer wrap. She comes in the room.*)

ROSE. Where are the Ellises?

SOPHIE. They went to the party, Mrs. Griggs.

ROSE. No! Without me? I *must* say that's very rude. They can't have done that, Sophie— (*She hurries to the hall, looks out. Then she comes back in, goes to the porch*) Ben. (*He looks up*) The Ellises left without me, Ben!

GRIGGS. Yes?

ROSE. You'll have to walk me over. I just won't go in, alone.

GRIGGS. It's across the street, Rose. Not a very dangerous journey.

ROSE (*Gently*). Ben. (*He rises, comes in*) You know, I think it's shocking. In front of other people. God knows what they know or guess this summer. (*Suddenly notices* SOPHIE *who is collecting cups*) Sophie. Don't wait here listening.

(SOPHIE *turns, surprised, but before she can speak* . . .)

GRIGGS (*Sharply*). Rose!

ROSE (*Who is always charming at this point. To* SOPHIE) I am sorry, my dear. Please most earnestly I ask your pardon—

SOPHIE. Yes, ma'am.

ROSE (*Tries to catch her at door*). I'm just a nervous old silly these days. Now say you forgive me—

(SOPHIE *disappears.*)

GRIGGS (*Smiles, as if he has seen this before*). All right, Rose. You're charming.

ROSE. You won't even walk over with me, just to the door?

GRIGGS. Certainly I will.

ROSE (*Smiles*). No, you don't have to. I just wanted to see if you would. Will you call for me, at twelve, say?

GRIGGS. No.

ROSE. Then will you meet me at twelve, at the tavern?

GRIGGS. No. What mischief is this, Rose?

ROSE. Is it mischief to want to talk with you?

GRIGGS. Again? Tonight? And every night and every day? The same things over and over? We're worn out, Rose, both of us. (*Kindly*) There is no more to say.

ROSE (*Softly*). No more to say. Do people get divorces, after twenty-five years, by just saying they want them and that's all and walking off?

GRIGGS. I suppose some men do. But I haven't walked off and I have said all I know how to say.

ROSE. But you haven't really explained anything to me.

You tell me that you want a divorce— And I ask why, why, why. We've been happy together.

GRIGGS (*Looks at her*). You don't believe that.

ROSE. When people get our age, well, the worst is over— and what else can one do? (*Exasperated*) I never really heard of such a thing. I'm just not taking you seriously and I do wish you'd stop talking about it. (*After a pause*) You've never given me a good reason. I ask you ten times a day if there's another woman. I could understand that. Of course you say no, naturally—

GRIGGS. There is no other woman.

ROSE (*Giggles*). You know what I think? I think it's that little blonde at the drugstore, and the minute my back is turned—

GRIGGS. Please, Rose. Please stop that.

ROSE. Never at any time, during this divorce talk, have you mentioned them. You'd think we didn't have sons, and the awful effect on them. Did you write them today?

GRIGGS. I did not write them because you begged me not to.

ROSE. Oh, yes, I forgot. It will break their hearts.

GRIGGS. Their hearts won't be broken. They won't even bother to finish the letter.

ROSE (*Softly, shocked*). You can't love them, to speak that way.

GRIGGS. I don't love them. I did love them but I don't now. They're hard men to love.

ROSE. Oh, I don't believe a word you say. You've always enjoyed shocking me. You've been a wonderful father and you're just as devoted to them as they are to you.

GRIGGS. They aren't the least devoted to me—when they think about me it is to find my name useful and when it isn't useful they disapprove of me.

ROSE (*Moving to door*). Look, Ben. I just can't stay and talk all night. I'm late now. There's no use our saying the same things over and over again— (*He laughs*) If you won't come to the party what are you going to do?

GRIGGS. I am going down by the water, sit on a bench and study from a Chinese grammar.

ROSE. You'll be lonely.

GRIGGS. Yes, but not for parties.

ROSE. It's very hard to take seriously a man who spends the evening with a Chinese grammar. I'll never forget that winter with the Hebrew phonograph records. (*Pats his arm*) Now, good night, darling. And don't worry about me: I am going to try to have a good time. We'll talk about all this another day.

(*She starts out.*)

GRIGGS (*Sharply*). No. No, we're not going to do that. You're turning it into a pleasure, Rose, something to chatter about on a dull winter night in the years to come. I've told you it isn't going to be that way. (*She is in the hall*) It isn't going to be that way. When you go back to town next week I'm not going with you.

(*He turns to see that she has gone.*)

ROSE'S VOICE (*From the hall*). Good night, darling.

GRIGGS (*He stands still for a minute. Then he turns, sees his book on the porch table. Goes out to the porch, realizes the doors have been open. To* CROSSMAN). I guess we thought the doors were closed. I am sorry.

CROSSMAN. Don't be.

GRIGGS. There are so many things I want to do that I don't know which to do first. Have you ever thought about starting a new life?

CROSSMAN (*Smiles*). I've often thought that if I started all over again, I'd go right back to where I started and start from there. Otherwise, it wouldn't prove anything.

GRIGGS (*Laughs*). Where'd you start from?

CROSSMAN (*Laughs*). Nowhere. That's the trouble.

GRIGGS. I started with mathematics. Seems strange now, but that's why I went to West Point—wonderful mathe-

matics department. So I got myself two wars instead.
I want to go somewhere now and study for a few years,
or— (*Smiles*) Anyway, sit down by myself and think.

CROSSMAN. Europe?

GRIGGS. I don't think so. Europe seemed like a tourist joint
the last time. With all the aimless, dead bitterness of—
tourist joints. I don't want sentimental journeys to old
battlefields. I'll start tame enough: I've written my sister
that I'd like to stay with her for a month or two.

CROSSMAN. Isn't that a sentimental journey?

GRIGGS. I suppose it is. I really want to see her because she
looks like my mother. The last six months I've thought
a lot about my mother. If I could just go back to her for
a day. Crazy at my age—

CROSSMAN. I know. We all do at times. Age has nothing to
do with it. It's when we're in trouble.

GRIGGS. I don't know why I want to say this but, well, don't
think too badly of my wife.

CROSSMAN. Why should I think badly of anybody?

GRIGGS (*As he turns to go*). All professional soldiers marry
Rose. It's in the Army Manual. She is as she always was.
It is my fault, not hers.

CROSSMAN. Haven't you lived in the South long enough to
know that nothing is ever anybody's fault?

(GENERAL GRIGGS *laughs, starts out as* CONSTANCE *comes
downstairs.* CONSTANCE *has on a different dress and is
buttoning the belt as she comes into the room.* GENERAL
GRIGGS *crosses the room and exits by the stage left windows.* CONSTANCE *looks around, finds the room is neat,
goes out to the porch, talking as she goes.*)

CONSTANCE. I *think* everything is ready. I've put Nick in
Sophie's room— Sophie says she doesn't mind sleeping
down here. Anyway it happens every summer. And I've
given Mrs. Denery the yellow room. They wanted *two*
rooms, Nick said on the phone.

CROSSMAN. Fashionable people don't sleep together, don't you know that? It's not sanitary.

CONSTANCE (*Sits down*). I'm tired, Ned.

CROSSMAN. Have a brandy.

CONSTANCE. No. It would make me nervous.

CROSSMAN. Remarkable the things that make people nervous: coffee, brandy, relatives, running water, too much sun, too little sun. Never anything in themselves, eh, Constance?

CONSTANCE. They have a maid and a chauffeur. I'll have to put them in the boathouse. It's all so much work at the end of the season. Sophie's been cleaning all day, and I've been cooking— Why did I say they could come?

CROSSMAN (*Smiles*). I wonder why.

CONSTANCE. Well, of course, I want to see Nick again. But I am nervous about meeting her. (*Points to his glass*) Do you think perhaps a sip?

CROSSMAN. Only drunkards borrow other people's drinks. Have one of your own.

(*Through her next speech he pours her a drink and hands it to her. When she finishes it, he will take back the glass and pour himself a drink.*)

CONSTANCE. I got out Mama's good, old linen sheets. I don't care how rich the Denerys are, or where they've been, they never could have had finer linen. And I've stuffed some crabs and there's white wine— Remember how Nick loved stuffed crabs?

CROSSMAN (*Smiles*). No. I don't remember.

CONSTANCE. It was twenty-three years ago, the eighteenth of next month. I mean the night he decided to go to Paris to study. Not so many young men from New Orleans went to Paris in those days.

CROSSMAN. Just as many young men met rich young ladies on boats.

CONSTANCE (*Sharply*). *He fell in love.* People can't be

blamed for changing their hearts—it just happens. They've had a fine marriage, and *that's* given me happiness all these years.

CROSSMAN. How do you know they've had a "fine" marriage?

CONSTANCE (*Smiles*). I know.

CROSSMAN. The rest of us don't know anything about any marriage—but you know all about one you've never seen. You're very wise, Constance. It must come from not thinking.

CONSTANCE. Is this dress all right?

CROSSMAN. You've changed your dress three times since dinner.

CONSTANCE. My dresses are all sort of— She'll think they're cheap. (*Smiles*) Well, and so they are. (*There is silence. Then*) Have we changed much, Ned?

CROSSMAN. Yes, my dear. You've changed, I've changed. But you're still handsome, if that's what you mean.

CONSTANCE. Ned, you don't look so well this summer. (*He is pouring himself another brandy. She points to bottle*) I wanted to tell you— Don't you think—

CROSSMAN (*Very pleasantly*). Don't I think you should mind your business? Yes, I do.

(SOPHIE *comes into living room carrying sheets, a quilt, a pillow, puts them down and moves to porch.*)

CONSTANCE. Isn't what happens to you my business?

SOPHIE. You look pretty, Aunt Constance.

CONSTANCE (*To* CROSSMAN). Sophie made this dress for me. Last winter. What could the girls at school have thought? Sophie sitting sewing for an old country aunt when she could have been out dancing—

SOPHIE. I sew better than I dance.

CONSTANCE (*To* CROSSMAN). Sophie's mother taught her to sew. You know that Ann-Marie is a modiste?

SOPHIE (*Laughs*). Oh, she is not. She is what you call here a home-seamstress, or sometimes a factory worker.

CONSTANCE. But she *designs*. She wrote me and you told me—

SOPHIE (*Laughs*). Oh no. You did not understand. She does—

(*Outside the house there is the noise of a car coming to a stop. CONSTANCE turns towards the room, then steps back, moves around the table and suddenly runs into the house. CROSSMAN turns to stare at her.*)

SOPHIE (*Timidly, pointing out towards living room*). Should I— Should I stay, Mr. Ned?

CROSSMAN. I don't know the etiquette of such meetings.

SOPHIE. Why is Aunt Constance so nervous about the visit of this lady and gentleman?

CROSSMAN. Because she was once in love with Nicholas Denery, this gentleman.

SOPHIE. Oh. Such a long, long time to stay nervous. (*Sententious*) Great love in tender natures. And things of such kind. (*As he turns to stare at her*) It always happens that way with ladies. For them it is once and not again: it is their good breeding that makes it so.

CROSSMAN. What is the matter with you?

SOPHIE (*Laughs*). I try very hard to sound nice. I try too hard, perhaps?

(*She begins to move out into the room; then, as she hears voices, she runs out of the room, exits off porch.*)

NICK'S VOICE (*Offstage*). Constance!

(*NICK appears in the hall and comes into the room. He is about forty-five, handsome, a little soft-looking and in a few years will be too heavy. He is followed by NINA DENERY, who is a woman of about forty, good-looking, chic, tired and delicate. She stops and stands in the doorway.*)

NICK (*Calling*). Constance!

(*NICK and NINA are followed by a maid, HILDA, who stands waiting in the hall. She is carrying a jewelry case, an overnight bag, two coats.* CROSSMAN *starts to come forward, changes his mind, draws back.*)

HILDA (*In German*). Shall I take the bags upstairs, madame?

NINA (*In German*). We don't where upstairs is.

NICK. Oh, I know where upstairs is. I know every foot of this house. (*Examining the room*) It was *the* great summer mansion and as kids we were here more than we were at home— (*Softly*) The great summer mansion! Did the house change, or me? (*Sees* NINA *in doorway*) Come on in.

NINA. Perhaps it would be pleasanter for you to see old friends without me. In any case, I am very tired—

NICK. Oh, now don't get tired. We've just come. What have you got to be tired about? Do you realize how often these days you're tired?

NINA. I realize it very well. And I know it bores you.

NICK. It *worries* me. (*By this time,* NICK, *wandering around the room, has reached the porch.* CROSSMAN *turns and, realizing that he has been seen, now comes forward*) Could you tell me where we could find Miss Tuckerman?

CROSSMAN. Hello, Nick. Good to see you.

NICK (*After a second*). My God, Willy. How many years, how many years? (*He puts his arm around* CROSSMAN, *embraces him*) Nina, this may be my oldest and best friend in the world. Nina, tell Willy how often I've talked about him and what I said.

CROSSMAN (*Who is shaking hands with* NINA, *amused*). Then I hope he told you that my name is Edward, not Willy.

NINA (*Amused*). I hope so—but I am not sure.

NICK. Your mother always called you Willy. Don't you remember?

CROSSMAN (*Goes out into the hall*). No. I thought it was my brother's name. (*Calls out, loudly*) Constance, Nick is here.

NICK (*Coming to* CROSSMAN). Tell me before I see her. What has happened here? I don't know anything.

CROSSMAN. There's very little to know. Old man Tuckerman surprised everybody by dying broke. Constance sold the New Orleans house and managed to hang on to this by turning it into what is called a summer guest house. That's about all, Nick.

NICK. Where is Mrs. Tuckerman? I was crazy about her, Nina: she had style.

CROSSMAN. I don't know where she is, although I've asked myself often enough. She died shortly after Mr. Tuckerman—just to show him anybody could do it.

NICK (*Laughs, pats* CROSSMAN). Good to see you, boy. You know, if anybody had asked me, I would have said this room was as large as an eighteenth-century ballroom and as elegant. I think it shrank. All the fine things were sold?

CROSSMAN. The size hasn't changed. And nothing was sold.

NICK. Could I have been so wrong all these years? Seems so shabby now and—

NINA (*Quickly*). I think it is a pleasant room.

NICK. Does Sam live here?

CROSSMAN. Sam died during the war. He went to Europe, oh, in the thirties, married there and never came back. You'll meet his daughter. Constance imported her five years ago.

NICK. Well, Sam was always the devoted brother until it came to being devoted. And Constance sacrificed her life for him.

CROSSMAN (*To* NINA). Nick is still a Southerner. With us every well-born lady sacrifices her life for something: a man, a house, sometimes a gardenia bush. Is it the same where you come from?

NINA (*Smiles*). New York is too cold for gardenias.

(*Through* CROSSMAN's *speech,* CONSTANCE *appears in the*

*hall. As she moves into the room, she trips, recovers her-
self, smiles nervously and waits for* NICK *to come to her.
He takes her face in his hands and kisses her. Then he
stands back to look at her.*)

NICK. This is a good hour of my life, Constance.

CONSTANCE (*Softly*). And of mine.

NICK (*Holds her face*). You've changed and you've
changed well. Do you still have the portrait, Constance?

CONSTANCE (*Smiles*). *Still* have the portrait! It's the only
important thing I have got— (*Then she remembers*
NINA, *becomes confused, moves away from him and
comes to* NINA) Forgive me, Mrs. Denery.

NINA (*Puts out her hand, warmly*). Hello.

CONSTANCE (*Flossy*). I should have been here to make you
as welcome as you truly are. I was reading when you
arrived, reading a book, and I didn't hear the car.

(*She sees* CROSSMAN *is staring at her and she looks nervously away from him.*)

NICK. I had expected you standing in the driveway with
the sun in your face, in the kind of lovely pink thing
you used to wear—

NINA. The sun is not usually out at night—even for you.

NICK (*To* CONSTANCE). Instead, you are reading. As if you
were waiting for the groceries to come.

CONSTANCE (*Quickly*). I wasn't reading. It was a silly lie.
I was just pretending— (*Embarrassed*) Well, I'm even
forgetting my manners. You must be hungry, Mrs.
Denery, and I've got—

NICK (*Laughs, takes her hands, pulls her to the couch*). No,
no. Stop your manners, girl. There's a great deal I want
to know. (*They sit down*) Now. Is the portrait as good
as I remember it? I want Nina to see it. Nina knows a
great deal about painting. Sometimes I think she knows
more than I.

CONSTANCE (*Smiles to* NINA, *nods. Then to* NICK). You

know, Nick, I subscribe to the New York Sunday *Times*. Because of the art section. I wanted to follow your career.

NICK (*Carefully*). You haven't often found me in the *Times*. I've only exhibited in Europe.

CONSTANCE (*Relieved*). Oh. That explains it.

(*There is a slight, awkward pause.*)

I like painting. I like Renoir best. The summer ladies in the gardens, so very, very pretty.

NICK (*Bored*). Yes, very pretty. This is the same wonderful place— My God, we had happy summers here, all of us. We loved each other so very much. Remember, Ned?

CROSSMAN. I don't remember that much love.

NINA (*Laughs*). I like you, Mr. Crossman.

NICK. Of course you like him. These are my oldest friends. I think as one grows older it is more and more necessary to reach out your hand for the sturdy old vines you knew when you were young and let them lead you back to the roots of things that matter. (NINA *coughs.* CROSSMAN *moves away, smiling. Even* CONSTANCE *is a little overwhelmed*) Isn't that true, Ned? Now what have you been up to all these years?

CROSSMAN. I still work in the bank and come here for my vacation. That's about all.

NICK. I bumped into Louis Prescott in Paris a couple of years ago and he told me you and Constance had never married—

(*Pats* CONSTANCE's *hand;* CONSTANCE *looks embarrassed.*) Couldn't understand it. No wonder you drink too much, Ned.

CROSSMAN. Louis Prescott go all the way to Paris to tell you that?

NICK (*Anxious, gets up*). Oh, look old boy. I didn't mean anything— I drink too much myself. I only want to know about you and have you know about me. I hope you didn't mind, Ned.

CROSSMAN. Not a bit. I want to know about you, too. Ever had syphilis, Nick? Kind of thing one has to know right off, if you understand me.

CONSTANCE (*Gets up, very disturbed.*) Ned, how can you speak that way?

NICK (*Smiles*). You've grown edgy. I didn't remember you that way.

CROSSMAN (*Pleasantly*). Oh, I don't think I've changed. See you in the morning.

NICK. Hope you'll take me around, show me all the old places—

CROSSMAN. Of course I will. Good night, Mrs. Denery. (*He exits up staircase.*)

NICK (*To* CONSTANCE, *meaning* CROSSMAN). I'm sorry if I said anything—

CONSTANCE. You know, for years I've been meeting you and Mrs. Denery—in my mind, I mean—and I've played all kinds of roles. Sometimes I was the dignified old friend, and sometimes I was a very, very old lady welcoming you to a gracious table. It was so important to me—our first meeting— (*Sadly*) And now when it happens—

NICK (*Heartily*). Nonsense. My home-coming is just as it should be. It's as if I had gone away yesterday. We took up right where we left off: even Ned and I. Let us be as we were, my dear, with no years between us, and no pretending.

CONSTANCE (*Delighted with him, warmly*). Thank you. (*Goes to* NINA) All these years I wanted to write you. I did write but I never sent the letters. It seemed so intrusive of me. I could see you getting the letter and just not knowing who I was.

NICK. I told Nina about you the first night I met her and

through the years she has done quite a little teasing—
You are too modest, Constance. (*Suddenly*) Now are
you going to let me do another portrait of you?

CONSTANCE (*Laughs*). Another portrait? No, no, indeed.
I want to remember myself as I was in the picture upstairs.

NICK. Go and get it for me. I want to look at it with you.
(*She smiles, exits. There is silence*) You haven't been
too warm or gracious, Nina.

NINA. What can I do when I don't even know the plot?

NICK. What are you talking about?

NINA. You told me about Constance Tuckerman the first
night we met? And about dear Willy or Ned, and I've
done quite a little teasing about her all these years?

NICK. I did tell you about her immediately—

NINA. You mentioned her very casually, last week, years
after the night you met me and you said that you could
hardly remember anything more about her than a rather
silly—

NICK (*Quickly*). Are you going to be bad-tempered for
our whole visit here? For years I've looked forward to
coming back—

(NINA *laughs*.)

NINA. So you came to do her portrait?

NICK. No, I didn't "come to do her portrait." I thought
about it driving down here. If the one I did is as good
as I remember, it would be wonderful for the show. The
young girl, the woman at forty-five. She's aged. Have
we changed that much? I don't think you've changed,
darling.

NINA. I've changed a great deal. And I wouldn't want it
pointed out to me in a portrait to be hung side by side
with a picture of what I used to be. (*He doesn't answer
her*) That isn't a nice reason for being here and if I had
known it—

NICK. We have no "reason" for being here. I just wanted to come back. Nothing mysterious about it—

NINA. You're simply looking for a new area in which to exercise yourself. It has happened many, many times before. But it *always* happens when we return from Europe and spend a month in New York. It's been too important to you, for many years, that you cannot manage to charm my family. And so, when our visit is finished there, you inevitably look around for— Well, you know. You know what's been and the trouble.

NICK (*Cheerfully*). I don't know what the hell you're talking about.

NINA. I'm tired of such troubles, Nick—

NICK. Do you know that these sharp moods of yours grow more sharp with time? Now I would like to have a happy visit here. But if something is disturbing you and you'd prefer not to stay, I'll arrange immediately—

NINA (*As if she were a little frightened*). I'd only prefer to go to bed. Sorry if I've been churly about your— home-coming. (*She starts out, meets* CONSTANCE *who comes in carrying portrait*) Will you excuse me, Constance? The long drive gave me a headache.

CONSTANCE. I am sorry. Will I bring you a tray upstairs?

NINA. No, thank you.

(CONSTANCE *moves as if to show her the way.*)

NICK. Come, I want to see the picture. Nina will find her way.

(*He takes the picture from* CONSTANCE.)

CONSTANCE. The yellow room on the left. Your maid is unpacking. I peeked in. What lovely clothes. Can I come and see them tomorrow?

NINA (*Going up the stairs*). Yes, of course. Thank you and good night.

(CONSTANCE *watches her and then comes into room.*)

NICK (*Who is looking at the picture*). I was nervous about seeing it. Damn good work for a boy eighteen.

CONSTANCE. You were twenty-two, Nick.

NICK. No, I wasn't. I—

CONSTANCE. You finished it the morning of your birthday. (*She points to windows*) And when you put down your brushes you said damn good work for a boy of twenty-two, and then you asked me to marry you. Don't you remember— (*She stops, embarrassed*) Why should you remember? And I don't want to talk that way.

NICK (*Who is preoccupied with the picture*). Oh, nonsense. Talk any way you like. We were in love, very much in love, and why shouldn't we speak of it?

CONSTANCE (*Hastily, very embarrassed*). After I die, the picture will go to the Delgado Museum.

NICK (*Laughs*). I want to borrow it first. I'm having a retrospective show this winter, in London. I've done a lot of fancy people in Europe, you know that, but I'll be more proud of this— And I want to do another portrait of you as you are now. (*Moves toward window, excited*) You standing there. As before. Wonderful idea; young girl, woman at— Be a sensation. Constance, it's fascinating how faces change, mold firm or loose, have lines that start in youth and—

CONSTANCE (*Amazed*). Oh, Nick. I don't want to see myself now. I don't want to see all the changes. And I don't want other people to stand and talk about them. I don't want people to laugh at me or pity me. (*Hurt*) Oh, Nick.

NICK. I see. (*Turns*) Well, it would have meant a lot to me. But that's that. I'll be off to bed now—

CONSTANCE (*Coming after him*). But we haven't had a minute. And I have supper all ready for you—

NICK. Good night, my dear.

CONSTANCE (*Slowly*). You think I'm being selfish and vain? I mean, am I the only woman who wouldn't like—

NICK. No, I think most women would feel the same way. (*He starts out.*)

CONSTANCE. Do you prefer breakfast in bed? And what shall I make for your dinner? Pompano—

(*He is at the door as* CARRIE *and* ROSE *come into the hall.* CARRIE *is holding* ROSE's *arm.*)

CARRIE. Hello, Nick.

NICK (*Takes her hands*). My God, Carrie. I didn't know you were here. How come? It's wonderful—

CARRIE. We come every summer.

NICK. You're handsome, Carrie. But you always were.

CARRIE (*Smiles*). And you always remembered to say so. (ROSE *coughs delicately*) This is Mrs. Griggs. (*To* CONSTANCE) Mrs. Griggs didn't feel well, so I brought her home. She became a little dizzy, dancing.

ROSE (*To* NICK, *who is shaking hands with her*). You're a famous gentleman in this town, sir, and I've been looking forward so to seeing you. We lead dull lives here, you know—

NICK (*Laughs*). *You* don't look as if you do.

ROSE. Oh, thank you. But I don't look well tonight. I became suddenly a little ill—

CARRIE (*Tartly*). Yes. Well, come along. If you still feel ill.

NICK. Can I help you, Mrs. Griggs?

ROSE (*Delighted*). Oh, thank you. That would be nice. I haven't been well this summer—

(NICK *starts into hall.*)

CONSTANCE. Nick—

(*He pays no attention.* CARRIE *moves quickly ahead of him, takes* ROSE's *arm.*)

CARRIE. Come. Good night, Nick. I look forward to seeing you in the morning. Hope you're staying for a while.

NICK. I think we'll have to leave tomorrow.

ROSE. Oh, don't do that. (*Then*) Constance, if Ben comes in would you tell him I was taken ill?

(CARRIE *impatiently pushes her ahead and up the steps.*)

NICK (*Meaning* ROSE). Pretty woman, or was. (*Looks at* CONSTANCE) What is it, Con?

CONSTANCE. How can you talk of leaving tomorrow? (*He doesn't answer*) Don't be mad with me, Nick.

NICK. I don't get mad, darling.

CONSTANCE (*Catches him as he is almost out the door*). Please, Nick, please let me change my mind. You are welcome to take this picture and I am flattered you wish to do another. But I'll have to pose early, before they're all down for breakfast—

NICK (*turns casually*). Good. We'll start in the morning. Do you make a living out of this place, darling?

CONSTANCE (*Gaily*). Not much of one. The last few years have been a little hard. I brought Sam's daughter from Europe—she and her mother went through the occupation and were very poor—and I've tried to send her to the best school and then she was to make her debut only now she wants to get married, I think, and—

NICK. The girl expected all that from you?

CONSTANCE. Oh, no. Her mother didn't want to come and Sophie didn't want to leave her mother. I finally had really to *demand* that Sam's daughter was not to grow up— Well, I just can't describe it. At thirteen she was working in a fish store or whatever you call it over there. I just *made* her come over—

NICK. Why didn't you ever marry Ned?

CONSTANCE. I can't answer such questions, Nick. Even for you.

NICK. Why not? I'd tell you about myself or Nina.

CONSTANCE. Oh, it's one thing to talk about lives that have been good and full and happy and quite another— Well, I don't know. We just never did marry.

NICK (*Bored*). Well, then, tomorrow morning. I'll do a

good portrait of you because it's the face of a good woman—

(*He stops as* SOPHIE *comes in. She sees* NICK *and* CONSTANCE *and draws back a little.*)

CONSTANCE. Sophie. (SOPHIE *comes into the room*) This is Sam's daughter.

NICK (*Very warmly to* SOPHIE). I've been looking forward to meeting you for many years.

(CONSTANCE *turns, puzzled.*)

SOPHIE. How do you do, sir?

NICK. You follow in the great tradition of 'Tuckerman good looks.

SOPHIE. Er. Er.

CONSTANCE (*Smiles*). Don't er, dear. Say thank you. (GRIGGS *enters from left porch*) Do come in. (GRIGGS *comes in*) This is General Griggs. My very old friend, Nicholas Denery.

NICK. Are you General Benjamin Griggs? I've read about you in Raymond's book and Powell's.

GRIGGS (*As they shake hands*). I hear they disagree about me.

NICK. We almost met before this. When your boys marched into Paris. I was in France during the German occupation.

(SOPHIE *turns sharply.*)

GRIGGS. That must have been unpleasant for you.

NICK. Yes, it was. But in the end, one has to be just; the Germans were damn smart about the French. They acted like gentlemen.

GRIGGS (*Pleasantly*). That's a side of them I didn't see. (*Looks over at* SOPHIE) You didn't either, Sophie?

(*During his speech* HILDA, *the maid, appears in the doorway.*)

HILDA (*In German*). Excuse me, Mr. Denery. Mrs. Denery would like you to come for a minute before you retire.

She has a little surprise gift she bought for you in New Orleans.

NICK (*In German*). No. Tell Mrs. Denery I will see her in the morning. Tell her to take a sleeping pill.

HILDA (*In German*). Thank you, sir.

CONSTANCE (*Who hasn't understood the German but who is puzzled because* SOPHIE *is frowning and* GRIGGS *has turned away*). Can I— Does Nina want something?

NICK. No, no, she's fine. (SOPHIE *begins to make up the couch.* NICK *turns to her*) That means one of us must have put you out of your room. I'm sorry and I thank you.

SOPHIE. Not at all, sir. It is nothing.

NICK (*Comes to her*). You're a sweet child and I look forward to knowing you. Good night. (*To* GRIGGS) Good night, sir. A great pleasure. (GRIGGS *bows.* NICK *kisses* CONSTANCE) Wonderful to be here, darling.

(*He goes out.* CONSTANCE *moves to help* SOPHIE *make up the couch. There is silence for a minute while they arrange the bedclothes.* GRIGGS *watches them.*)

CONSTANCE. I suppose I shouldn't ask but what did the German maid want? Something from the kitchen or— (*No answer*) Sophie. (*No answer*) Sophie.

SOPHIE (*Slowly*). Mrs. Denery wanted to say good night to Mr. Denery.

GRIGGS. Mrs. Denery had bought a little gift for him in New Orleans and wanted to give it to him.

CONSTANCE. After all these years. To have a little gift for him. Isn't that nice? (*She looks at* GRIGGS *and* SOPHIE. *Neither answers her. She becomes conscious of something strained*) What did Nick say?

SOPHIE. He said she should take a sleeping pill and go to sleep.

CONSTANCE. Just like that?

SOPHIE. Down at the beach there is the frankfurter concession. I think I will get the sleeping-pill concession and grow very rich.

CONSTANCE. Why, Sophie. Are you disturbed about something, dear? (*Looks at her dress*) You didn't go to the party! I've been so busy, I didn't realize— Why, where's Fred and—

SOPHIE. I did not wish to go to the party, Aunt Constance. And Frederick had a most important appointment.

CONSTANCE. More important than being with you? Young people get engaged and act toward each other with such— I don't know. (*To* GRIGGS) In our day we made marriage more romantic and I must say I think we had more fun. If you can't have fine dreams now, then when can you have them? (*Pats* SOPHIE) Never mind. I guess the new way is more sensible. But I liked our way better. (*To* GRIGGS) Didn't you? Oh, what's the matter with me? I forgot. Rose came back from the party. She said she was ill. I mean, I think she just didn't feel well— Carrie is upstairs with her. (*He doesn't move*) I think Carrie probably wants to go back to the party and is waiting for you to come.

GRIGGS. Yes. Of course. Thank you. Good night.

(*He exits.*)

CONSTANCE (*She kisses* SOPHIE). You'll be comfortable? See you in the morning, dear.

(*She exits through the hall.* SOPHIE *finishes with the couch, goes out. After a second,* CROSSMAN *comes down the stairs. He sticks his head in the door, sees nobody, crosses the room, goes out to the porch, takes the bottle of brandy and a glass, moves back into the room and crosses it as* SOPHIE *returns carrying pajamas and a robe.*)

CROSSMAN (*His voice and his manner are slightly different now*). I needed another book and another bottle. Royalty gone to bed? Does anybody improve with age? Just tell me that, Sophie, and I'll have something to lie awake and think about.

SOPHIE. I do not know, Mr. Ned.

CROSSMAN. For God's sake, Sophie, have an opinion about *something*. Try it, and see what comes out.

SOPHIE (*Laughs*). Some people improve with age, some do not.

CROSSMAN (*Nods, amused*). Wonderful, Sophie, wonderful. Some improve with age, some do not. Medical statistics show that 61 per cent of those who improve have bought our book on Dianetics and smoke Iglewitz cigarettes. You're beginning to talk like an advertisement, which is the very highest form of American talk. (*Sharply*) It's not *your* language, nor your native land. You don't have to care about it. You shouldn't even understand it.

SOPHIE. Sometimes I understand.

CROSSMAN. That's dangerous to admit, Sophie. You've been so busy cultivating a pseudo-stupidity. Not that you'd ever be a brilliant girl, but at least you used to be normal. Another five years and you won't be *pseudo-*stupid.

SOPHIE (*Smiles*). I will not mind. It will be easier. (*Carefully*) You notice me too much, Mr. Ned. Please do not feel sorry or notice me so much.

CROSSMAN. You came here a nice little girl who had seen a lot of war and trouble. You had spirit, in a quiet way, and you were gay, in a quiet way, which is the only way women should be gay since they are never really gay at all. Only serious people are ever gay and women are very seldom serious people. They are earnest instead. But earnestness has nothing to do with seriousness. So. (*Suddenly*) What the hell is this marriage business between you and Fred Ellis?

SOPHIE (*Softly*). It is the marriage business between me and Fred Ellis.

CROSSMAN. But what's the matter with you? Haven't you got sense enough to know—

SOPHIE (*Quickly*). I do the best I can. I do the best I can. And I thank you for worrying about me, but you are an educated man with ideas in English that I am not qualified to understand.

CROSSMAN. Listen to me, Sophie. Sometimes when I've had enough to drink—just exactly enough—I feel as if I were given to understand that which I may not understand again. And sometimes then—but rarely— I have an urge to speak out. Fewer drinks, more drinks, and I'm less certain that I see the truth, or I get bored, and none of my opinions and none of the people and issues involved seem worth the trouble. Right now, I've had just enough: so listen to me, Sophie. I say turn yourself around, girl, and go home. Beat it quick.

SOPHIE. You take many words to say simple things. All of you. And you make the simple things—like going to sleep—so hard, and the hard things—like staying awake —so easy. Go home, shall I? Just like that, you say it. Aunt Constance has used up all her money on me, wasted it, and for why and what? How can I go home?

CROSSMAN. If that's all it is I'll find you the money to go home.

SOPHIE (*Wearily*). Oh, Mr. Ned. We owe money in our village, my mother and I. In my kind of Europe you can't live where you owe money. Go home. Did I ever want to come? I have no place here and I am lost and homesick. I like my mother, I— Every night I plan to go. But it is five years now and there is no plan and no chance to find one. Therefore I will do the best I can. (*Very sharply*) And I will not cry about it and I will not speak of it again.

CROSSMAN (*Softly, as if he were moved*). The best you can?

SOPHIE. I think so. (*Sweetly*) Maybe you've never tried to do that, Mr. Ned. Maybe none of you have tried.

CROSSMAN. Sophie, lonely people talking to each other can make each other lonelier. They should be careful because maybe lonely people are the only people who can't afford to cry. I'm sorry.

(*He exits through the hall, goes up the stairs as the curtain falls.*)

Curtain

ACT TWO

SCENE I

SCENE: The same as ACT ONE. *A week later, eight-thirty Sunday morning.*

AT RISE: CONSTANCE *is standing against the outside edge of the porch, leaning on the railing.* NICK *is standing in front of an easel.* CONSTANCE *has on a most unbecoming house dress and her hair is drawn back tight. She looks ten years older. In the living room,* SOPHIE *has finished folding her bedclothes and is hurrying around the room with a carpet sweeper. After a second,* LEON *appears from the direction of the dining room with a tray and dishes and moves out to the porch. He puts down the tray, moves the table, begins to place the dishes.* CONSTANCE *tries desperately to ask him if everything is all right in the kitchen. She does this by moving her lips and trying not to move her head.* LEON *sees her motions but doesn't understand what she is trying to say. The noise of the rattling dishes, and the carpet sweeper, becomes sharp.*

NICK. Constance, please ask them to stop that noise. (*Waves his hand to* LEON *and* SOPHIE) Go away, both of you.
CONSTANCE. They can't, Nick. I explain it to you every morning! We simply have to get ready for breakfast. (*Quietly*) Sophie, is everything all right in the kitchen?
SOPHIE. Yes, ma'am. Everything is fine.
NICK (*To* CONSTANCE, *sharply*). Please keep the pose. Just a few minutes more.

CONSTANCE (*To* LEON). Tell Sadie not to cook the liver until everybody is downstairs, like she always does. Did she remember about the grits this Sunday? (*To* NICK, *sees his face*) All right. I'm sorry. But really, I can't run a boardinghouse and pose for—

(*She sighs, settles back.* SOPHIE *picks up her bedclothes and exits through the hall.* LEON *finishes with the porch table and comes back into the living room as* MRS. ELLIS *comes down the steps.*)

MRS. ELLIS (*To* LEON). My breakfast ready?

LEON. No, ma'am. We'll ring the bell.

MRS. ELLIS. What's the matter with my breakfast?

LEON. Nothing the matter with it. It will be like always.

MRS. ELLIS. It gets later and later every day.

LEON. No, ma'am. That's just you. Want it in the dining room or on the porch?

MRS. ELLIS. Too damp on the porch. Whole house is damp. I haven't slept all summer, Leon.

LEON. Just as well not to sleep in summer.

MRS. ELLIS (*As* LEON *exits*). You're going to have to explain that to me sometime. (*She turns, goes toward porch, comes around in front of* CONSTANCE) Constance, he's made you look right mean and ten years older. Why have you done that, Nicholas?

(SOPHIE *comes back into living room with a large urn of coffee and small cups. She puts the tray on a table.*)

NICK (*To* MRS. ELLIS). Shoo, shoo. This is forbidden ground.

MRS. ELLIS (*Calls*). Sophie, give me a cup. I have to stay awake for church. (*To* CONSTANCE) Ten years older. When you pay an artist to paint your portrait he makes you ten years younger. I had my portrait done when I was twenty-one, holding my first baby. And the baby looked older than I did. Was rather a scandal or like those people in Tennessee.

NICK. You know if you wouldn't interrupt me every morning, I think I'd fall in love with you.

MRS. ELLIS (*She goes toward* SOPHIE *to get her coffee. During her speech,* SOPHIE *puts three spoons of sugar in the small cup*). I wouldn't like that. Even if I was the right age I wouldn't like it. Although I realize it would make me dangerously different from every other woman in the world. You would never have been my dish of tea, and isn't that a silly way of saying it? (*To* SOPHIE: *she is now in the living room*) You're the only one who ever remembers about my sugar. Sophie, will you come up to town (CROSSMAN *comes down the steps and into the room*) and stay with me for a few weeks while Carrie and Frederick are in Europe?

SOPHIE. I would like that.

MRS. ELLIS. Ned, what shall I give Sophie for her wedding present? My pearls or my mother's diamonds?

CROSSMAN (*To* SOPHIE). The rich always give something old and precious to their new brides. Something that doesn't cost them new money. Same thing true in your country?

SOPHIE (*Smiles*). I do not know the rich in my country.

MRS. ELLIS. He's quite right, Sophie. Not only something old but something so old that we're sick of it.

CROSSMAN. Why don't you give her a nice new check?

MRS. ELLIS. Only if I have to.

CONSTANCE (*On porch*). Nick, my neck is breaking—

NICK. All right. All finished for this morning.

(*Turns the picture around so that* CONSTANCE *cannot see it.* SOPHIE *brings two cups of coffee to the porch.*)

CONSTANCE (*Collapsing in a chair*). Whew.

(*Takes the coffee from* SOPHIE, *pats her arm.* SOPHIE *takes the other cup to* NICK.)

NICK. You're the girl I want to paint. Change your mind and we'll start today. Why not, Sophie?

(*He is holding her hand.*)

SOPHIE. I am not pretty, Mr. Nicholas.

NICK. You are better than pretty.

(CROSSMAN *comes out to the porch.* SOPHIE *disengages her hand, moves off.*)

CROSSMAN (*staring at* CONSTANCE). My God, you look awful, Constance. What did you get done up like that for? You're poor enough not to have to pretend you are poor.

NICK (*Laughing*). Go way, Ned. You've got a hangover. I know I have.

(NINA *comes down the steps, comes into the room, says good morning to* MRS. ELLIS *who says good morning to her. She pours herself a cup of coffee. She is close enough to the porch to hear what is said.*)

CONSTANCE. You know, I waited up until twelve o'clock for you both—

NICK. We were late. We had a good get-together last night. Like old times, wasn't it, Ned? (*To* CONSTANCE) If you have the normal vanity you'd be pleased at the amount of time we spent on you. Ned loosened up and talked—

CROSSMAN. I did? I thought that was you.

NICK (*Laughs*). I knew you wouldn't remember what you'd said— Don't regret it: did you good to speak your heart out—for once.

CROSSMAN. My heart, eh?

NICK. In a juke-box song called Constance.

CONSTANCE. What? I don't understand.

CROSSMAN (*Who has turned sharply, then decided to laugh*). Neither do I. The stage of not remembering, or speaking out my heart, will come in time, I am sorry to say. But I hope it hasn't come yet.

(*As he turns to go out,* LEON *appears in the hall with a bell and begins to ring the bell.*)

NINA (*A little timidly*). Good morning, Mr. Crossman.

CROSSMAN. Good morning, Mrs. Denery. I'm sorry you

didn't join us last night—to hear me pour my heart out.

NINA. I'm never invited to the pouring of a heart.

CROSSMAN. I looked for you, but Nick said you had a headache.

NINA. Nick always says I have a headache when he doesn't want me to come along, or sees to it that I do have one.

MRS. ELLIS (*Gets up quickly*). All right, Leon. I'm ready. I haven't eaten since four this morning. (*Goes out. As she passes stairs, she shouts up*) Carrie! Frederick! I simply won't wait breakfast any longer.

(CROSSMAN *follows her out.*)

CONSTANCE (*Gets up*). Well, they seemed to have managed in the kitchen without me. I reckon I better change now. Where'd you get this dress, Nick?

NICK. Place on Dreyenen Street.

CONSTANCE. In a Negro store! You bought this dress in a Negro store! (*He looks at her and laughs*) I don't mean that. I mean Ned's right. You must have wanted to make me look just about as awful as— For some reason I don't understand. Nick, what *are* you doing? And why won't you let me see the portrait?

NICK. Haven't you yet figured out that Ned is jealous?

CONSTANCE. Jealous of what?

NICK. He's in love with you, girl. As much as he was when we were kids. You're all he talked about last night. How lonely he's been, how much he's wanted you, how often he asked you to marry him—

CONSTANCE. I just don't believe you. Ned never talks about himself. I just don't believe he said such things—

NICK. You know damn well he loves you and you know he's rotting away for you. He said last night—

CONSTANCE (*Prissy*). Nick, if he did talk, and it's most out of character, I don't think I should hear what he said in confidence just to you.

NICK. Oh, run along, honey. You're pleased as punch. When you're not pretending to be genteel.

CONSTANCE (*Laughs*). Genteel? How awful of me. Mama used to say gentility was the opposite of breeding and— (*She has started to move out of the room*) Did Ned say—er—

(NICK *laughs, she laughs, and exits.* NICK *begins to put away portrait and to fold easel as* NINA *puts down her coffee and comes out to the porch.*)

NICK (*Kisses her*). Morning, darling. (NINA *sits down, watches him*) What's the matter?

(LEON *appears with breakfast dishes. He serves* NICK *and* NINA *during the next few speeches.*)

NINA. Why have you done that? To Constance?

NICK. Done what? Tell her the truth?

NINA. How could you know it to be the truth? I don't believe Crossman talked to you—

NICK. Look, it makes her happy—and if I can get a little sense into her head it will make him happy. I don't have to have an affidavit to know what's going on in the human heart.

(*He leans over, kisses her, sits down to eat his breakfast.*)

NINA (*Laughs*). Oh, you are enjoying yourself so much here. I've seldom seen it this hog-wild. (LEON *exits*) You're on a rampage of good will. Makes me nervous for even the trees outside. But there's something impertinent about warning an oak tree. How should I do it?

NICK (*Laughs*). First tell me how to understand what you're talking about.

(*They eat in silence for a minute.*)

NINA. Are we staying much longer, Nick?

NICK. A few more days. The house officially closes this week, Constance says. The Ellises go tomorrow and the Griggses on Tuesday, I think. Just till I finish.

NINA. Finish what?

NICK (*Carefully*). The portrait, Nina.

(ROSE GRIGGS *comes down the stairs, carrying a small over-*

night case. She is done up in a pretty, too fussy, hat and a pretty, too fussy, dress. She looks in the room, puts the case down, comes hurrying out to the porch.)

ROSE. Oh, good morning. Sorry to interrupt. You look so handsome together. (*Makes a gesture to* NICK *meaning "Could you come here?"*) Nick—

NICK (*Hospitable*). Come on out.

ROSE. I'd rather. Could you—

NICK. Come and join us.

ROSE (*Hesitantly*). Well, I wanted to tell *you* but I don't want to worry Nina. You see—

NINA. I'd go away, Mrs. Griggs, but I've been dismissed from so many meals lately that I'm getting hungry.

ROSE (*Smiles to* NINA. *Speaks to* NICK). I called him last night. Just like you advised. And I'm driving right over now. He's the executor of my trust fund, you know. He's very wise: I've got gilt-edged securities.

NICK. Who is this?

ROSE. My brother, of course. Henry, like I told you. (*To* NINA) It sounds so mysterious, but it isn't. He's much older. You know he builds ships, I mean during our wars. I'll tell him the whole story, Nick, and he'll know what to do.

NICK (*Amused*). Of course he will.

ROSE. I'm going to drive over to my doctor's. He's going to wait for me on a hot Sunday. It'll be expensive— (*To* NINA) I had a heart murmur. They had to take me out of school for a year.

NINA. Recently?

(NICK *chokes back a laugh.*)

ROSE (*Giggles*). That's charming—"recently." (*To* NICK) There's so much I wanted to consult you about. I waited up for you last night, but—well. Should I do *just* as you told me yesterday?

NICK (*Who doesn't remember what he told her*). Sure.

ROSE. Everything?

NICK. Well—

NINA. I think, Mrs. Griggs, you'll have to remind Nick what he told you. Yesterday is a long time ago when you have so many ladies to attend to—

ROSE (*As* NICK *laughs*). I shouldn't have brought it up like this. Oh, Mrs. Denery, you might as well know: it's about a divorce, and Nick has been most kind.

NINA. I am sure of it.

ROSE. Just one more thing. What should I do about our boys? Should I telephone them or let Henry? One of our sons works on the atom bomb, you know. He's the religious one and it will be traumatic for him. What do you think, Nick?

NINA (*Gets up quickly, trying not to laugh, moves away*). Goodness.

NICK. I think you should go and have your breakfast. It's my firm belief that women only look well in hats after they've eaten.

ROSE (*To* NICK, *softly, secretly*). And I'm going to just *make* Henry commission the portrait—and for the very good price that he can afford to pay. You remember though that I told you she can't take the braces off her teeth for another six months.

NICK (*Laughs*). Go along now, my dear.

ROSE (*Pleased*). Thank you for all you've done. And forgive me, Nina. I'll be back tonight, Nick, before you go to bed because you'll want to know how everything turns out.

(*She exits through room.* NINA *stands without speaking.*)

NICK (*Looks up at her*). There was a day when we would have laughed together about this. Don't you have fun any more?

NINA. I don't think so.

NICK. She's quite nice, really. And very funny.

NINA. I suppose it's all right to flirt with, or to charm, women and men and children and animals but now-

adays it seems to me you include books-in-vellum and
sirloin steaks, red squirrels and lamp shades.

NICK (*Smiles*). Are you crazy? Flirt with that silly woman?
Come and eat your breakfast, Nina. I've had enough
seriousness where none is due.

(*Through this speech,* CARRIE *has come down the steps.
She meets* SOPHIE *who is going through the hall to the
dining room.* SOPHIE *is carrying a tray.*)

CARRIE. Good morning, dear. Is Frederick in the dining
room?

SOPHIE. No. He has not come down as yet.

(*She goes on past.* CARRIE *comes into the room, continues
on to the porch.*)

CARRIE (*To* NICK *and* NINA). Good morning. Your maid said
you wanted to see me, Nick.

NICK (*Hesitantly*). Carrie, I hesitated all day yesterday.
I told myself perhaps you knew, but maybe, just maybe,
you didn't.

NINA (*Laughs*). Oh, it sounds so serious.

CARRIE (*Smiles*). It does indeed.

NICK (*Carefully*). Don't you know that man's reputation,
Carrie? You can't travel around Europe with him.

CARRIE. Travel around Europe with *him*? I'm going to
Europe with Frederick. (*Then sharply, as she sees his
face*) What do you mean, Nick?

NICK. I—

(SOPHIE *comes into room, goes out to porch. During next
speeches, she pours coffee.*)

CARRIE. Please tell me.

NICK. I saw Frederick in the travel agency yesterday with
a man I once met in Europe. Not the sort of man you'd
expect to see Frederick with.

CARRIE. Are you talking about Mr. Payson?

NICK. Yes, I am. Well, I waited until they left the travel
place and then I went in.

NINA. Why did you go in?

NICK. Luther hadn't seen me since we were kids and we got to talking. He said he had booked your passage on the *Elizabeth* and now he had another for Mr. Payson and Fred had just paid for it— (CARRIE *gets up, turns sharply, does not speak*) I didn't know whether you knew, Carrie, or if I should tell you—

CARRIE. I didn't know. I thank you for telling me. (*After a second, she turns*) What did you mean, Nick, when you asked me if I knew Payson's reputation? I don't like to press you for gossip, but—

NINA. He didn't mean anything, Mrs. Ellis—

NICK. Oh, look here, Nina, you know he's part of Count Denna's set, and on the nasty fringe of that.

(SOPHIE, *very quietly, leaves the porch.*)

CARRIE. What does that mean: Count Denna's set and the nasty fringe of that?

NINA (*Quickly*). It means very little. The Count is a foolish old man who gives large parties—

NICK (*To* NINA). Would you want your young son with such people at such parties?

NINA (*Angrily*). I have no son. And I don't know: perhaps I would have wanted only to leave him alone—

CARRIE (*Gently*). All people who have no children think that, Mrs. Denery. But it just isn't true. (*To* NICK) I don't know much about Mr. Payson but I've been worried for a long time that he's taken Frederick in. Frederick admires his writing, and— Yet I know so little about him. He stayed with us a few weeks in town last winter. He'd just come back from Europe then—

NICK. He'd just come back from a filthy little scandal in Rome. It was all over the papers.

NINA. You don't know it was true.

CARRIE. What kind of scandal? (*No answer. Softly*) Please help me. I don't understand.

NICK (*Gets up*). Look, Carrie, there's nothing to understand. The guy is just no good. That's all you need to know. He's nobody to travel around Europe with.

CARRIE. How could Fred have— (*She hesitates for a minute*) It was kind and friendly of you to tell me. I am grateful to you both.

(*She goes slowly across the room and into the hall toward the dining room. There is a long pause:* NICK *takes a sip of coffee, looks around at* NINA.)

NICK. What would you have done?

NINA (*Idly*). I don't know. Have you ever tried leaving things alone?

NICK. I like Carrie. She doesn't know what the hell it's all about—and the chances are the boy doesn't either. I'm sorry for them. Aren't you? (*When she doesn't answer*) What's the matter, Nina?

NINA. I can smell it: it's all around us. The flower-like odor right before it becomes troublesome and heavy. It travels ahead of you, Nick, whenever you get most helpful, most loving and most lovable. Down through the years it runs ahead of us—I smell it—and I want to leave.

NICK (*Pleasantly*). I think maybe you're one of the few neurotics in the world who didn't marry a neurotic. I wonder how that happened?

NINA. *I want to leave.*

NICK (*Sharply*). Then leave.

NINA (*After a second*). You won't come?

NICK. I told you: we'll go Friday. If you want to go before, then go. But stop talking about it, Nina. Or we'll be in for one of your long farewells—and long returns. I don't think I can stand another. Spare yourself, darling. You pay so heavy, inside. (*Comes to her, puts his arms around her*) Friday, then. And in the meantime, gentle down to the pretty lady you truly are.

(*He kisses her. Exits.* NINA *stands quietly for a minute*

SOPHIE *comes onto the porch, begins to gather the dishes.*)

SOPHIE (*Gently*). Would you like something, Mrs. Denery?

NINA (*Softly*). No, thank you.

(*She moves off, through the room and toward the staircase. As she starts up the stairs,* FREDERICK *comes down.*)

FREDERICK. Good morning.

NINA. Good morning, Mr. Ellis. (*Stops as if she wanted to tell him something*) I—er. Good morning.

(*She goes up as* SOPHIE, *who has heard their voices, leaves the dishes and comes quickly into the room.*)

SOPHIE (*Calling into the hall*). Fred. Fred. (*He comes in. Shyly*) Would you like to have your breakfast on the kitchen porch?

FREDERICK. Sure. Why?

SOPHIE. Your mother is—er— (*Points toward dining room*) She has found out that— Come.

FREDERICK. Denery told her he saw me in the travel agency. I was sure he would. There's nothing to worry about. I intended to tell her this morning.

SOPHIE. But perhaps it would be more wise—

FREDERICK (*Smiles to her*). We'll be leaving here tomorrow and for Europe on the sixteenth. You and I won't see each other for six months. Sophie, you're sure you feel all right about my going?

SOPHIE (*Quickly*). Oh, I do.

FREDERICK. We will visit your mother. And—

SOPHIE (*Very quickly*). No, no, please do not do that. I have not written to her about us—

FREDERICK. Oh.

SOPHIE. You see, we have as yet no date of time, or—

FREDERICK (*Smiles*). I don't think you want a date of time, Sophie. And you don't have to be ashamed of wishing you could find another way. But if there isn't any other way for you, then I'll be just as good to you as I know how. And I know you will be to me.

SOPHIE. You are a kind man. And I will also be kind, I hope.

FREDERICK. It isn't any deal for you. You are a girl who should love, and will one day, of course.

SOPHIE (*Puts her hand up to her mouth*). Shssh. Such things should not be said. (*Cheerfully*) It will be nice in your house with you, and I will be grateful for it.

FREDERICK. I have no house, Sophie. People like me never have their own house, so-to-speak.

SOPHIE. Never mind. Whatever house. It will be nice. We will make it so.

(*He smiles, pats her arm.*)

FREDERICK. Everybody in the dining room? (*She nods. He starts for hall*) Might as well face it out.

SOPHIE. I would not. No, I would not. All of you face out too much. Every act of life should not be of such importance—

FREDERICK (*Calling into dining room*). Mother. (SOPHIE *shrugs, smiles, shakes her head, and exits.* FREDERICK *comes back into room, pours himself a cup of coffee. After a minute,* CARRIE *appears. She comes into the room obviously very disturbed. But she does not speak*) There's nothing to be so upset about.

CARRIE (*After a pause*). You think that, really?

(MRS. ELLIS *appears in the hall.*)

FREDERICK. We've going to have a companion. That's all. We know nothing of traveling and Payson knows all of Europe.

MRS. ELLIS. Of course. You're lucky to get Mr. Payson to come along.

(*Both of them turn to look at her.*)

FREDERICK (*After a second, to* CARRIE). What is it, Mother?

CARRIE. I can't say it. It's shocking of you to take along a guest without consulting me. You and I have planned this trip for three years and—

FREDERICK. I didn't consult you because the idea came up

quickly and Payson had to get his ticket before the travel office closed for the week end—

CARRIE. *Payson* had to get *his* ticket?

FREDERICK. I thought you'd given up going through my checkbooks.

CARRIE. *Please don't speak that way to me.* (*Pause, quietly, delicately*) We are not going to Europe.

FREDERICK (*After a second, quietly*). I am.

CARRIE. We are not going, Fred. We are not going.

MRS. ELLIS. Your mother's feelings are hurt. She had looked forward to being alone with you. Of course.

FREDERICK (*Uncomfortably*). We'll still be together.

CARRIE (*To* MRS. ELLIS). I don't wish to be interpreted, Mother. (*To* FREDERICK) There's no sense talking about it: we'll go another time.

FREDERICK (*Laughs, unpleasantly*). Will you stop acting as if you're taking me back to school? I will be disappointed if you don't wish to come with me but I am sailing on the sixteenth. (*Then, quietly*) I've never had much fun. Never seen the things I wished to see, never met the people I wanted to meet or been the places where I could. There are wonderful things to see and to learn about and to try to understand. We're lucky to have somebody who knows about them and who is willing to have *us* tag along. *I'm* not much to drag around— (*Softly*) I'll come back, and you can take up my life again. Six months isn't much to ask.

MRS. ELLIS. Six months? Sad to ask so little.

CARRIE (*As if she recognized a tone of voice*). Mother, please. I—

MRS. ELLIS. Perhaps you won't want to come back at all? I wouldn't blame you.

CARRIE (*Nervously*). Fred, don't make a decision now. Promise me you'll think about it until tomorrow and then we'll talk quietly and—

MRS. ELLIS (*To* FREDERICK). Don't make bargains with

your mother. Everything always ends that way between you. I advise you to go now, or stay.

FREDERICK. I am going. There is nothing to think about. I'm going.

(*He turns and exits, goes up staircase. There is a pause.*)

CARRIE (*Angry*). You always do that, Mother. You always arrange to come out his friend and make me his enemy. You've been amusing yourself that way all his life.

MRS. ELLIS. There's no time for all that, Carrie. I warned you to say and do nothing. I told you to make the best of it and go along with them.

CARRIE (*Softly*). How could I do that? That man is a scoundrel and Fred doesn't know it, and won't believe it. What am I to do now?

MRS. ELLIS. You're to go upstairs and say that you are reconciled to his leaving without you but that Frederick is to make clear to his guest that his ten thousand a year ends today and will not begin again. Tell him you've decided young people have a happier time in Europe without American money—

CARRIE (*Sharply*). I couldn't do that. He'd hate me for it. Maybe we'd better let him go, and perhaps I can join him later. Time will— (*Sees* MRS. ELLIS's *face*) I will not cut off his allowance.

MRS. ELLIS. I didn't know it was you who wrote the check.

CARRIE (*With dignity*). Are you quite sure you wish to speak this way?

MRS. ELLIS. Relatively sure.

CARRIE. Then I will say as sharply that the money is his father's money, and not yours to threaten him, or deprive him, in any proper sense.

MRS. ELLIS. In any *proper* sense. There is no morality to money, Carrie, and very immoral of you to think so.

CARRIE. If you stop his allowance, Mother, I will simply send him mine.

MRS. ELLIS. Then I won't give you yours. (CARRIE *turns*

sharply, as if she were deeply shocked. MRS. ELLIS *now speaks, gently*) Yes, old people are often harsh, Carrie, when they control the purse. You'll see, when your day comes. And then, too, one comes to be bored with those who fool themselves. I say to myself—one should have power, or give it over. But if one keeps it, it might as well be used, with as little mealymouthness as possible. Go up now, and press him hard, and do it straight. (CARRIE *turns slowly to exit*) Tell yourself you're doing it for his own good.

CARRIE (*Softly*). I wouldn't be doing it otherwise.

MRS. ELLIS. Perhaps. Perhaps not. Doesn't really matter. (*Laughs, amused*) I'm off to church now. You can skip church today, Carrie.

CARRIE. Thank you for the dispensation.

(*She begins to move off toward hall and toward stairs as* ROSE *comes from the direction of the dining room and into the room.*)

MRS. ELLIS (*To* CARRIE, *as* CARRIE *moves off*). Quite all right. You have God's work to do. (*She turns to watch* ROSE *who is elaborately settling herself in a chair as if she were arranging for a scene—which is what she is doing*) What are you doing, Mrs. Griggs? (ROSE *nervously points to left window.* MRS. ELLIS *looks toward it, watches* ROSE *fix her face*) Is it Robert Taylor you're expecting or Vice-President Barkley? (GRIGGS *comes in from the left windows. He has on riding pants and an old shirt*) Oh.

GRIGGS (*To them both*). Good morning.

MRS. ELLIS. Your wife's getting ready to flirt. You'd be safer in church with me.

(*She exits as* GRIGGS *laughs. He goes to coffee urn.*)

ROSE (*Meaning* MRS. ELLIS). Nasty old thing. (*Then*) I'm driving over to see him. I'm sorry I had to make such a decision, but I felt it was necessary now.

GRIGGS. Are you talking about your brother?

ROSE. Yes, of course. Now, I know it will be bad for you, Ben, but since *you're* being so stubborn, I didn't know what else to do.

GRIGGS. I think you should see Henry.

ROSE. But he's going to be very, very angry, Ben. And you know how much influence he has in Washington.

GRIGGS (*Turns, carefully*). Tell him to use his influence. And tell him to go to hell.

ROSE (*Giggles*). On a Sunday?

GRIGGS (*Gently*). Rose, no years will make you serious.

ROSE. You used to like me that way.

GRIGGS. So you always wanted to believe.

ROSE. How can I just walk into Henry's happy house and say Ben wants a divorce, and I don't even know the reason. I *ask* him and I *ask* him but he says there is no reason—

GRIGGS. I never said there was no reason. But it isn't the reason that you like, or will accept. If I were in love with another woman you'd rather enjoy that. And certainly Henry would.

ROSE. It would at least be human. And I am not convinced it isn't so. I've done a good deal of thinking about it, and I've just about decided it's why you stayed in Europe so long.

GRIGGS. I didn't arrange World War II and don't listen to the rumors that I did.

ROSE. He said it at the time. He said he had known a good many professional soldiers but nobody had managed to make so much fuss about the war as you did, or to stay away so long. Henry said that.

GRIGGS. I guessed it was Henry who said that.

ROSE (*Laughs*). But you didn't guess that it was Henry who got you the last promotion.

GRIGGS. Rose, stop that. You're lying. You always do it

about now. (*Turns to her*) Give Henry this reason: tell him my wife's too young for me. For Henry's simple mind, a simple reason.

ROSE. I've wanted to stay young, I've—

GRIGGS. You've done more than stay young: you've stayed a a child.

ROSE. What about your mother, Ben, have you thought of her? It would kill her—

GRIGGS. She's been dead sixteen years. Do you think this will kill her?

ROSE. You know what I mean. She loved me and she was happy for our marriage.

GRIGGS. No, she didn't. She warned me not to marry— (*With feeling*) I began my life with a serious woman. I doubt if any man gets over that, or ever really wants any other kind of woman.

ROSE. *Your mother loved me.* You have no right to malign the dead. I say she loved me, I know she did.

GRIGGS (*Wearily*). What difference does it make?

ROSE. You never think anybody loves me. Quite a few men have found me attractive—

GRIGGS (*Quickly*). And many more will, my dear.

ROSE. I always knew in the end I would have to tell you although I haven't seen him since you came home. That I promise you. I told him you were a war hero with a glorious record and he said he wouldn't either any longer—

GRIGGS (*Who is at the left window*). Henry's chauffeur is outside, Rose.

ROSE. He was very, very, very, very much in love with me while he was at the Pentagon.

GRIGGS. Good place to be in love. The car is outside, Rose.

ROSE. Even after we both knew it, he kept on saying that you didn't make love to a friend, more than a friend's, wife.

GRIGGS (*Gently*). Rose, don't let's talk this way.

ROSE. Does it hurt you? Well, you've hurt me enough. The third time you went to Europe was when it really began, maybe the second. Because I, too, wanted affection.

GRIGGS (*Gently*). I can understand that.

ROSE. Ask me who it was. Ask me, Ben, and I will tell you. (*No answer*) Just ask me.

GRIGGS. No, I won't do that, Rose.

ROSE. Remember when the roses came from Teheran, I mean wired from Teheran, last birthday? That's who sent them. You didn't even like Teheran. You said it was filthy and the people downtrodden. But he sent roses.

GRIGGS. He sounds like the right man. Go to him, Rose, the flying time is nothing now.

ROSE (*Angrily*). You just stop being nasty. (*Then*) And now I am going to tell you who it is.

GRIGGS (*Begins to move toward door, as if he were backing away from her*). Please, Rose. We have had so many years of this— Please. (*As she is closer to him*) Do I have to tell you that I don't care who it is?

ROSE (*She begins to move on him*). I'd like to whisper it. I knew if I ever told you I'd have to whisper it. (*He begins now really to back away*) Ben, you come right here. Ben stand still. (*He starts to laugh*) Stop that laughing. (*Very loudly, very close to him*) It was your cousin, Ralph Sommers. There. (*She turns away*) There. You won't ever speak with him about it?

GRIGGS. You can be sure of that.

ROSE (*Outside an automobile horn is sounded*). Oh, I'm late. I can't talk any more now, Ben. (*She starts for door, stops*) What am I going to tell Henry? Anyway, you know Henry isn't going to allow me to give you a divorce. You know that, Ben. (*Carefully*) And therefore I won't be able to do what you want, and the whole day is just wasted. Please tell me not to go, Ben.

GRIGGS (*As if he has held on to himself long enough*). Tell Henry that I want a divorce. But in any case I am going away. I am leaving. That is all that matters to me or need matter to you or him. I would prefer a divorce. But I am going, whatever you and Henry decide. Understand that, Rose, the time has come to understand it.

ROSE (*Gently, smiling*). I am going to try, dear. Really I am. It's evidently important to you.

(*She exits through hall.* GRIGGS *sits down as if he were very tired. A minute later,* CROSSMAN *comes from the direction of the dining room, carrying the Sunday papers. He looks at* BEN, *goes to him, hands him the front page.* BEN *takes it, nods, sits holding it.* CROSSMAN *crosses to a chair, sits down, begins to read the comic section. A second later,* NINA *comes down the stairs, comes into the room, starts to speak to* BEN *and* CROSSMAN, *changes her mind and sits down. Then* CONSTANCE, *in an old-fashioned flowered hat and carrying a large palmetto fan, comes through the hall and into the room.*)

CONSTANCE. I'm off to church. Anybody want anything just ring for Leon or Sophie. (*Bravely*) Want to come to church with me, Ned? (*He peers over his paper, amazed*) All right. I just thought— Well, Nick told us that you told him last night—

CROSSMAN (*Laughs*). I think perhaps I shall never again go out at night.

CONSTANCE. Oh, it's good for all of us to confide in somebody— (*She becomes conscious of* NINA *and* GRIGGS, *smiles awkwardly and then with great determination leans over and kisses* CROSSMAN) Good-by, darling.

(*Surprised, he gets up, stands watching her leave the room. Then he sits down, staring ahead.*)

NINA (*After a minute, hesitantly*). I've got a car and a full picnic basket and a cold bottle of wine. Would you— (*Turning to* CROSSMAN *and then to* GRIGGS) like to come along? I don't know where to go, but—

CROSSMAN. Got enough in your picnic basket for lunch *and* dinner?

NINA (*Smiles*). I think so.

CROSSMAN. Got a mandolin?

NINA (*Smiles*). No. Does that rule me out?

CROSSMAN. Almost. But we'll make do. The General whistles very well.

GRIGGS (*Smiles, gets up*). Is one bottle of wine enough on a Sunday?

NINA (*Laughs as she goes toward hall*). Not for the pure in heart. I'll get five or six more.

(GRIGGS *follows her out through hall.* CROSSMAN *gets up, folds the comic section, puts it under his arm, exits through hall. As he exits,* SOPHIE *comes on the porch. She begins to pile the breakfast dishes on a tray. She sees a half-used roll and a piece of bacon, fixes it for herself, goes out carrying the tray and chewing on the roll as the curtain falls.*)

Curtain

ACT TWO

SCENE II

SCENE: *The same. Nine-thirty that evening.*

AT RISE: NICK *is lying on the couch. Next to him, on the floor, is an empty champagne glass. On the table, in a silver cooler, is a bottle of champagne.* CONSTANCE *is sitting at the table playing solitaire and humming to the record on the phonograph. On the porch,* SOPHIE *is reading to* MRS. MARY ELLIS.

NICK (*Looks up from couch to* CONSTANCE, *irritably*). Please don't hum.

CONSTANCE. Sorry. I always like that so much, I—

NICK. And please don't talk. Mozart doesn't need it.

CONSTANCE. Haydn.

NICK. Mozart.

CONSTANCE (*Tartly*). I'm sorry but it's Haydn.

NICK. You know damn well I know what I'm talking about.

CONSTANCE. You don't know what you're talking about. Go look.

NICK (*Gets up, picks up his glass, goes to phonograph, shuts it off, looks down, turns away annoyed, picks up a champagne bottle, pours himself a drink, then brings the bottle to* CONSTANCE). Ready for another?

CONSTANCE. I haven't finished this.

(NICK *carries the bottle out to the porch.*)

MRS. ELLIS (*Looks up at him*). For the fourth time, we don't want any. Please go away. We're having a nice time. We're in the part I like best.

498

NICK. A nice time? Will I think such a time is a nice time when I am your age? I suppose so.

MRS. ELLIS. No, Mr. Denery. If you haven't learned to read at your age, you won't learn at mine.

NICK (*Laughs, pats her shoulder*). Never mind, I like you.

MRS. ELLIS. You must be damn hard up. People seldom like those who don't like them.

NICK (*Pleased*). You haven't forgotten how to flirt. Come on inside and talk to me. My wife disappears, everybody disappears— (*Stretches*) I'm bored, I'm bored.

MRS. ELLIS. And that's a state of sin, isn't it?

NICK. Unfortunately, it isn't. I've always said I can stand any pain, any trouble—but not boredom.

MRS. ELLIS. My advice is to try something intellectual for a change. Sit down with your champagne—on which you've been chewing since early afternoon—and try to make a paper hat out of the newspaper or get yourself a nice long piece of string.

NICK (*Goes to* SOPHIE). Sophie, come in and dance with me.

MRS. ELLIS (*Calls in*). Constance, whistle for Mr. Denery, please.

NICK (*To* SOPHIE). You don't want to sit here and read to Mrs. Ellis.

SOPHIE. Yes, sir, I do. I enjoy the adventures of Odysseus. And the dollar an hour Mrs. Ellis pays me for reading to her.

NICK (*Laughs, as* MRS. ELLIS *laughs*). Give you two dollars an hour to dance with me.

MRS. ELLIS. It's not nearly enough, Sophie.

NICK (*Pats* MRS. ELLIS). You're a corrupter of youth—you steal the best hours.

MRS. ELLIS (*Shakes his hand off her shoulder*). And you're a toucher: you constantly touch people or lean on them. Little moments of sensuality. One should have sensuality whole or not at all. Don't you find pecking at it ungratifying? There are many of you: the touchers and the leaners. All since the depression, is my theory.

NICK (*Laughs, pats her again*). You must have been quite a girl in your day.

MRS. ELLIS. I wasn't. I wasn't at all. (NICK *wanders into the room.* MRS. ELLIS *speaks to* SOPHIE) I was too good for those who wanted me and not good enough for those I wanted. Like Frederick, Sophie. Life can be hard for such people and they seldom understand why and end bitter and confused.

SOPHIE. I know.

MRS. ELLIS. Do you? Frederick is a nice boy, Sophie—and that is all. But that's more than most, and precious in a small way.

SOPHIE. Yes, I think so.

(MRS. ELLIS *smiles, pats her hand;* SOPHIE *begins again to read.*)

NICK (*Near the phonograph, to* CONSTANCE). Dance with me?

CONSTANCE. I don't know how any more.

NICK (*Turns away from the phonograph*). Has it been wise, Constance, to lose all the graces in the service of this house?

CONSTANCE. Do you think I wanted it that way?

NICK. I'm not sure you didn't. You could have married Ned, instead of dangling him around, the way you've done.

CONSTANCE. Ned has come here each summer because, well, because I guess this is about the only home he has. I loved Ned and honored him, but—I just wasn't in love with him when we were young. You know that, and you'd have been the first to tell me that you can't marry unless you're in love— (*He begins to laugh*) What are you laughing at?

NICK. "Can't marry unless you're in love." What do you think the rest of us did? I was in love with you. I've never been in love again.

CONSTANCE (*Very sharply*). *I don't want you to talk to me that way.* And I don't believe you. You fell in love with Nina and that's why you didn't come back— (*Desperately*) You're *very* much in love with Nina. Then and now. Then—

NICK. Have it your way. What are you so angry about? Want to know something: I've never been angry in my life. (*Turns to her, smiles*) In the end, we wouldn't have worked out. You're a good woman and I am not a good man.

CONSTANCE. Well, whatever the reason, things turned out for the best. (*Carefully*) About Ned. What did he say last night? I mean did he really talk about me?

NICK (*Expansively*). He said he loved you and wanted you and had wasted his life loving you and wanting you. And that he wasn't coming here any more. This is his last summer in this house.

CONSTANCE (*She turns, pained, startled*). His last summer? He said that? He really said it was his last summer—

(CARRIE *comes quickly into the room.*)

CARRIE. Has Fred come back?

NICK (*To her*). Well, where have *you* been? Come and have a drink and talk to me.

(*He moves to pour her a drink as she crosses to the porch.*)

CARRIE (*Softly, to* MRS. ELLIS). I've been everywhere. Everywhere possible. I even forced myself to call on Mr. Payson.

MRS. ELLIS. And what did he say?

CARRIE. That Fred came in to see him after he left here this morning, stayed a few minutes, no more, and he hasn't seen him since.

MRS. ELLIS. Ah, that's good.

CARRIE. What's good about it? It means we don't know where he's been since ten this morning. (*Softly, as she sits down*) I don't know what else to do or where else to look. What should I do? Shall I call the police, what else is there to do?

MRS. ELLIS. Nothing.

CARRIE. How can I do nothing? You shouldn't have made me threaten him. We were wrong. It wasn't important that he wanted to go to Europe with a man his own age. What harm was there in it?

MRS. ELLIS. All his life you've been plucking him this way and plucking him that. Do what you like. Call the police.

NICK (*Who has come to the door carrying a glass for* CARRIE. *He hears the last few speeches; gently*). Can I do anything, Carrie?

CARRIE. I don't know, Nick. I only found one person who had seen him, down by the water—

NICK. Is he—would he have—is that what you're thinking, Carrie?

CARRIE. I'm afraid, I'm afraid.

NICK (*Quickly, the kind of efficiency that comes with liquor and boredom*). Then come on, Carrie. You must go to the police right away. I'll get a boat. Tell the police to follow along. Right away.

(CARRIE *gets up. Starts toward* NICK. SOPHIE *gets up.*)

SOPHIE (*Angrily, in French, to* NICK). Do not enjoy the excitement so much. Stop being a fool.

NICK (*Amazed*). What?

SOPHIE (*In German*). I said don't enjoy yourself so much. Mind your business.

CARRIE. What? What is it, Sophie?

SOPHIE (*To* CARRIE). Frederick is in the cove down by the dock. He has been there all day.

NICK (*To* SOPHIE). You said I was a fool. I don't like such words, Sophie. I don't.

CARRIE (*Carefully, to* SOPHIE). You've let me go running about all day, frantic with terror—

SOPHIE. He wanted to be alone, Mrs. Ellis. That is not so terrible a thing to want.

CARRIE. How dare you take this on yourself? How dare you—

MRS. ELLIS. I hope this is not a sample of you as a mother-in-law.

SOPHIE (*Gently, to* CARRIE). He will return, Mrs. Ellis. Leave him alone.

NICK (*Softly*). Sophie, I think you owe me an apology. You are by way of being a rather sharp little girl underneath all that shyness, aren't you? I'm waiting. (*No answer*) I'm waiting.

MRS. ELLIS. Well, wait outside, will you?

(*He stares at her, turns, goes in the room.*)

NICK (*Very hurt, to* CONSTANCE). I don't think I like it around here, Constance. No, I don't like it.

(*He goes out left windows as* CONSTANCE *stares at him.*)

CARRIE. Since Frederick has confided in you, Sophie, perhaps you should go to him.

SOPHIE. He has not confided in me. Sometimes his troubles are his own.

(*She gets up, walks through room, sits down near* CONSTANCE, *who looks at her curiously. On the porch,* MRS. ELLIS *leans over and whispers to* CARRIE.)

CARRIE. Not tonight.

MRS. ELLIS. Why not tonight? We'll be leaving in the morning.

CARRIE. Because I've changed my mind. I think it best now that we let him go to Europe.

MRS. ELLIS (*Gets up*). He will not want to go to Europe. Haven't you understood that much?

CARRIE (*Hesitantly*). How do you know what he wants or feels—

MRS. ELLIS. I know. (*She comes into room, sits near* CONSTANCE *and* SOPHIE. *After a second* CARRIE *follows her in, stands near them*) Sophie, I think a decision had best be made now. There should be no further postponement.

CARRIE (*Very nervous*). This isn't the time. Fred will be angry—

MRS. ELLIS (*To* SOPHIE). I don't want to push you, child, but nothing will change, nothing. I know you've wanted to wait, and so did Frederick, both of you hoping that maybe— But it will all be the same a year from now. Miracles don't happen. I'm telling you the truth, Sophie.

SOPHIE. Yes, Mrs. Ellis, and I agree with you. Nothing will change. If Frederick is willing for an early marriage then I am also willing.

CONSTANCE. Is this the way it's been? *Willing* to marry, *willing* to *marry*—

SOPHIE (*Looks at her*). I do not use the correct word?

CONSTANCE (*To* MRS. ELLIS *and* CARRIE). If that's the way it is, then I am not willing. I thought it was two young people who—who—who loved each other. I didn't ever understand it, and I didn't ask questions, but— Willing to get married. What have you been thinking of, why— (*Sharply, hurt*) What kind of unpleasant thing has this been?

CARRIE. I—I know. I can't—

MRS. ELLIS (*To* CONSTANCE *and* CARRIE). Why don't you take each other by the hand and go outside and gather in the dew?

SOPHIE. I think Aunt Constance is sad that we do not speak of it in the romantic words of love.

CONSTANCE. Yes. I am. And shocked. When Carrie first talked to me about the marriage, I asked you immediately and you told me you were in love—

SOPHIE. I never told you that, Aunt Constance.

CONSTANCE. I don't remember your exact words but of course I understood— You mean you and Frederick have never been in love? Why? Then why have you—

SOPHIE. Aunt Constance, I do not wish to go on with my life as it has been. I have not been happy, and I cannot continue here. I cannot be what you have wished me to be, and I do not want the world you want for me. It is too late—

CONSTANCE (*Softly*). Too late? You were thirteen years old when you came here. I've tried to give you everything—

SOPHIE. I came from another world and in that world thirteen is not young. I know what you have tried to give me, and I am grateful. But it has been a foolish waste for us both.

CONSTANCE (*Softly*). Were you happy at home, Sophie?

SOPHIE. I did not think in such words.

CONSTANCE. Please tell me.

SOPHIE. I was comfortable with myself, if that is what you mean, and I am no longer.

CONSTANCE (*Gently, takes her hand*). I have been so wrong. And so careless in not seeing it. Do you want to go home now?

SOPHIE. No. My mother cannot— Well, it is not that easy. I do not— (*As if it were painful*) I do not wish to go home now.

CONSTANCE (*Puzzled*). It's perfectly simple for you to go home. Why, why isn't it?

SOPHIE. I do not want to say, Aunt Constance. I do not want to. (*With feeling*) Please do not talk of it any more. Please allow me to do what I wish to do, and know is best for me. (*Smiles*) And don't look such a way. Frederick and I will have a nice life, we will make it so.

(*Goes out.*)

CARRIE (*Sharply*). Don't be too disturbed, Constance. I have decided that Frederick should go to Europe and this time I am not going to allow any interference of any kind.

(FREDERICK *appears in the hall, comes into the room.*)

FREDERICK. I'm not going to Europe, Mother.

CARRIE (*Turns to him*). I have had a bad day. And I have thought of many things. I was mistaken and you were right. You must go wherever you want—however you want to go.

FREDERICK. I am not going, Mother. Payson made that very clear to me this morning.

MRS. ELLIS. Don't, Frederick. It's not necessary. I know.

FREDERICK. But evidently Mother doesn't. . . . Payson made it clear to me that I was not wanted and never had been unless I supplied the money.

(CONSTANCE *gets up, moves off to the porch.*)

CARRIE (*After a second*). I— Er— I don't believe he meant that. You just tell him that it's all been a mistake and there will certainly be money for the trip. Just go right back and say that, Frederick—

FREDERICK (*Very sharply*). Mother! I don't want to see him again! Ever.

CARRIE. You often imagine people don't like you for yourself. *I'll* go and tell Mr. Payson that it's all fixed now—

MRS. ELLIS. Carrie, you're an ass. (*To* FREDERICK) But I hope you haven't wasted today feeling bitter about Mr. Payson. You have no right to bitterness. No right at all. Why shouldn't Mr. Payson have wanted your money, though I must say he seems to have been rather boorish about not getting it. People like us should pay for the interest of people like him. Why should they want us otherwise? I don't believe he ever pretended to feel anything else about you.

FREDERICK (*Softly*). No, he never pretended.

MRS. ELLIS. Then understand that you've been the fool, and not he the villain. Take next week to be sad: a week's long enough to be sad in, if it's true sadness. Plenty long enough.

FREDERICK (*Smiles*). All right, Grandma. I'll take a week.
(SOPHIE *appears at the hall door.*)

SOPHIE (*To* FREDERICK). You have had no dinner? (*Puts out her hand*) Then come. I have made a tray for you.
(*He turns, goes to her, takes her hand, goes out.*)

MRS. ELLIS (*Gets up, looks at* CARRIE). Are you going to interfere this time, Carrie? (*No answer. Gently*) I hope not.

(*She goes out.* CARRIE *stands for a minute near the porch. Then she goes out to* CONSTANCE.)

CARRIE. I don't like it either.

CONSTANCE (*Wearily*). Whole thing sounds like the sale of a shore-front property. I don't know. Seems to me I've been so mixed up about so much. Well, maybe you all know what you're doing.

CARRIE. I don't know what I'm doing.

CONSTANCE. Why did you want the marriage, Carrie? I mean a month ago when you spoke to me—

CARRIE. I don't even know that.

CONSTANCE. You always seem so clear about everything. And so strong. Even when we were girls. I envied you that, Carrie, and wanted to be like you.

CARRIE (*Laughs*). Clear and strong? I wish I could tell you what I've missed and what I've wanted. Don't envy me, Con.

(*She exits toward hall and staircase. As she does,* NICK *comes in. He is now a little more drunk than when he went out.*)

NICK. Come on out, Carrie. It's wonderful night. Take you for a sail.

CARRIE (*Laughs*). Good night, Nick.

NICK (*As she goes up steps*). I'm lonely, Carrie. I wouldn't leave you if you were lonely. (*When she doesn't answer, he goes into room, looks around, sees* CONSTANCE *sitting on the porch, goes over, stands in the door looking out.*

After a second) I wish I wanted to go to bed with you, Con. I just can't want to. I don't know why. I just don't want it.

CONSTANCE (*Very sharply*). Stop talking that way. You've had too much to drink.

(*She gets up, comes into room. He grabs her arm.*)

NICK. Now you're angry again. (*Puts his arms around her*) I'll sing you a lullaby. Will you like that?

CONSTANCE. Look, Nick, you've been rather a trial tonight. Do go to bed.

NICK. I'm not going to bed. I'm lonely. I'm—

(*The phone rings,* CONSTANCE *goes to it.* NICK *pours himself a glass of champagne.*)

CONSTANCE. Yes? General Griggs isn't in, Rose. Oh. Yes. Just a minute. (*To* NICK) Rose Griggs wants to talk to *you.*

NICK. What's the matter, she got some new trouble?

CONSTANCE (*Annoyed*). Do you want the call or don't you?

NICK. Tell her I'm busy.

CONSTANCE (*In phone*). He's busy drinking, Rose. Shall I leave a message for General Griggs— Oh. (*She puts the phone down, annoyed*) She says it's absolutely and positively urgent that she speak with *you.* Not her husband. Absolutely and positively.

(*She exits through hall.* NICK *rises and goes to phone.*)

NICK. Look here, my dear, don't be telling people you want to speak to me and not to your husband. Sounds awful. (*Laughs*) Oh. A most agreeable doctor. Must get to know him. Look, you don't have to convince me. Save it for your husband. Oh, come on. You're getting like those people who believe their own press agents. Anyway, I once knew a woman with heart trouble and it gave her a nice color. You didn't go to the doctor to believe him— (*Sighs, listens*) All right, of course I'm sorry. It sounds jolly nice and serious and I apologize. (*Listens*) Oh. Well, that is kind of you. Yes, tell your brother I'd like to stay with him. Oh, by Friday, certainly. How old is your niece? Is she the one with the braces on her teeth? (NINA *appears from the hall entrance. She is followed by* GRIGGS *who is carrying the picnic basket*) No, I won't paint anything out. That big a hack I'm not. Yes, we'll have plenty of time together. You're a good friend. (*To* NINA *and* GRIGGS) Had a nice day? (*Into phone*) No, I'm talking to your husband. Oh. Good-by. Take care of yourself. (*He hangs up. To* GRIGGS) That was Rose. (*Gaily, to* NINA) I've had a dull day, darling. (CROSSMAN *comes in*) Where'd you skip to?

NINA. We drove over to Pass Christian.

NICK. Did you put the car in the garage?

CROSSMAN (*Gives* NINA *the keys*). Yes, all safe.

NICK. Did you drive, Ned? That heavy Isotta? (*To* NINA) Nobody who drinks as much as Ned should be driving that car. Or any car belonging to me.

NINA. And nobody as tight as you are should talk that way.

NICK (*Laughs*). Have a drink, Ned.

(*He brings* CROSSMAN *a glass.*)

CROSSMAN. Thank you, no.

(NICK *turns, hands glass to* GRIGGS.)

GRIGGS. No, thank you.

NICK. What the hell is this? Refusing to have a drink with me— (*To* CROSSMAN) I'm trying to apologize to you. Now take the drink—

NINA. Nick, please—

NICK. Stay out of it, Nina. Women don't know anything about the etiquette of drinking.

CROSSMAN (*Laughs*). Has it got etiquette now? (*As* NICK *again hands him glass. Shakes his head*) Thank you.

NICK (*Drunk, hurt*). Look here, old boy, I say in the light of what's happened, you've just got to take this. It's my way of apologizing and I shouldn't have to explain that to a gentleman.

(*He grabs* CROSSMAN'S *arm, playfully presses the glass to* CROSSMAN'S *lips.*)

CROSSMAN (*Quietly*). Don't do that.

NICK. Come on, old boy. If I have to pour it down you—

CROSSMAN. Don't do that.

(NICK, *laughing, presses the glass hard against* CROSSMAN'S *mouth.* CROSSMAN *pushes the glass and it falls to the floor.*)

NINA (*Sits down*). Well, we got rid of that glass. But there are plenty more, Nick.

NICK (*Sad, but firm to* CROSSMAN). Now *you've* put *yourself* on the defensive, my friend. That's always tactically unwise, isn't it, General Griggs?

GRIGGS. I know nothing of tactics, Mr. Denery. Certainly not of yours.

NICK. Then what the hell are you doing as a general?

GRIGGS. Masquerading. They had a costume left over and they lent it to me.

NICK (*To* CROSSMAN). I'm waiting, Ned. Pour yourself a drink, and make *your* apologies.

CROSSMAN. You are just exactly the way I remember you. And that I wouldn't have believed of any man.

(*He turns, goes out.*)

NICK (*Like a hurt child*). What the hell does that mean? (*Calling*) Hey, Ned. Come on back and have it your way. (*Gets no answer, turns, hearty again*) Come on, General. Have a bottle with me.

NINA. Are we going to start again?

NICK. General, got something to tell you: your wife telephoned but she didn't want to speak to you.

GRIGGS. That's most understandable. Good night, Mrs. Denery, and thank you for a pleasant day.

NICK. But she'll want to speak to you in the morning. Better stick around in the morning.

GRIGGS (*Stares at him*). Thank you. Good night.

NICK (*Following him*). I think you're doing the wrong

thing, wanting to leave Rose. You're going to be lonely at your age without—

GRIGGS. If my wife wishes to consult you, Mr. Denery, that's her business. But I don't wish to consult you.

(*He exits.*)

NICK. Sorry. Forget it.

(NICK *turns, takes his drink to the couch, lies down.*)

NINA (*After a pause*). You know, it's a nasty business hating yourself.

NICK. Who's silly enough to do that?

NINA. Me.

NICK (*Warmly*). Come on over here, darling, and tell me about yourself. I've missed you.

NINA. To hate yourself, all the time.

NICK. I love you, Nina.

NINA (*Gets up*). Here we go with that routine. Now you'll bait me until I tell you that you've never loved any woman, or any man, nor ever will. (*Wearily*) I'll be glad to get out of this house before Constance finds you out. She can go back to sleeping with her dreams. (*After a second*) You still think you can wind up everybody's affairs by Friday?

NICK. Oh, sure. Friday. Then we're going up to spend a month with Rose's brother, Henry something or other. In New Orleans.

NINA (*Carefully*). What are you talking about?

NICK. Rose fixed it for me. I'm going to do a portrait of her niece, the heiress to the fortune. The girl is balding and has braces. (*Looks at her*) Five thousand dollars.

NINA. Are you crazy?

NICK. Not a bit.

NINA. It's all right to kid around here—

NICK (*Gets up*). I *don't* know what you mean.

NINA (*Violently*). Please don't let's talk this way. Just tell Mrs. Griggs that you've changed your mind—

NICK. I demand that you tell me what you mean.

NINA (*Angrily*). How many years have we avoided saying
it? Why must you walk into it now? (*Pauses, looks at
him*) All right. Maybe it's time: you haven't finished a
portrait in twelve years. And money isn't your reason
for wanting to do this portrait. You're setting up a silly
flirtation with Mrs. Griggs. I'm not going to New Orleans, Nick. I am not going to watch it all again. I can't
go on this way with myself— (*Then softly*) Don't go.
Call it off. You know how it will end. Please let's don't
this time— We're not young any more, Nick. Somewhere
we must have learned something.

NICK (*Softly, carefully*). If I haven't finished every picture
I started it's because I'm good enough to know they
weren't good enough. All these years you never understood that? I think I will never forgive you for talking
that way.

NINA. Your trouble is that you're an amateur, a gifted amateur. And like all amateurs you have very handsome
reasons for what you do not finish—between trains and
boats.

NICK. You have thought that about me, all these years?

NINA. Yes.

NICK. Then it was good of you and loyal to pretend you
believed in me.

NINA. Good? Loyal? What do they mean? I loved you.

NICK. Yes, good and loyal. But I, too, have a little vanity—
(*She laughs; he comes to her*) And no man can bear to
live with a woman who feels that way about his work.
I think you ought to leave tomorrow, Nina. For good
and forever.

NINA (*Softly*). Yes. (*She turns*) Yes, of course.

(*She starts to exit. He follows behind her, talking.*)

NICK. But it must be different this time. Remember I said
years ago— "Ten times of threatening is out, Nina," I
said—the tenth time you stay gone.

NINA. All right. Ten times is out. (*Quietly, desperately*) I promise for good and forever.

NICK (*She is climbing the staircase*). This time, spare yourself the return. And the begging and the self-humiliation and the self-hate. And the disgusting self-contempt. This time they won't do any good. (*He is following her but we cannot see him*) Let's write it down, darling. And have a drink to seal it.

(*On the words "disgusting self-contempt,"* CONSTANCE *comes into the hall. She hears the words, recognizes* NICK's *voice and stands, frowning, and thoughtful. Then she turns out the lights on the porch, puts on all lights except one lamp, comes back into the living room and begins to empty the ashtrays, etc.* SOPHIE *comes into the room carrying pillow, sheets, quilts, a glass of milk, and crosses to couch. Without speaking,* CONSTANCE *moves to help her and together they begin to make the couch for the night.*)

SOPHIE (*After a minute, smiles*). Do not worry for me, Aunt Constance.

CONSTANCE. I can't help it.

SOPHIE. I think perhaps you worry sometimes in order that you should not think.

CONSTANCE (*Smiles*). Yes, maybe. I won't say any more. I'll be lonely without you, Sophie. I don't like being alone, any more. It's not a good way to live. And with you married, I'll be alone forever, unless— Well, Ned's loved me and it's been such a waste, such a waste. I know it now but—well— I don't know. (*Shyly, as a young girl would say it*) You understand, Sophie? (SOPHIE *stares at her, frowning. Then* CONSTANCE *speaks happily*) Sleep well, dear.

(*She comes to* SOPHIE, *kisses her, exits, closing door.* SOPHIE *finishes with the bed, brings her milk to the bed table, takes off her robe, puts it around her shoulders, gets into* bed, and lies quietly, thinking. *Then she turns as she hears footsteps in the hall and she is staring at the door as* NICK *opens it. He trips over a chair, recovers himself, turns on a lamp.*)

NICK (*Sharply*). Constance! What is this—a boys' school with lights out at eleven! (*He sees* SOPHIE) Where's your aunt? I want to talk to her. What are you doing?

SOPHIE. I think I am asleep, Mr. Denery.

NICK. You're cute. Maybe too cute. (*He pours himself a drink*) I'm going down to the tavern and see if I can get up a beach party. Tell your aunt. Just tell her that. (*Going toward door*) Want to come? You couldn't be more welcome. (*She shakes her head*) Oh, come on. Throw on a coat. I'm not mad at you any more. (*He comes back toward her, looks down at her*) I couldn't paint you, Sophie. You're too thin. Damn shame you're so thin. (*Suddenly sits down on bed*) I'm sick of trouble. Aren't you? Like to drive away with me for a few days? (*Smiles at her*) Nobody would care. And we could be happy. I hate people not being happy. (*He lies down. His head is now on her knees*) Move your knees, baby, they're bony. And get me a drink.

SOPHIE. Take the bottle upstairs, Mr. Denery.

NICK. Get me a drink. And make it poison. (*Slowly, wearily, she gets up, takes his glass, goes to bottle, pours drink. He begins to sing. She brings glass back to him. He reaches up to take the glass, decides to pull her toward him, and spills the liquid on the bed*) Clumsy, honey, clumsy. But I'll forgive you.

(*He is holding her, and laughing.*)

SOPHIE (*Calmly*). Please go somewhere else, Mr. Denery.

NICK (*Springs up, drunk-angry*). People aren't usually rude to me, Sophie. Poor little girls always turn rude when they're about to marry rich little boys. What a life you're going to have. That boy doesn't even know what's the matter with him—

SOPHIE (*Very sharply*). Please, Mr. Denery, go away.

NICK (*Laughs*). Oh, you know what's the matter with him? No European would be as innocent of the world as you pretend. (*Delighted*) I tricked you into telling me. Know that?

SOPHIE. You are drunk and I am tired. Please go away.

NICK (*Sits down across the room*). Go to sleep, child. I'm not disturbing you. (*She stares at him, decides she can't move him, gets into bed, picks up a book, begins to read*) I won't say a word. Ssh. Sophie's reading. Do you like to read? Know the best way to read? With someone you love. Out loud. Ever try it that way, honey? (*He gets up, comes to bed, stands near her, speaking over her shoulder*) I used to know a lot of poetry. Brought up on Millay. My candle and all that. "I had to be a liar. My mother was a leprechaun, my father was a friar." Crazy for the girl. (*Leans over and kisses her hair. She pulls her head away*) Ever wash your hair in champagne, darling? I knew a woman once. (*Tips the glass over her head*) Let's try it.

SOPHIE (*Sharply*). Let us not try it again.

NICK (*Sits down beside her*). Now for God's sake don't get angry. (*Takes her shoulders and shakes her*) I'm sick of angry women. All men are sick of angry women, if angry women knew the truth. Sophie, we can always go away and starve. I'll manage to fall in love with you.

SOPHIE (*He is holding her*). Mr. Denery, I am sick of you.

NICK (*Softly*). Tell me you don't like me and I will go away and not come back.

SOPHIE. No, sir. I do not like you.

NICK. People have hated me. But nobody's ever not liked me. If I thought you weren't flirting, I'd be hurt. Is there any aspirin downstairs? If you kiss me, Sophie, be kind to me for just a minute, I'll go away. I may come back another day, but I'll go all by myself— (*Desperately*) Please, Sophie, please.

SOPHIE (*Sighs, holds up her side face to him*). All right. Then you will go, remember. (*He takes her in his arms, pulls her down on the bed. She struggles to get away from him. She speaks angrily*) Do not make yourself such a clown. (*When she cannot get away from him*) I will call your wife, Mr. Denery.

NICK (*Delighted*). That would be fun, go ahead. We're getting a divorce. Sophie, let's make this night our night. God, Julie, if you only knew what I've been through—

SOPHIE (*Violently*). Oh shut up.

(*She pulls away from him with great effort. He catches her robe and rolls over on it.*)

NICK (*Giggles as he settles down comfortably*). Come on back. It's nice and warm here and I love you very much. But we've got to get some sleep, darling. Really we have to.

(*Then he turns over and lies still. She stands looking at him.*)

SOPHIE (*After a minute*). Get up, Mr. Denery. I will help you upstairs. (*No answer*) Please, please get up.

NICK (*Gently, half passed-out*). It's raining out. Just tell the concierge I'm your brother. She'll understa— (*The words fade off.* SOPHIE *waits a second and then leans over and with great strength begins to shake him*) Stop that. (*He passes out, begins to breathe heavily. She turns, goes to hall, stands at the foot of the steps. Then she changes her mind and comes back into the room. She goes to the couch, stands, looking at him, decides to pull him by the legs. Softly*) I'll go away in a few minutes. Don't be so young. Have a little pity. I am old and sick.

(SOPHIE *draws back, moves slowly to the other side of the room as the curtain falls.*)

Curtain

ACT THREE

SCENE: *Seven o'clock the next morning.* NICK *is asleep on the couch.* SOPHIE *is sitting in a chair, drinking a cup of coffee. A minute after the rise of the curtain,* MRS. ELLIS *comes down the steps, comes into the room.*

MRS. ELLIS. I heard you bumping around in the kitchen, Sophie. The older you get the less you sleep, and the more you look forward to meals. Particularly breakfast, because you've been alone all night, and the nights are the hardest— (*She sees* NICK, *stares, moves over to look at him.*) What is this?

SOPHIE. It is Mr. Denery.

MRS. ELLIS (*Turns to stare at her*). What's he doing down here?

SOPHIE. He became drunk and went to sleep.

MRS. ELLIS. He has been here all night? (SOPHIE *nods*) What's the matter with you? Get him out of here immediately.

SOPHIE. I cannot move him. I tried. Shall I get you some coffee?

MRS. ELLIS (*Staring at her*). Are you being silly, Sophie? Sometimes it is very hard to tell with you. Why didn't you call Constance or Mrs. Denery?

SOPHIE. I did not know what to do. Mr. and Mrs. Denery had some trouble between them, or so he said, and I thought it might be worse for her if— (*Smiles*) Is it so much? He was just a little foolish and sleepy. (*Goes toward door*) I will get Leon and Sadie and we will take him upstairs.

MRS. ELLIS (*Crosses to door*). You will not get Leon and Sadie. Rose Griggs may be President of the gossip club for summer Anglo-Saxons, but Leon is certainly President of the Negro chapter. You will get this, er, out of here before anybody else sees him. (*She crosses back to bed, pulls blanket off* NICK) At least he's dressed. Bring me that cup of coffee. (SOPHIE *brings cup*) Mr. Denery! Sit up! (NICK *moves his head slightly. To* SOPHIE) Hold his head up.

(SOPHIE *holds* NICK's *head;* MRS. ELLIS *tries to make him drink.*)

NICK (*Very softly*). Please leave me alone.

MRS. ELLIS (*Shouting in his ear*). Mr. Denery, lisen to me. *You are to get up and get out of here immediately.*

NICK (*Giving a bewildered look around the room; then he closes his eyes*). Julie.

SOPHIE. He has been speaking of Julie most of the night.

MRS. ELLIS (*Very sharply*). Shall I wake your wife and see if she can locate Julie for you, or would you rather be cremated here? Get up, Mr. Denery.

(*He opens his eyes, shuts them again.*)

SOPHIE. You see how it is? (*She tries to pull her robe from under him*) Would you get off my robe, Mr. Denery?

MRS. ELLIS (*Stares at her*). Sophie, you're a damned little ninny. (*Very loudly, to* NICK) Now get up. You have no right to be here. You must get up immediately. I say *you*, you get up. (*Shouting*) Get to your room. Get out of here.

NICK (*Turns, opens his eyes, half sits up, speaks gently*). Don't scream at me, Mrs. Ellis. (*Sees* SOPHIE, *begins to realize where he is, groans deeply*) I passed out?

SOPHIE. Yes, sir. Most deeply.

MRS. ELLIS. I'm sure after this he won't mind if you don't call him "sir."

NICK. Champagne's always been a lousy drink for me. How did I get down here? (*He turns over*) I'm sorry, child. What happened?

SOPHIE. You fell asleep.

NICK (*Hesitantly*). Did I— God, I'm a fool. What did I— Did I do anything or say anything? Tell me, Sophie.

MRS. ELLIS. Please get up and get out of here.

NICK. I'm thirsty. I want a quart of water. Or a bottle of beer. Get me a bottle of cold beer, Sophie, will you? (*Looks around the bed*) Where'd you sleep? Get me the beer, will you?

MRS. ELLIS (*Carefully*). Mr. Denery, you are in Sophie's bed, in the living room of a house in a small Southern town where for a hundred and fifty years it has been impossible to take a daily bath without everybody in town advising you not to dry out your skin. You know that as well as I do. Now get up and go out by the side lawn to the boathouse. Put your head under water, or however you usually treat these matters, and come back through the front door for breakfast.

NICK (*Laughs*). I couldn't eat breakfast.

MRS. ELLIS. I don't find you cute. I find only that you can harm a young girl. Do please understand that.

NICK. Yes, I do. And I'm sorry. (*He sits up, untangling himself from the robe*) What's this? Oh, Sophie, child, I must have been a nuisance. I am *so* sorry.

MRS. ELLIS (*Very loudly*). Get up and get the hell out of here.

(*The door opens and* ROSE, *carrying her overnight handbag, sticks her head in.*)

ROSE (*To* MRS. ELLIS, *who is directly on a line with the door*). You frightened me. I could hear you outside on the lawn, so early. Oh, Nick. How nice you're downstairs. I never expected it— (*Her voice trails off as she sees* SOPHIE *and realizes* NICK *is on the bed*) Oh. (*Giggles, hesitantly*) You look like you just woke up, Nick. I mean, just woke up where you are.

MRS. ELLIS (*To* NICK). Well, that's that. Perhaps you wanted it this way, Mr. Denery.

(*She starts out as* LEON *appears carrying the coffee urn.* ROSE *stands staring at* NICK.)

LEON (*Very curious, but very hesitant in doorway*). Should I put it here this morning, like every day, or—

MRS. ELLIS. Who told you, Leon?

LEON. Told me what, Mrs. Ellis? Sadie says take on in the urn—

MRS. ELLIS. I'm not talking about the urn. Who told you about Mr. Denery being here?

LEON. Told me? Why Miss Sophie came in for coffee for them.

MRS. ELLIS (*After a second, shrugs, points to coffee urn*). Take it into the dining room.

LEON. You want me come back and straighten up, Miss Sophie?

MRS. ELLIS (*Waves him out*). Mrs. Griggs will be glad to straighten up.

(*She exits.*)

ROSE (*Softly to* NICK). You were here all night? I come back needing your help and advice as I've never before needed anything. And I find you—

NICK. Rose, please stop moving about. You're making me seasick. And would you go outside? I'd like to speak to Sophie.

ROSE. I am waiting for you to explain, Nick. I don't understand.

NICK. There is no need for you to understand.

ROSE. I'm not judging you. I know that there's probably a good explanation— But please tell me, Nick, what happened and then I won't be angry.

NICK. What the hell are you talking about? What's it your business? Now go upstairs, Rose.

ROSE (*Softly, indignant*). "Go upstairs, Rose," "What's it

your business?" After I work my head off getting the commission of the portrait for you and after I go to the doctor's on your advice, although I never would have gone if I had known, and I come back here and find you this way. (*Sits down*) You've hurt me and you picked a mighty bad day to do it.

(*The door opens and* CONSTANCE *comes in. She goes to* NICK, *stands looking at him.*)

CONSTANCE. Nick, I want you to go to that window and look across the street. (*He stares at her. Then he gets up slowly and slowly moves to the window*) The Carters have three extra guests on their breakfast porch, the Gable sisters are unexpectedly entertaining— (*With feeling*) This house was not built to be stared at.

NICK (*Gently*). It can't be that bad, Constance.

CONSTANCE. It is just that bad.

NICK. I'm sorry. I was silly and drunk but there's no sense making more out of it than that.

CONSTANCE. I am not making anything out of it. But I know what is being made out of it. In your elegant way of life, I daresay this is an ordinary occurrence. But not in our village. (*The telephone rings.* CONSTANCE *picks up phone, says "Hello," pauses, "Hello, Mrs. Sims." Then her face becomes angry and she hangs up. She stands looking at the phone, and then takes it off the hook. Turns to* NICK) Please explain to me what happened. (*Points to telephone and then across the street*) I only know what they know.

SOPHIE. Mr. Denery came down looking for someone to talk to. He saw me, recited a little poetry, spoke to me of his troubles, tried to embrace me in a most mild fashion. He was uncertain of my name and continued throughout the night to call me Julie although twice he called for Cecile. And fell into so deep a sleep that I could not move him. Alcohol. It is the same in my country, every country.

CONSTANCE (*Softly, as if it pained her*). You are taking a very light tone about it, Sophie.

SOPHIE (*Turns away, goes toward couch, and through the next speeches will strip the bed and pile the clothes*). I will speak whichever way you think most fits the drama, Aunt Constance.

CONSTANCE. Will you tell me why you stayed in the room? Why didn't you come and call me, or—

NICK. Oh, look here. It's obvious. The kid didn't want to make any fuss and thought I'd wake up and go any minute. Damn nice of you, Sophie, and I'm grateful.

CONSTANCE. It was the most dangerous "niceness" I've ever heard of.

(SOPHIE *looks up, stares at* CONSTANCE.)

NICK. I know it's hard for you, Constance, but it's not all that much.

CONSTANCE. Isn't it? You've looked out of the window. Now go down to the drugstore and listen to them and I think you'll change your mind.

NICK. Look. A foolish guy drinks, passes out—

ROSE (*Amazed as she turns to look at* SOPHIE). Why look at Sophie. Just as calm as can be. Making the bed. Like it happened to her every night.

CONSTANCE (*Turns, realizes* ROSE *is in the room*). What are you doing here, Rose?

ROSE. Sitting here thinking that no man sleeps in girl's bed unless she gives him to understand— (CONSTANCE *stares at her*) You can blame Nick all you like. But you know very well that a nice girl would have screamed.

CONSTANCE. How dare you talk this way? Whatever gave you the right— I hope it will be convenient for you to leave today. I will apologize to the General.

ROSE (*Softly*). That's all right, Constance. I must leave today, in any case. You see, I have to— (*Sighs, sincerely*) You won't be mad at me for long when you know the story. Oh, I'm very tired now. Could I have my breakfast in bed? Doctor's orders. (*She goes out, passes* CROSSMAN *who is coming in. In sepulchral tones*) Good morning, dear Ned. (*Then in a sudden burst*) Have you heard—?

CROSSMAN (*cheerful*). Good morning. Yes, I've heard. I'm not the one deaf man in town.

(*Passes her. She stares at his back, reluctantly exits.*)

CONSTANCE (*Turns*). Ned, what should we do?

CROSSMAN. Is there always something that can be done, remedied, patched, pulled apart and put together again? There is nothing to "do," Con. (*Smiles to* SOPHIE, *amused*) How are you, Sophie?

SOPHIE. I am all right, Mr. Ned.

NICK. Ned, is it as bad as (*Gestures toward window and* CONSTANCE) Constance thinks?

CONSTANCE. What's the difference to you? You're just sitting there telling yourself what provincial people we are and how you wish you were in the Ritz bar with people who would find it amusing with their lunch. (*Very angrily*) You came here as my friend and in our small life—in our terms—you have dishonored my house. It has taken me too many years to find out that you—

CROSSMAN. All right, Con, maybe that's the truth; but what's the good of discussing Nick's character and habits now?

NICK (*Sincerely, to* CONSTANCE). Whatever you think of me, I didn't want this. I know what it will mean to Sophie and I'll stay here and face anything that will help you. Anything I can say or do—

SOPHIE (*She finishes folding the clothes*). What will it "mean" to me, Mr. Ned?

CONSTANCE (*Softly*). You're old enough to know. And I believe you do know.

SOPHIE. I want to know from Mr. Ned what he thinks.

CROSSMAN (*To* SOPHIE). I know what you want to know: the Ellis name is a powerful name. They won't be gossiped about out loud. They won't gossip about you and they won't listen to gossip about you. In their own way they'll take care of things. (*Carefully*) You can be quite sure of that. Quite sure.

SOPHIE (*After a second*). And that is all?

CROSSMAN. That is all.

SOPHIE (*Softly, carefully*). Thank you, Mr. Ned.

CONSTANCE. Take care of things? She hasn't done anything. Except be stupid. The Tuckerman name is as good as the Ellis name—

CROSSMAN. Yes, yes. Sure enough.

(SOPHIE *looks at* CROSSMAN, *exits. She passes* LEON *in the hall. He is carrying his hat.*)

LEON. Mrs. Ellis is cutting up about her breakfast. And Sadie's waiting for orders. We're messed this morning, for good.

CONSTANCE. Not at all. Tell Sadie I'm coming. (*She goes toward door*) What's your hat for, Leon?

LEON. Well, kind of a hot sun today.

CONSTANCE. Not in here. Rest your hat: you'll have plenty of time to gossip when the sun goes down.

(*She goes out.*)

NICK (*Miserably*). Ned. Ned, you understand I never thought it would make all this— Is Constance being— I mean, is she being old-maid fussy or is it really unpleasant—

CROSSMAN. It is unpleasant. She loves the girl, and she's worried for her.

NICK (*Groans*). If I could do something—

CROSSMAN. You did; but don't make too much of it.

NICK (*The first kind word he's heard*). Thank you, boy.

CROSSMAN. Or too little. (NICK *groans*) Nobody will blame

you too much. The girl's a foreigner and they don't understand her and therefore don't like her. You're a home-town boy and as such you didn't do anything they wouldn't do. Boys will be boys and in the South there's no age limit on boyishness. Therefore, she led you on, or whatever is this morning's phrase. You'll come off all right. But then I imagine you always do.

NICK. You think this is coming off all right?

CROSSMAN. No, I don't.

NICK. I didn't even want her. Never thought of her that way.

CROSSMAN (*Too sympathetic*). That *is* too bad. Better luck next time. You're young—in spirit.

(*He exits into hall toward dining room as* HILDA, *carrying a jewel case, and hat box, comes down the steps. She has on her hat and gloves.*)

NICK (*Who is sitting on a line with the door and sees her, speaks in German*). Where you going?

HILDA (*In German*). Good morning, sir. I am taking madame's luggage to the nine-thirty train.

(*She moves off as* NINA *appears.* NINA *has on a hat and gloves. On her heels is* ROSE *in a fluffy negligee.* ROSE *is talking as she follows* NINA *down the steps.*)

ROSE. I'm not trying to excuse him. Of course it was indiscreet but you're a woman of the world, Nina, and you know what young girls are with a tipsy man. Nina, do believe that I saw them this morning and he didn't have the slightest interest in her. Nina—

NINA (*Turns to her, very pleasantly*). I know it's eccentric of me, Mrs. Griggs, but I dislike being called by my first name before midnight.

ROSE (*Hurt, softly*). You shouldn't allow yourself such a nasty snub. I'm only trying to help Nick. I know him well enough to know that he didn't do a thing— (NINA *laughs*) He's been my good friend. I'm trying to be a friend to him.

NINA. You will have every opportunity.

NICK (*Very angry*). Will you please not stand there in the hall discussing me?

ROSE. Oh! (*Looks at* NICK, *then at* NINA, *steps back into hall, calls toward kitchen*) Leon! Could I have my tray upstairs? (*As she goes past room and upstairs*) Anybody seen my husband this morning?

(*Exits.*)

NICK. Nina. (*She comes in*) I just want to say before you go that they're making an awful row about nothing—

NINA. You don't owe me an explanation, Nick.

NICK. Nothing happened, Nina, I swear. Nothing happened.

NINA. Try out phrases like "nothing happened" on women like Mrs. Griggs.

NICK (*Smiles*). I'm sorry as all hell but they sure are cutting up—

NINA. Well, it is a tasty little story. Particularly for a girl who is going to be married.

NICK. My God, I'd forgotten about the boy. I must say he's an easy boy to forget about. Now I'll have to take *him* out and explain—

NINA. Don't do that, Nick. He isn't a fool.

NICK (*Looks around, thinking of anything to keep her in the room*). Shall I get you a cup of coffee, darling?

NINA. No. Darling will have it on the train.

(*She turns.*)

NICK. Nina, I swear I didn't sleep with her.

NINA. I believe you. The girl doesn't like you.

NICK. Doesn't she? She's been very kind to me. She could have raised hell. That doesn't sound as if she doesn't like me. (NINA *laughs*) Don't laugh at me this morning. (*After a second*) What can I do for her, Nina?

NINA. You used to send wicker hampers of white roses. With a card saying "White for purity and sad parting."

NICK. Stop being nasty to me. (*Then he smiles and comes toward her*) Or maybe it's a good sign.

NINA. It isn't. I just say these things by rote. (*Turns*) I don't know how long I'll be in New York, but you can call Horace and he'll take care of the legal stuff for us.

NICK (*Close to her*). I told you last night that I would agree to the separation because I knew with what justice you wanted to leave me.

NINA (*Coldly*). That's not at all what you said.

NICK. I was tight. It was what I meant to say—

NINA (*Very angry*). You're lying. You said just what you meant to say: I was to leave. And not make you sick with my usual begging to come back—

NICK. Stop, Nina. Take any kind of revenge you want, but—please—some other day. (*Leans down, puts his face against her face*) Don't leave me. Don't ever leave me. We've had good times, wild times. They made up for what was bad and they always will. Most people don't get that much. We've only had one trouble; you hate yourself for loving me. Because you have contempt for me.

NINA. For myself. I have no right—

NICK. No, nobody has. No right at all.

NINA. I wouldn't have married you, Nick, if I had known—

NICK. You would have married me. Or somebody like me. You've needed to look down on me, darling. You've needed to make fun of me. And to be ashamed of yourself for doing it.

NINA (*Softly*). Am I that sick?

NICK. I don't know about such words. You found the man you deserved. That's all. I am no better and no worse than what you really wanted. You like to—to demean yourself. And so you chose me. You must say I haven't minded much. Because I've always loved you and known we'd last it out. Come back to me, Nina, without

shame in wanting to. (*He leans down, kisses her neck*)
Put up with me a little longer, kid. I'm getting older
and I'll soon wear down.

NINA (*She smiles, touched*). I've never heard you speak
of getting old.

NICK (*Quickly*). Yes. (*Then*) The *Ile* sails next week.
Let's get on. We'll have fun. Tell me we're together
again and you're happy. Say it, Nina, quick.

NINA. I'm happy.

(*He takes her in his arms, kisses her. Then he stands away,
looks at her, and smiles shyly.*)

NICK. There'll be no more of what you call my "home-
comings." Old friends and all that. They are damn
bores, with empty lives.

NINA. Is that so different from us?

NICK. If we could only do something for the kid. Take her
with us, get her out of here until they get tired of the
gossip—

NINA (*Laughs*). I don't think we will take her with us.

NICK (*Laughs*). Now, now. You know what I mean.

NINA. I know what you mean—and we're not taking her
with us.

NICK. I suppose there isn't anything to do. (*Softly, his
hand to his head*) I feel sick, Nina.

NINA. You've got a hangover.

NICK. It's more than that. I've got a sore throat and my
back aches. Come on, darling, let's get on the train.

NINA. You go. I'll stay and see if there's anything I can do.
That's what you really want. Go on, Nicky. Maybe it's
best.

NICK. I couldn't do that.

NINA. Don't waste time, darling. You'll miss the train. I'll
bring your clothes with me.

NICK (*Laughs, ruefully*). If you didn't see through me so
fast, you wouldn't dislike yourself so much. (*Comes to*

her) You're a wonderful girl. It's wonderful of you to take all this on—

NINA. I've had practice.

NICK. (*Hurt*). That's not true. You know this never happened before.

NINA (*Smiles*). Nicky, it always confuses you that the fifth time something happens it varies slightly from the second and fourth. No, it never happened in this house before. Cora had a husband and Sylvia wanted one. And this isn't a hotel in Antibes, and Sophie is not a rich Egyptian. And this time you didn't break your arm on a boat deck and it isn't 1928—

NICK. This is your day, Nina. But pass up the chance to play it too hard, will you? Take me or leave me now but don't—

NINA. You're right. Please go, darling. Your staying won't do any good. Neither will mine, but maybe—

NICK. When will you come? I tell you what: you take the car and drive to Mobile. I'll get off there and wait at the Battle House. Then we can drive the rest of the way together. Must be somewhere in Mobile I can waste time for a few hours—

NINA (*Gaily*). I'm sure. But let's have a week's rest. Now go on.

NICK (*Takes her in his arms*). I love you, Nina. And we'll have the best time of our lives. Good luck, darling. And thank you. (*He kisses her*) They won't rag you, nobody ever does. We'll get the bridal suite on the *Ile* and have all our meals in bed. (*He moves away*) If you possibly can, bring the new portrait with you. I can finish it now. And try to get me the old portrait, darling. Maybe Constance will sell it to you—(NINA *laughs*) All right. Think what you want and I'll be what I am. I love you and you love me and that's that and always will be.

(*He exits. She stands quietly.*)

NINA. You love me and I love you and that's that and always will be. (*Then she turns, goes to the bell cord, pulls it. After a second,* CONSTANCE *appears in the hall.* NINA *does not turn*) Leon, could I have breakfast on the porch?

CONSTANCE (*In the doorway. She is carrying a tray*). Yes, of course. I'll tell Leon to bring it.

(NINA *turns, stares at her.*)

NINA. I am very sorry, Constance.

CONSTANCE. I am sorry, too, my dear.

NINA. I don't know what else to say. I wish—

CONSTANCE. There's nothing for us to say. (*There is an awkward pause*) Well. I'll tell Leon. Old lady Ellis is having her second breakfast. She always does on her last day. I don't know why. (*She starts out as* CARRIE, *followed by* FREDERICK, *comes down the steps.* CARRIE *has on her hat, etc., as if she were ready for traveling.* FREDERICK *is carrying two valises*) Shall I send breakfast up to Nick?

NINA (*Very quickly*). No, no. I'll just have mine and—

FREDERICK (*Calling to* CONSTANCE). Where's Sophie?

CONSTANCE. I'll send her in.

FREDERICK (*Smiles*). Don't sound so solemn, Miss Constance.

CONSTANCE (*Sharply*). I didn't mean to.

(*She disappears in the direction of the dining room.* FREDERICK *and* CARRIE *come into the room.*)

NINA. Mr. Ellis, I should be carrying a sign that says my husband is deeply sorry and so am I.

(*He smiles at her. She turns, goes out on the porch, closes the door behind her.*)

CARRIE (*Hesitantly*). She's a nice woman, I think. Must be a hard life for her.

FREDERICK (*Laughs*). I don't think so. (*Turns as he hears*

SOPHIE *in the hall*) Now remember, Mother. (SOPHIE *appears in the door*. FREDERICK *goes to her, takes her chin in his hand, kisses her*) I want to tell you something fast. I don't know how to explain it but I'm kind of glad this foolishness happened. It makes you seem closer to me, some silly way. You must believe that, although I can't make it clear. Now there are two things to do right away. Your choice.

SOPHIE. I have made bad gossip for you, Frederick. We must speak about that. Right away.

FREDERICK. There's no need to speak about it again. It's a comic story and that's all. And you must begin to laugh about it.

SOPHIE (*Smiles*). I did laugh but nobody would laugh with me. And nobody will laugh in New Orleans, either. Is that not so, Mrs. Ellis?

CARRIE. I think you should travel up with us, Sophie. Right now. Whatever is to be faced, we will do much better if we face it all together and do it quickly.

FREDERICK (*Looks at her, as if they had had previous talk*). You're putting it much too importantly. There's nothing to be faced.

CARRIE. I didn't mean to make it too important. Of course, it isn't—

SOPHIE (*Puts her hand on his arm*). It is important to you. And you must not be kind and pretend that—

FREDERICK (*Firmly*). I'm not being kind. I told you the truth. I've been in trouble, now you've been in a little. That's all, now or ever. (*Shyly*) As far as I'm concerned, it makes us seem less like strangers. I'd hope you'd feel the same way—

CARRIE (*Quickly*). Run and pack a bag, Sophie. It's a lovely day for driving and we'll be in town for lunch. I think you and I will have it at the club— Now let's not talk about it any more—

SOPHIE. No. It would be most mistaken of me to come now. My leaving here would seem as if I must be ashamed and you shamed for me. I must not come with you today. I must stay here. (*Smiles*) It must be faced.

FREDERICK. All right. That makes sense. Mother and Grandma will drive up and I'll stay here—

SOPHIE (*Very quickly*). No, no. You must not stay here. (*Points to window, meaning town*) They knew you had made plans to leave today as usual. And so you must leave. We must act as if nothing had happened, and if we do that, and are not worried, it will all end more quickly. (*Goes to* FREDERICK) Believe me, Frederick. You know what I say is true. All must seem to be as it has been. (*To* CARRIE) You tell him that, please, Mrs. Ellis.

CARRIE. I don't know. You belong with us now, Sophie. We don't want to leave you, or Constance. I think she should come along and—

SOPHIE. Oh, she would not do that. You know she would not. (*Smiles, very cheerfully*) Now. You are both very kind. But you know what I say is best for us all, and of no importance whether I come one week or the next. (*Takes* FREDERICK'S *arm*) You have said I must laugh about it. I do laugh, and so it will be nothing for me to stay.

(MRS. ELLIS *comes to the door from the direction of the dining room.*)

CARRIE. Good-by, Sophie. We will be waiting for you.

(*She exits, passing* MRS. ELLIS *without speaking.*)

FREDERICK (*Unhappily*). You all seem to know what's right, what's best, so much faster than I do. I—

SOPHIE (*Smiles, puts her hand over his mouth*). This is best. Please.

FREDERICK. Then let us come back this week end. Can I do that?

SOPHIE (*She touches his face*). I think so. You are a nice man, Frederick.

FREDERICK (*Kisses her*). And you're a nice girl to think so. See you in a few days. (*Turns to go out, passes* MRS. ELLIS) I feel happy, Grandma.

(MRS. ELLIS *nods, waits for him to exit.* SOPHIE *sits down.*)

MRS. ELLIS (*After a second*). Sophie.

SOPHIE (*Smiles as if she knew what was coming*). Yes.

MRS. ELLIS. Did *Carrie* ask you to leave with us? (SOPHIE *nods*) Ah. That's not good. When Carrie gets smart she gets very smart. Sophie, Frederick meant what he said to you. But I know them both and I would guess that in a week, or two or three, he will agree to go to Europe with his mother and he will tell you that it is only a postponement. And he will believe what he says. Time and decisions melt and merge for him and ten years from now he will be convinced that you refused to marry him. And he will always be a little sad about what could have been.

SOPHIE. Yes. Of course.

MRS. ELLIS. Carrie never will want him to marry. And she will never know it. Well, she, too, got cheated a long time ago. There is very little I can do—perhaps very little I want to do any more. Don't judge him too harshly, child.

SOPHIE (*Smiles*). No, I will not judge. I will write a letter to him.

MRS. ELLIS. That's my girl. Don't take from us what you don't have to take, or waste yourself on defeat. (*She gets up*) Oh, Sophie, feel sorry for Frederick. He is nice and he is nothing. And his father before him and my other sons. And myself. Another way. Well. If there is ever a chance, come and see me.

(*She moves out.* SOPHIE *remains seated. After a second* CONSTANCE *comes in from the hall. She looks at* SOPHIE.)

CONSTANCE (*Hesitantly*). Carrie tells me you'll be going up to town in a few weeks to stay with them. I'm glad. (*No answer*) Er. Why don't you go up to my room, dear, and lie down for a while? (*Points to porch*) She's on the porch. I'm going to ask the Denerys to leave today. I am sure they will want to, anyway. And the Griggses will be going and then just you and I—

SOPHIE. I will not be going to New Orleans, Aunt Constance, and there will be no marriage between Frederick and me.

CONSTANCE (*Stares at her*). But Carrie told me—

SOPHIE. Now she believes that she wants me. But it will not be so.

CONSTANCE (*After a second*). I wish I could say I was surprised or angry. But I'm not sorry. No marriage without love—

SOPHIE (*Pleasantly*). Yes. Yes.

CONSTANCE (*Gently*). You're not to feel bad or hurt.

SOPHIE. I do not.

CONSTANCE. I'm— I'm glad. Mighty glad. Everything will work out for the best. You'll see. After everybody goes, we'll get the house and the accounts cleaned up and straightened out as usual. (*Gaily*) And then I think you and I will take a little trip. I haven't seen Memphis in years and maybe in a few months— (*Gently*) You know what? We can even sell, rent, the place, if we want to. We can pick up and go anywhere we want. You'll see, dear. We'll have a nice time.

SOPHIE (*Almost as if she were speaking to a child*). Yes, Aunt Constance. (CONSTANCE *goes out.* SOPHIE *turns to watch* LEON *who, during* CONSTANCE's *speech, has come out on the porch and is serving breakfast to* NINA. SOPHIE *rises and goes out to the porch. She takes the coffee pot from* LEON—*he has finished placing the other dishes*—*nods to him, and pours* NINA's *coffee.* LEON *exits.*

NINA *turns, sees* SOPHIE, *turns back*) You are a pretty woman, Mrs. Denery, when your face is happy.

NINA. And you think my face is happy *this* morning?

SOPHIE. Oh, yes. You and Mr. Denery have had a nice reconciliation.

NINA (*Stares at her*). Er. Yes, I suppose so.

SOPHIE. I am glad for you. That is as it has been and will always be. (*She sits down*) Now could I speak with you and Mr. Denery?

NINA (*Uncomfortably*). Sophie, if there is anything I can do— Er. Nick isn't here. I thought it best for us all—

SOPHIE (*Softly*). Ah. Ah, my aunt will be most sad.

NINA. Sophie, there's no good my telling you how sorry, how— What can I do?

SOPHIE. You can give me five thousand dollars, Mrs. Denery. American dollars, of course. (*Demurely; her accent from now on grows more pronounced*) I have been subjected to the most degrading experience from which no young girl easily recovers. (*In French*) A most degrading experience from which no young girl easily recovers—

NINA (*Stares at her*). It sounds exactly the same in French.

SOPHIE. Somehow sex and money are simpler in French. Well. In English, then, I have lost or will lose my most beloved fiancé; I cannot return to school and the comrades with whom my life has been so happy; my aunt is uncomfortable and unhappy in the only life she knows and is now burdened with me for many years to come. I am utterly, utterly miserable, Mrs. Denery. I am ruined. (NINA *bursts out laughing.* SOPHIE *smiles*) Please do not laugh at me.

NINA. I suppose I should be grateful to you for making a joke of it.

SOPHIE. You make a mistake. I am most serious.

NINA (*Stops laughing*). Are you? Sophie, it is an unpleasant and foolish incident and I don't wish to minimize it. But don't you feel you're adding considerable drama to it?

SOPHIE. No, ma'am. I did not say that is the way I thought of it. But that is the way it will be considered in this place, in this life. Little is made into very much here.

NINA. It's just the same in your country.

SOPHIE. No, Mrs. Denery. You mean it is the same in Brussels or Strasbourg or Paris, with those whom you would meet. In my class, in my town, it is not so. In a poor house if a man falls asleep drunk—and certainly it happens with us each Saturday night—he is not alone with an innocent young girl because the young girl, at my age, is not so innocent and because her family is in the same room, not having any other place to go. It arranges itself differently; you have more rooms and therefore more troubles.

NINA. Yes. I understand the lecture. (*Pauses*) Why do you want five thousand dollars, Sophie?

SOPHIE. I wish to go home.

NINA (*Gently*). Then I will be happy to give it to you. Happier than you know to think we can do something.

SOPHIE. Yes. I am sure. But I will not accept it as largesse —to make you happy. We will call it a loan, come by through blackmail. One does not have to be grateful for blackmail money, nor think of oneself as a charity girl.

NINA (*After a second*). Blackmail money?

SOPHIE. Yes ma'am. You will give me five thousand dollars because if you do not I will say that Mr. Denery seduced me last night. (NINA *stares at her, laughs*) You are gay this morning, madame.

NINA (*Shocked*). Sophie, Sophie. What a child you are. It's not necessary to talk this way.

SOPHIE. I wish to prevent you from giving favors to me.

NINA. I intended no favors. And I don't like this kind of talk. Nick did not seduce you and I want no more jokes about it. (*Pleasantly*) Suppose we try to be friends—

SOPHIE. I am not joking, Mrs. Denery. And I do not wish us to be friends.

NINA (*Gets up*). I would like to give you the money. And I will give it to you for that reason and no other.

SOPHIE. It does not matter to me what you would like. You will give it to me for my reason—or I will not take it. (*Angrily,* NINA *goes toward door, goes into the room, then turns and smiles at* SOPHIE.)

NINA. You are serious? Just for a word, a way of calling something, you would hurt my husband and me?

SOPHIE. For me it is more than a way of calling something.

NINA. You're a tough little girl.

SOPHIE. Don't you think people often say other people are tough when they do not know how to cheat them?

NINA (*Angrily*). I was not trying to cheat you of anything—

SOPHIE. Yes, you were. You wish to be the kind lady who most honorably stays to discharge—within reason—her obligations. And who goes off, as she has gone off many other times, to make the reconciliation with her husband. How would you and Mr. Denery go on living without such incidents as me? I have been able to give you a second, or a twentieth, honeymoon.

NINA (*Angrily*). Is that speech made before you raise your price?

SOPHIE (*Smiles*). No. A blackmail bargain is still a bargain. (CROSSMAN *appears in the hall,* SOPHIE *sees him.*)

NINA. How would— How shall we make the arrangements?

SOPHIE (*Calling*). Mr. Ned. (*Pleasantly, to* NINA) Mr. Ned will know what to do.

NINA (*After a second to* CROSSMAN). I'd like to get a check cashed. It's rather a large check. Could you vouch for me at the bank?

CROSSMAN. Sure. That's easy enough. The bank's just around the corner.

SOPHIE. Would you like me to come with you, Mrs. Denery?

NINA (*Smiles*). You know, I think perhaps it's wisest for you to stay right here. You and I in a bank, cashing a check, this morning, could well be interpreted as a pay-off, or blackmail.

(*She goes out.*)

SOPHIE. I will be going home, Mr. Ned.

CROSSMAN (*Smiles*). Good. (*Looks at her, turns to stare at* NINA, *as she passes him and goes into hall*) At least I hope it's good.

SOPHIE. I think it is more good than it is not good.

(*He goes out.* ROSE *comes down the steps. Her manner is hurried, nervous. She goes immediately to windows. She looks out as if she saw somebody coming. Then she turns and sees* SOPHIE.)

ROSE (*Very nervous*). Oh. Good morning, Sophie.

SOPHIE. We have seen each other earlier this morning, Mrs. Griggs.

ROSE. Oh. It's like a nightmare to me, as if a year had gone by. I've asked for my breakfast tray twice and nobody pays any attention. And the doctor says that's the way it *must* be.

SOPHIE (*Exiting*). I will get it for you.

ROSE (*Back at the window, speaks to* SOPHIE *who has left the room*). Not you, Sophie. You have your own troubles, God knows. I don't know how any of us can eat anything today. (GRIGGS, *in riding pants and old shirt, comes in through the windows. Because she is upstage of the windows, he does not see her until she speaks*) I've been looking everywhere for you, Ben.

GRIGGS (*Turns*). Rose. You knew where I was.

ROSE. That was all we needed here today: a telephone call

to the stables. Oh, Ben, it was I who found them. But you don't know about it—

GRIGGS. I've heard all about it.

ROSE. Terrible, isn't it?

GRIGGS. Not very.

ROSE. He's been a disappointment to me. I've been lying on the bed thinking about it. Nick Denery, I mean.

GRIGGS. I'm sorry.

ROSE. You know, Ben, I've just about come to the conclusion that I'm often wrong about people, mostly men.

GRIGGS. And what did you and Henry—ah—put together, Rose?

ROSE. It was so hot in town. Henry's got that wonderful air conditioning, of course, but it's never like your own air. I think Sunday's the hottest day of the year, anyway. Athalia's braces cost twenty-five hundred dollars at that Greek dentist's and believe me they don't make anybody look prettier—

GRIGGS. What point did you come to about my decision?

ROSE. Decision? Your decision—

GRIGGS (*Tensely*). Please stop playing the fool. I'm afraid of you when you start playing that game.

ROSE. *You* afraid of *me*?

GRIGGS. Yes, me afraid of you. This very minute. Be kind, Rose, and tell me what has been decided for me.

ROSE (*Softly, very nervous*). It wasn't like that. Before I saw Henry I went to see Dr. Wills. You know he won't ever see patients on Sunday.

GRIGGS. Not unless the fee is over a hundred.

ROSE. I've always been sorry you didn't like Howard Wills. He's known as the best man in the South, Ben. He gave up a beach picnic with that woman, you know. Only that famous a man could buck having an open mistress—

GRIGGS. I don't want to hear about Wills. Come to the point. What did you and Henry—

ROSE (*Grows sober, recognizing the tone*). I've been un-
easy. I've sometimes been in pain, all summer. But I
guess I knew because I guess I've known since that
army doctor in 1934—I didn't want to talk about it—
(*Moves toward him, frightened*) I have bad heart
trouble, Ben.

GRIGGS. (*After a second, as if he were sick*). Don't play
that trick, Rose. It's just too ugly.

ROSE. I am not playing a trick. Wills wrote you a letter
about it.

(*She reaches in the pocket of her robe, hands him a
folded paper. He takes it from her, reads it.*)

GRIGGS (*Violently*). How much did Henry pay Wills for
this?

ROSE (*Gently, seriously*). It wasn't bought. Even Henry
couldn't buy it.

(*She turns, goes toward door, as if she were a dignified
woman.*)

GRIGGS (*Softly*). Tell me about it.

ROSE. There isn't much to tell. I've known some of it for
years, and so have you. I just didn't know it was this
bad, or didn't want to. Wills says I must lead a—well,
a very different life. I'll have to go to the country somewhere and rest most of the day—not climb steps or go
to parties or even see people much. I like people, I—
Well, I just don't understand what I can do, except sit
in the sun, and I hate sun— Oh, I don't know. He said
worse than I am saying— I can't say it—

GRIGGS. Yes. (*After a second*) I'm sorry.

ROSE. I know you are. You've been my good friend. I'm
frightened, Ben. I play the fool, but I'm not so big a fool
that I don't know I haven't got anybody to help me.
I pretend about the boys and what they're like but I
know just as well as you do that they're not very kind
men and won't want me and won't come to help me.

(*With feeling*) And of course I know about Henry—
I always have. I've got nobody and I'm not young and
I'm scared. Awful scared.

GRIGGS. You don't have to be.

ROSE (*Who is crying, very quietly*). Wills says that if I
take good care I might be, probably will be, in fine
shape at the end of the year. Please stay with me this
year, just this year. I will swear a solemn oath—believe
me I'm telling the truth now—I will give you a divorce
at the end of the year without another word. I'll go and
do it without any fuss, any talk. But please help me
now. I'm so scared. Help me, please. One year's a lot
to ask, I know, but—

(GRIGGS *comes to her, presses her arm.*)

GRIGGS. Of course. Of course. Now don't let's speak of it
again and we'll do what has to be done.

(*She turns, goes out. He stands where he is. A minute
later,* CROSSMAN *comes in, stares at* GRIGGS *as if he knew
something was wrong. Then he speaks casually.*)

CROSSMAN. Seen Sophie?

GRIGGS (*As if it were an effort, idly*). In the kitchen, I
guess. Tough break for the kid, isn't it?

CROSSMAN. Perhaps it isn't. I don't know.

(*He watches as* GRIGGS *takes out a cigarette and lights it.*
GRIGGS's *hands are shaking and as he puts out the match,
he stares at them.*)

GRIGGS (*Smiles*). My hands are shaking.

CROSSMAN. What's the matter?

GRIGGS. Worst disease of all. I'm all gone. I've just looked
and there's no Benjamin Griggs.

CROSSMAN (*After a second*). Oh, that. And you've just
found that out?

GRIGGS. Just today. Just now.

CROSSMAN. My God, you're young.

GRIGGS (*Laughs*). I guess I was. (*Slowly, carefully*) So at any given moment you're only the sum of your life up to then. There are no big moments you can reach unless you've a pile of smaller moments to stand on. That big hour of decision, the turning point in your life, the someday you've counted on when you'd suddenly wipe out your past mistakes, do the work you'd never done, think the way you'd never thought, have what you'd never had—it just doesn't come suddenly. You've trained yourself for it while you waited—or you've let it all run past you and frittered yourself away. (*Shakes his head*) I've frittered myself away, Crossman.

CROSSMAN. Most people like us.

GRIGGS. That's no good to me. Most people like us haven't done anything to themselves; they've let it be done to them. I had no right to let it be done to me, but I let it be done. What consolation can I find in not having made myself any more useless than an Ellis, a Denery, a Tuckerman, a—

CROSSMAN. Say it. I won't mind. Or a Crossman.

GRIGGS. The difference is you've meant to fritter yourself away.

CROSSMAN. And does that make it better?

GRIGGS. Better? Worse? All I know is it makes it different. Rose is a sick woman. But you know I'm not talking only about Rose and me, don't you?

CROSSMAN. I know.

GRIGGS. (*Very slowly*). I am not any too sure I didn't partly welcome the medical opinion that made it easier for me to give up. (*Then in a low voice as if to himself*) And I don't like Rose. And I'll live to like her less.

(*He starts toward door.* CONSTANCE *appears in the hall carrying a tray. She is followed by* SOPHIE *who is carrying a carpet sweeper and a basket filled with cleaning rags, etc.* CONSTANCE *comes to the door. She speaks wearily.*)

CONSTANCE (*To* GRIGGS). Sorry about Rose's breakfast. I forgot it. Sophie is going to help Rose to get packed. I don't mean to sound inhospitable but since you were going tomorrow, anyway—(*Gently*) I'm just tired and it would be easier for us. Please forgive me but you're an old friend and you will understand.

GRIGGS (*Smiles, pats her arm*). I'll take the tray.

(*He takes it from her, goes up the steps.* CONSTANCE *comes in the room, sighs, sits down.*)

CROSSMAN. Sophie. (SOPHIE *comes to him*) I was asked to give you this.

(*He hands her an envelope.*)

SOPHIE. Thank you, Mr. Ned.

CONSTANCE (*Idly, without much interest*). Secrets?

CROSSMAN. That's right. Secrets. Old love letters or something.

(SOPHIE *laughs, goes out.*)

CONSTANCE (*After a silence*). I hate this house today.

CROSSMAN. Well, they'll all be gone soon.

CONSTANCE. You won't go? Please.

CROSSMAN. I'll stay for a few days if you'd like me to.

CONSTANCE. Oh, yes. I need you to stay.

CROSSMAN (*Points out of window*). Don't worry about what the town thinks. Just act as if nothing had happened and they'll soon stop talking.

CONSTANCE. Oh, I'm not worrying about that. (*Pauses*) I feel so lost, Ned. As if I distrusted myself, didn't have anything to stand on. I mean, right now, if you asked me, I just wouldn't know what I thought or believed, or ever had, or— (*Shyly*) Well, what *have* I built my life on? Do you know what I mean?

CROSSMAN. Sure. I know.

CONSTANCE (*As if she had trouble with the words*). It's— it's so painful. (*Then as if she wished to change the subject quickly*) Sophie will be going back to Europe. She just told me. She *wants* to go. Did you know that?

CROSSMAN. Is that so?

CONSTANCE. I was so sure I was doing the right thing, bringing her here. You see? That's part of what I mean by not knowing the things I thought I knew. Well. She wants me to come with her and live with them, but I told her I'd be no happier in a new life than she was. (*Pauses as if she were coming to something that frightens her*) Nick said you wouldn't be coming here next summer. Did you say anything like that, or was it one of Nick's lies? (*He does not answer her. She stares at him*) Why, Ned?

CROSSMAN. Hasn't anything to do with you, Con. Just think I'd be better off. You know, it's kind of foolish— two weeks a year—coming back here and living a life that isn't me anymore. (*Laughs*) It's too respectable for me, Con. I ain't up to it anymore.

CONSTANCE. Oh. It's what I look forward to every summer. What will I— (*Very quickly*) Where is Nick? I haven't seen him. I wish they'd leave—

CROSSMAN. They've gone.

CONSTANCE (*Stares at him*). Without a word to me? Exactly the way he left years ago. I didn't ever tell you that, did I? We had a date for dinner. He didn't come. He just got on the boat. I didn't ever tell anybody before. (*Violently*) What a fool. All these years of making a shabby man into the kind of hero who would come back some day all happy and shining—

CROSSMAN. Oh, don't do that. He never asked you to make him what he wasn't. Or to wait twenty years to find him out.

CONSTANCE. No, he didn't. That's true. (*She rises, goes to the portrait and stands staring at it*) Do I look like this?

CROSSMAN. You look nice.

CONSTANCE. Come and look at it.

CROSSMAN. No. I don't want to.

CONSTANCE. Much older than I thought or— And I don't look very bright. (*Puts the picture away from her*) Well, I haven't been very bright. I want to say something to you. I can't wait any longer. Would you forgive me?

CROSSMAN. Forgive you? For what?

CONSTANCE. For wasting all these years. For not knowing what I felt about you, or not wanting to. Ned, would you have me now?

CROSSMAN (*After a second*). What did you say?

CONSTANCE. Would you marry me? (*There is a pause. Then* SOPHIE *comes from the direction of the dining room carrying a carpet sweeper and a cleaning basket. As she goes up the steps she is singing a cheerful French song.* CONSTANCE *smiles*) She's happy. That's good. I think she'll come out all right, always.

CROSSMAN (*Stares at* CONSTANCE, *then slowly, carefully*). I live in a room and I go to work and I play a game called getting through the day while you wait for night. The night's for me—just me—and I can do anything with it I want. There used to be a lot of things to do with it, good things, but now there's a bar and another bar and the same people in each bar. When I've had enough I go back to my room—or somebody else's room—and that never means much one way or the other. A few years ago I'd have weeks of reading—night after night—just me. But I don't do that much anymore. Just read, all night long. You can feel good that way.

CONSTANCE. I never did that. I'm not a reader.

CROSSMAN (*As if he hadn't heard her*). And a few years ago I'd go on the wagon twice a year. Now I don't do that anymore. And I don't care. (*Smiles*) And all these years I told myself that if you'd loved me everything would have been different. I'd have had a good life, been worth something to myself. I wanted to tell myself that. I wanted to believe it. Griggs was right. I not only wasted myself, but I wanted it that way. All my life, I guess, I wanted it that way.

CONSTANCE. And you're not in love with me, Ned?

CROSSMAN. No, Con. Not now.

CONSTANCE (*Gets up, goes to him*). Let's have a nice dinner together, just you and me, and go to the movies. Could we do that?

CROSSMAN. I've kept myself busy looking into other people's hearts so I wouldn't have to look into my own. (*Softly*) If I made you think I was still in love, I'm sorry. Sorry I fooled you and sorry I fooled myself. And I've never liked liars—least of all those who lie to themselves.

CONSTANCE. Never mind. Most of us lie to ourselves, darling, most of us.

Curtain

The Best of the World's Best Books
COMPLETE LIST OF TITLES IN
THE MODERN LIBRARY

83 WILDE, OSCAR: *The Plays of Oscar Wilde*
84 WILDE, OSCAR: *Poems* and *Fairy Tales*
126 WODEHOUSE, P. J.: *Selected Stories*
268 WORDSWORTH: *Selected Poetry*

44 YEATS, W. B. (Editor): *Irish Fairy and Folk Tales*
179 YOUNG, G. F.: *The Medici*

207 ZIMMERN, ALFRED: *The Greek Commonwealth*
142 ZOLA, ÉMILE: *Nana*

MISCELLANEOUS

288 *An Anthology of Irish Literature*
330 *Anthology of Medieval Lyrics*
326 *The Apocrypha*
201 *The Arabian Nights' Entertainments*
87 *Best American Humorous Short Stories*
18 *Best Russian Short Stories*
129 *Best Spanish Stories*
Complete Greek Tragedies
310 Vol. I (Aeschylus I); 311 Vol. II (Aeschylus II); 312 Vol. III (Sophocles I); 313 Vol. IV (Sophocles II); 314 Vol. V (Euripides I); 315 Vol. VI (Euripides II)
101 *A Comprehensive Anthology of American Poetry*
226 *The Consolation of Philosophy*
94 *Eight Famous Elizabethan Plays*
224 *Eighteenth-Century Plays*
73 *Famous Ghost Stories*
139 *The Federalist*
30 *Five Great Modern Irish Plays*
144 *Fourteen Great Detective Stories*
108 *Great German Short Novels and Stories*
168 *Great Modern Short Stories*
238 *Great Tales of the American West*
203 *The Greek Poets*
118 *Stories of Modern Italy*
217 *The Latin Poets*
149 *The Making of Man: An Outline of Anthropology*
183 *Making of Society*
133 *Medieval Romances*
1 *The Modern Library Dictionary*
258 *New Voices in the American Theatre*
152 *Outline of Abnormal Psychology*
66 *Outline of Psychoanalysis*
287 *Restoration Plays*
337 *Roman Comedies*
158 *Seven Famous Greek Plays*
57 *The Short Bible*
276 *Six Modern American Plays*
38 *Six American Plays for Today*
127 *Twentieth-Century American Poetry—revised*
341 *Twenty German Poets*

MODERN LIBRARY GIANTS

A series of sturdily bound and handsomely printed, full-sized library editions of books formerly available only in expensive sets. These volumes contain from 600 to 1,400 pages each.

THE MODERN LIBRARY GIANTS REPRESENT A
SELECTION OF THE WORLD'S GREATEST BOOKS